SCRIPTURE
INSIGHTS
FROM
SCIENCE AND
ARCHAEOLOGY

SCRIPTURE INSIGHTS
FROM
SCIENCE AND ARCHAEOLOGY

PAUL MCCOY

Pleasant Word
A Division of WinePress Group

Pleasant Word (a division of WinePress Publishing, PO Box 428, Enumclaw, WA 98022) functions only as book publisher. As such, the ultimate design, content, editorial accuracy, and views expressed or implied in this work are those of the author.

The text of the Revised Standard Version of the Bible (RSV) and quotations therefrom are copyright 1946, 1952 by Division of Christian Education of the National Council of the Churches of Christ in the United States of America. Scripture quotations designated "ASV" are from the American Standard Version of the Revised Bible, copyright renewed 1929 by the International Council of Religious Education.

Pentateuch and Haftoras Edited by Dr. J.H. Hertz Sec. Ed. Soncino Press London 1992

Cover image with author showing Hazor Area G Canaanite glacis and fosse, attacked by Joshua. Courtesy David Livingston.

ISBN 13: 978-1-4141-1340-1
ISBN 10: 1-4141-1340-4
Library of Congress Catalog Card Number: 2008911235

To my wife Carol who has been with me on four of my seven digs to Israel, loving the Biblical sites and the country as much as I.

CONTENTS

INTRODUCTION

I DEVELOPED THIS material for a four-year Bible study, which I gave at the Cities Service Research and Development Center in Cranbury, New Jersey. I began the project in 1975 and added to it over the years. I do not intend for this to be all-inclusive. (For instance, I may cover only a major verse in question, though others may carry the same problems as duplicates.) Rather I intend to cover the major Biblical problem verses, and to illustrate new knowledge from recent Semitic language studies, archaeology, and scientific areas.

Each chapter can still be used for a Bible Study session. The discussion of each point that I cover is brief, to point the instructor in the right direction. I also provide previous objections and the best answers available today, with references for further information or background study.[1]

As a Christian and a scientist, I have had to deal with the scientific aspects of miracles, as well as statements that might imply supernatural conclusions, but may be easily explained by other aspects; some involve better understanding of the wording itself. Not all miracles can be rationally explained.[2] We must let God be God—he is after all, by definition, supernatural. Evolutionists take comfort in that given enough time, all things are possible—this, though they have a built-in limit of the age of the Universe to work with. The Laws of Compound Probability of Statistics show quite clearly that *chance does not even have a chance,* and they have run out of time for the events to occur. Without getting into the numbers here, the analogy for comparison would be: Suppose you were deposited on the Moon with a set of blueprints for a Boeing 747 and nothing else—no protective suit, atmosphere, tools, raw materials or fuel. The instructions were to build a working plane in 24 hours and fly it off the surface. What would be the chance for completion of the project? Less than the proverbial chance of the snowball in Hell. Even these odds would be better than for chance to assemble a single working strand of DNA to start the life process in the time allowed for the Earth's existence. Evolution assumes there is enough time, as a given fact. However, statistics gives hard evidence that it won't fly, pardon the pun.

The agnostics among us are at least honest in that they do not know if there is a God. The atheists have put themselves between a rock and a hard place. In fact, there is no such thing as an atheist. They would need to possess perfect knowledge (thereby, becoming a god) in everything. Admitting there was something they did not know would leave the door open for God to reside in those spaces. Sorry atheists, you are sorely misguided.

If an astronomer were to look at the Universe and contemplate the order he sees, it would violate the Second Law of Thermodynamics (if chance were in charge), which states that the entropy (disorder) of the Universe tends to a maximum. This is why your shiny new red XLR 1500 after 15–20 years has rust, dings, dents, and the brakes and steering aren't so good. Even though it has a computer and battery, it won't change from a ten mile per gallon beast into a plasma powered solar generated whiz-bang.

A brief look at the laws of thermodynamics: the term "law" is not applied until enough time has passed to test all possible exceptions. This is essentially Plank's Principle, TEEB p.118. I know of no scientist who does not accept them all.

Law	Scientific Definition	Common Definition	Humorous Definition
0th	Two systems in equilibrium with a third are in equilibrium with each other	The common factor is temp.	Temperature scales are all over the place: °C, °F, °K
1st	Energy cannot be created or destroyed only changed	Perpetual motion is impossible	You can't win or get something for nothing
2nd	See above	Energy is required to run a refrigerator	Don't even try
3rd	Absolute zero is impossible to obtain	Absolute zero is –273.16°C or 0 °K	You're still warm. We have only reached -273.15999999955°C on Sept. 2003 at MIT

The proposal of black holes was thought to violate the Second Law. If nothing can escape from a black hole, throwing something into it would cause the entropy to decrease. A disagreement arose between Hawking and Jacob Bekenstein in which all experts lined up with Hawking, except Bekenstein and his mentor and thesis advisor John Wheeler. It turned out the entropy resides in the hole's surface area. Bekenstein and the

Second Law won. In fact, if you replace the term Horizon Areas with Entropy in Hawking's law of Area Increase, it becomes the Second Law of Thermodynamics, but it took from 1970 to 1974 to prove it, (Thorne pp. 422–446). The black hole laws are the thermodynamic laws in disguise, Thorne p.422. Wormholes were first proposed in questions to Thorne from Carl Sagan in 1985, Thorne p. 483. These would be necessary to speed up travel to other galaxies via Star Trek, Babylon 5 and Star Gate SG 1. After all, what fun is it to be stuck in your own little corner of the universe? Nevertheless, take heart; warp drive at speeds faster than the speed of light will not occur. Sorry Enterprise, we are thus stuck in our own galaxy. The recently proposed theory is that there were speeds faster than the speed of light in the first second of the universe, (Magueijo pp. 156–163). If I read his book right these are not operating now. In that, Omega is the ratio between the gravitational energy of the universe and the energy contained in its outward motion. At one second old the value of Omega must have been between 0.99999999999999999 and 1.00000000000000001. Any greater deviation would have led to a crunching or emptiness of the universe, leading to its destruction, (Magueijo pp. 94: 96). Who was in charge of this fine-tuning? Have we made another case for God?

Wormholes, well maybe, if one can be found to exist. Magueijo's Cosmological Perturbation Theory runs to some 50 p. of intricate algebra, which was later cut to 30 p. by tricks and shortcuts. More tricks reduced the calculation to 10 p. for three different versions. All three answers agreed with the first one. The main equation for a variable speed of light is $E=MC^2/1+MC^2/Ep$ where Ep is the Planck energy, (Magueijo pp. 176; 252).

Hawking's formula is $S=AkC^3/4hG$ where S is the entropy, and directly proportional to the area, A is area of the event horizon of the black hole, h is Boltzman's constant, C is the speed of light, h is Planck's constant, and G is Neuton's gravitational constant, Shun p. 63. Now at least you know it. He also showed that the temperature of a black hole is inversely proportional to the mass in that $T = hC^3/8\Pi kGM$. The symbols are the same where Π equals 3.14159 and M equals mass, SHUN p. 118. A black hole of only a few solar masses will have a temperature of about 0.000001°K. Thus, the smaller the black hole the higher the temperature. When the background microwave radiation of the universe was found to be a relative high 2.7°K, it would swamp the average black hole temperature. Thus, they could not be found by present methods. Only small ones might show up, but apparently they are few in number, SHUN p. 39. The Schwarzchild solution of Einstein's Theory of Relativity in 1916 showed that a black hole radius of the event horizon $R = 2GM/C^2$ or if the mass was the same as the Sun, the radius would be two miles, (SHUN pp. 111; 118).

The statistical problem would be similar to the classical Billiard case with no pockets. With the 15 balls arranged in order (maximum order for the table), the break is made. The result is disorder. With the next shot, what is the chance for the balls to return to the exact initial positions before the break? The similar problem exists for the geneticist—to figure out how DNA came into being and why nature uses only the L form of amino acids to form proteins. The complimentary D form of man is possible, but you don't find him running around. Since all plant and animal life forms on Earth use the L forms, he would not be able to digest them as food. In fact, remove any one of the essential amino acids from the diet and you can starve to death on a full stomach.

The paleontologist and geologist must figure out the where, why, and how of fossils. We are given comfort in Daniel 12:4 "in that knowledge will increase," so much so that we have been able to figure out the human genome and determine where the genetic defects reside. More knowledge will come, and God will get His due in spite of us.[3] With an advanced degree in Organic Chemistry, and knowing how to get around in the scientific literature, it is natural to transfer this understanding to the archaeological and theological literature. Similarly, Nobel Prize winner (1965) Richard Feynman could go from astrophysics to deciphering Mayan hieroglyphs (SHUN p. 83). My 40 years' interest in archaeology led to seven seasons of excavation in Israel as a square supervisor, six from 1979–1994 at ABR's site of Khirbet Nisya, the final excavation report of which has been published. Moreover, our group was privileged to spend one season at Herod the Great's Winter Palace at Jericho in 1980 under Ehud Netzer.[4]

Ultimately, though, the Bible's message is of Christ. C.S. Lewis summed it up brilliantly this way:

> If you had gone to Buddha and asked him, "Are you the son of Bramah?" he would have said, "My son, you are still in the vale of illusion." If you had gone to Socrates and asked, "Are you Zeus?" he would have laughed at you. If you had gone to Mohammad and asked, "Are you Allah?" he would first have rent his clothes and then cut your head off. If you had asked Confucius, "Are you Heaven?" I think he would have probably replied, "Remarks, which are not in accordance with nature, are in bad taste." The idea of a great moral teacher saying what Christ said is out of the question. In my opinion, the only person who can say that sort of thing is either God or a complete lunatic suffering from that form of delusion, which undermines the whole mind of man. If you think you are a poached egg, when you are looking for a piece of toast to suit you, you may be sane, but if you think you are God, there is no chance for you. We may note in passing that he was never regarded as a mere moral teacher. He did not produce that effect on any of the people who actually met him. He produced mainly three effects: Hatred—Terror—Adoration. There was no trace of people expressing mild approval (p. 311).

Peter Larson expressed it this way: "Despite our efforts to keep him out, God intrudes. The life of Jesus is bracketed by two impossibilities: a virgin's birth and an empty tomb. Jesus entered our world through a door marked "No Entrance" and left through a door marked "No Exit" (Christianity Today Dec. 2005, p. 62; or Prism Jan/Feb 2001).

Finally, my mantra is, *A day spent without learning something new is a day wasted.* So comments or questions are welcomed at (304) 258-6759 or pacmccoy@peoplepc.com or pacmccoy@hughes.net

ABBREVIATIONS

AD	anno Domini, in the year of our Lord
b.	ben (son of)
BC	before Christ
C&EN	Chemical and Engineering News
ca.	circa, about
ch.	Chapter
d.	died
DSS	Dead Sea Scrolls
e.g.	example gratia, for example
fr.	fragment
ibid.	in the place cited
KJV	King James Version
LXX	Septuagint or Seventy
par.	paragraph
p.	page
pl.	plural
pp.	pages
RSV	Revised Standard Version
v.	verse or verses
vol.	volume
#	chapter or section

CHAPTER 1

THE BIBLE—ORIGINAL LANGUAGES

THE OLD TESTAMENT was written in Hebrew except for Genesis 31:47, Daniel 2:4–7:28, Ezra 4:8–6:18, 7:12–26, and Jeremiah 10:11, which are in Aramaic. Aramaic (or Syriac) is still spoken in two villages in Lebanon, as well as in Mosul, Iraq, and in Malula and Edessa, Syria. With continued persecution of Jews, many of the dispersed groups in Syria, Azerbaijan, Kazakhstan, and Kurdistan immigrated to Israel; as of 1998, 20,000 people conversed in Aramaic. Since then there are many more now studying the language, causing a revival, especially in Malula.

Aramaic was the official and everyday language of the Chaldeans of South Babylonia, and it is related to Hebrew. The Lord spoke Aramaic as a common language in 30 AD. An Aramaic letter from King Adon of Ascalon to Pharaoh Necho (ca. 600 BC) was discovered in 1942 and published in 1948, showing that Aramaic was an official language of diplomacy before the Chaldean conquest of Palestine.[5]

Hebrew developed from the Phoenician culture and era (Wight p. 175).

The New Testament was written in Greek. It was the official language of the Roman Empire and was widely used even in Rome itself. All letters and treatises intended for wide circulation were written in Greek, e.g. Josephus and the Septuagint (LXX).

Bible Development

Old Hebrew: This included the Samaritan Pentateuch, which developed before the Masoretic text, was written from ca. 430 BC. Although quoted by Eusebius of Caesarea, Cyril of Alexandria, and the Talmud (contemptuously), no copy had been seen by Westerners until 1616. It is very close to the Masoretic text.

Modern square Hebrew characters developed from Aramaic in Babylon during the time of Ezra (ca. 425 BC).[6]

The Isaiah Dead Sea Scroll dates from (ca. 150 BC); it is the oldest complete Hebrew manuscript known.[7] Before the 1st century, the jot (Hebrew yod, Gk. Iota, was not a small letter in Phoenician or Old Heb.) and tittle (accent mark) of Matthew 5:18 were introduced. The Masoretes about the 6th century AD added the vowel points, although vowels created from consonants such as yod, heh, and vav (scripto plena—full writing) were in use by 700 BC (Burrows p. 112). The oldest complete Hebrew Old Testament dates from approximately 930 and comes from Aleppo Syria.[8] The first printed Hebrew Old Testament was in 1488 at Soncino, England. The first printed Greek New Testament was done by Erasmus in 1516.

Masoretic Text: Well before 70 AD, Jewish scribes were aware of alternate manuscript versions with different readings. No official list of Scripture had established the Canon of the Old Testament. This was settled about 150 AD and the text with vowel points was being used by 600 AD. This resulted in all variant texts being withdrawn from use.[9]

The Septuagint (LXX): This Greek version of the Old Testament was translated during the reign of Ptolemy II Philadelphus (285–246 BC)—the Torah was completed in 250 BC, and the rest of the Old Testament was completed by (ca.) 130 BC. History records that a group of Jewish scholars carried the Torah from Jerusalem to Alexandria, where it was to be translated from Hebrew into Greek.[10] The oldest copy is Codex Vaticanus of 340 AD, composed of 759 leaves, of which 142 are from the New Testament up to Hebrews 9:13. The New Testament of Codex Sinaiticus is the oldest complete text and dates to 350 AD (ca.). The Chester Beatty Papyrus contains three sets. Set I **p**[45] contains parts of nine Old Testament books and four Gospels plus Acts (Mt 20–Acts 17) and dates to 225 AD; but the Old Testament dates to the 4th century. Set II **p**[46] contains Romans–2 Thessalonians and dates to (ca.) 200 AD. Set III **p**[47] contains Revelations 9:10–17:2 from (ca.) 275 AD (Metzger p. 37–8).

Codex Vaticanus appeared in the Vatican library catalog in 1481. However, it was not studied until 1843. The Pentateuch is accurate, but Psalms (with Ps 151) and Isaiah show signs of incompetence. The last part of Jeremiah is literally unintelligible, and Daniel is a Midrash paraphrase. Most New Testament quotes are from the Septuagint.[11]

The Vulgate of 404 AD: Some old Latin versions of unequal value originating from Africa were in use before 250 AD. Jerome (340?–420 AD) first revised the New Testament from Greek to Latin and began the Old Testament from the LXX but later settled in Bethlehem so as to visit some of the actual places mentioned in the Bible stories. By working with the Hebrew manuscripts, he revised his earlier work. This became the official Bible of the Roman Catholic Church; it included the Apocrypha (from the LXX). The Gutenberg Bible of 1455 is the Vulgate. A revision by Alcuin in 802 attempted to preserve the Vulgate from the numerous corruptions of old and Jerome Latin, which were creeping in. Continued corruptions required the corrections of Lanfranc of Canterbury 1089, Cardinal Niccolaus 1150 and Abbot (Cistercian) Stephanus of 1150. Revisions of the Gutenberg Bible of 1455 included various readings; there was a Paris edition of 1504, a Venice edition of 1511, and the Lyons edition of 1513.

Further work by Cardinal Ximenes in 1517 placed the revised Latin between the Hebrew and Greek. R. Stephens had two editions in 1528 and 1532. Erasmus in 1516 corrected the Latin from the original texts, as did Pagninus in 1518–28 and Cardinal Cajetanus and Steuchius in 1529. Clarius in 1542 and Josephine Campensis in 1533 made a new Latin version. R. Stephens in 1540 used 20 manuscripts and altered his former text. Josephine Benedictus in 1541 made a Paris edition based on a collection of manuscripts and editions. The Biblia Ordinaria with glosses (notes) was published at Lyons in 1545 (sources of manuscripts are not known). The Council of Trent on Feb. 4, 1545 appointed a committee to make a revision. Under Sictus V in 1587, an edition of the LXX was made. Sictus V in 1590 personally corrected the copy of the new Latin Vulgate and forbade publication of other readings.

A revision by Toletus under Clement VIII was issued in 1592. Pope Pius X authorized a revision in 1909 (nine volumes from Genesis [1926] to Esther-Job [1951] have appeared). In 1941, Rome began a translation of the Psalms directly from the Hebrew, which appeared in 1944; in 1945, a second edition with the 17 Canticles in Old and New Testaments was used in the Roman Breviary. Augustinus Bea in 1950 published his Latin book of Ecclesiastes.

English Versions: Early versions in the English vernacular were burned in the 4th century, along with the English martyrs. Versions translated from the Latin include:

- Caedmon, 689—a minstrel versification of an English translation sung as a paraphrase.

- St. Cuthbert, 689—a Latin translation with interlinear English.
- St. Aldhelms, 709—a translation of the Psalms from the Latin.
- Eadfurth, 720—a translation from the Latin.
- Venerable Bede, 649–735—a translation of the Gospel of John in Anglo Saxon.
- King Alfred, 901—translated from the Latin, the first complete Bible in Anglo Saxon.
- Aelfric, 995—a translation from the Latin.

After the Norman Conquest, 1066, Old English almost disappeared from use.

John Wycliffe, 1380—along with his associates, published one hand-written edition based on Jerome's Vulgate. John Purvey independently published one in 1388. Wycliffe died in 1384, but 44 years later (1428) angry priests led by Bishop Fleming dug up his bones, desecrated, and burned them on order of Pope Martin V following a decree of the Council of Constance in 1415.

William Tyndale, 1525—after the fall of Constantinople to Turks in 1453, many Greek scholars fled to Europe and Britain. This revived interest in Greek and Hebrew. Tyndale then sought support for a new translation, which was not based on Roman doctrine and interpretation as in the Vulgate. The Bishop of London, Tunstall, would not support him, so he left for Hamburg, Germany in 1524. His English New Testament was then printed in Cologne, but he was forced to flee to Worms taking several unbound sheets with him. In 1525, Peter Schoeffer (one of Gutenberg's workers) printed 3,000 copies of the New Testament. In 1526, these copies were sent to London, where they were gathered up and burned in front of St. Paul's Cathedral. The Bishop of London bought up one whole shipment, whereupon the merchant Augustine Packynton sent the money to Tyndale who used it to print an enlarged and improved edition. Several editions were printed between 1534–36. While working on the Old Testament at Antwerp, he was tricked into leaving his house (where he was safe from arrest) by a cleric "convert" and was arrested. He continued to work on the Old Testament during his 16-month imprisonment (possibly through Chronicles) but had published previously only the Pentateuch in 1530 and Jonah in 1531. On October 6, 1536, he was strangled and his body burned at the stake.

Myles Coverdale, 1535—under the influence of Cromwell, he republished the first complete English Bible, Tyndale's New Testament, and retranslated the Vulgate and Luther's German (Dutch) into English, since he did not know Hebrew or Greek. He did not relish the task, and it shows haste and carelessness. He had it dedicated to Henry VIII. His translation of the Psalms with some modernizing is still used in the Book of Common Prayer. He also placed the Apocrypha between the Old and New Testaments.

John Rogers, 1537—wrote under the name Thomas Matthew for safety. He was a friend of Tyndale who had been entrusted with the Old Testament unpublished work, notes and New Testament revisions; he used Coverdale for the rest. Archbishop Cranmer (1539) secured a license from Henry's Prime Minister, Thomas Cromwell; thus it was now lawful to publish Scripture in English.

Richard Taverner, 1539—at the request of Cromwell and ecclesiastical opposition, he revised and expunged the Matthew Bible and for the first time had it printed in English.

Great Bible, 1539—commissioned by Cromwell at request of the Anglican Church and directed by Coverdale. He removed controversial margin explanation notes and had it printed on large paper as a "Pulpit Bible." It often was chained to the reading desk to keep men from walking off with it (cost at that time was about $30).

Geneva Bible—the New Testament appeared in 1557, and the complete Bible in 1560. When the Puritans fled to Geneva, William Whittingham, Calvin's brother-in-law, published a small, inexpensive Bible using Roman type with verses and marginal notes. This was the Bible brought to America; it was also read by Shakespeare, Milton, Bunyan, and Cromwell. British sea captains took it around the world. It excluded the Apocrypha and had over 180 editions; eight appeared after the KJV of 1611.

Bishops Bible, 1568—Matthew Parker, Archbishop of Canterbury, after the accession of Queen Elizabeth, sought to secure an official Anglican Church Bible to replace the Great Bible. They could not accept the Geneva Bible in spite of its better scholarship due to the notes and interpretations. He collated and edited the eight clerics' and other scholars' work, which differed in ability and quality. It was a large, well-bound work but did not supersede the Geneva among the people; it included the Apocrypha.

Rheims-Douai Catholic Bible, New Testament, 1582; Old Testament, 1609—with the success of the Geneva and Bishops Bibles, the Catholics wished to have a laity version with translation and notes in accord with the Doctrine of Rome. Due to "hindrance," Gregory Martin of Oxford started the work in an English R.C. College in (Douai) Flanders and later in Rheims and finally at Douai again, when the college moved back. This sorry version ignored the scholarship of the ages and simply retranslated the Vulgate into complex words with copious notes.[12] They did not encourage the laity to read it. The New American Bible is the first Catholic English translation from Greek and Hebrew.

King James Version, 1611—the work of 47 scholars[13] at Oxford and Cambridge, over a seven year period; the actual writing took two years and nine months. The purpose was to placate differences of the Puritans over the mistranslations of the Bishops' and the Puritans' anticlerical bias in the Geneva, which was antagonistic to the Anglicans. It is based on versions from Tyndale and the Greek New Testament of Robert Estienne of 1550. It has been estimated that 4% came from the Wycliffe of 1380, 18% from the Tyndale of 1525 (where 90% of the New Testament is word for word), 13% from the Coverdale of 1535, 19% from the Geneva of 1560, 4% from the Bishops of 1568, 3% others (Rhemes-Douai, Cranmer, etc.), leaving only 39% for the original work of the KJV.

Revisions of 1613, 1615, 1629 and 1638 with an incomplete one of 1653 were to correct inconsistencies of spellings, grammar, and awkward sentence construction. There was a Cambridge revision of 1762 under Dr. Thomas Paris, and an Oxford revision of 1769 (the one used today) by Dr. Benjamin Blayney, to include modernization of spelling, punctuation, and expression. Few changes, mainly in spelling, have occurred since. The 1901 revised version is actually worse than the KJV.[14]

Chapter Divisions

Stephan Langton, Archbishop of Canterbury (died in 1228) is credited with establishing the Bible's chapter divisions. (He also added to the Magna Carta the phrase "Taxation without Representation.") Cardinal Hugo Caro in 1238 (died in 1263) used them in a concordance of the Latin Vulgate. Wycliffe and all others since have used them. Some Psalms were numbered early (see Acts 13:33).

Jewish scholars picked them up and used the same chapter divisions for their Old Testament. Some order is changed, actually for the better.[15]

Verse Divisions

Masoretes used some verse divisions in the 10th century. Rabbi Nathan used them in the Old Testament in 1448. Robert Estienne (Stephanus) of Paris, a printer, used them in a Greek New

Testament, and his Latin Vulgate of 1551 was the first complete Bible to contain both chapter and verse divisions. The Geneva Bible of 1560 was the first English Bible to have them.

Paragraph Divisions ¶

The King James Version was the first to use paragraph divisions to divide subject or story matter. They are usually longer than a verse but shorter than a chapter. They conform to lessons of Lectionaries more than they do chapter divisions. They cease at Acts 20:36. Some recent printings continue to the end of Acts but no further. The reason is not known; maybe some committee did not finish its work.

Italic Words

Certain words within the King James Version were italicized, since equivalents in Hebrew or Greek are lacking. They were added to make a sentence clearer or read smoother. Italics were first used in the Geneva Bible of 1560. Some are in error (see Deuteronomy 33:6, which reads better as "but let his men be few."[16] Using these words where they are not intended can also result in bad doctrine.[17]

Marginal Notes

In the King James Version, sectarian or controversial notes were omitted. Of 17,000 notes, 9,000 are cross references, 5,300 are more literal meanings of Hebrew or Greek, 600 are more literal meanings of proper names or defined unfamiliar terms (coins, weights, plants or animals), 250 are variant readings from other manuscripts. Later notes have been expanded greatly and in some editions replaced by new material. The 1769 edition had 65,000.

Chronology of Ussher

James Ussher was the Archbishop of Armagh of the Irish Protestant Church (ca. 1654) but was published posthumously in 1660; it attempts to fix dates. Beyond the fall of Samaria in 722 BC, he is not off by more than a few years. Many dates are shrewd guesses. His calculation of creation in 4004 BC is badly off, since "begat" is not a literal father to son descent, but refers to having as a descendant. The first Bible to contain the chronology was the Bishop Lloyd King James Version of 1701.

Why New Translations Are Necessary

1. Language is living and changes with time. For instance, in the English King James Version, "let" means "hinder," but now "let" means "allow" (except for tennis buffs, where a let ball does not make it over the net).[18]
2. Knowledge of Greek and Hebrew has vastly improved since the Middle Ages.
3. Better texts are now known: Codex Vaticanus was known of since 1481 and partly used for the King James Version, but not really studied until 1843. Codex Sinaiticus has been known of since 1844, when 43 leaves were found at St. Catherine's Monastery at Mt. Sinai. The other 347 leaves were found at the same place in 1859. It also contains the complete New Testament as well as the Epistle of Barnabas and the Shepherd of Hermas. Codex Alexandrinus was known of since 1078. It reached King Charles I as a gift from Patriarch Cyril Lucar of Constantinople in 1627. Moreover, it just missed being used by the King James Version committee. The Chester Beatty Papyrus was purchased on November 19, 1931, which included nine of Paul's Epistles, the four Gospels, and Acts. It contains the oldest copy of Luke (ca. 200 AD). Finally there was the discovery of the Dead Sea Scrolls, which is discussed in a separate chapter.

CHAPTER 2

AUTHORITY FOR THE BIBLE

SOURCE IS GOD: Phrases such as "the word of the Lord came," "the Lord spoke," "the word of God," "God said," "the Lord commanded," and "thus saith the Lord" occur nearly 700 times in the Pentateuch alone and 3,000 times in the Old Testament.[19]

Who Used Men as His Instrument: Matthew 1:22 refers to Isaiah 7:14 as fulfilled prophesy. Acts 1:16 refers to Psalm 41:9 and 109:8. In addition, 2 Peter 1:21 describes authors as "moved" or "borne along" (compare the reading of vv. 20–21 from the Amplified New Testament).

Inspiration

Their Words Were His Media: In 2 Timothy 3:16, "inspiration of God" means God-breathed. 1 Corinthians 2:13 uses the word "comparing" (only occurs here and 2 Cor 10:12); can also have the since of interpreting, thus explaining spiritual things to spiritual men. For doctrine, Isaiah 28:9,10,13, as shown here requires things be done in pairs. Thus, two clear verses are needed to form a doctrine. What is the inspiration or authority in the thoughts the words express? The Bible itself takes very seriously its own accuracy and trustworthiness. It consistently teaches that to change the voice, mood, or tense of a verb, to change a single word or number of a noun, or to alter or omit a phrase would be to break the Scriptures.[20] Scriptures are God-breathed revelations.[21]

Selection: Only parts of the history of Israel and Judah are given (see Lk 1:1–3; Jn 20:30). Sometimes even the prophets did not comprehend what they were asked to say, as shown by Jeremiah 4:10 (from the Amplified Bible): "Then I [Jeremiah] said, Alas Lord God! Surely you have greatly deceived and misled this people and Jerusalem, [for the prophets represented You as] saying to your people, you shall have peace, whereas the sword has reached to their very life."[22]

What of Difficulties? Tregelles, a textural critic, said, "No difficulty in connection with a proved fact can invalidate the fact itself." A man once said to D.L. Moody, "I cannot accept your Bible because there are so many difficulties in it." Moody replied, "Do you like fish?" "Yes," was the answer. "Do you find bones in it?" "Yes," he said. "Do you eat them?" "No," he said, "I put them on the side of my plate." "That is what I do with the difficulties of the Bible, and I find quite enough fish without bones."

Interpretation:

The interpretation of Science and the interpretations of the Bible frequently disagree. However, Science and the Bible come from the same God.

Criticism—How Do We Know?

1. **Lower or Textual:** This includes exegesis to interpret (grammar, manners, customs of literary and rhetorical forms of

expression), as well as conjectured emendation and usually requires translation of Hebrew and Greek.

2. **Higher or Literary:** This includes scholarship involving authorship, date of writing, character of a book, historical setting, and ascertaining accuracy.[23]

3. **Highest:** This involves motive (see Is 66:2 and Heb 4:12). A critics motive can badly mistreat a verse and make it say the opposite. James Hamilton said, "A Christian on his knees sees farther that a philosopher on his tiptoes."[24]

The Bible is . . .

- eternal (Is 40:8; Mt 24:35);
- a judge (Jn 12:48; Heb 4:12);
- God's seed (Lk 8:11; Jas 1:21);
- the source of our new birth (1 Pt 1:23);
- the means of our growth (1 Pt 2:2);
- the means of our cleansing (Jn 15:3);
- the source of sanctification (Jn 17:17);
- our protection (Eph 6:17);
- edifying (Acts 20:32);
- illuminating (Ps 119:105);
- the means of conversion (Ps 19:11);
- satisfying (Ps 119:103); and
- healing (Ps 107:20).

The proof of the pudding is in the eating. However, keep in mind 1 Corinthians 2:14: "The natural man does not welcome and cannot experience the deep truths and insights of God." He must be changed spiritually.

The Theme of the Bible is simply Christ (Lk 24:25–27). The whole Bible must be seen and studied in this light. He endorsed the Old Testament in Matthew 23:35 and Luke 11:51.[25]

Also Jesus made the statement in John 5:46, "Moses wrote of me."

Admittedly, this is a condensed synopsis, but illustrates why some of these points are controversial. Some of these words can be challenged on every front.

CHAPTER 3

BIBLE STUDY

Background for the Bible

Objectives

INSPIRED BY GOD and without error in the original writings.

1. Used over 22 authors for 39 Old Testament books, and eight or nine different authors for 27 New Testament books.
2. Covered a period from Genesis (ca. 1450 BC) to Revelation (ca. 95 AD), or 1545 years. Job may be the oldest book in the Bible, and could have been written as early as 2000 BC since the setting is in the Patriarchal period. (Job lived 140 years and saw four generations of sons.) The development of poetry in it may place it as late as the Solomonic period (ca. 900 BC). Hebrew poetry is not metrical as ours, but relies on parallelism to link thoughts.[26] There is a 450-year silence between Malachi (400 BC) to James (ca. 50 AD), the first New Testament book.

3. Written in three languages: Hebrew, Aramaic, and Greek (Koine, common).

Purpose

1. To reveal God's purpose and plan for the Christian's life (Jn 10:10).
2. To teach man the folly and result of sin by historical example (Gn 2:25–3:21; 1 and 2 Chr; Is 64:5–7; and Rom 3:23).
3. To grow the Christian in grace and knowledge of our Lord and Savior Jesus Christ (Mt 4:4; Eph 4:14; 2 Pt 3:18; and Jer 15:16).
4. To cleanse us from sin by His Word (Jn 15:3; and Ps 119:9, 11).
5. To reveal future events of the world, so that we will be prepared. (Prophesy must and will be fulfilled, according to Daniel and Revelation, etc.)[27]
6. To grant us eternal life, through belief in Christ Jesus as God's son (Jn 3:16 and14:6; Eph 2:8).

This is why the Bible is the all time best seller. Many people have read the Bible completely through many times. What book(s) have you thought enough of to read more than once? The Bible is the only Book that changes with each reading, because as we grow in Christ we continue to find new truths yearly.

A Bible Study on the Bible

Observe: What do I see?

1. Genesis 1: The creation account is not consistent with what should be its mythological setting. Moses was trained in the Egyptian court as an Egyptian. The Egyptian creation myth says the world began from the egg of the Celestial Goose: the Great Cackler, or else from the Ibis (Thoth), which was laid

on the primeval mound of Hermopolis (opposite Amarna).
Nothing like this appears in the Bible.

2. Compare Genesis 1:1 and John 1:1–3. Who did the creating?
Who was the Word? See John 1:14.

3. Compare Genesis 1:25 and 1:31. These good verses were
said only after man was made.

4. Compare Galatians 5:22–23. Fruit is . . .: These are singular;
we cannot have one without the others, if we are Spirit led
Christians and not carnal. The corresponding list in vs.
19–21 is plural. Each sin stands by itself.

5. Compare Acts 9:3–5 and Galatians 2:1. Galatians 1:11–24
recounts Paul's visit to Jerusalem, after being away anywhere
from a year and two months to three years.[28] Paul was
bringing from the scattered churches a financial collection,
due to a severe famine in Judea in 46 AD (known from
Roman records of Josephus, and Acts 11:28–30). Thus,
Paul's conversion was in 46-16= 30 AD, or shortly after the
death of Jesus.

6. Compare John 8:58 and 18:6 with Exodus 3:14, noting the
statements, "I am." In John 10:30–33, why did the crowd
react to this statement as it did?

7. Compare Isaiah 53 with 1 Peter 2:21–24. Who is Isaiah
speaking of? Note also that his back was beaten and his
beard plucked out (Is 50:6), and his face beaten to a pulp
(Is 52:14).

8. Compare Revelation 2:4 with 2:8–11. Ephesus was a strong
church. Paul taught there three years. Smyrna Christian
Jews were undergoing strong persecution from Jews (v. 9).
In verse 10, "ten days" may refer to the persecutions under
Diocletian from 295–305. Compare the above verses with
Revelation 2:16: repent, or else.

9. In Acts 1:8, there were over 200 observations found for this
verse. Prof. Hendricks at Dallas Theological Seminary has
620!

Interpret: What does it mean?

1. Proverbs 26:4–5 Is there a contradiction here? Are there times when a rascal should and should not be answered?
2. Daniel 1:5 indicates three years, but 2:1 indicates two years. In Babylon, the accession year was not counted as the first year of reign.
3. Daniel 3:1 comments on the size of the image. Would this have been a solid gold statue, or a gold plated one? A quick calculation would show that a 90-foot high statue would greatly exceed the size of the solid gold statue of Marduk in the Esagila temple that Herodotus said weighed 800 talents, or 20 tons of gold and stood 12 cubits, or 18 feet high. Xerxes melted it down in 482 BC (Eydoux p. 73, TLBM p. 139 and Wellard p. 155). Thus it would have to be gold plated. A 90-foot solid-gold statue would exceed the world's gold supply at that time.
4. Daniel 3:19 describes the furnace as seven times hotter, but hotter than what? Probably the temperature of a bread oven is intended. If this were 350°, then the furnace would have been at 2450° F, unless the seven times is only an expression of completion as in other Scripture. If literal, the temperature is typically above that to melt cast iron or to fire pottery.

Apply: How does it work in my life, or how should it work?

1. 1 Corinthians 8:9–13 (meat offered to idols) and 1 Corinthians 10:27–31.
2. 1 Corinthians 13 describes *agape* love, which is all giving and comes only from God. This is the only Greek word not translated in the New Testament. Other Greek words for love are *eros* (sexual love, which is not used in the Bible), *phileo* (brotherly, friendship love) and *storge* (family love, also not

used in the Bible). See also the change from *agape* to *phileo* in John 21:15–17.

Try the following for yourself. How can you apply these? Are there any contradictions?

Drinking

1. Deuteronomy 14:26 and 1 Thessalonians 5:22
2. Proverbs 23:29–35 and 1 Corinthians 8:13
3. Isaiah 28:7 and 1 Corinthians 6:19–20 (the body is the temple of the Holy Spirit).
4. 1 Timothy 5:23 or in John 2 (the Greek *oinos* can be either wine or grape juice; only the context or time of year can distinguish these).

Immorality

1. Exodus 20:5, The Mosaic Covenant: Sins of the father are visited upon children; compare Jeremiah 31:30, which declares everyone will die for his own iniquity; and furthermore, consider the expected New Covenant in Jeremiah 31:31–34.
2. Leviticus 18:22–23, regarding homosexuality and bestiality: God's remedy is 1 Corinthians 10:12–13; he provides *the* way of escape.
3. Romans 1:18–32 refers to homosexuality and idolatry, with God's same remedy (above).
4. 1 Corinthians 6:9 speaks to the effeminate or abusers of themselves with mankind, specifically referring to transvestites and/or homosexuals.
5. 1 Corinthians 3:12–17 speaks to false teaching and gay pastors, with true repentance described in 2 Corinthians 7:12 (especially vv. 9–11).
6. 1 Corinthiains 5:1–7 speaks to incest.

Effect of Sin on You

1. Jeremiah 17:9: The heart is deceitful above. . . and the Author of Sin: Jeremiah 17:10
2. Romans 5:12: Wherefore, as by one man sin . . .
3. 2 Corinthians 4:3–5: God of this world; and 2 Corinthians 11:14–15: the god of this world is Satan.

Sin Does Not Pay

1. Proverbs 16:25: There is a way that seemeth. . .; and God's plan for sins in John 3:16–17.
2. Isaiah 13:11: And I will punish the world for their evil and the wicked. . .; and God's way of Ephesians 2:8–10.
3. Mark 8:36: For what shall it profit a man. . .; same as above.
4. Galatians 6:7–8: Be not deceived, God is not mocked. . .; same as above.

What does the Bible say about gambling? Nothing as such (do not include casting lots, as this was prophetic). However, see Matthew 6:25–34. God's Word condemns covetousness and materialism; both of these are at the core of gambling. Matthew 10:29–30 says God is sovereign in the direction of human events; gambling looks to luck. Matthew 22:37–40 insists our main goal should be love for God and neighbor; gambling seeks personal gain and pleasure at others' loss and pain. Ephesians 4:27 and 2 Thessalonians 3:10–13 teach that man should work creatively and use his possessions for the good of others; gambling fosters a something-for-nothing attitude and a poor stewardship of possessions.

As a means of opening up alternate ways of thinking about Scripture, you could try playing the "What if" game. For example, what if Adam had been stronger in Genesis 2:15–19?

What would be the consequences if he had not eaten the fruit?

1. Eve was doomed to a spiritual death; would she have died physically sooner?
2. Eve punished, but not Adam.
3. What potential problems would arise from her being smarter than Adam in areas of good and evil?
4. Would Adam want her as a wife?
5. Could Adam complain to God about Eve and demand a replacement? Since God hates divorce, how would this work (especially in view of Deut. 24:1)?
6. How would he relate to her?
7. If half-pure and half-corrupted, what would be the sin nature of the children?
8. Would God comply? If Adam refused to consummate the marriage, would not this be the end of the human race?
9. Would they still be expelled from Eden? (The answer to this one is yes. Because of the tree of life, Eve would need to be shielded from it.)

CHAPTER 4

MASORETIC TEXT

Ancient Translations

THE ORIGINAL OLD Testament scrolls from Genesis through Joshua were written from ca. 1420–1375 BC, and the rest of the Old Testament (Judges through Malachi) were written from 1020–400 BC, originally in Hebrew but with certain words and parts in Aramaic.[29] The old Hebrew version used in 432 BC later resulted in the Samaritan Schism under Nehemiah (13:28) when a son of Joiada married a daughter of Sanballat, and he was driven out of Judah. It is said he took a copy of the Torah with him, from which the Samaritan Pentateuch derives: the oldest copy we have dates to 655 AD.

The Jewish Aramaic later gave rise to the Targums, first oral in form from 800 BC to 30 AD, then the written form from 30 to 600 AD; the oldest copy, Onkelos dates to 700 AD. At this point translations began to be made. The Septuagint (or LXX), written in Greek, was translated in 250 BC (the oldest copy we have dates to 350 AD; see New Testament manuscripts). The old Syriac was translated in 150 AD (which became known as the *Peshita*: "Simple" Aramaic, the oldest copy dating to ca. 600 AD). A Latin translation was written in 175 AD, which became the Vulgate of Jerome's 404 AD version. He used the LXX for some parts (the oldest copy dates to ca. 810 AD). The Egyptian Coptic version, derived from the LXX, dates to 350 AD. Other versions followed.

At the Academy of Jamina in 90 AD, the Jews were faced with a decision: what was Scripture? The new Christians were calling their books Scripture, but the Jews had never finalized their collection. Copies of scrolls were beginning to be found, which had variant readings, omissions, and some errors. It was decided to standardize the text; the others that failed scrutiny were culled out. This process of refinement (addition of vowels, vocalization, and cantillation) continued under the group known as the Masoretes (tradition) from 400–900 AD, the oldest copy known dating to 1010 AD. The oldest manuscript is a Book of the Prophets from Cairo of 895 AD. The oldest pieces of the Old Testament are the two silver scrolls from Tomb chamber 25 at St. Andrews in Jerusalem; both contain part of the Priestly Benediction of Numbers 6:24–26 and scroll one also contains Deuteronomy 7:9 dating from ca. 605 BC. This section of Numbers from 1:1–10:28 is said to be by the "P" redactor (as is the Dt 7:9 reference) written from 500–450 BC (so much for the "P" redactor theory). BAR 35: 22 (09).

The Dead Sea Scrolls furnished a huge trove of scrolls and fragments in old Hebrew that are older than the Masoretes collection, dating back to 250 BC in the Leviticus fragments and 225–200 BC for the Samuel fragments. The great Isaiah scroll dates to 150 BC. Before these, the oldest Hebrew fragment was the Nash papyrus "Shema Yisrael" of Deuteronomy 6:4 and the 10 commandments dating to 100 BC.

Copying Errors

No handwritten Biblical or classical manuscript is without errors. Scarcely a page can be found on which some note or correction has not been added. John Mill (1645–1707) found 30,000 variant readings in the New Testament alone. Now, of 7,917 verses in the New Testament, only about eight are in serious question, but no doctrinal position is affected by any of them. This is by far the best record of any ancient manuscripts known. Since the printing press of Gutenberg, we can now copy our mistakes by the hundreds of thousands at a time. Proofreaders are still missing some.

Many problem verses are easily corrected. Codex 109 of the 14th century is the worse case known: it was apparently copied from a manuscript that had Luke's genealogy of Jesus (3:23–38) in two columns of 28 lines each. The scribe copied the genealogy by following the lines across both columns. The result is that almost everyone is the son of the wrong father. The last column was apparently not full; the name of God is within the list instead of closing "Adam, the son of God." Here God is the son of Aram and the source of the human race is Phares and not God. A scribe may be learned in Greek but not necessarily the Bible. His general knowledge should have caught this mistake. Few of us can recite the genealogy of Christ, but many would be familiar with the list covering Nahor-Perez at least to five generations.

Even Shakespeare is not immune, in that some type of error occurs as is this drivel in the first quire of King Lear in Act III, Scene IV: 'Swithald footed thrice the old a nellthu night more and her nine fold bid her, O light and her thoth plight and arint thee, with arint thee'. Can anyone in his right mind tell me what this is supposed to mean? Although the Harvard Classics Edition of 1968 makes a good stab at it. Edgar: "St. Withold footed thrice the 'old (open country); he met the night-mare, and her nine fold (familiar spirits); bid her alight, and her troth plight, and, aroint (avaunt) thee, witch, aroint thee. Recovery of the text is often possible.

Types of Copying Errors

1. **Faulty eyesight:** Scribes afflicted by astigmatism (or in some cases, sloppy writing) failed to distinguish certain letters, such as in the Hebrew, *dalet* and *resh*: for instance, as in Genesis 10:4 and 1 Chronicles 1:7, where *Dodanim* should be *Rodanim,* or *he* should be *heth*, and *beth* should be *kaph*. In Greek uncial script the lunar Sigma, Epsilon, Theta and Omicron (C, E, ϑ,O) look alike, causing confusion in passages such as 1 Timothy 3:16—some manuscripts read *OC* ("he who") rather than ϑ*C* ("God"), Similar confusion has occurred over Gamma, Pi, and Tau (Γ,Π,Τ) when a crossbar is carelessly drawn or a leg is drawn too short; such was the case in 2 Peter 2:13, in which "love feasts" was unfortunately then translated "deceptions." Likewise, when two Lambdas are written too close together, they could be perceived as a Mu (ΛΛ,Μ), which was the case for some translations of Romans 6:5, rendering "but" as "together."

   A Lambda written too close to an Iota may become Nu (ΛΙ, Ν as in 2 Pt 2:18, where "scarcely" becomes "really"). In this latter case Tau and Gamma (Τ,Γ) were also confused. Sometimes Delta and Lambda (Δ,Λ) are confused, as in Acts 15:40 where "having chosen" became "having received." Similar mistakes account for the 1 Corinthians 12:13 "to drink of one Spirit" being mistranslated as "to drink of one drink," or in Romans 12:11 the accepted "serving the Lord" became "serving the time." Similar mistakes can occur in the later minuscule cursive script.

2. **Inverting Letter Order—Metathesis:** Similar to dyslexia today, scribes sometimes reversed characters, creating a

different word. Some of these are clearly nonsense words
and are known to be mistakes.

3. **Copying a Word, Phrase or Letter Twice—Dittography:**
   In Acts 19:34 the phrase, "Great is Artemis of the Ephesians"
   is copied twice.

4. **Copying a Word or Letter Once—Haplography:** In 1
   Samuel 10:1 the words from "over his heritage" have omitted
   what follows "And you shall reign over the people of the
   Lord and you will save them from the hand of your enemies
   round about. And this shall be the sign to you that the Lord
   has anointed you to be prince over his heritage." The scribe's
   eye jumped from one heritage to the other, missing what was
   in between. The LXX, Vulgate, DSS and Josephus all have
   the longer version. This is usually the case where a longer
   text is known, also known as **parablepsis** (a looking to the
   side) combined by **homoioteleution** (a similar ending of
   lines).

5. **Omitting a Phrase Which Began the Same—
   Homoioarchton:** As in Isaiah 2:3: [the mountain of the
   Lord to] the. The material in brackets was omitted from
   the 1st "the" to the 2nd.

6. **Omitting a Phrase Which Ends the Same—
   Homoioteleution:** As in Isaiah 4:5–6: by day [and the
   smoke. . . by day]; 33 words have been left out. Both 5 and
   6 result in the eye jumping ahead to the second occurrence.

7. **Mistakes of Memory—Memoriter:** Our memory can play
   tricks on us, as in Isaiah 49:6 reversing the "tribes of Israel"
   and the "preserved of Jacob."

8. **Errors of Reading:** These occur when a scribe reads to a
   group who copy new manuscripts. Did the copying scribe
   hear Adoni when the text had YHWH (which would not be
   spoken as such)? Spoken homonyms could also be confused,
   as would be with English, for example: *there* or *their, great*
   or *grate, led* or *lead.* On the other hand consider this effect

of wrong word division: The notable surgeon was not able to operate because there was no table. Was it attendance or were we to at ten dance? Was it unionized or un-ionized. In Revelation 1:5, *Lousanti* = "Washed," as in the KJV; or *Lusanti* = "released or freed," as in the oldest manuscripts. Both words would be spoken the same. In Revelation 4:3 the word "rainbow" would be pronounced the same as "priests" as the older manuscripts have it. Thus, we know of a group of manuscripts copied by hearing, while a scribe working individually from a scroll before him copied the others. Each has its own set of errors.

9. **Errors of the Mind:** These occur when the scribe holds a clause in his mind before writing it down. These include substitutes of synonyms, transposing the sequence of words as in Mark 1:5 "and were all baptized" to "and baptized were all." Adding words from one passage to another as in Colossians 1:14 "in whom we have redemption the forgiveness of sins (through his blood)" is added from Ephesians 1:7. Anyone who memorizes Scripture will often remember the extra words contained in the other verse.

10. **Errors of Judgment:** These occur most often in which marginal notes were often added to the text, because the scribe did not know what to do with it. For example, a note at John 5:7 was added at John 5:3b–4.

11. **Changes for Completeness; Historical or Geographical Difficulties:** Examples are adding "unto repentance" from Luke 5:32 to Matthew 9:13, adding "the scribes" to "the chief priests" in Matthew 26:13, or "Pharisees" to "scribes" in Matthew 27:41, or adding "openly" to Matthew 6:4, 6. Changing "6th hour" of John 19:14 to "3rd hour" as in Mark 15:25, not realizing that John uses Roman time. Changing Bethany of John 1:28 to Beth Abara by Origen and thus into several manuscripts and the KJV.

12. **Conflation of Readings:** A scribe faced with two manuscripts both reading differently might combine both readings as in Luke 24:53 where "blessing God" and "praising men" were independent, becoming "praising and blessing God."

13. **Additions of Missing Details:** Scribes sometimes would fill in the blanks, adding names to fill out Jesus' genealogy in Matthew 1:8; changing the 14 generations of Matthew 1:17; giving the names of Onesiphorus's household in 2 Timothy 4:19; naming Cleopas's companion on the Emmaus road of Luke 24:18; and naming the two thieves in Matthew 27:38, Mark 25:27, and Luke 23:32.

14. **Deliberate Euphemisms:** Offensive or inelegant words were sometimes replaced, as in 1 Samuel 24:3 or 2 Chronicles 16:12. (Asa didn't have gout!) **Synonyms** may be used. Alternatively, **Glosses** may be added, as in Genesis 10:14 and 14:8. **Sectarian** changes may be made, in that the Samaritan scribes changed Mt. Ebal in Deuteronomy 27:4 to Mt. Gerizim. Also, see the 18 scribal changes (see the Tiqqune Sopherim) of which six are uncertain.

15. **Wrong Word Division or Connection:** In Jeremiah 46:15 the LXX reads, "Why has Apis (sacred bull) fled?" or "Why did not your bull stand?" compare v 20. Early Hebrew and Greek had few spaces and Hebrew had no vowels. In English GDSNWHR could become God is nowhere, but the other division, into God is now here, may depend on whether the writer is a theist or atheist.

16. **Hapax Legomena:** "Words used once." Several words in Hebrew are unknown, in that 21.3% of the words occur only once. This is a nightmare for translators. Recovery of other Semitic documents and archaeological discoveries has filled in large numbers of these. Even so, we still are not sure what a *Sinnor* is in 1 Samuel 5:8. In Arabic, it relates to "hook," and a close word in Hebrew also refers to a hook, rather than "gutter", as it is commonly translated, (see below

and Metzger for more complete information; BR 1[1]: 28 [85]).

Other Ancient Manuscripts

Bible scrolls and codices of all types far outnumber some of our historic writings. As of 1988 there were 88 partial or complete papyrus manuscripts, 274 uncial codices and 2,795 miniscule as well as 2,209 lectionaries. For example, Homer holds first place with some 643 copies, the oldest dating to 400 BC, separated from the author by only 400 years. Yet Caesar's Gallic War is known only from ten copies, the oldest copy dating to 850 AD. Thucydides' History of 460–400 BC is known by eight fragment copies from 900–950 AD; and the oldest of eight copies of Herodotus (480–415 BC) dates to 900 AD.

Further discoveries of ancient biblical manuscripts can always be expected, such as the discovery in 1990 of a 490-page book in Coptic, complete with wooden covers containing all 150 Psalms from ca. 392 BC. It was found in a 12-year-old girl's tomb at Al-Mudil 25 mi N of Oxyrhynchus. Few scholars can read the old Coptic. The present Coptic Orthodox church uses a modernized version.

Notes in Masorite Text:

There is a treasure trove of material in the margins, notes and annotations that include:

- *Tiqqune Sopherim*: Scribal corrections in which 18 verses have been changed (see below).
- *Puncta Extraodinaria*: Fifteen words in which every letter has a dot above it, usually to draw attention to doubted words or statements.

- *Pisqa:* Twenty-eight blank spaces or omissions, such as 1 Samuel 13:1.
- *Qaryan Walo Kethibhan:* The Masorite marks the text to be read this way, but the word is not actually in the text and mark omissions; I know of five).
- *Kethibhan Walo Quryan:* Word is written, but must be omitted (mistaken scribal addition; I know of three).
- *Qere:* Suggested as improvements. Several hundred are known (see *Sebhirim* below).

Orthography Peculiarities:

- Anomalous Forms: Two hundred defective forms, usually by omission, of the *Matres Lectionis* or wrong insertion of the same.
- *Literae Majusculae:* Thirty large letters (mark middle letter of a book, such as Leviticus 11:42, in belly is the middle letter in the Pentateuch and Jeremiah 6:7, the middle letter of the Old Testament. In the Shema of Deuteronomy 6:4 the large ayin in "Hear" prevents interchange with *aleph*, which means "perhaps," and the large *daleth* in "one"prevents interchange with *resh*, which means "another." Combined, these would cause the verse to read, "Perhaps O Israel, the Lord our God is another God." Both Letters form the word *witness*, which every Israelite becomes when uttering the Shema (Hertz p. 769.)
- *Literae Minusculae:* Thirty-two small letters that end and begin adjacent words with the same letter. In the old Hebrew, one letter could stand for two in such cases.
- Inverted and Reversed *Nun*: Nine known, significance debated.
- Oddities: Letters cut off or inserted at beginning, middle, or end of a word; six are known. In Genesis 2:7 "formed"

in Hebrew (*vayitzer*) has two *yods,* but in v. 19 it has only one. The Rabbis explained that man has a *yetzer tob,* or good inclination, and a *yetzer ra,* or evil inclination, whereas animals do not. Man also has a soul and spirit, (Hertz p. 6).

- *Literae Suspensae:* These are letters that are written above the line; four are known.

Masorah:

- Statistical: Used to count letters and check accuracy. All letters had to be accounted for when new scrolls were made.
- *Lamad:* Used to mark *Hapax Legomena.* Of 8,000 Hebrew words, 1,700 or 21.25% occur only once in the Bible. Sometimes the meaning is found in other secular writings. Several dozen have been rediscovered recently.
- Exegetical *Pahashiyot:* Open and closed text divisions. This is a type of paragraphing that allows the Pentateuch to be read in one year.
- Vocalization—*Metres Lectionis* (mother of writings) or *Scripto Plena* (full writing): Letters used as vowels to give the correct pronunciation.
- Accentuation: Used for pronunciation and cantillation. Remember all Scripture can be sung, even the headings to the Psalms and others.
- Admonition: Guidance on the divine name YHWH where Adoni is to be read instead, or where it is to be spoken, or to read the next to last line over again for the end of a book (eg., Isaiah, Malachi, Lamentations, and Ecclesiastes).
- *Sebhirim:* Variant readings from other known texts; some 350 are recorded.

- *Paseq:* Divider occurs 500 times; the significance is unknown.
- *Curiosa:* For example, all but eight verses of Ruth start with *vaw* (or W). Redundant letters and years covered by events mentioned in a section.

Of 23,085 verses in the Old Testament, 1,287 (5.6%) are defective in at least one way. Some of these represent unusual or obscure words.

Tiqqune Sopherim

There were scribal changes made at certain places. The Sopherim introduced marginal notes in the Masoretic Text about 100 AD. These changes mainly introduced euphemisms for Hebrew words the Sopherim considered offensive or inelegant. Eighteen of these are recorded. In 2 Chronicles 16:12 Asa was diseased in his "feet," but it wasn't gout, and it wasn't his feet. Even though this is not one of the 18, this was done almost everywhere feet are mentioned.

Verse Changed	Probable Hebrew Original
Gn 18:22	"——while YHWH passed in front of Abraham"
Nm 11:15	Change uncertain: "my" may have been "thy"
Nm 12: 12	Change uncertain: the word changed was "not"
1 Sm 3:13	the sons "brought a curse on God"
2 Sm 16:12	"Lord will look on and return good. . ."
2 Sm 20:1	Change uncertain
1 Kgs 12:16	Change uncertain

2 Chr 10:16	Change uncertain: these three have the same context; an ancient cry for rebellion.
Jb 7:20	"So that I am a burden to thee"
Ps 106:20	"Thus they exchanged the glory of God"
Lam 3:20	Change uncertain: possibly "cheek"?
Eze 8:17	"Twig" should be some other word
Hos 4:7	"they" exchanged "their" Glory
Hb 1:12	"Thou does not die."
Zec 2:8	". . .touches the apple of My eye"
Mal 1:12	Change uncertain

For these and other problems in the Hebrew text, see A. Jeffery (IB Vol. I p. 46). (Note: this should be enough for those looking for hidden Bible Codes a la Michael Drosnin to realize that any change would throw the computer code off and make finding any hidden words or phrases impossible, since an unaltered text would be required. (See also BR 13[4]: 22 [97].))

Kabbalah

I approach this section with fear and trembling. The Christian is abysmally ignorant of this branch of Judaism. I will draw heavily on the book by Franck for the discussion. See also the *Kabbalah for Dummies* book. Closely related to the Masoretic Text development, was the mystical element of the Kabbalah from around 100 AD. It is claimed that every word and letter carries a special significance. "Woe to the man who sees nothing but simple stories and ordinary words in the Law" (Franck p. 80).

The Kabbalah is said to have been given to Adam by angels to explain how he could recover his primal nobility and bliss. Another school says it was given to Moses during the 40 days on Sinai, who transmitted it to 70 elders, who in turn passed it on orally until Ezra wrote it down (see II Esdras 12:37; 14:45 [Franck p. 13]). It consists of two parts: the *Sefer Yetzirah,* or Book of Formation, and the *Zohar* or Book of Brightness or Splendor. It teaches the three names of God: The Tetragrammation (YHWH), which was spoken once per week in the schools. The name of 12 letters was spoken daily (under the breath) by the priests to their brethren during the benediction. Moreover, there also was the name of 42 letters, a close comparison of which is Isaiah 9:6, which Jewish scholars would translate as: "Wonderful of counsel is God the mighty, the Everlasting Father, the Ruler of Peace" (see Hertz p. 305). Maimonides concluded that there was no name in Hebrew composed of 42 letters (without vowels) and that they formed several words. The final observation made on this complicated subject: Counting the letters of the sacramental Hebrew names, the names of the ten Sefiroth of the Kabbalah and adding the conjunctive particle "v" as a prefix, adds up to 42 (Franck, pp. 19–20).

The antiquity of the kabbalistic ideas goes back at least to the Babylonian translation of the Torah by Onkelos, which was regarded as a divine revelation. The original source is to be found in the theology of the ancient Persians starting with Zoroaster, who had already began his religious mission in 549 BC at age 40 and continued until 539. He had already converted the entire court of Hystaspis, the father of Darius. The Brahmins of India sent an entourage to the court to challenge Zoroaster on the new teachings, but they were overcome. Zoroaster finally taught in Babylon and converted the capital to his own doctrines. This is where Ezra would have picked it up about 536–530 BC in the reign of Cyrus. Many of the concepts are found in the Send Avesta, (Franck pp. 201–224).

Other admonitions were given in the Mishna—Haggiga Sect 2. In Genesis, the "Story of Creation" is not to be explained (because it taught the science of nature) to two men. The Merkaba (Heavenly Chariot of Ezekiel 1:4–28) could not be taught even to one, "unless he is wise and can deduce wisdom of his own accord" (because it contained a treatise on theology). All Kabbalists accepted this opinion. Rabbi Zerah in the Talmud is even more severe, saying even the chapter headings may be divulged only to men "who carry within them a heart full of solicitude" (Franck pp. 15–16). Today the beginning and end of Ezekiel is not read in the Synagogues due to these points. When the Mishna was edited (in 185 AD), there already existed a secret doctrine concerning the Creation and the Divine Nature, which evoked religious awe even among the outsiders who were not privy to the actual knowledge.

The Babylonian Talmud contains another interesting story:

> The teachers taught that four persons entered the Garden of Delight (this Kabbalah teaching), ben Azai, ben Zoma, Aher and Rabbi Akiba. Ben Azai looked around and died (Ps 116:15 was quoted for him). Ben Zoma looked around and went crazy (Prv 25:16 was quoted for him). Aher made ravages in the plantations. (His real name was Elisha ben Abua, one of the wisest teachers in Israel. His name was changed to Aher, which literally means that he became "another man," by becoming an open infidel. He threw over morality, betrayed his faith, led a scandalous life, and was even charged with the murder of a child.) Akiba entered in peace and came out in peace." The Jerusalem Talmud states that Aher recognized in Heaven two supreme principles. The Babylonian Talmud states that Aher saw in Heaven the power of Metatron, the angel next to God, by exclaiming, "Perhaps there are two supreme powers." Metatron in the Kabbalist system was an archangel who governs the visible world, and resides over the spheres, planets and celestial bodies suspended in space, as well as the angels who control them. The numerical

value of his name is the same as the Almighty, and therefore interchangeable (Franks, pp. 16–18).

Not only in Babylon but also in Sura, Pompadita and Nehardea, religious schools were established. Hiller the Babylonian, who died about 44 BC, was the teacher of Yohanan ben Zakai mentioned often in the kabbalistic stories. These same schools produced the Babylonian Talmud.

The Persian *Send Avesta* tells of the fate of the dead at the hands of the demons. The Kabbalists tell of the seven tests: 1. The separation of body and soul; 2. The recapitulation of the deeds of our life; 3. The time of burial; 4. The ordeal or judgment of the grave; 5. The time when the dead, still animated by the vital spirit, feels the biting of the worms; 6. The punishment of hell; 7. The metempsychosis. These have been taken almost literally from the Zohar. The Parsee in the *Send Avesta* must not take four steps upon leaving his bed without putting on the sacred belt called the Kosti, and washing his hands and face three times. Those of rabbinical law follow the same procedures. The practice of defending the dead and the newborn are the same, except the Jews' ceremony of keeping at bay the night demon Lilith ([Franks pp. 209–210], which is mentioned in Isaiah 34:14, but translated as screech owl—she is also the one responsible for killing new born babies, and who plagues young men and boys with nocturnal emissions) is described in the book of Raziel (see NUBD p. 922). Lilith is also credited with being Adam's first wife—by insisting on the top position for intercourse, she was forced to leave Eden and stand in the Euphrates up to her neck. She later became the consort of Samael, the same as Satan in the Zohar 3:19; 7:34. (See the *Encyclopedia Judica* for further information.) The Assyrian version of her is Lamashtu, "Who keeps going after women about to give birth" (TLBM p. 69).

The Kabbalist is also much concerned with the numerical value of words, since each letter of the Hebrew alphabet also stands for a number. This is best brought out in Michener's book (p. 864), where Rabbi Zaki, in fiddling with the alphabet, saw all the letters but two fall away (*shin* and *aleph*, which means fire, and whose value is 301). Zaki, who saw the numbers appear in odd places, was convinced that he was to go to Rome. There he would confront the Pope and be burned at the stake.

Other systems were established, including the *Gematria* (the oldest example is an inscription of Sargon III [721–705], who built the wall of Khorsabad 16,283 cubits long to correspond with the numerical value of his name), wherein one word can be exchanged for another with the same numerical value (see above); the *Notarikon,* wherein each letter of a word becomes the initial for another word; and the *Tomurah,* wherein the value of the letters are changed the last for first and vice versa (Franks p. 82). This is also known as *Athbash.* Three examples are actually present in Jeremiah 25:26 and 51:41 (wherein *Sheshack* is equivalent to Babylon, as *beth beth lamed* becomes *shin shin kaph*), and 51:1 (wherein *Leb-qamai* is equivalent to *Caldea*; IB p. 1003). The Samaritan Pentateuch also has an acrosticon-cryptogram called *Tashqil* down the middle columns (see BR 7[5]: 13 [91]).

The *Sefer Yetzirah* lacks a title and author, but concludes with the statement that it was given to Abraham and is found in the oldest commentaries. Today the honor has spread to Rabbi Akiba. The Talmud gives him a rank even above Moses.

The Zohar's author was also kicked around; some claim it is not the work of Rabbi Simeon ben Yahai but rather was published under his name in 1290. Others claim it to be the work of Moses de Leon of Aragon, who wrote under the name of R. Yahai. Yahai died about the year 140, but there are statements in the Zohar that the Mishna is divided into six parts, when the Mishna was not written until sixty years after his death. It named the vowel signs and other innovations of the Tiberias School, which did not invent them until the 6th century. It also contains the interesting statement: "The earth turns upon itself like a sphere; that some people are above, others below; that all creatures adapt their appearance to the climate of the region, although always keeping the same position; that certain places on earth are light, while others are in darkness; that some have daylight while others have night, and that there are countries where it is always daylight, or at least, where night lasts only a few moments." Copernicus did not know this until 1500 and the Zohar dates to about 1300 in the oldest copies. R. Yahai says that he had predecessors and that he only collected the material. How far back before his death does it go (Franks pp. 35–41 and 61)?

In the Sefer Yetzirah the central theme is the Sefiroth, which represent the ten categories of the universe, stated this way: "There is no end to the ten Sefiroth, neither in the future or in the past, either in good or in evil, either in height or in depth, either in the east or in the west, either in the south or in the north." The paired Sefiroth, even if opposite, are part of one idea—one infinite.

One, the first Sefiroth, is the spirit of the living God. The Spirit, the Voice, and the Word, that is the Holy Spirit.

Two is the breath, which issues from the Spirit; it contains 22 letters and forms a single breath.

Three is water, which issues from breath or from air.

Four is fire, which issues from water, and with which He made the throne of His glory, the celestial wheels (Ophanim), the Seraphim and the angelic hosts. From these three He built His habitation.

Five is east.
Six is west.
Seven is north.
Eight is south.
Nine is height.
Ten is depth.

Their symbols are the different combinations, which may be formed with the first three Hebrew letters of the name of Yahweh (YHW). It expressly states that the Holy Spirit, the Voice and the Word, are one and the same. This part of the Kabbalah deals only with the universe and not with man.

The 22 letters by giving them form and figure, and by mixing and combining them in different ways, God made the soul of all that is formed and his holy name. Through them the Holy Spirit reveals Itself in nature (Franks p. 73). One should look for the numbers 3, 7, and 12 in the three areas of nature:

1. In the general composition of the world
2. In the division of the year or in the distribution of time
3. In the structure of man

Three represents the elements water, air, and fire—the symbols of moral man.

Seven are doubles or contraries or opposite ends, seven planets (as of 1843) for good or evil, seven days of the week, and seven openings in the head.

Twelve corresponds to the twelve signs of the Zodiac, the twelve months of the year, and the twelve parts of the human body: sight, hearing, smell, speech, nutrition, generation, action or touch, locomotion, anger, laughter, thought, and sleep.

Intelligence is represented by the 22 letters of the alphabet.

"One prevails over the three, the three over the seven, and the seven over the twelve; but each is inseparable from the others. The Celestial Dragon is the center of the universe, the heart the center of man, and the revolutions of the Zodiac constitute the basis of the year. The first is said to be comparable to a king upon his throne; the second to a king among his subjects; the third to a king at war" (Franks p. 75).

The Kabbalists had their own abstract form of a kind of Trinity: "Wisdom is called Father, Intelligence is Mother, and the firstborn son is knowledge or Science." Among their writing is a picture of a man wearing a crown. The head is wisdom, the left shoulder is intelligence, the chest is beauty, the left arm is fear, the right arm is love, the genitals is foundation, the left leg is splendor, and the right leg is firmness and the feet is kingdom. The right hand has a cross in the palm.

The first three Sifiroth—Crown, Wisdom and Intelligence—are regarded as identical. Of the last seven, all but Kingdom exists in pairs: one active or male, the other passive or female. The last Sefiroth Kingdom, also called Malkuth, expresses the harmony that exists between all the others, (Franks pp. 99–102).

The Zohar states that Samael is the angel of death; evil desire, Satan, and the serpent that seduced Eve are one and the same. He and his "wife" Lilith combined are called the beast (Franks p. 120). The custom of the Orthodox Jew of looking at the fingernails and fingertips when blessing the candle at the end of Sabbath is also based on a Zohar passage (Franks p. 135).

As Kabbalists encountered Christianity, they began to collect passages from the Zohar and the New Testament that were similar. Many of them converted to Christianity in the medieval period, including Paul Ricci, Conrad Otton, and Rittangel, the last editor of the Sefer Yitzirah, all around 1600. Around 1760, The Polish Jew Jacob Frank (HJP p. 767), who was founder of the sect of the Zoharites, converted to Catholicism along with several thousand of his followers. Rittangel, after converting, regarded the Kabbalah as the most potent means of lowering the barrier that separates church from synagogue. This was also shown by the vast conversions of the followers of Sabbatai Zevi (who himself converted to Islam [JP p. 703]) in 1660 and the sect of the Neo-Hassidim of Hungary and Poland (see the *Encyclopedia Judica* for more information.).

Several in the movement declared themselves a Messiah, or were proclaimed as such by followers: Solomon Molcho "the Messenger" of David Reubeni in 1515; Sar David Reubeni (from the tribe of Reuben) in 1528; Shabbetai Zevi, 1626–1676 (his marriages and sexual orgies at his court, as well as licentiousness, show his deviance); Barukhyan Russo (Osman Bala), d. 1721; and R. Israel ben Eliezer Ba'al Shem Tov (Master of the Good Name), 1700–1760. All *ba'al Shems* were credited with miracle powers. And then Jacob Frank, 1726–1791. Some of his organized festivities deteriorated into sexual orgies. After his death, his daughter took over his movement (HJP, pp. 703–770).

Jerome and Clement said that Simon Magus the Magician of Samaria (Acts 8:9–25) claimed, "I am the Divine Word, I possess true beauty, I am the comforter, I am the Almighty, I am all that is in God." Each statement can be found in a Sefiroth of the Kabbalah as well as those in Acts 8:10, (Franks pp. 194–95).

Today we still see the mystical element as in the Masonic Order identification of the 1st degree Mason with Jachan, the 2nd degree with Boaz, and the 3rd degree with Tubal-Cain. The modern interest in Tarot cards also finds their place in this realm.

CHAPTER 5

THE TALMUD

AFTER THE KABBALAH, this is the next great area of Christian background about which Christians know very little. This is of far more importance and interest than the Kabbalah. The Talmud is the oral tradition that shaped the New Testament in the Herodian period and makes much of the "Traditions of the elders or Pharisees" comprehensible.

For instance, when the statement was made in Exodus 20:10, "thou shall not do any work on the Sabbath," the word *work* was not defined, and it became necessary to clarify what was allowed and what was not. The final result was a compendium of 2.5 million words, larger than the Encyclopedia Britannica.

Talmud means learning or teaching, coming from the root *lamad:* "he learned." It is composed of three parts: the *Mishna,* or oral teaching, which include 63 tractates or books embodying the interpretation of Scripture and rabbinic decisions from 10–220. The *Gemara* is an interpretation of the earlier decisions by a later group of rabbis who lived from 220–499 AD. The *Tosafot* (or additions) were not added until the 12–13th centuries, usually to clean up loose ends.

The Mishnah contains no quotes from Obadiah, Nahum, Habakkuk, Zephaniah, Daniel or Nehemiah.

There are two Talmuds: The Babylonian, which was written in Eastern Aramaic and composed in the major academies of Nehardea, Sura, Pumbedita, Mahoza, Naresh, and Mata Mehasya (often work was done in two or more of the centers at the same time and switched back and forth due to political persecution); the other is the Jerusalem Talmud (written in Hebrew and Western Aramaic, mostly by Rabbi Judah ha-Nasi). Although called the Jerusalem Talmud, it was actually written mostly in Caesarea (as indicated by the tractates Nezikin, Shabbat, and the three Babas). The rest was written from Tiberias—the last rabbi to work on it was Hiyya ben Adda, who finished in Sepphoris; and a small amount was done at Lydda. It contains only four of the six orders and the first three chapters of tractate Niddah. It was finished about 150 years before the Babylonian and was then used to refine the Babylonian, which became "the Talmud." Further details are found in the *Encyclopedia Judica* and Coburn (pp. 624–635).[30]

ORDERS and TRACTATES (Books) of the MISHNA

Order I, *ZERA'IM:* Seeds (agricultural law) Covers:

- *Berakhot:* Benedictions, prayers, and worship of Israel
- *Pe'ah:* Corner of fields to be left for the poor (Lev 19:9–10)
- *Demai:* Doubtful if tithes have been set aside
- *Kil'ayi:* Mixtures of plant, animal, and garments (Dt 22:9–11)
- *Shevith:* Seventh rest of land and release of debts (Ex 23:10–11)
- *Teremoth:* Heave offerings, harvest assigned to the priest (Nm 18:21)

- *Ma'aseroth:* Tithes, 1st tithes for the Levite (Nm 18:21)
- *Ma'aser Sheni:* 2nd tithe in the 1st, 2nd, 4th, and 6th year (Dt 14:22–27)
- *Hallal:* Dough offering for the priest (Nm 5:17–21)
- *'Orlah:* Uncircumcision of trees, 1–3 yr; and treatment in 4th (Lev 19:23–25)
- *Bikkurim:* First fruits in the temple and ceremony (Lev 26:1–11)

Order II, *MO'ED:* Appointed Seasons

- *Shabbat:* Sabbath and Hanukkah rules
- *'Erubin:* Blendings, freedom of movement within limits
- *Pesahim:* Paschal lambs, destroying leaven and seder service
- *Shekalem:* Shekels, contributions (Ex 30:11–16)
- *Yoma:* The day, of atonement, and ceremonies of the High Priest
- *Sukkah:* Booth, feast of tabernacles and the four plants
- *Bezah:* Egg, festival, limitations on food preparation
- *Rosh Hashanan:* New year, new moon, and *shofar*
- *Ta'anith:* Fasting rules for fast days
- *Megillah:* The scroll, puram and *Torah* in public worship
- *Mo'ed Katan:* Minor feast, mourning day prior to Passover, and tabernacles
- *Hagigah:* Festival offering, esoteric teaching of Torah

Order III, "*NASHIM:* Women

- *Yebamoth:* Sisters in law, leviarate and prohibited marriage

- *Kethuboth:* Marriage settlements, bride, seduction, and the widow
- *Nedarim:* Vows (Nm 30)
- *Nazir:* Nazirite (Nm 6)
- *Sotah:* Suspected adulteress (Nm 5:11–31)
- *Gittin:* Bills of divorcement
- *Kiddushin:* Consecrations, marriage

Order IV, *NEZIKIN:* Damage

- *Baba Kamma:* Baba= gate or chapter, property, injuries
- *Baba Mezi'a:* Sales, interest, rent, hire, or bailments
- *Baba Bathra:* Divisions of property, rights of ownership[31]
- *Sanhedrin:* Courts of justice, judges
- *Makkoth:* Perjures, cities of refuge, regulations on lashes (Dt 25:2)[32]
- *Shebu'oth:* Oaths
- *Eduyyoth:* Traditional testimonies, decisions, when R. Eleazer ben Azariah became head of the Academy
- *'Abodah Zarah:* Idolatry, in festivals, rites, and association with heathens
- *Aboth:* Ethical maxims, aphorisms of men of the Great Assembly onwards
- *Horayoth:* Erroneous ruling of the court (Lev 4:22–35)

Order V, *KODASHIM:* Holy Things

- *Zebahim:* Animal offerings, preparations, and procedures
- *Menahoth:* Meal offerings, meal and drink, barley, sheaf, and showbread
- *Hullin:* Non-holy, animals for food, and dietary laws

- *Bekoroth:* Firstling, men and cattle, tithing of cattle
- *'Arakin:* Estimations, amount to fill a vow, Jubilee year
- *Temurah:* Substitutions
- *Kerithoth:* Excisions, offences, and penalty (Lev 18:29)
- *Me'ilah:* Trespass, unlawful use of consecrated things
- *Tamid:* The continual offering, Temple service
- *Middoth:* Dimensions, measurements of Temple, and service of priests
- *Kinnim:* [bird] Nests, what to do if birds for different offerings are mixed

Order VI, *TOHOROTH:* Cleanness

- *Kelim:* Vessels, uncleanness of articles
- *Oholath:* Tents, contact with dead, conveyed to persons or vessels
- *Naga'im:* Leprosy (Lev 13; 14)
- *Parah:* Heifers, the red heifer (Nm 19)
- *Tohoroth:* Cleanness, foods and liquids
- *Mikva'oth:* Pools of immersion, dimensions, volumes; types of water
- *Niddah:* The menstruant
- *Makshirin:* Predispositions, foods in contact with liquids (Lev 11:37–38)
- *Zabim:* Fluxes, running issues
- *Tebul Yom:* Immersed at daytime, uncleanness that clings to one who has immersed during the day, until the setting of the sun
- *Yadayim:* Hands, canon of Bible, controversies between Sadducees and Pharisees, unwashed hands
- *'Ukzin:* Stalks of plants, effect on uncleanness

As you can see, everything is covered. Any question you have can be found by consulting the appropriate section. Some questions are answered in other sections because of overlap. Although the material has no logical beginning or end, it reads more like a court record. I will give only one example from Sanhedrin 36a–36b (footnotes are included from the text in parentheses). R. Abbahu said:

> In ten respects do civil suits differ from capital charges, and none of these is practiced in [the trial of] the ox that is stoned (but the trial is similar to that of the owner), save that twenty-three [judges are necessary]. Whence is this derived? —R. Aha b. Papa said, "Scripture states, 'Thou shall not wrest (incline or bend) the judgment of thy poor in his cause (judgment must not be inclined in favor of conviction by a majority of only one)'"; but thou mayest do so in the case of the ox that is stoned (the object of particularly applying that procedure in capital cases was to achieve the acquittal of the accused. Not so with an ox).
>
> Ten? But there is only nine! ([You say that there are only nine,] but indeed, ten are taught! —The laws that not all [persons] are eligible, (e.g, bastards may not try capital cases) and that 23 judges are necessary, are but one) (So making the total nine given in the Mishna. People of illegitimate birth are ineligible as judges in capital cases because a court of 23 is a minor Sanhedrin, with whom pure descent is essential; hence, they are counted as one). —There is yet another [difference]: for it has been taught: "We do not appoint as members of the Sanhedrin, an aged man, a eunuch or one who is childless (because such are more or less devoid of paternal tenderness). R. Judah includes also a cruel man. It is the reverse in the case of a *Mesith'* (idolater), for the Divine Law states, neither shall thou spare, neither shall thou conceal him " (Dt 13:9).

For civil cases, only three judges are necessary (HJP p. 340–42).

From this, you get an insight into some background material. Paul was appointed by the Sanhedrin to round up Christians in Acts 9:1–3. Only another Sanhedrin member could be appointed to do this. He also voted for Stephen's death, as recounted in Acts 8:1 and 26:10–11. To vote a death sentence required that he be married, a father, and at least 30 years old. Though Paul never mentions a wife, she and the child were probably dead. This qualification was probably already in force during the time of Paul.

Other qualifications for Sanhedrin members were that they had to know the seventy languages of the world (Menahoth 65:1), know about other religions, the occult arts, astrology, astronomy, mathematics, biology, and be in near perfect health. Why would anyone want the job? By the time of Christ, most High Priests would serve only for about two years due to the pressures of the job.

In Pesahim 62b, the interesting statement is made that a Rabbi from Lod in Israel was living in Nehardea and wanted to learn the Book of Genealogies in three months. The answer was given that Beruriah the wife of R. Meir and daughter of R. Hanina b. Teradion studied 300 laws from 300 teachers in one day but could not study the Law adequately in three years. Thus women were not restricted from wide scholarship if they so desired. Home duties, in the case of children to care for, excluded them from synagogue attendance if they so desired. If they did come they were relegated to the upper balcony behind a curtain to avoid distractions to the men and to provide privacy for nursing mothers.

In Yadayim 3:5 is recorded the dispute at Jamina over whether Ecclesiastes and the Song of Songs "defiled the hands"; that is, were they considered scripture. Other disputes in the Gemara occur over the scripture status of Proverbs, Esther, Ezekiel and Ruth.

Also there is the statement in Sanhedrin 97b: Abaye said, "The world must contain not less than 36 righteous men in each generation who are vouchsafed the sight of the Shekinah's countenance; for it is written, 'Blessed are they that wait lo for him; the numerical value of *lo* is 36.'"

During the *Tannim* (repetition) Period of 4 BC–220 AD, eyewitnesses must have written down the details of the Temple and the rituals presented in a minute fashion before or shortly after 70 AD.

There are a number of interesting statements about the Temple and priestly ritual. It asks and answers many questions that seem foolish:

1. Why has an ox a long tail? Why has an ass a short tail?
2. What is the reason that the lower eyelids of a hen turn up?
3. For ceremonial purification before each meal, what kind and amount of water was to be used; which hand must be put in the basin first; what is the place to put the napkin?
4. How must the dough be kneaded for unleavened bread; how it must be baked?
5. What oil and wicks may be used in the lamps on the Sabbath?
6. Can a light be put out on the Sabbath, for fear of an accident or to afford rest for the sick?
7. May a chair be dragged across a dirt floor on the Sabbath? This would be plowing.
8. Can food that is left in the oven (therefore cooked on the Sabbath) be eaten?
9. For the Sabbath walk, how long may steps be?
10. May a man with a wooden leg go out at all? Would he not be carrying his burden with him?

11. Could any assistance be given to a woman in labor on the Sabbath?
12. Can anything be removed from a burning building on the Sabbath? (Yes, the Torah.)
13. What can be done for an animal falling in water on the Sabbath?
14. Can a bath be taken on the Sabbath, or only to wash each limb separately?
15. Is it lawful to use soap on the Sabbath?
16. Can a corpse's eyes be closed on the Sabbath? Or can a body be moved on the Sabbath to save it from fire?
17. May one warm himself by a hearth fire on the Sabbath?
18. May one rend one's clothes upon hearing of the death of a relative on the Sabbath?

Mark 11:16, about not carrying goods through the Temple, has a similar restriction in the Mishnah Berakhoth 9:5, when it forbids those who enter the Temple to wear their traveling or working clothes and says, "A man may not enter the Temple with his staff or his sandal or his wallet, or with dust upon his feet; nor may he make a short cut of it."

Various Rabbis gave various answers to these and other questions. However, there was agreement that no tailor could go out with his tools on Friday evening. Nothing could be sold to a Gentile, nor money lent to him, late in the week. No Jew could heat water on the Sabbath, although a Gentile cook could do this, as well as kindle fires and cook food, which could then be partaken of by the family. A woman could wear a small gold hairpin, but could not go out with a seal ring or carry a perfume bottle or a key. You may not chop ice on the Sabbath, but chopped ice (by a Gentile) can be put in a pitcher. Gold teeth or fillings were generally forbidden, but silver was permitted. Amulets were permitted. One Rabbi stated that grasshopper eggs should be carried for toothache, the tooth of a fox to cure sleeplessness, or a nail from a gallows as a remedy for tumor. If an animal falls into a cistern or lake on the Sabbath, he may push something into it for it to climb out. Gentile nurses may be hired for the sick. If an Israelite says grace, say Amen to it; but if a Gentile, be careful. If a Gentile shaves you, keep your eye on the mirror. In fact, there are ways around most of the prohibitions in the law.

References to Christ and the Messiah

One Rabbi said, "Make my funeral sermon impressive, for I shall be present." In addition, that the "appointed times" for the appearance of the Messiah have already passed, and that repentance and good deeds are essential (Cobern p. 630).

Even in the present day, we find this strange prayer from A. Th. Philips (1931 ed.) in the *Prayer Book for the Day of Atonement*: "Our righteous anointed is departed from us: horror hath seized us, and we have none to justify us. He hath borne the yoke of our iniquities, and our transgressions, and is wounded because of our transgressions. He beareth our sins on his shoulder, that he may find pardon for our iniquities. We shall be healed by his wound, at the time that the Eternal will create him (the Messiah) as a new creature. O bring him up from the circle of the earth. Raise him up from Seir, to assemble us the second time on Mount Lebanon, by the hand of YHWH (YAHWEH)." This is saying that the Messiah has died, but will be resurrected.

Jesus is mentioned but never well or by name. In Sanhedrin 107b, he is called an idolator who worshiped a brickbat (idol). He is called "that man," Son of Stada, Son of Pandera (an anagram for the Greek parthenos or virgin), dead dog, the hanged one, the sorcerer, Balaam and Seducer. Mary, it says, has the hinge of hell's gate fastened to her ear. The Talmud does specify his healing the crippled, blind, and lepers as sorcery learned in Egypt and mentions his walking on the water. Several of the disciples are mentioned by name and the death of Christ by crucifixion at the time of the Feast of Passover is mentioned.

Tractate Sanhedrin is the one to look at to find the entire procedure for a legal Jewish trial involving a capital offence. Consider the trial of Jesus, which is illegal on almost all counts. Held at night (Tosephta Sanhedrin 7.1) on the eve of a major festival (Sanhedrin 4.1), in a private house instead of the hall Gazith (on the Temple Mount although the Temple Mount gates were closed after sundown [Sanhedrin 11a]). Although a provision was available that in an emergency, it might be held elsewhere; for example, if the high priest was confined to his house for illness or injury. The death sentence occurred on the same day as the trial, instead of the next day (Sanhedrin 4.1; 5.5) etc.

At least 23 members of the Sanhedrin needed to be present (for civil cases only three were needed). The Bible gives no number but indicates that the chief priests, elders and scribes (the whole council) were present (Mk 15:1; Mt 27:1). These accounts say the final trial took place in the morning (which would be legal, except this day was a feast day), but John 18:28 says they went immediately to Pilate after the trial, the first thing in the morning. John was an eyewitness to the events, but the other disciples were not.

Each member was pledged to impartiality (the High Priest was not impartial [he was actually supposed to act as counsel for the accused] nor did he try to protect the accused, even having him beaten and slapped [not even murderers could be treated in this manner]) and kindness of thought. The search for hostile witnesses was illegal (Sanhedrin 4.1). The accused could not be convicted on his own evidence, as He was. Otherwise, there was no valid legal evidence presented against Him. Other witnesses had to be searched for, since the star witness for the prosecution, Judas Iscariot, had disappeared. No prior indictment had been prepared, which was usually read at the opening of a case. The

Mishnah stated that seven basic questions were to be asked of the witnesses about the event in question. In what septenate of the Jubilee did the crime occur, what year, what month, what day of the month, which day of the week, at what hour and at what place (Sanhedrin 40a)?

The Sanhedrin did reject this obviously erroneous testimony. False witnesses were to be put to death. However, there is no hint that any were. The charge of blasphemy did Him in. To remain silent in reply to the direct question of Caiaphas would have been a declaration of guilt. There must be a distinct majority of two to convict, but only one to acquit. If the vote for guilty was 12 to 11, two additional members were added and continued to be added, with the trial redone each time until at least two convicted him or he was acquitted. The vote of guilty would be retaken the next day to give the members time to reflect, and gather any new evidence, before it became binding. If the vote of guilty was unanimous, the accused went free. This would be taken as proof of personal enmity of the jury. How would that rest with today's courts?

The whole purpose of a Jewish trial was to find for the accused at all costs if any doubt existed. Gamblers, usurers, tax collectors and government contractors were disqualified as witnesses (all were looked upon as crooked and therefore sinners), of which there must be at least three. Voting started with the youngest so that the older members would not sway them, but Caiaphas asked for an oral expression of opinion, which was illegal.

At this point the setting shifted to a Roman court and procedures, otherwise, a herald must go before the convicted one (on his way to death) giving his name, the charges in the case, and crying aloud that anyone who had evidence in his defense should speak up at once. The procession had to stop at least twice to allow such to come forward. If such was offered the party went back and a retrial was held *de novo*, or as new. In other words, the appeal trial was held immediately. Again, how would this sit today?

Pilate's trial was also illegal since Roman custom also dictated that trials were not held on feast days. The charge was changed from blasphemy to treason. The Romans would not even hear a charge of blasphemy, as it did not concern them. Again no witnesses were brought, no accuser put under oath to testify, and no jury was called. Pilate could have demanded all of these. Jesus' answer to Pilate was that he was a prophet; there was no crime in being a prophet. As a result, Pilate found him innocent.

Pilate sought a sneaky way out of the problem by sending him to Herod Antipas. Herod had no jurisdiction in Judea since his kingdom was in Galilee. Herod found him innocent but did not send Pilate any report to this effect that he should be released. At the next appearance before Pilate, for the fourth time, Pilate found him innocent. Pilate reversed his position when a charge of treason was brought against Pilate. The hand washing is yet another declaration of innocence.

Pilate was later banished to Vienna in 36 AD, because of this and two other mistakes in his administration. His later military action against the Samaritans did him in. Similar facts can be found in Wilkinson (pp. 131–144).

Jewish law knows only four types of capital punishment. Decapitation was mainly a Roman form of execution for murderers, rebels, etc. (according to tradition, such was Roman citizen Paul's death). Burning was for gross sexual crimes, carried out by pouring molten lead down the throat. In later times, this was done by a lighted string after the man had been partially or wholly strangled. Strangling was for adultery, striking a parent, kidnapping, giving false prophecy, or prophesying in the name of an idol. This was done by a scarf twisted around the neck. Stoning was for blasphemy and adultery, of which the chief witness dropped the first stone (frequently this was done in a quarry—the cliff edges provided the required height of two times a man's height—and where plenty of freshly prepared stones were available). The size of the stone required two of the witnesses to lift. Crucifixion was strictly a Roman practice, although used earlier in various forms by the Assyrians, Persians, Egyptians, Greeks, Carthaginians, Scythians, Indians, and the early Germans or Gauls. Roman citizens were exempted and usually beheaded. Frequently they were allowed to commit suicide.

Other Jewish Sayings

Pirke Aboth is the celebrated chapter today used as the Orthodox Jewish Prayer Book, written from 30 BC–300 AD. Some of its mottos are well known and include the following:

"Talk not much with thy wife . . . So long as the man talks much with the wife he causes evil to himself and desists from the words of Torah and his end is that he inherits Gehennah." R. Hiller said, "In a place where there are no men, strive to be a man." R. Eleazar said, "Be not easily wroth, and repent one day before thy death." R. Jose said, "Let the wealth of thy associate be dear to thee as thine own." R. Tarhon said, "The day is short, and the work is great, and the laborers few, and the hire is much, and the master of the house is urgent," R. Halaphta said, "When ten are seated and occupied with Torah, the Shechinah is among them." R. Judah said "At five years old one is fit for Scripture, at ten for Mishna, at 13 for the commandments, at 15 for the Talmud, at 18 for marriage, at 20 for retribution, at 30 for power, at 40 for discernment, at 50 for council, at 60 for elderhood, at 70 for gray hairs, at 80 for strength, at 90 for decrepitude."

Other sayings: "There are four types of men: 1. He that says what is mine is mine, and what is thine is thine. This is the average type; some would say it is the type of Sodom. 2. What is mine is thine, and what is thine is mine. This is the word of the vulgar. 3. What is mine and what is thine are thine. He is pious. 4. What is thine and what is mine are mine. He is wicked."

"There are four types of men who sit before the wise: a sponge, a funnel, a strainer, and a sieve. A sponge, because it sucks up everything; a funnel, because it receives at one end and lets out at the other; a strainer, because it lets out wine and keeps back the dregs; a sieve because it lets out the course meal and keeps back the fine flour."[33]

The Talmud preserves 316 controversies between the schools of Shammai and Hiller ca. 100 BC. Hiller became the head of the Sanhedrin and Shammai vice president. Gamaliel of Acts 5:34–39 was a grandson of Hiller and the teacher of Paul (Acts 22:3). Early church tradition says he was converted by Peter and Paul, whereas the Clementine Recognition 1:65 says he was a secret Christian at this time. However, this is doubted (see the Open Bible p. 886).

The summary given in Coburn (p. 626) sums it up nicely: Although, as Goldsmidt says, "this vast work until very recently was hidden in an obscurity more mysterious than any Egyptian hieroglyphics, yet it is now open to scholars. There is today no written record or oral tradition known to any Hebrew rabbi which is not known by some Christian scholar."

ANGELOLOGY

There was a great interest in angels, especially found on amulets, in addition to Michael and Gabriel from the Bible, as well as Raphael and Uriel (who are referenced in the Apocrypha and the Metatron in the Kabbalah). These and others are found on Aramaic amulets in gold and silver from Syria dating to the Byzantine period. It is said in *The Wisdom of the Chaldeans* (a 14th century manuscript) that gold amulets (for writing curative and protective charms) were to be written on a Sunday, the day of Helois, and ruled by the archangel Raphael etc. Many magical names are included such as Abrasax (whose numerical value is

365, as for the year). The total angels listed is 31 the maximum number of days in a month using a solar calendar, these are:

Michael, also associated with Mercury.

Gabriel, associated with the moon.

Raphael, associated with the sun or Sunday, a master of healing (see DSS of Tobit).

'Anael, God hears (who answers prayer), associated with Venus and Friday.

Sadqiel, angel of justice, associated with Jupiter and Thursday. The S is a Hebrew *Shin*.

Uriel, means flame of God or light.

Nahariel, means to shine or be bright as God.

Seraphiel (Seraphim), fiery beings who burn or consume.

Barqiel, means Bright, shine, or flask of God.

Yakonel, means to establish or determine by God.

Suriel, means God is my rock or protection. The S is the Hebrew letter *Shin* (there are two letter S's).

Suriel (the other letter), means to turn to God.

Rahabiel, no meaning for the name is given.

Ramiel, the meaning of this name is unsure.

Harbiel, means word of God.

Satqie, means to be silent (a demon or affliction). His place is on the 7th step of the 2nd firmament.

Doliel, means to relieve (affliction) by God.

Yahobel, means God gives.

Sitriel, means hiding place of God.

'Azriel, means angel of help/protection.

Sammael, means (healing) drug, medicine or potion, associated with Mars and Tuesday. Usually this is an angel of death, as is Qaspiel, an angel of destruction, associated with Saturn and Saturday.

'Azazel, means to be strong, bright or intense.

Hazaqel or Yehezqel, means God is strong.

Yaqtiel, means Strength, the meaning of this name is unsure.
Amsiel, means to make strong or strengthen.
'Uzziel, means to be strong.
Nuriel, means angel of fire.
'Am(a)tiel, means angel of truth.
'Amoriel, means in firmament.
'Emuniel, means firmness or security.
'Anaqiel, means to choke (afflictions?).

The first six, except for Sadqiel (the S is the Hebrew letter Shin), are archangels in other lists. Most of the names are associated with light or fire. Those from 'Azazel —Uzziel refer to strength.'Am(a)tiel-'Anaqiel all begin with aleph, and others form a loose alphabetic sequence as though taken from some pre-existing manual. In the DSS 4Q285 we find "Michael, Gabriel, Sariel and Raphael," (Vermes p. 189). In Sefer ha-Razim, each of the 12 angels of the 5th firmament governs a month of the year (see IEJ 41: 267 [91]). Other angel names Qum'iel and Qut'iel are found on incantation bowls (see BASOR 223: 23 [76].) In BAR 15(2): 30 (89) a bronze amulet buried under the threshold of the Meroth synagogue asked the angel Hatoaa to give him power over the village—apparently a power struggle was going on. On the floor was part of a mosaic Zodiac. At least seven synagogues including Beth Alpha, Hammath Tiberias, Sepphoris, Ein Gedi, Khirbet Suseya, Naaran near Jericho and a Byzantine monastery of the Lady Mary near Beth Shean contained mosaic Zodiacs, in many cases complete with the Sun god Helios riding in his celestial chariot. The most famous amulets (although not containing angel names) were the two silver ones from Tomb chamber 25 at Ketef (shoulder of) Hinnom at St. Andrews in Jerusalem. These contain the oldest piece of Scripture known, the priestly blessing from Numbers 6:24–26 dating to 605 BC (see ABR Premiere Issue Autumn p. 20 [87]). Many amulets contain parts of Psalm 90 and 91, especially vs. 1–8.

CHAPTER 6

PERCEIVED BIBLE ERRORS— MINOR

MOST OF THE past perceived biblical errors were misconceptions or faulty understanding of the Hebrew or Greek, which is better understood now. Most originate in the KJV, which has propagated them.

Gn 1:6–8 "Firmament" as a solid vault (as in Josephus *Antiquities* 1.1, or KJV) is a mistranslation from the Greek Septuagint LXX. The Hebrew word is *Rakia* and means stretched out, extended or better, expanse. In modern terms, it is clearly the atmosphere.

4:8 Cain said, "Let us go out to the field." Hebrew omits this clause, but the LXX and other texts contain it (for clarity, perhaps, since this is implied in the Hebrew). The sentence is actually incomplete in the Hebrew.

10:11 "Out of that land went forth Asshur." This is better translated; He [Nimrod] went out into Assyria.

10:14 (Out of whom came the Philistines), and Caphtorium. Better read, "And Caphtorium [Crete] out of whom came the Philistines). See also Jeremiah 47:4 and Amos 9:7.

28:12 Jacob's ladder is actually a stairway, perhaps like that of a Ziggurat or a terrace up a mountainside. Israel is full of these, which from a distance look like stairs.

37:28 "20 pieces of silver." As recorded in the Hebrew and Samaritan Pentateuch. The LXX has 20 pieces of gold. The Testament of Gad has 30 pieces of gold. Vulgate has 30 pieces of silver. Josephus has 20 pounds. "Pieces" is missing and in this case understood to be shekels, thus silver is the correct form.

Ex 13:18 Red Sea. The Hebrew is *Yam Suph*, which means the Reed or Marsh Sea. Since reeds will not grow in salt water, the area of the Bitter Lakes (which is 36 feet deep) is indicated near Lake Timsah (about ten feet deep). This brackish inlet, closed from the sea, has changed since the building of the Suez Canal. Some of the lakes have disappeared. Do not go looking for a crossing by the children of Israel in the Gulf of Suez (which is up to 90 feet deep down to Ras Abu Darag, 45 miles from Suez) or the Gulf of Aqaba (about 1,000 feet deep). Only the north ends of both are relatively shallow, but would be utterly impossible to cross due to steep cliffs. There were only eight hours for all to cross. How wide the crossing point was, we are not told.

20:5 versus Jer 31:30—a result of sins visited upon children? This is one of the Old Testament provisions, which has been altered by the "New Covenant" of Jeremiah 31:31–34, which was fulfilled at the birth of Christ. With no mention of a final blood sacrifice being given, it is a legal contract but unsigned.

Lev 11:5–6 and Dt 14:7. The coney is the rock badger or hyrax, and the hare is in Hebrew, *arnebeth*, which is a rodent. Neither chews the cud, but the chewing motion resembles it. Most of the plants and animals here in chapter 11 are not the ones we know.

Nm 28:11 versus Eze 46:6—the New Moon Offering. In Numbers, it is two bullocks, one ram, and seven lambs; but in Ezekiel, it is one bullock, one ram, and six lambs. The Talmud (Shabbath 13b, Hagigah 13a, and Menahoth 45) recounts how Hananiah Ben Hezekiah, head of the school of Shammai, "commissioned 300 jars of oil setting in his upper chamber". As we would say now, "He burned the midnight oil," trying to figure out the difference. In Samuel, Kings, and Chronicles where parallel numbers occur 150 times, only 25 disagree.

Jos 1:4 Lebanon even unto the river Euphrates. A strange command, since Lebanon and the area up to the Euphrates were never in control of Israel under Joshua. Everything up to "Euphrates" may have been added as a gloss. If this is left out, the rest makes perfect sense. The Hittites would be those isolated areas of the mountains around Hebron and elsewhere (Gurney p. 58).

Jgs 5:30 Damsel: This is a *hapax legomena,* or a word used once in the Hebrew; the word is *racham,* a rare word meaning "womb." Hebrew can be quite graphic and blunt. Actually it is used in a derogatory sense, as one would use a common four-letter vulgarity today. Another one the KJV has prettied up is Isaiah 64:6. "Filthy" is Hebrew *'ed,* or menstrual period.

1 Sm 6:19 Fifty thousand and seventy men killed. This figure is a scribal error. In the Hebrew text the 70 stands before the 50,000 (which is rare), and the linking copula Waw = and, is absent. The Beth-Shemesh population was not this large. Josephus *Antiquities* 6.1.4 says 70 men were killed.

1 Sm 11 Some 52 words have been lost from all previous Hebrew manuscripts. See the chapter on the Dead Sea Scrolls for the correct reading. It was known that this reading was incorrect but Josephus knew of the missing words (see also ABR 5: 109 [92]).

1 Sm 13:1 . . . years and he reigned—and two years. These numbers are missing from all present Hebrew manuscripts. Jonathan was already of military age, as in verse three Saul's age was about 40 at his accession.

13:21 "file with mallows etc." The Hebrew words were obscure when the KJV was written. One is now known: *Pym,* a weight, 2/3 of a shekel of silver. In addition, for mattock read plow tip (approximately 8–10 inches long), a high price to pay—about four days' wages (UOT p. 199). The best reading is the RSV: "and the charge was a pym for the plowshares (bottom runner) and for the plow tip, and 1/3 of a shekel for sharpening the axes and for setting the goads." About 50 pym weights or sets of weights are now known (Stern p. 196). In Assyria about 1900 BC, iron which was of meteoric origin, was worth eight times the value of gold (TLBM p. 47).

1 Sm 17:40 Five stones. Some commentators mention that Goliath had four brothers. The verses in 2 Samuel 21:19–22; 1 Chronicles 20:5–8, 16, "the brother of" Goliath is supplied in italics (otherwise Elhanan is listed as the slayer of Goliath), or is listed as sons of the giant. Apparently some corruption of the text has occurred in 2 Samuel.

17:54 Goliath's head brought to Jerusalem. This presents a problem since Jerusalem had not been taken by David at this time and was still in Jebusite hands, at least all within the walls. The Israelite presence indicated in Joshua 15:63 and Judges 1:21 was probably on the present Mt. Zion to the west. No artifacts of the 10th century have been found in this area, but little excavation has been done. Some remains of the 8th century have been found in five areas.

2 Sm 1:21 "fields of offering." The Ras Shamra (Ugarit) tablets of the 14th century BC contains the phrase "Seven years may Baal fail, even eight the Rider of the Clouds (see Ps. 68:4); nor dew, nor rain, *nor upsurgings of the deep*, nor sweetness of the voice of Baal." Thus, above one would expect some parallel reference to water. The Hebrew words *field* and *upsurging* would look alike, also *offering* and *deep* are similar, thus a better reading would be "upsurging of the deep (mountain springs)." For similar poetical expressions, see Proverbs 6:16 and 30:18–19.

5:8 "water shaft." This word *tsinnor* is now known to mean *hook* (after the Aramaic and Arabic word). There may be an allusion to this in David's poem in 2 Samuel 22:30. This does not refer to the use of "Warren's shaft" at the Gihon spring as once thought; see BAR 21(1): 78 (95); 25(1): 22 (99); 29(5): 70 (03). Rather the walls were probably scaled using grappling hooks. See Simons pp. 168–73 for a complete discussion of the Hebrew words and verbs.

11:11 "The Ark. . .abideth in (*succoth*) tents." Never is the Ark said to abide in succoth (booths or canopies). The Hebrew for tents is better rendered *ohel*. Thus, this is a place name Succoth, or Tell Deir Alla (Yadin p. 274–5).

24:9 and 1 Chr 21:5 Israel 88,000 and 1,100,000 vs Judah 500,000 and 470,000. Josephus has 900,000 and 400,000. The problem has to do with the Hebrew term, '*elep* and '*alep;* without the vowels, as originally written in Hebrew, these would be 'lp. 'Elep means thousand, clans or families; and '*alep* means chieftains. The same problem exists anywhere large numbers are mentioned, as in Exodus, Joshua, Kings, Chronicles, Ezra and Nehemiah (see EHB p. 191 for an excellent discussion).

24:24 and 1 Chr 21:25. Fifty shekels paid for the threshing floor (Goren), versus 600 shekels for the place (Maqom). This discrepancy disappears when the difference between these places is understood (which would require a different price).

1 Kgs 6:2 and. 2 Chr 3:4. Height of the house = 30 cubits and height of a porch = 120 cubits. Inside and outside measurements may be mixed up, or may be an error of numbers. Josephus in *Antiquities* 8.3.2 has 60 and 120 cubits; the LXX and Syriac have 20 cubits for the porch.

7:26 and 2 Chr 4:5. 2,000 Baths vs. 3,000 baths. The bath equals an *ephah* (dry measure), or about 7½ gallons. Josephus in *Antiquities* 8.3.5 has 3,000 baths.

10:22 Apes and peacocks. These products are African or Arabian; the monkeys have Egyptian names and should probably read apes and baboons (see NUBD p. 76).

10:28 "droves" (Amp Bible) or "linen yarn" (KJV). It is now known that this word is a place name and not a common noun. Read . . .Egypt and from QWH and the kings merchants received them from QWH at a price. In Assyrian records, KUE is Cilicia (north of Tarsus in Turkey). Thus, Solomon was a middleman and made his profit from both ends of the transaction.

2 Ki18:9 Shalmaneser V (727–722 BC) or Sargon III [A. Poebel in JNES 2(1), 86 (43) has found a new Sargon who ruled between 1812–1727 BC, so it is necessary to reassign the numbers. He is still known in most sources as Sargon II] 721–705), versus Hezekiah (727–698 BC). The year is 724 BC, and Samaria fell in 721, Sargon's records boasts of taking the city, thus the conquest may have been started by Shalmaneser but upon his death was completed by Sargon, or else he took credit for it. Shalmaneser may have adopted Sargon, because he took over without opposition but he never lists any of his ancestors.

1 Chr 6:28 Samuel the Ephraimite (1 Sam.1:1) is credited as being a Levite, as is Obed-edom the Gittite in 13:13. Apparently, "Levite" resembles the Hebrew word *lawah*, meaning "to attach." It might in time, as "attached persons," become credited with Levitical ancestry. In Deuteronomy the phrase "the priests, the Levites" became changed later by the insertion of a *waw*, which means "and" into the expression "the priests and the Levites," resulting in later confusion.

7:6 "Benjamin"; but Zebulun is meant; otherwise, this tribe is not listed. The Hebrew spelling is somewhat similar. The Benjamin list is 8:1–40.

2 Chr 2:2, 17–18 These verses refer to the same group of people.

8:18 and 1 Kgs 9:28. "Four hundred fifty talents of gold" versus 420 talents. LXX has 120 and Josephus has 400.

16:1 The 36th year dates from the beginning of the Southern Kingdom; the actual date is the 15th year of Asa (15:10), or 893 BC, since Baasha died in 883 BC (1 Kgs 15:33).

22:2 Hebrew says 42, but it is an error: his age was 22 (see 2 Kgs 8:26, LXX and Syriac). His father died at 40 (v. 21:20 and 2 Kgs 8:17). If age 42, he was older than his father was at his father's death.

36:9 The age of Jehoiachin was 18 years. See also 2 Kings 24:8 and I Esdras 1:43. Thus no co-regency of ten years as previously thought. The Yod = 10 is easily lost from manuscripts (NUBD p. 658).

36:10 "brother." Is actually uncle or kinsman (see 2 Kgs 24:17).

36:22–23 Is actually the same as Ezra 1:1–3a, except the final sentence is incomplete. Frequent practice was to copy the first words from the next scroll as an indexing method. Since 2 Chronicles ends the Hebrew Bible, this must have occurred when Chronicles, Ezra and Nehemiah formed a literary unit.

Ezr 4:7–23 Chronologically this belongs after Chapter 10, but was placed here by Ezra to finish the subject.

Neh 10:20 "Leaders of the people" Hezir. Hezir was a priest in the 17th course (1 Chron. 24:15). Since many in this list are priests, he may be one also, but misplaced among the leaders. If so, his family tomb is known in the wadi Kidron at Jerusalem south of Absalom's pillar.

Est 1:9 Queen Vashti. Secular history does not know of her. Herodotus says Amestris was Xerxes' (Ahasuerus') queen. There were many wives but only one was called queen. Esther and Vashti were probably secondary queens ranking just above concubines.

2:6 Mordecai's age. He was taken captive in 597 BC. Xerxes' 12th year was 474 BC (3:7). At least 123 years had passed. Dates in Apocrypha additions to Esther agree. However, the relative pronoun in 2:6 "who" can refer to Kish, Mordecai's great grandfather (see NUBD p. 378). However, some people still lived to a great age; Jehoiada the High Priest in 2 Chronicles 24:15 died at 130 in 798 BC.

2:20 "she obeyed Mordecai's command to her." "To fear God and execute His commands." The LXX contains this, but the Hebrew does not mention God anywhere directly in the text. There are five places where acrostics are used. Four times YHWH is hidden: in 1:20 *all the wives shall give;* 5:4 *let the King and Haman come this day;* 5:13 *this availeth me nothing;* and 7:7 *that there was evil determined against him;* and once for EHYEH I Am that I Am; in 7:5 *Who is he, and where is he.* In three manuscripts, the letters are written large so that they stand out (Tenney footnote1, chapter 12 p. 218).

Jb 3:8 The Leviathan is now identified as the Crocodile.

39:9–10 The Unicorn is not the one horned medieval mythical animal. The Hebrew *Rᵉ'EM* has two horns as shown by Numbers 23:22; 24:8 and Deuteronomy 33:17. The animal is the now extinct Auerochs described by Julius Caesar and shown depicted by Tiglath-Pileser I (1115–1077 BC).

40:15–24 The Behemoth is now known to be the Hippopotamus.

Ps 14 In the Psalms considerable overlapping and consolidating occurred within the four sets of books making up the Psalms, and the order varied considerably (see the DSS). Except for verse 6, this Psalm is identical to Psalm 53. Psalm 14 is considered older, in that YAHWEH is preferred (272 times verses 15 times for ELOHIM in Ps 3–41).

40:12 Joined two separate poems (see Ps 70, which was added to the end).

43 is combined with Psalm 42 in several Hebrew manuscripts.

60:6–12 Is identical to Psalm 108:7–13.

72:20 Ends Book II of the Psalms, but see 86, 101, 103, 108–110, 122, 124, 131, 133, and 138–145, which are said to be by David.

114 and 136 The last Hallelujah should begin this Psalm as in the LXX.

137 In verses 1–3 the verbs are in the past tense, thus it dates to after 538 BC as the latest. The curse for a blessing contrasts the New Testament teaching in verse 9.

145 In this acrostic poem, the line beginning with Nun has been omitted between 13 and 14. It is present in the DSS and the LXX. It reads, "The Lord is faithful in all his words, and gracious in all his deeds."

Prv 11:31 Proverbs has the same overlap and rearrangement as Psalms. "If the righteous are barely saved what will become of the ungodly and wicked?" This is present in the LXX and quoted by Peter from the LXX in 1 Pet. 4:18.

14:12 and 16:25 are identical.

18:9b The LXX adds "and he who does not use his endeavors to heal himself is brother to him who commits suicide." The Hebrew would not have considered it necessary to say this. Note: this is a direct answer to Christian Scientists.

22:3 and 27:12 are identical.

30:5 is identical to Psalm 18:30 except the Aramaic form of *God* is used rather than *Lord.*

Sg 1:9 "my mare." This allusion is obscure, but the subject is a woman, since all chariot corps used only stallions. One way to disrupt a cavalry charge was to loose a mare in heat as a battle tactic. See the account of Thutmose III at Kadesh in WERE p. 59.

Is 7:22 "milk and honey." In the 20 other places where the expression "a land of milk and honey" is used, we usually think of an abundance of provision. However, there is another abstraction, which would be in the back of the mind of any Israeli. Only a wasteland or uncultivated land is in view, for only this would lead to cattle having ample feed in fields unplowed and where bees can build nests unbothered. Throughout the Pentateuch, this is the picture of a people that have not resorted to cultivation on any grand scale. The horror for an Israeli is that if he leaves the land he will return to it overgrown with weeds and briers (see Eerdmans p. 381).

Isaiah 34:14 "screech owl." This word is in Hebrew *Lilith*, the night demon, and she is associated with owls. She was said to be Adam's first wife, who was banished after disputing with Adam for the top position in intercourse and was made to stand in the Euphrates River up to her neck. Later she became the demon who sought out women about to give birth, to strangle the babies, and who plagued young men and boys with nocturnal emissions from which she conceived other demons. She appears in the Babylonian myths as Lilitu or Lamashtu (see Saggs p. 241; articles in *Encyclopedia Judica*).

49:12. "Sinim" was thought to refer to the Chinese. The Isaiah DDS reads a matres lectionis "w" after the S for the reading "Aswan" in Egypt, as was expected by scholars and supported by the Targum, which supplied "the land of the South." "Afar" always refers to the East, and North and West are mentioned, leaving only the South, which Aswan supplies.

Jer 1:13 "a boiling pot with its face toward the north." The correct reading is "its face away from the north." The Assyrians and Babylonians would descend on the land from the north as a raging conflict symbolized by the boiling pot.

10:5 "upright like the palm tree." From the DSS Letter of Jeremiah it is now known this verse should read "like a scarecrow in a melon patch."

17:6 and 48:6 "heath." In Psalm 102:17, "desolation." The Hebrew is *Ar'Ar*, which is now known to be the Sodom apple, which grows only in the Arabah valley. It is a member of the milkweed family, spoken of by Josephus as dissolving into smoke and ashes when touched. This is the vine of Sodom of Deuteronomy 32:32.

27:1 Jehoiakim should be Zedekiah as in vs. 3 and 12. Both were sons of Josiah.

31:31–34. The "new covenant" with no mention of a final blood sacrifice being given; this is a "legal contract left unsigned."

Chapter 52 is recopied from 2 Kgs 24:18–25:30. In verse 11, the LXX gives the word *mill* rather than *prison*. The fate of Zedekiah may have been the same as that of Samson in Jgs 16:21.

Eze 4:5 and 9 "390 days." However, in the LXX only 190 days. The Hebrew is probably correct. However, it is uncertain what it refers to. The days are thought of as actually years as in v. 6.

26:1 Month is not given. LXX has twelfth year, first day and eleventh month. Jerusalem fell in 586 BC and some time was needed for word to reach Babylon, so it may have been in the twelfth.

29:1 The year as in 33:21. LXX gives the twelfth year rather than the tenth year.

32:17. Month is not given. The LXX gives the first month.

33:21 The LXX, eight Hebrew manuscripts and the Syriac gives the eleventh year. All dates are in agreement with an autumnal reckoning.

39:2 1/6 of Gog to be kept alive. This is a mistaken translation of the KJV. Compare verses 4 and 11: "all" are to be struck down.

Jl 2:23 "The former rain in just measure." Actually, the Hebrew with a different word division can be read "the teacher of righteous." Actually, 23b makes better sense with the former.

Am 4:4 Three years in the KJV is a mistake. The Hebrew is best read "in the morning and on the third day."

7:14 "sycamore." The addition of figs makes it clear that the sycamore is actually the sykamine fig, the same one in Luke 19:4. This variety of inferior fig needed to be punctured before it would ripen.

9:12 "Remnant of Edom," the LXX has men as in Acts 15:17.

Na 1:12 "quite and likewise many." Actually correct but not understood. Scofield p. 950 shows this is an Assyrian legal formula; dozens of tablets found at Nineveh contain this formula. It means that there is a joint responsibility for carrying out an obligation. Even though the scribes may not have understood what it meant, they still copied it carefully.

Zep 1:14 "the voice etc." This is a classic case of wrong word division in the Hebrew and loss of one letter. The better reading would be "Swifter than a runner the day of the Lord and speedier than a warrior."

Mt 1:6 and Lk 3:31. Compare Jeremiah 22:30, no descendant of Coniah = Jehoiachin will ever sit on David's throne. Thus, Jesus cannot be a descendant from Joseph's family, which stems from Solomon, whereas Mary's family stems from Nathan. From David to Joseph there are 32 generations listed, but from David to Mary there are 42 generations. Levirate marriage is assumed by some scholars to account for some of the differences. Normal difference in genealogies accounts for the rest. In Jeremiah 36:30 "sit" implies some degree of permanence. Jehoiachin ruled only three months and ten days (2 Chr 36:9). It is also quite clear that Mary's mother was actually a Levite, if her mother and Elizabeth, the wife of Zacharias were sisters. A priest can only marry a priest's daughter. Mary's mother Anna was apparently married outside the tribe to a Judahite, which was permitted.

1:8 Names omitted. After Joram should come Ahaziah, Joash and Amaziah (1 Chr 3:10–16).

1:11 After Josiah should come Jehoiakim. Thus, "begat" only means in the line of descent. The list was probably shortened to obtain three groups of 14 names as a means to aid memory (v. 17). Note: Jehoiachin = Jeconiah = Coniah as in 2 Kings 24:6 and Jeremiah 22:24.

Mt 1:12–16 has 14 generations, but only 13 are listed. Dr. H.J. Schonfield in *"Those Incredible Christians"* (Bernard Geis Assoc. p. 117, 1968) states that an old Hebrew manuscript at v. 13 gives Abner between Abiud and Eliakim, which was later lost due to a scribal error in likeness of the Hebrew spelling of Abner (Abiner) and Abiud (Abiur).

Verse 12 "Shealtiel's son Zerubbabel." Compare Ezra 3:2, 8; 5:2, Nehemiah 12:1, Haggai 1:1, 12, 14 and 2:2 and Josephus Antiquities 11.3.10. The Pedaiah of 1 Chronicles 3:18–19 may be the brother of Shealtiel. If Shealtiel died childless and Pedaiah performed the Levirate duty, the laws of heritage would relate Zerubbable as Shealtiel's son, see Deuteronomy 25:5–6 and NUBD p. 1171.

9:21 "Permit me to go and bury my father." Since the dead were buried within 24 hours, why was he even in the crowd? A better understanding would be "Let me remain here until my old father actually dies, so I can clear up the estate."

10:29 and Luke 12:6, two sparrows for one farthing vs. 5 for two farthings. The custom is the same as today—buy four and get one free.

23:24 This is the only typo not corrected in revisions of the KJV since 1611 the New KJV has made the change. Strain "at" should read "out." This refers to the Jewish custom of straining wine to prevent any unclean insect being swallowed. Note: the camel was the largest unclean animal under Jewish law.

Jn 7:53–8:11 The woman caught in adultery. The first manuscript to contain it is Codex Bezae of about the 6th century, and found at the Monastery of St. Irenaeus of Lyons. Eusebius of Caesarea stated it was from the "Interpretations of the Words of the Lord" of Papias, a disciple of John ca. 130. This fragment appeared to wander about in the Gospels, showing they did not know where it belonged, BAR 34(4): 28 (08). It also contains Jesus' statement on the Sabbath: "At that time Jesus seeing a man working on the Sabbath said to him; man, if you know what you are doing, blessed are you. But if you do not know, you are accursed and a transgressor of the Law."

Acts 19:8 and 10 vs 20:31 Two years and three months versus three years. Roman custom, as well as Jewish, counted any part of a year as a full year. The three years were just rounded off.

vs. 9 One manuscript at the end adds "from 11 (A.M.) to 4 (P.M.)"

27:12 Phoenicia. The word should be Phoenix, a harbor on the western part of the southern shore of Crete.

Phil 4:3 *Syzygus* is probably a proper name but simply means yokefellow.

1 Jn 5:7 The last part of this verse was inserted in the Latin manuscripts and is not found in the Greek texts. Should read, "Because there are three that bear record and there are three that bear witness in earth——etc." Some Bibles (NAS) make 6b to become v. 7 (Finnegan p. 57). Erasmus compiled the first printed Greek N.T. in 1516 at the insistence of his Swiss printer Froben (in competition with Cardinal Jimenez Steunica in Spain). See IB Luke p. 20. Cardinal Jimenez version, began in 1502, was delayed until 1520 (he used the Vatican copies which had to be returned before publication was allowed): these contained I John 5:7.

Erasmus refused to include it "until he could be shown a Greek manuscript that contained it." Therefore, Frani of Oxford "made" a manuscript to contain this verse, actually written on paper. Erasmus then included it in his third edition. Of 5,000 New Testament manuscripts, only three late ones contain it (lecture by Prof. Metzger of Princeton Theological Seminary 2-17-74). It is never quoted during the controversies over the Trinity for example the Council of Nicea in 325 AD, or during the first 450 years of the Church era. It is first known from a Latin quotation by the Spanish heretic Pricillian who died in 385 (Finnegan p. 57). No manuscript before the 15th century contains it.

5:13 . . . that you may have eternal life. The rest: "and that you may believe," etc., was recopied.

Rev 22:19 "Book of life" A good example of how mistakes can creep into a text. Erasmus only had one defective copy of Revelation in Greek and it lacked the last six verses, so he translated from a Latin manuscript back into Greek, since then about 200 manuscripts are known which do not read this way. Instead read, "tree of life" (the tree of life is mentioned in Egypt at the beginning of the 18th Dynasty also see ECIAT p. 230). If your name can be erased from the Book of Life, this would be loss of salvation. Many in the Charismatic movement and Church of God have used this to support their position. The correct reading would remove this difficulty, to establish a doctrine on this point a second equally clear verse would be needed.

CHAPTER 7

PERCEIVED BIBLE ERRORS—
MAJOR

THESE "ERRORS" ARE more controversial and involve supposed inaccuracies of facts or historical information.

Of man's account: Archbishop James Ussher (1581–1656) of Ireland assumed unbroken father/son relationships in the genealogical lists of Genesis 5 and 11, placing the creation of man at 4004 BC. The same data from the Septuagint gives a date of 5411 BC. This is untenable in view of Archaeological finds at Jericho, Jarmo, Tepe Gawra and other sites. The North American Indian civilization of 10,000 years has been established for Cro -Magnon Man in Clovis, New Mexico and Texas. Scripture indicates that only major persons are mentioned in Genesis. Also, Hebrew has no word for grandfather or grandson. Thus, son of . . . could cover generations. Begot means became an ancestor of (compare Mt 1:8), so Jehoram begot Uzziah but this omits Ahaziah, Joash, and Amaziah (1 Chr 3:10–16); this is likewise the case in Ezra 7:3 as well as with 1 Chronicles 6:7–11 and Matthew 1:1, where Jesus is the son of David and the son of Abraham, leaving out all others between.

Gn 1:5 Twenty-four hour days for creation. Some creationists make much of the statement "and it was evening and morning." This is not a well-defined statement and would actually refer to twelve hours. The more accurate statement is found in Leviticus. 23:32 where from "even unto even" is used. Furthermore, the sun (which was probably obscured until the fourth day by a thick haze or fog) could not have been used to mark off time intervals until the fourth day. Light simply separated day from night, but the sun itself couldn't be seen. Consider Peter's statement in 2 Peter 3:8 that a day to the Lord is as a thousand years (or any other large time interval). Thus, there are no good ways to identify what time interval is being used. To attempt to compress the time into twenty-four hour days is pushing the envelope. While it could be, it could be something else, such that the reference point could shift between Genesis 1:2–11.

We like to think that everything remains constant as we are familiar with, but we know that such wasn't that way in the beginning. Man was created fully formed and not as a baby, animals didn't come from embryos, the trees didn't come from seeds, and grass was in place as though it had been there for some time. Carnivores cannot eat grass (their stomachs cannot digest it, and if they do it acts as a laxative: compare your dog or cat eating grass) and expect to live; but death is equated with sin. So how did they eat meat before the fall? Fish, sharks, and whales all eat meat, but what did they live on from Genesis1:20 until the fall? They were probably pretty hungry by this time. Supernovas as much as 150,000 light years away can be seen today, but was the light traveling for 150,000 years to get here today? Dozens of similar problems abound for young-earth advocates.

Gn 4:2 Abel may have been a twin, since the statement that Adam "knew his wife" is not said of his birth as for Cain and Seth, MCOCB p. 97. Other commentaries such as John Calvin's Critical Commentary on Genesis, the IB, Int. Critical

Commentary of Skinner on Genesis and the Int. Bible of Simpson on Genesis, as well as others, mention this.

4:14 and 17 Cain's wife and "whosoever finds me will slay me." This indicates that considerable time had passed for Cain to marry a sister (who was at least 15) and for others to inhabit the earth as potential slayers. The Talmud and The Life of Adam and Eve in the Pseudepigrapha state that Adam and Eve had 33 sons and 30 daughters (the Talmud says 23 daughters). The Book of Jubilees says there were nine sons and daughters and that Cain married Awam and Seth Azura. Josephus says it would be tedious to name them; which may indicate the names were available.

12:9–20 Abraham in Egypt (ca. 2000 BC). Diodorus the Greek historian stated that Egypt was a closed country to strangers until 700 BC. However, the tomb painting at Beni Hassan dated (ca.) 1892 BC shows 37 Semitic traders arriving in Egypt to trade stibnite (Finnegan p. 93 and Wright p. 46).

12:16—Abraham's camels. Since Egyptian tomb paintings did not show camels, some have said that the camel was not introduced into Egypt until 300 BC. Dr. J.P. Free, however, has found in Egypt camel figurines and statuettes, plaques and rock carvings, bones, a skull, and a camel hair rope dating from 3000–700 BC. A petroglyph near Aswan shows a man leading a Dromedary from the 6th Dynasty 2423–2263 BC, [ABR Premiere Issue p. 26, (87)]. Tiglath Pileser I (1115–1077 BC), on his Broken Obelisk, mentions his breeding of Bactrian camels. In addition, the Black Obelisk of Shalmaneser III of Assyria dated about 841 BC shows two Bactrian camels. The Tell Halaf monument dated about 1000–850 BC shows a man seated on a saddled Dromedary (Free p. 170). The camel is hard to domesticate and it probably had to be relearned in several places many times. The first might have been in Saudi Arabia.

13:10—Lot in the Jordan Valley. The temperature in this area often runs from 110–120°. Why did he not choose the more pleasant maritime plain? Excavations in this region by Nelson Glueck have found over 70 ancient sites, many of which go back over 5000 years. Thus, the Jordan valley was not empty during this time. The climate has been shown to be wetter, and thus able to support a larger population. The cemeteries at Bab edh-Dhra and Numeira, the most likely sites of Sodom and Gomorrah, contained about 1,000,000 bodies each and were in use for over 1,000 years. Zoar, Feifa, and Khanazir represent the other three Cities of the Plain; Feifa also has as large a cemetery as Bab edh-Dhra (see BAR 6[5]: 27 [80]).

Gn Chapter 14—4 Kings against 5. Objections were raised that (1) the Mesopotamian Kings are fictional; (2) no such extensive travel was used in those days; and (3) there was no line of march east of Palestine, as described in verse 5. The answers to these supposed problems are (1) the Babylonian Mari texts tell of Amutpiel who was king of Qatanum (this may be a variation of Amurpiel, which would be equivalent to Amraphel); (2) a Mari tablet, dating from the era of Abraham, was a contract from what would have amounted to the local "Hertz" agent, which leased a wagon for a year but on condition that it not be driven to Kittim (the whole coast land of the Mediterranean Sea), about 320 miles to the nearest point—thus extensive travel was so common that such a journey ran the risk of having a wagon worn out on the round trip; and (3) While W.F. Albright considered this line of march a purely legendary narrative, he has since found a number of large mounds, the remains of old cities indicating an ancient trade route. The places mentioned in Genesis 14:5 and 6 are located in this territory.

19:9—Lot's mob-proof door. Critics have said such doors were not needed, since houses from David to Solomon 900–600 BC did not even have doors, but rather archways or curtains. When Albright and Kyle excavated Tell Beit Mirsim (equated with Debir, but this is now untenable) WSW of Hebron, it showed occupation from 2200–1600 BC with strong walls and great doors in use (one large door socket was found in place). If a strong central government is in force, strong walls are not necessary. However, the smaller and weaker the police force, the greater the doors need to be. Free states "The critics date the writing of the accounts of Abraham in the 9th and 8th centuries BC. However would a late writer know about the conditions 1,000 years or more before his time?" (p. 63). Human authors without inspiration are prone to these errors. Compare the error of Shakespeare in Julius Caesar Act II Scene II line121, where Caesar asks, "What is't o'clock?" and Brutus answers "Caesar, "tis strucken eight." Clocks had not been invented in Roman times. Similar errors occur in Act II Scene I, and in Troilus and Cressida Act II Scene II, which has a reference to Aristotle who was born 800 years after the Trojan War. In The Two Gentlemen of Verona, Valentine is traveling by ship from Verona to Milan in Act I Scene I, when neither is a seaport.

37:10— "thy mother." According to 35:19, Rachel was already dead. If the dream of chapter 37 occurred before the birth of Benjamin, this is no help because Rachel never got to Egypt (probably Bilhah, Zilpah and Leah were dead also).

Ex 12:37—Number of men leaving Egypt. The problem is in the Hebrew terms 'alep and 'eleh which can reduce thousand to mean clan. This would make for a more manageable number of people. Something approximately 70,000 total or about 18,000 armed men. The total number indicated in Exodus would have been near 2,500,000, an impossible number to move around, provide water, and feed, in the limited area of Sinai. As late as 1850, the total population of the Sinai was only about 5,000. In 14:7, the 600 chariots plus an unspecified number of others would have been lost against such a large hoard of people to plow through and provide no competition for the Israelites.

An army marches inversely proportional to its size; the more there are the slower the march and the more room it takes up. The full Macedonian army of Alexander at Gaza of 52,000 infantry, 6,600 cavalry plus followers, at one point covered 137 miles at a rate of 19.6 miles per day. Infantry at ten abreast and cavalry at five abreast would still extend 16.5 miles deep with no provision for followers or baggage animals or carts. If this were what the experienced army of Alexander could do, what would be the rate for a mob of Israelites, which included women, children, wagons and cattle? Water requirements of a minimum are two quarts per person plus eight gallons per day for a horse or mule. The army of Alexander above needed 100,000 gallons per day, but had no sheep or cattle to contend with (see Engels and Murnane p. 95). The Israelis would be so spread out it would be impossible to move the entire group past an obstacle such as the Reed Sea crossing in the 8-hour period allotted. Road conditions also limit speed and the smallest obstacle acts as a funnel to reduce the flow past it. See the discussion Thutmose III had about the Aruna pass at Megiddo where the troops had to go single file, ANE Vol. 1 p. 176. Herodotus said it took Cyrus three months to march his army from Susa to Sardis in Lydia some 1700 miles, or a rate of 18.8 mi/day. These rates are for an experienced army.

24:4—Moses wrote all the words. Older views claimed that the Phoenicians invented alphabet writing about 900 BC. The oldest known alphabetic script was discovered in 1904 by Sir Flinders Petrie at Serabit-el-Khadem (probably the eighth stopping place during the exodus known as Dophkah, [smelting, see Keller p. 131] Nm 33:12), which is 2/3 of the way from Suez to Mt. Sinai. This is an old Egyptian turquoise mine that had been worked from the early dynasties. The nearby hill contains an old Semite temple or shrine to Hator, where literate workers in a proto-Semitic alphabet cut about 40 inscriptions or graffiti. Albright (p. 189) dates these as ca. 1500 BC. Note: this early Sinai-Hebrew script was found in the very region where Moses was instructed to write (17:8–14; see NUBD p. 1373). Albright had this to say (Wight p. 100), "Somewhere around 2000 BC we may suppose, Semites in close contact with Egypt invented the alphabet by application of a simple acrophonic principle, e.g., they took the Egyptian hieroglyph for "house," simplified it, and used it to write the first consonant for the Semitic word *bet* ("house"), which continued to be employed as the name of the letter (Heb. *beth*, Greek *beta*). It is interesting to note in Genesis 26:5 that oral and probably written laws and commandments were given before Moses.

Jos 6:20–24—Jericho's Walls and Rahab's House. Objections are: (1) battering rams would force walls inward, but the Bible says they fell flat or outward; (2) a city of stone and mud brick could not burn; and (3) if the walls fell, Rahab's house would have fallen also. Answer: (1) Garstang found old outer walls having fallen outward down a slope, although these may date to an earlier period; (2) a large extensive fire occurred about 1400 BC, in which pots containing grain were crushed by blackened timbers from the roof. Plenty of wood was used in construction, and then there were the various combustibles (furniture, olive oil and clothing) already present; and (3) the inner wall had houses built on top, but some walls were still standing. Only sections of walls need have fallen.

The next city (E) was not rebuilt until 860 BC in the time of Ahab by Hiel (1 Kgs 16:34).

Jgs—Good Stories, or God's Word?

1:10 The Cannanite names Ahi'man and Tal'mai occur in the Ras Shamra Tablets dated about 1400 BC, written in alphabetic cuneiform, related to Hebrew.

1:21 Jerusalem was not taken as shown by the Amarna Tablets (found 200 miles S. of Cairo), written in Accadian cuneiform to Akhenaten indicating that Jerusalem was still secure from the marauding Habiru (probably included the Hebrews). Whereas Bethel (vs. 1:23–25) was destroyed, excavations at Betein (which may not be the correct site of Bethel) in 1924 by Albright showed the town completely destroyed during this period. But Bethshan, Megiddo and Gezer were not subject to the Israelites (vs. 1:27–29). Excavations bear out that these cities were not held by Israel during this period.

4:2 Hazor existed during this time and actually reached its peak about 1800 BC.

8:14 Writing was not well developed until about 800 BC. Evidence from the Lachish fosse temple, Beth-Shemesh and Megiddo indicates that the Hebrew alphabet was already in use by as early as 1400 BC.

Jgs Chapter 13–16—Philistines in Samson's day. The monuments of Ramses III (1198–1166 BC) depict his sea battle with Philistines trying to land in the Nile delta. Repulsed, they then landed in Palestine, joining those who were there from the time of Abraham (Gn 21:32 and 34). Then there is the Egyptian story of Wenamon, who went from Egypt to Byblos (including Lebanon) to buy cedar, and had contact with a kindred people of the Philistines who had no esteem for Egyptian power in that region about 1100 BC when Egypt was in decline. This was at Dor, in the Mt. Carmel region, "a town of the Tjeker" (sea people; see ANE, Vol. I p. 16–24).

20:40—Burning of Gibeah. The strata remains of the fortress dating from this period show the result of burning.

1 Sm 16:17, 21 and 23; 1 Chr 25—David's Music and Guilds. Critics claim that music guilds did not originate until after the exile, or 538 BC, and that the attribution to David is aetiological (invented to explain a fact, e.g. robin red breast and the fire). However, (1) the Beni-Hassan tombs dated to about 1892 BC show Asiatic Semites carrying a lyre about 1000 years before David; (2) Thebes Tomb #38 about 1420 BC shows a girl with a lyre and another with a double oboe; (3) a vase from Megiddo about 1025 BC shows a lyre from the time of David; (4) at Ur beautiful ivory harps and lyres with 3–11 strings dated from about 2500 BC (5) the guild name Chaicol (Calcol). 1 Chronicles 2:26 was also found on the Megiddo ivories of about 1300 BC. Ethan and Herman (1 Chr 2:6) are the same as numerous abbreviated names found at Ras Shamra (Ugarit) dating from about 1400 BC. The Hebrew word for singer is *sharim*, which is a Canaanite word, indicating that David used the local term by which these musicians were known (Bible and Spade 1:53 [72]). In Psalm 88 and 89 (intro.) *Ezrahite* means "native born" or Canaanite proselytes used in the guilds. The oldest heptonic scale dates to 1800 BC on a tablet found at Nippur, Iraq, deciphered by Dr. Duchesne-Guillemin in 1966/7.

1 Chr 29:7 seems an anachronism, as the Daric (see the next section) was not in existence in David's time. Unless this is a scribal change that slipped into the text, it may represent a clue to when the "Chronicler" wrote. Even the Jews did not trust Chronicles, in that neither book is read aloud in Synagogue services. Note that Ishbaal has not been changed in 1 Chronicles 8:33 as in 2 Samuel 2:8. There are other places like it that retain the Baal ending, showing that it didn't get much editing.

2 Chr 33:11—Manasseh in Babylon. Thought to be an error: would an Assyrian king take a prisoner to Babylon and not Nineveh? Although the king is not named, we know that Sennacherib was involved with Manasseh's father Hezekiah. At this point in time Esarhaddon was on the throne. He was the only Assyrian king to live in Babylon, as shown by his son Ashurbanipal's library found at Nineveh. (See also ARAB Vol. I, # 639–708 for the restoration of Babylon, Baxter p. 35.)

Ezr 2:69 and Neh 7:70—Daric. In Hebrew, a Greek drachma—a coin said not to be in use until after Alexander the Great (330 BC). Critics say Ezra, Nehemiah, and Chronicles were all written by the "Chronicler" about 250 BC. The daric was first minted in Persia by Darius who copied it from the Lydians about 512 BC. The coin shows a king with bow in a bent-knee position commonly called "archers." Thus when the Spartan king Agesilaos says he was driven out of Asia by ten (or thirty) thousand archers he may have been talking about his bribe to leave. Zenophon in 400 BC says it was a month's pay for a mercenary soldier. The Babylonian shekel was taken from the Median sigloi (Cook p. 103).

Albright has shown that the Attic or Athens drachma was a standard coin in Palestine from about 450 BC. Excavations at Beth-Zur (S. of Jerusalem) yielded six drachmas from the Persian level.

Ezr 4:2—The adversaries are confused, not the Bible. Shalmaneser V (726–722 BC) repopulated Samaria not Esarhadon (680–669; see ARAB Vol. II p. 2).

4:7–24—Opposition to the temple during the reign of Artaxerxes I Longimanus (464–424 BC). It is possible this section should follow at the end of Ezra Chapter 10. Note: all of Ezra is found in I Esdras.

4:7—Aramaic used in correspondence. Earlier scholars have denied this use and thus the authenticity of Daniel and Ezra. The Elephantine Papyri record correspondence between the Jewish colonies from 500–400 BC in Aramaic. In 411 BC, an uprising occurred and their temple was destroyed. They wrote to the Persian governor Bigvia at Jerusalem in 408 BC seeking aid. These letters also mention Sanballat's sons dated in the 17th year of Darius II (407 BC) and confirm Sanballat being governor when Nehemiah came to Jerusalem in 444 BC (Neh. 2:10). Nehemiah's brother Hanani (Neh 7:2) and the high priest Johanan (Neh 12:22) are also mentioned in these letters.

"Tobias (Neh 2:10) governor of Ammon" (probably a descendant of Nehemiah's foe) wrote to Zeno (Zeno Papyri archives of an Egyptian official) under Ptolemy II Philadelphus (285–246 BC), dealing with Palestinian affairs. The Tobiad tombs and the name Tobiad in Aramaic script were found at Araq el Emir in Trans-Jordan near Amman. "Gesham the Arabian," also called Gash'mu (Neh 6:1 and 6), has been identified by Albright as a Persian governor of NW Arabia in a Lihyanic inscription found at Hegra (Edomites are equivalent to Arabs during the Persian period).

In 1947, several silver offering bowls and coins dated about 400 BC were found at Tell el-Maskhuta in N. Egypt. Four bowls bear Aramaic inscriptions to the goddess Han-Ilat. One reads, "That which Qaynu bar Gash'mu, King of Qedar, brought in offering to Han-Ilat." This reference to the son of Nehemiah's adversary verifies a Biblical character from a historical record and authenticates Nehemiah's account from a source outside the Bible. This and other additional information about the little known Arabian nation of Qedar shows that Qedar was a force to be reckoned with from Sennacherib's time (BC 704–681) to the Nabataean period (550 BC–106 AD). Her confederate or allied people were distributed from the Syrian Desert to N. Arabia and during the Persian period from S. of Palestine to the Delta of Egypt. (See Bible and Spade 1: 82 [72]).

An Aramaic letter from King Adon of Ashkelon to Pharaoh Necho of Egypt about 600 BC, confirms that Aramaic was the official language of Palestine before the Chaldean conquest as indicated in 2 Kings 18:26.

Ezr 4:10—Osnappar; In more correct Hebrew it is Asenapper, a Hebraized form of Ashurbanipal (668–627 BC) who collected the great library of 100,000 tablets found at Nineveh, which contained the Babylonian Creation and Flood stories.

Ezr 6:14 Artaxerxes I Longimanus (464–424 BC) is meant, but he only contributed to the maintenance, not the building. From the date of completion of the Temple, the 6th year of Darius (Feb–Mar 516 BC) in verse 15 (Josephus has the 9th year) to the 7th year of Artaxerxes in 7:7, 59 years lapsed. Josephus does not give this additional chronology.

Eze 1:2—Jehoichin, called King of Judah. C.C. Torrey claims that this basis of dating by King Jehoiachin's captivity (when he ruled only three months and was taken to Babylon, his uncle

Zedekiah was then placed on the throne by Nebuchadrezzar) is unusual and should be dated in the late 3rd Century BC and not the 6th.

Jar handles stamped "Eliakim steward of Yaukin [Jehoiachin]" were found at Tell Beit Mirsim and Beth-Shemesh, indicating that crown property still belonged to the exiled king.

The Babylonians also considered him still King of Judah when receipts dated 592 BC (same year as Ezek 8:1) listing Yaukin king of the land of Yahud (Judah) and his sons for their royal rations, along with other kings and nobles of Egypt, etc., were found. One would expect that Jews in Babylon would date by the year of their sovereigns' captivity (UOT p. 297).

Dn 5; 7:1 and 8:1—Belshazzar king in Babylon? Critics state Cyrus's record indicated that Nabonidus was the last king of Babylon, that the Bible is in error, and that there was no such person as Belshazzar as a son of Nebuchadrezzar.

Discovery of the Nabunaid Chronicle (published in 1882; see ANET p. 305) indicated that he did have an eldest son named in Akkadian Bel-Shar-Usur ("Bel protect the king") and that in the 3rd year of Nabonidus's reign (553 BC) he was made co-regent and continued until the fall of Babylon (539 BC). The Chronicle reports that in the 7th, 9th, 10th and 11th year, Nabonidus was at Tema, his provincial capital in Arabia. He entrusted actual kingship to Belshazzar as follows: "He entrusted a camp to his eldest, first-born son; the troops of the land he sent with him. He freed his hand, he entrusted the kingship to him. Then he himself undertook a distant campaign, the power of the land of Akkad advanced with him; towards Tema in the midst of the Westland, he set his face . . . He himself established his dwelling at Tema . . . That city he made glorious . . . They made it like a palace of Babylon."

The Chronicle expressly states that the New Year Festival was not celebrated in those years the king was absent, but was observed in the 17th year when the king returned home from (self imposed?) exile (ANET p. 306 and Wiseman p. 75).

Nabonidus had taken Nebuchadrezzar's daughter Nitocris as his wife. Her son would thus be related to Nebuchadrezzar ("son of" is equivalent to "successor of" since Caldean has no word for grandson or grandfather). Note: The Black Obelisk records Jehu as the "son of Omri" actually; Jehu was only a royal successor with no lineal relationship at all. Nabonidas is mentioned in a Hebrew manuscript for the first time in DSS 4Q 242 "The Prayer of Nabonidus" (see Vermes p. 573).

Cyrus's inscription states that Nabonidus was not present in Babylon on the night of the attack, confirming Daniel chapter 5, where Nabonidus is not named. It reads, "In the month of Tashritu (Sept/Oct), when Cyrus attacked the army of Akkad in Opis on the Tigris, the inhabitants of Akkad revolted but he [Nabonidus] massacred the confused inhabitants." The 15th day, Sippar was seized without battle. Nabonidus fled. The 16th day Gobryas [Ugbaru], the governor of Gutium and the army of Cyrus entered Babylon without battle (Oct 13). Afterward Nabonidus was arrested in Babylon when he returned [there] . . .In the month of Arahshamnu, the 3rd day, Cyrus entered Babylon. Green twigs were spread in front of him—the state of "Peace" [shulmu] (Hebrew Shalom) was imposed upon the city. Cyrus sent greeting to all Babylon. Gobryas, his governor, installed [sub-] governors in Babylon . . . In the month of Arashshamnu on the night of the 11th day, Gobryas died. In the month [Arashamnu, the . . . th day, the wi]fe of the king died. From the 27th day of Arahshamnu till the 3rd day of Nisanu (Hebrew Nisan) an official weeping was performed in Akkad, all the people [went around] with their hair disheveled." (See ANET p. 203.) The mutilated state of the text makes it impossible to determine if it was the king, the wife of the king, or son of the king who died. Evidence favors the wife of the king. Grief, because of her age and the death of her son, with the passing of

Babylon into foreign hands, may have caused her death. Both Daniel 5 and Xenophon in the Cyropaedia VII, 5, 30 agree on Belshazzar's death coinciding on the fall of Babylon.

Jon 3:3 and 4—Size of Nineveh. Critics claim that Nineveh was not 60–75 miles across, and did not contain such a large population as in 4:11.

Actually, Nineveh's walls enclosed 1800 acres (2.8 mi²). The Kuyunjik mound covering Sennacherib and Assurbanipal's and other palaces covers an area one mile wide and is 90 feet high. (It is so huge it will never be completely explored). Just as New York City is spoken of as a whole, Nineveh was also spoken of as consisting of its suburbs such as Calah 18 miles S., Resen (between Calah and Nineveh, Rehobeth-Ir (probably same as Rebit-ninua) W. of Nineveh. (Both names have the same meaning.) Other suburbs such as Tarbisu, Dursharrukin (Sargonsburg) were probably also included. Note: Nineveh in Assyrian is Nuna or Ninua. In Jonah 1:2, 3:2 and 4:11 it is called "the great city."

"Three days journey" refers to time for official delegation to visit an important city (see BAR 16[5]: 63 [90] and NIV).

3:3 Nineveh "was" is not necessarily past tense (compare Luke 24:13, where Emmaus was from Jerusalem about seven miles).

4:11—120,000 people. Jonah was there about 775 BC. Ashurnasirpal II (883–859 BC) on his Monument at Nimrud (Calah), states that a 10-day banquet at the dedication of his palace was given for 69,574 of the "chief" people of Nimrud. Nineveh was twice as large as Nimrud [see NUBD, Bible and Spade 1: 118 (72), and ANE Vol. II p. 99].

At Ur, Woolley found the walled city had 4,250 houses and at eight persons per house gives a population of 34,000 and was only about 1/6 the size of the "Greater Ur." The Larsa period ruins (about 2000 BC) or suburbs were found 4–5 miles away in several directions. The Greater Ur could easily have had a population of 500,000.

Mt 27:9—Spoken by Jeremiah the Prophet. The reference is to Zechariah 11:12–13. In some Hebrew canon lists, Jeremiah is the first book in the Prophets (see Talmud, Baba Bathra 14b) and would be cited as the Title. See also Luke 24:44 where all three sections of the Old Testament are referred to, with Psalms standing as the first scroll in the poetry section.

CHAPTER 8

DEAD SEA SCROLLS

THIS IS THE most important manuscript discovery of all time. Within the liberal school, the argument has been, "Show me a really old manuscript, and I will show you how the mistakes occurred." Only some of this has actually happened. Lost words, variant readings and information lost from the accepted manuscripts has been our greatest source of new information.

The first scrolls were discovered in 1947 by Muhammad edh-Dhib "the Wolf," at Cave One about 0.88 miles north of the site of Khirbet Qumran. Caves One, Two, Three and 11 are all north of Qumran. To date, over 475 caves have been thoroughly examined (see BAR 16(6): 75 (90)). Bedouins of the Ta'amara tribe found Caves One, Two, Four, Six, and 11. Archaeologists found Three, Five, and Seven-Ten. Caves Four through Ten were found at Qumran. Most of the small fragments found by the Bedouin were bought for $1 per cm² or $11 per in². The total manuscripts represent 930. No codex has been found at Qumran.

Cave One contained a complete copy of Isaiah, 1 foot x 24 feet, dated 125–100 BC, and 47 of 66 chapters (about 70%)

of another. Also present was a commentary on Habakkuk dated at 120–5 BC, thus removing previous New Testament allusions for a later date (actually a Midrash), and Genesis written in Aramaic, which contains only chapters 5–15 along with a poetical description of Sarah. The Manual of Discipline of the Essenes was found in two sections (also known as the Community Rule). The enigmatic passage in Matthew 5:43–44, "to hate your enemies," is found in no Jewish writing except the Essene Manual of Discipline. Jesus may have been including them by way of example for a summary (see BAR 10[5]: 46 [84]). Also present was the War of the Sons of Light with the Sons of Darkness (called the War Scroll). Thanksgiving Psalms are in four sections, three fragments of Daniel are from two separate manuscripts, and there are eleven other biblical fragments.

Writing used *scriptio plena,* or full writing (creation of vowels from consonants, first used ca. 700 BC), and most resembled the Nash papyrus dating from 100 BC. Carbon-14 tests on the linen covering were dated 33 AD (+/-200 yrs.).

Cave Two contained fragments from Exodus, Leviticus in old Hebrew, Numbers, Deuteronomy, Psalms, Ruth, and Jeremiah. Ben Sira and Jubilees are in Hebrew with approximately 40 other non-biblical manuscripts (Fritch p. 40).

Cave Three the furthest north, contained Ezekiel, Psalms, Lamentations, an Isaiah midrash, Jubilees, seven miscellaneous scrolls, and the copper scroll in two pieces containing a hidden treasure list of 160 tons of gold and silver in 64 caches (from ca. 70 AD). It states another copy also existed.

Cave Four contained a hoard of fragments of about 575 manuscripts, 90 of which are biblical. Only Esther is missing. Included are 12 Isaiahs, 13 of Deuteronomy, 110 individual Psalms, seven Minor Prophets, five Pentateuchs, and the Testament of Levi, Tobit in Aramaic, and Hebrew, Enoch, and Jubilees. Ecclesiastes dates to 150 BC. Three copies of Samuel representing about 35% of the book dating to about

250 BC, whereas Jeremiah dates to (ca.) 200 BC. The Prayer of Nabonidus in Aramaic is the only Jewish source to mention Nabonidus. Four fragments from Daniel, including a pseudo-Daniel in Aramaic, show a lively interest in a book most scholars date as late. A total of eight Daniel manuscripts are known. Also present are numerous Messianic proof texts.

Cave Five contained Deuteronomy, Kings, Isaiah, Amos, Psalms, Lamentations, and an Apocryphal Malachi, as well as 15 miscellaneous manuscripts.

Cave Six contained Genesis and Leviticus in old Hebrew, Deuteronomy, Kings, Psalms, Song of Songs, and Daniel on papyrus, as well as several apocryphons (three on papyrus).

Cave Seven contained fragments only in the Greek LXX of Exodus, and the Letter of Jeremiah (vs. 43–44), as well as 17 unidentified fragments. Jose O'Callaghan, a Jesuit priest, identified these as from the New Testament written in Zierstil Greek of 50 BC to 50 AD (see the articles in Bible and Spade 1: 35 7[2], 2: 15, 57 [73], 3: 55 [74]). Other scholars take issue with this identification. Cave Seven is to be re-excavated for additional fragments.

Cave Eight contained Genesis, Psalms, and three miscellaneous.

Caves Nine and Ten contained a papyrus fragment and an ostracon respectively.

Cave 11, which is between Cave One and three to the north, contained two copies of Leviticus, one in old Hebrew, along with Deuteronomy, Ezekiel, 41 Psalms, the Targum of Job, seven Apocryphal Psalms and Psalm 91, Jubilees, Melchizedek, Berakhah, Songs of the Sabbath Sacrifice, New Jerusalem, and the most famous one, the Temple Scroll—the largest at 26.9 ft and the thinnest at 0.1 mm. About 75% is preserved. Two previously unidentified fragments of another copy are now known from Cave Four. Yigael Yadin, who published the scroll in 1977, has dated the original composition at 150–125 BC.

The interesting point is that it is written in the first person, as if by God (BAR 10[5]: 32 [84]).

Some 13 paleo-Hebrew scrolls are known, covering Genesis, Exodus, Leviticus, Deuteronomy, and Job. According to the Talmud Yadiam 4:5, these could only be used for study and not liturgical purposes. The Tetragrammation YHWH was also often in paleo-Hebrew.

Khirbet Qumran excavations indicated three main occupations, the earliest from the Iron Age, 8–6th century BC; after several centuries of abandonment the Hasmoneans used the site from 134 BC until the earthquake mentioned by Josephus, which occurred on the day of the battle of Actium in 31 BC. The site was revived after repair of the aqueduct and water system and remained in use until destroyed by the Xth Legion in June 68 AD. The Roman garrison withdrew after the fall of Masada in 73 AD. Several coins from the Bar Kokhba War show that the site served as a hiding place from 132–135 AD. This settlement was the main base of the Jewish Essene sect.

Some 750 coins have been found from the reign of John Hyrcanus, 135–104 BC, down to the end of the Hasmonean period of 39 BC. These include coins of Archelaus 4 BC–6 AD down to the Jewish revolt of 70 AD. A few coins from 70–86 AD, including one of Vespasian of year 70, two of the city of Ascalon 72–73, three Judea Capta 78–81 and one of Agrippa II 86, were left by the Xth Legion garrison stationed here and in Jericho. Thirteen coins of Hadrian, 132–135 AD, indicate the ruins were used by Jewish guerillas in the 2nd revolt.

A cemetery of 1,200 graves in three parts is to the east. Only 53 were excavated, with ten women and three children's graves found in the northern and southern part of the far east subsidiary cemetery.

The caves also yielded 202 jars and 97 lids that were used to store the scrolls (several whole jars from Cave One were probably stolen by Bedouins). At least five inkwells were also found. An interesting point is that the caves around Qumran are man made. West of Cave Four are at least three others that have never been excavated due to roof collapse. Possibly other scrolls are yet to be found. More than 35 fragments are in the hands of private collectors who bought them from the Bedouins. James H. Charlesworth has recently published three of them (BAR 33[5]: 62 [07]).

General references

W.H. Brownlee, The Meaning of the Qumran Scrolls for the Bible, Oxford Univ. Press, 1964.

C.F. Pfeifer, *The Qumran Community*, Weathervane Books, New York, 1969.

C.T. Fritch, *The Qumran Community*, Biblo and Tannen, New York, 1972.

G. Vermes, *The Complete Dead Sea Scrolls in English*, Allen Lane, New York, 1997.

J. Magness, *Archaeology of Qumran and the Dead Sea Scrolls*, Eerdmans, Grand Rapids, Michigan, 2002.

Dead Sea Scrolls Bible

The major problem for Bible scholars has always been, "what was the original text?" If there is a Murphy's Law in manuscript copying it is, "If any error can be made, it will be . . .over and over." Ever since the King James Bible of 1611, we have attempted to solve the problem of the authentic text. One would think that the problem would not be that difficult. Just find the oldest copy known. It should contain fewer errors than newer, more copied versions. But the oldest copy of the Old Testament, the Aleppo codex, dates only to 930 AD and is not complete (originally 490 leaves); but after the fire of 1947 the beginning and end were burned. Today only 294 leaves are intact.

The oldest complete codex is the Leningrad codex of 1008 AD; it has 491 leaves. Both copies are derived from the Masoretic text of Aaron ben Moshe ben Asher, which was the final standardization of the 6th–9th centuries. As early as 90 AD at Jamina, just north of Ashdod, Rabbi Akiba and his associates met to standardize the text of the Old Testament, as to which books would be the official ones. This was done to counter the New Testament's rise and to place the Apocrypha on the outside. Since several different scrolls were known with different readings, it was decided that the two, which read the same, were the official ones and the others were removed from circulation and copying. The Masoretes' work completed the task of "building a hedge" around the text.

The discovery of the Dead Sea Scrolls pushes the time period for Hebrew and Aramaic scrolls back in one fell swoop from 1000–1205 years, a quantum jump. The only other way to get beyond the Masoretic text was to use the translated versions: the Septuagint (LXX) Greek version, originally of 250 BC (the oldest copy Vaticanus dates to 340 AD, although the John Rylands papyrus 458 has some text of the 2nd century BC, and the papyrus Fouad 266 has some of ca. 100 BC); the Samaritan Pentateuch, originally of 430 BC (the oldest copy dates to 655 AD); the Targums (oral sayings from 800 BC–30 AD, written from 30–600 AD); and the oldest copy is by Onkelos and dates to 700 AD, the Old Syriac from 150 AD (our oldest copy dates ca. 600 AD), as well as the Latin Vulgate which started in 175 AD, to Jerome's version in 404 AD (the oldest copy dates to ca. 810 AD). None of these are as old as the DSS.

The same problems are true for the New Testament, but the Septuagint, Syriac, and Vulgate also have the New Testament. The problem of which text is best still exists. The Septuagint Codex Alexandrimus of the 5th century AD did not reach England until 1627 and would have been a big help to the King James committee. An interesting observation is that most of the Old Testament quotations in the New Testament are from the Septuagint rather than the Hebrew. The Septuagint has its own problems; for example, Jeremiah is 13% shorter than the Masoretic.

The Dead Sea Scrolls Bible (M. Abegg, P. Flint, and E. Ulrich, Harpers San Francisco, 1999) uses all variations, additions, and corrections found in the Dead Sea Scrolls, as well as ten biblical manuscripts found at Masada, Nahel Hever, and Wadi Murabba. This brings the total biblical manuscripts to 225, dating from 250 BC–68 AD. Some scroll notations, or siglum, as currently used in the literature citations are 4Q Sam^c, referencing Cave Four Qumran Samuel scroll number 3, which in this case was copied by the same scribe that copied the Community Rule (1QS = sectarian). The similar handwriting became so familiar that it was used to join fragments of the same scroll. Only the complete great Isaiah Scroll 1QIsa^a and Psalms 11QPs^a have large parts preserved. Only Esther is missing. Nehemiah and 1 Chronicles are also missing, but since Ezra and 2 Chronicles are present, it is confidently assumed that Ezra-Nehemiah and 1 and 2 Chronicles were on the same scrolls and therefore present. Also present were Tobit, Ben Sira, and the Letter of Jeremiah.

The Qumran community probably viewed I Enoch and Jubilees as scripture at this time. Among the popular scrolls at Qumran were Psalms in 40 manuscripts, Deuteronomy in 33, and Isaiah in 22. Interestingly or coincidentally, in the New Testament, Psalms is cited 68 times, Isaiah 63 and Deuteronomy 39 as the largest number. The reader is referred to the DSSB for complete readings and only the more interesting points are presented here. The order follows the Hebrew Bible names. Based on verses preserved, the percentages are as listed.

Genesis—21.5% in 24 manuscripts. At least two contain both Genesis and Exodus. One is in paleo-Hebrew and dates to 150 BC; 4QGen^j, LXX, and the Samaritan Pentateuch contain a reading that may be original at 41:16: "Apart from me [Joseph], God will give no answer concerning the welfare of Pharaoh."

Exodus—72% in 18 manuscripts. One shows Exodus followed by Leviticus, and one has Genesis, Exodus. and Numbers One is in paleo-Hebrew.

1:5 reads 75 along with the LXX and Acts 7:14.

12:40 has 430 years for the time in Egypt only, and not the extra generation from Abraham to Jacob as in LXX, Samaritan Pentateuch and Galatians 3:17.

24:1, 9 add Eleazer and Ithamar.

38:18–22 4Q Ex-Lev^f and 4Q Sam^b both date to 250 BC as the oldest scrolls at Qumran.

Leviticus—58% in 16 manuscripts; 11QpaleoLev^a is in paleo-Hebrew. Only chapter 12 is missing in full. The nonbiblical manuscripts and the Temple Scroll quote all 23 chapters respectively for doctrine at Qumran.

1:13–2:1—4Q Ex-Lev^f date to 250 BC and over 1000 years older than the previous oldest copy known.

Numbers—43% in 11 manuscripts. Only chapters 6 and 14 are not represented; 4Q Lev-Num contains two scrolls, and 1QpaleoLev is in paleo-Hebrew and contains two passages from Numbers 1:48–50 and 36:7–8(?) between chapter 23 and 27; 4QNum^b from (ca.) 30 BC contains readings preserved in the LXX but not in the Masoretic text and represents a proto-Masoretic text before standardization; 4QLXX Num. is in Greek.

11:32 reads "all" the people.

13:15 reads *Micha* but *Maki* in the Masoretic text, *Miki* in the Samaritan Pentateuch, and *Makchi* in the LXX, showing the spoken form of words changes over time.

13:21 adds "and entered" and spied out.

16:8 adds, said to Korah, "and all his company."

Deuteronomy—21% in 33 manuscripts. One 4QLXXDeut is in Greek, two are in paleo-Hebrew, and one is on papyrus.

4:14 adds crossing over "the Jordan" to possess. Also in 11:8 in 4QDeut$^{k''}$ and in the LXX the object of a verb is needed. The NIV added it before these manuscripts were known.

8:6—4QDeut^n reads, his ways by "loving him."

15:2—4QDeut^c specifies no party can be exempted. This shows that legal differences arose early.

16:8 Specifies that unleavened bread be eaten for seven days as in v. 3.

26:19 Is not included in 4QpaleoDeut^c and some LXX.

32:43 Shows a different reading in the DSS. Rejoice, O heavens together with him, and bow down to him all you gods, for he will avenge the blood of his sons, and render vengeance to his enemies, and will recompense those who hate him, and will atone for the land of his people.

34:6 says, and "they" buried him (meaning the Israelites).

Jubilees—about 15 manuscripts, all in Hebrew; one on papyrus probably considered as Scripture at Qumran.

Joshua—8.5% in two manuscripts; 4QJos^a dates to (ca.) 100 BC.

3:15—4QJos^b adds wheat before harvest, as does the LXX.

8:35—4QJos^a has this verse at the end of Chapter 4 where it flows better; the LXX has it after 9:2. The Masoretic text requires a different introduction. This shows that Joshua already existed in two variant editions, one shorter and one longer.

Judges—8.3% in three manuscripts. Both 4QJudg$^{a \text{ and } b}$ has a shortened text, lacking Judg.6: 7–10.

6:5 adds "and camels."

21:18 "anyone who gives a wife to Benjamin is cursed" is missing from 4QJudg^b.

1 and 2 Samuel—35.2% and 16.3% is one scroll in four manuscripts; 4QSam^a (ca. 50 BC) is the largest fragment; 4QSam^b dates to (ca.) 250 BC.

1:24 correctly adds "a 3-year-old bull."

2:22 gives Eli's age as 98.

9:27 Some 44 words have been lost from the Masoretic text. The end should read, "And you shall reign over the people of the Lord, and you will save them from the hand of their enemies round about. And this shall be the sign to you that the Lord has anointed you to be prince over his inheritance."

10:27b—4Q Sam^a adds a whole paragraph that has been lost from all our texts, although Josephus (who had access to the Temple scrolls kept by Titus) knew of it. The KJV in 11:1 starts in a way known to be incorrect. The complete reading is "Nahash king of the children of Ammon, sorely oppressed the children of Gad and the children of Reuben, and he gouged out all their right eyes and struck terror and dread in Israel. There was not left one among the children of Israel beyond the Jordan whose right eye was not put out by Nahash king of the children of Ammon except that 7,000 men fled from the children of Ammon and entered Jabesh-Gilead. About a month later Nahash the Ammonite . . ." At present, the only Bibles to include this reading are NIB Vol. II Abingdon Press, Nashville 1998, the NAB of 1970, the Life Application Study Bible of 2004 and the NRSV.

11:8 reads, Judah "70,000" in 4QSam^a.

11:9—4QSam^a adds an entire line, deliverance "to you they will open the . . ."

12:8—4QSam^a has a longer text as shown by the spacing and in the singular, read as LXX: "When Jacob and his sons were in Egypt and Egypt abased them and your ancestors cried out."

13:1—The Samuel scrolls are all missing this series of verses, so there are no known manuscripts that give Saul's length of reign or age.

16:4—4QSam^b reads, "Seer do you come in peace?"

17:4—4QSam^a gives Goliath's height as "4 cubits and a span" (6 feet four inches) as does Josephus and LXX. Later LXX manuscripts give five cubits as does the Masoretic text and some later LXX give six cubits. This shows how narratives could "grow" over time. Just as the retelling of the fish we caught, which gets larger and larger. However, Josephus records from known records, a Jew named Eleazar presented to Tiberius by Artabanus king of Parthia, who was seven cubits (10.5 ft) tall in 36 AD (*Antiquities* 18.4.5).

2 Samuel 3:3—Chileab's name is given as Dalujah.

4:1—Mephibosheth is wrong; Ishbosheth, actually Ishbaal, was Saul's son. Baal (Lord) was changed to Bosheth (shame) in Herod's time.

11:3 adds, as well as Josephus, the wife of Uriah the Hittite, "the armor bearer of Joab."

12:16 adds, and "lay in sackcloth" on the ground.

13:20 adds, Absalom's house "desolate."

13:21 adds, he was furious. "But he would not inflict pain on his son Amnon's spirit, because he loved him, since he was his first born." Masoretic text lost 21 words when the scribe's eye jumped to the second negative.

14:30 adds, Field on fire: "So Joab's servants came to him with their clothes torn and said Absalom's servants have set the field on fire," which was lost from the Masoretic text by parablepsis.

15:7—4QSam[a and c] reads, after "four" years, as does LXX[L], Syriac, and Josephus.

24:17 adds 12 words: David said to the Lord, "Was it not I who ordered the census of the people? Look," I have sinned . . .

1 and 2 Kings—6.6% and 2% in three manuscripts. Variations show a text divergent from the Masoretic text as in Samuel.

8:16 adds, for my name to be there, "nor did I choose anyone to be a leader over my people Israel, but I chose Jerusalem for my name to be there" was added twice by dittography.

2 Kings 7:20 adds, Died, "just as the man of God has said." Also, present in two Vulgate manuscripts.

8:2 reads, arose "and left, following the instructions of the man of God, living in" the land of the Philistines seven years.

Isaiah—100% in 22 manuscripts. The oldest is the great Isaiah scroll 1QIsaᵃ (of ca. 125 BC). Thirteen of these readings were adopted by the RSV.

2:9b–10 Omitted from 1QIsaᵃ, but does appear in the later 4QIsaᵃ ᵃⁿᵈ ᵇ.

7:14 reads, "the young woman has conceived and is bearing a son . . ."

14:4 reads, oppressor has ceased! How his "assault" has ceased! This makes better sense.

19:18 end reads, City of the Sun (Heliopolis). City of "destruction" in Hebrew differs by only one letter. The correction is included in the NASB and NIV.

29:5 reads, multitude of "your enemies."

32:19 reads, the "wood" or thicket instead of "the city." The Hebrew words are *h'yr* and *hy'r* respectively.

40:14b–16—A blank was left here and these plus the first two words of vs. 20 were added by a different scribe.

48:4—The original scroll being copied probably read, "Because I knew that . . ." The incomplete line was not known by the scribe from any other manuscripts, so he changed it to read, "Because of my knowledge."

60:19–20—1QIsaᵇ left out by parablepsis the words between the phrase "everlasting light" in 19 and 20. Then it adds, you light "by night" in 19 in 1QIsaᵃ.

Jeremiah—26.6% in six manuscripts, with 4QJerᵃ may be older than (ca.) 200 BC. However, it contains more corrections than any other scroll. Twenty-one chapters are not preserved in any DSS manuscripts, including Chapter 1–4:3, 5–6, 16, 23–4, 28–9, 34–41, and 51 to the end.

Ezekiel—11.9% in seven manuscripts. A shorter text was used at two places 5:13 and 23:16–17.

Book of the Minor Prophets—10 manuscripts, 4QXII[a,b] may date to 150 BC. Seven manuscripts show that all 12 books were written on one scroll. 8HevXII has the order Joel, Amos, Obadiah, Jonah, Micah and 4QXII[a] has Malachi, Jonah as last.

Hosea—71.5% in three manuscripts.

13:4 and LXX add, Lord your God "who fortifies heaven and creates the earth whose hands made the whole host of heaven, but I did not show them to you to go after them but I brought you up" from the land . . .

Joel—88.6% in 13 manuscripts.

Amos—80.8% in four manuscripts.

1:3—5QAmos and LXX add, Threshed "the pregnant women of" Gilead.

Obadiah—100% in two manuscripts.

Jonah—100% in five manuscripts.

Micah—100% in three manuscripts.

Nahum—100% in three manuscripts.

Habakkuk—96.4% in three manuscripts.

Zephaniah—100% in five manuscripts.

Haggai—100% in three manuscripts.

Zechariah—37% in five manuscripts. 4QXII[a](scroll of Minor Prophets) dates to (ca.) 150 BC; is written in cursive script and placed in the final third of the collection, maybe even last, following Malachi.

Malachi—58.2% in two manuscripts.

I Enoch—20 manuscripts. All are in Aramaic, which may have been the original, and was considered Scripture at Qumran; also see Jude vs. 14 and 15.

Daniel—75.2% in eight manuscripts, dates from 125 BC to 50 AD. Four scrolls contain the switch from Hebrew to Aramaic at the same place.

7:1—The ending is awkward, 4QDan^b is the only scroll to contain this verse; it has a shorter ending: then "he wrote down the dream." This is similar to the LXX.

10:16—The LXX reads, Behold, "something in the likeness of a human hand" touched. Pap6QDan has "touched" in the feminine; the subject is likely hand but is not preserved.

Psalms—49.3% in 40 manuscripts, oldest is 150 BC. Some 15 noncanonical Psalms, nine completely unknown before, are found in four scrolls. Agreement and content were quite varied from what we are used to seeing. Psalm 32 is missing between 31 and 33 and may never have been included. Psalm 38 is followed by 71. Psalm 90 is not preserved and from 91 onward the order differs widely. That several collections make up our Psalter is evident at 41:13, 72:20, 89:52 and 106:48. Among the Qumran scrolls, three have large blank spaces at the end, indicating the end of the scrolls.

These occur at 91:16b, 150:6 and 151. The following are not preserved: Ps. 3, 4, 20, 21, 32, 41, 46, 55, 58, 61, 64, 65, 70, 72–75, 80, 87, 90, 108, 110, 111 and 117. The largest collections are 11QPs^a, 4QPS^a, 5/6HevPs, 4QPS^b, 4QPs^c, and 4QPs^e.

22:16 LXX and 5/6HevPs read, "They have pierced" my hands and feet; whereas the Masoretic text has, "Like a lion."

33:1—4QPs^q adds, Of David.

45:5—11QPs^d reads, Fall under you. "A thousand [some text missing]," thus a longer text.

69:3—4QPs^a reads, My throat is parched. "My teeth are consumed in anguish" for the God of Israel. This is unclear.

69:5—4QPs^a reads, O God "you do not know my crown." This is unclear.

71:3—4QPs^a reads, Habitation "my heart a lion [text missing] for you." This is unclear as it stands.

89:21—4QPs^x has this order: vs. 21, 25, 22, 26, 27 and 30, with a gap to 43.

91:1 Has a superscription "Of David." Both 90 and 91 are exorcism psalms. Before Psalm 91 in 11QApPs^c, from 50–70 AD, are three apocryphal Psalms, also exorcism type, unknown before now. One is attributed to Solomon. Column 5:1 is attributed to David, which mentions the archangel Raphael who is also known from the Apocrypha in the Book of Tobit. Column 5:6b–7 contains the earliest allusion to Satan having horns: "For your appearance is one of vanity and your horns are horns of illusion. You are darkness not light."

91:16b reads, "And he will show you his victory. Selah. Then they will answer Amen, Amen. Selah," then followed by a large blank space showing the end of the scroll.

93:1 In 11QPs^a is displaced and follows "The Apostrophe to Zion"; an unknown Psalm that is found here and in 4QPs^f, then by Psalm 141. It has a superscription, "Praise the Lord."

99:1 It has as a superscription, "Of David a Psalm."

101:1—11QPs^a begins the longest collection from 101–151 plus ten selections not found in the Masoretic texts with variations on their order.

103 is followed by 112 in 4QPs^b, 109 in 11QPs^a and 104 in 2QPs.

104 follows 118 in 4QPs^e and 11QPs^a and 147 in 4QPs^d; it has the superscription, "Of David."

105 follows 147 in 11QPs^a and 4QPs^e; it adds, Lord "for he is good; for his steadfast love endures forever!"

106 comes before 147 in 4QPs^d.

107 occurs only in 4QPs^f along with Ps. 22, 107, 108(?), 109, and three unknown pieces; The Apostrophe to Zion and Judah; and the Eschatological Hymn; possibly others dating to 50 BC, it omits v. 21.

109 in 11QPs^a followed 103.

112 (see 103).

113–118 The Hallel Psalms all found together in 11QPs^a. Missing is 117.

118:11 is missing by dittography in 4QPs[b].

119 occurs between 132 and 135 in 11QPs[a].

120–134—The Psalms of Ascent, 4QPs[e] and 11QPs[a], have only 120–132 with 133–4 appearing later in the collection.

121:5—11QPs[a] reads, "By night" the Lord is your keeper, "your shade" at your right hand.

132:11—11QPs[a] adds, Not turn back; "Surely one of your physical descendants" I will place.

133 is between 141 and 144 in 11QPs[a]. This ends with "Peace be upon Israel."

134 is between 140 and 151A in 11QPs[a].

135 follows 119 in 11QPs[a]. Verse two reads, "And exalt the Lord" you who . . . house of our God "and in your midst, O Jerusalem."

135:12—4QPs[n] has 136:22 and 23 at the end as an anomaly.

136 both 11QPs[a and b] have a longer ending called the *Catena* containing material from Ps. 118 in the order 1, 15, 16, 8, 9, 29.

137–8 in 11QPs[a] follows 139.

139:16—11QPs[a] end reads, Number of days, "for its formation even for it with its corresponding number from them all." This text as well as LXX and Masoretic text is disturbed here.

140 in 11QPs[a], is preceded by "David's last words" (also found in 2 Sam 23:1–7) and "David's Composition."

141 occurs between 93 and 133 in 11QPs[a and b].

142–3 occurs after 155 in 11QPs[a].

144 occurs between 133 and 155 in 11QPs[a].

145—This acrostic Psalm has only 21 verses instead of 22; the Nun is lost between 13–14. Only 11QPs[a], one Masoretic, the Syriac, and LXX contain it. It reads, "God is faithful in his words and gracious in all his deeds." Each verse also concluded with "Blessed be the Lord and blessed be his name forever and ever" and adds at end "This is for a memorial." Which is lost from all Masoretic texts and LXX? Probably it was recited or sung antiphonally. It is now included in NRSV, NAB, NIV and the Good News Bible.

146 follows 105 in 11QPs^a.

147 follows 104 in 11QPs^a.

148 follows 146 in 11QPs^a.

149 follows 143 in 11QPs^a.

150 follows 149 in 11QPs^a, but followed seven other compositions, including the Hymn to the Creator, David's Last Words, David's Composition, Psalm 140, 134, 151 A and B.

Ben Sira—found in three manuscripts; 51:13–30 is included in 11QPs^a and in the Apocrypha; 41:14b has the order 14b, 15, 14a, 16b, rather than LXX 14–16.

Job—8.4% in four manuscripts; one dates (ca.) 225–150 BC in paleo-Hebrew as with all the others of this age in the Books of Moses. Two are in Aramaic. Only parts of ten verses are preserved (8, 9, 13, 14, 31–33; 35–37).

33:25 in 4QJob^a has, Flesh "be xxx" than a child's. Preserved letters here cannot form the word used in the Masoretic text.

Proverbs—4.7% in two manuscripts, only five verses are preserved (1, 2, 13–15).

Ruth—48.2% in four manuscripts, dates from 50 BC–50 A.D; only vv. 1–4 preserved.

Song of Songs—48.7% in four manuscripts, which date from 30 BC–70 AD. In 4QCant^a the text from 4:7–6:11 is completely missing and may be deliberate, but is present in 4QCant^b.

3:6–8 in 4QCant^b is missing but present in "a and c."

4:4–7 in 4QCant^b is missing but present in "a."

5:1—4QCant^b probably ended here, as the last preserved letter is written large. The left edge seems to contain a Greek gamma as a diple obelismene used in Greek tragedies or comedies, appropriate for this section. It contains the chiastic pattern of hemistichs a-b-b-a whereas the LXX and Masoretic text uses a-b-a-b.

6:13—4QCant^a omits the second set of "come back, come back" since the lines would be too long.

Qohelet—12.6% in two manuscripts, one dates to 175–150 BC, only vs. 1, 5, 6 and 7 are preserved.

1:5—4QQoh^b before it breaks off, has two letters remaining, showing a text different from the Masoretic text.

6:4—4QQoh^a, the scribe left out "it goes, and with" between the words "darkness," then above the line corrected his mistake.

Lamentations—39.6% in four manuscripts, 3QLam is written in cola form of poetry but 4QLam and 5QLam^{a and b} are not, probably to save space.

1:1—4QLam begins a mid line with the upper margin clearly visible showing that this was not the first book of the scroll. Whether Ruth or Jeremiah is being determined by DNA testing on the Ruth and Jeremiah scrolls from Cave Four to see if the animal skin, from which the scroll is written, is the same.

1:15 in 4QLam v. 17 follows, then v. 16.

1:17—4QLam reads, "Zion" has "been banished" among them.

Epistle of Jeremiah—One fragment of this deuterocononical book, 6:43–44 is in Greek from Cave Seven, as were the other 19 manuscripts from this cave.

Esther—was not found and probably deliberate. The recently found Calendar Texts does not mention the late addition of Purim, which started in the story of Esther. Other reasons are: (1) the marriage of a Jewess to a Persian; (2) no mention of God; and (3) chapters 7–9 feature retaliation, which was against the Essene Code of the Community, as in 1QS 10:17–18, "Return to no man evil for evil."

Ezra and Nehemiah—5% in three fragments of Ezra from Cave Four dates to (ca.) 50 BC from chapter 4:2–6, 8–11, 5:17 and

6:1–5. None of Nehemiah has been found, but was presumed present.

2 Chronicles—0.5% in one fragment from Cave Four dated to 50–25 BC from chapter 28:27–29:3.

29:1—The Queen's name is given as Aybah.

Tobit—Five manuscripts from Cave Four; four are in Aramaic, and one in Hebrew. The oldest copy dates to 100 BC, 300 years older than previously thought for its composition, which now could have been (ca.) 210 BC. Ashmodeus the evil spirit and Raphael the archangel are also mentioned in this Apocryphal story.

At this point, let me insert an idea for thought. Recently several authors have put forth the idea that the Bible contains a hidden code relating to prophesy for the present (see J. Satinover, *Cracking the Bible Code*, William Morrow 1998 and Dr. Moshe Katz, *Computorah: On Hidden Codes in the Bible*, CompuTorah Jerusalem 1998). This is actually a take off on the Kabbalah idea of each letter in the Hebrew text being inspired and having a fixed position. If, as you can see above and in the section On How We Got Our Bible, words, sections of text or rearranged texts are missing, lost or changed, then any attempt to find a hidden code is doomed to fail from the outset for want of a single letter. The Bibles used by code seekers would all be later Masoretic texts. The original text is not known and will probably never be known. In addition, the Rabbis in the Tiqqune Sopherim changed 18 verses, and the original word is not known in seven cases. Nevertheless, we are closer to the original text than we have ever been before, which is the purpose of all scholarship.

CHAPTER 9

DEVELOPMENT OF THE OLD TESTAMENT

DUE TO THE Christians calling the early books of the New Testament "Scripture," the Jewish college or Academy of Jamnia (Jabnell), the present Yebna, nine miles NE of Ashdod in 90 AD, was called upon to determine what books would be the official ones for the Old Testament. Between the 1st and 2nd Jewish revolts (70–135 AD) it was settled. Many of the controversies are reported in the Talmud, the body of Jewish civil and canonical law or instruction consisting of three parts. The Mishnah —Text is mostly by Judah ha Nasi about 180–200 AD. The Gemara—Commentary and Tosefta—is a supplement to the Mishna. A Midrash is an exegesis on a book of the Old Testament.

Old Testament

Book	Author	Theme	Period Covered	Date of Writing (BC)
Genesis	Moses	Beginnings	? 1800	1440–1400

Book	Author	Theme	Period Covered	Date of Writing BC
Exodus	"	Going out	1800–1440	"
Leviticus	"	Holiness and Worship	1440	"
Numbers	"	Wilderness wanderings	1448–1440 _8 yrs_	"
Deuteronomy	"	Restatement of the Law	1480–1440 _40 yrs_	"
Joshua	Joshua	Conquest of Canaan	1400–1375 _125 yrs_	ca. 1375
Judges	Samuel (?)	300 yr History of Defeat & Deliverance	1375–1075 _300 yrs_	ca. 1020
Ruth*	?	Kinsman— Redeemer	one year	ca. 1020
Samuel	?	109 year History	Saul-David _109_	1070–ca. 961
Kings	Jeremiah (?)	400 year History Isr. and Jud.	961–560 _400_	ca. 560
Chronicles*	Ezra (?)	466 years History Saul; Bab. Cap.	1004–538 _466_	ca. 450
Ezra*	Ezra	Return and rebuilding of Temple	538–450 _88 yrs_	ca. 450
Nehemiah*	Nehemiah	Rebuilding wall of Jerusalem	445–430 _15 yrs_	ca. 430
Esther*	?	Jews staying in Persia	486–465 _21_	465–425
Job	Moses (?)	Why righteous suffer	25 yrs.	2000–900
Psalms	David + 7	Hymns of praise	—	1440–520
Proverbs	Solomon +2	Comparisons and Wisdom	—	965–687
Ecclesiastes*	"	Man's reasoning	—	ca. 930

S. of Solomon	"	Lyrics of the beloved	—	ca. 950
Isaiah	Isaiah	Prophesy on Messiah	740–680 *60 yrs*	ca. 680
Jeremiah	Jeremiah	Warning and Judgment	626–586 *40 yrs*	ca. 586
Lamentations*	Jeremiah	Mourning over Jerusalem	one year	586 *570 ?*
Ezekiel	Ezekiel	Comfort to Bab. captives	592–571 *21 yrs*	592–571
Daniel	Daniel	Rise and fall of world powers	604–536 *68 yrs*	ca. 536
Hosea	Same	Redeeming love for Israel	760–710 *50 yrs*	ca. 710
Joel	"	Day of the Lord	one year	850–700
Amos	" *Earthquake 736*	Judgment on sin of Israel	one year post	763
Obadiah*	"	Doom of Edom	two years	ca. 585
Jonah	"	God's mercy on Nineveh	one year	ca. 780
Micah	"	Judgment and Kingdom	740–687 *57 yrs*	pre 687
Nahum*	"	Nineveh's doom	one year	666–612
Habakkuk	"	Doubt to faith	one year	627–586
Zephaniah*	"	Day of the Lord/ Fall of Jerusalem	one year	640–622
Haggai	"	Temple rebuilt	four months	ca. 520
Zechariah	"	Messiah's advents	two years	520–518
Malachi	?	Formalism rebuked	one year	450–400

* Those books marked * are not quoted in the New Testament.

In Hebrew, the longest book is Jeremiah and the middle letter of the Old Testament is in Jeremiah 6:7. In Hebrew the last verse of Ecclesiastes, Isaiah, Lamentations, and Malachi usually ended with the preceding verse, to avoid having a curse ringing in the ears. Christ endorsed all Scripture in the Old Testament from Genesis 4:10 to 2 Chronicles 20:21 (Mt 23:35 and Lk 11:51). The Hebrew Old Testament ended with Chronicles. The Law, Writings and Prophets were covered in John 5:46 ("Moses wrote of me"); from Genesis 3:15, John 10:34 ("written in your law"); from Psalms 82:6 and John 12:34, "the Law" refers to Psalm 110:4, Isaiah 9:7, Ezekiel 37:25, and Daniel 7:14. Quotes from Old Testament otherwise unknown are Luke 11:49 the "Wisdom of God" and references to unknown Scripture in John 7:38, Ephesians 5:14 and James 4:5.

The Five Rolls, or Megilloth, contain The Song of Solomon, which was read at Passover on the 14th of Nisan (approximately April 1); Ruth was read at Pentecost, the 6–7th of Sivan (approximately May 21), Ecclesiastes was read at the Feast of Tabernacles, 15–22 of Tishri (approximately October 1), Esther was read at the Feast of Purim 14–15th of Adar (approximately March 1) and Lamentations or the Five Rules on the anniversary of the destruction of Jerusalem by Nebuchadrezzar on the 9th of Ab (approximately August 15).

Internal indications of the date when the books were written and other information bearing on the times at hand are shown for each book:

Genesis. 18:6 The meal for three guests. We let these details slip over our head. The three measures or seahs is about 25 quarts of flour to make unleavened ashcakes of bread, and to dress and barbeque a calf would take how long? I'll let the cooks figure out how long it took to prepare this meal for a party of four. A lot of bread being prepared.

18:21 "I will go down and see." A strange statement, if God is omniscient and omnipresent.

19:24–28 "Destruction of Sodom and Gomorrah."
The fire and brimstone is a perfect description of a natural gas
blowout. All the ingredients are present, cooking fires to ignite
the gas, oil and bitumen, known to be present in the area, pieces
of sulfur found all around the Dead Sea and the extensive salt
formations that underlie the Lisan peninsula and the whole
Dead Sea area. Fault lines bound the area on both sides of the
Lisan and across the Dead Sea in at least two places. The main
strike-slip fault on the east runs close to Bab edh-Drah and
Numeira, at present thought to be Sodom and Gomorrah (see
DSLS pp. 57, 82, 238; 249).

28:12 "Ladder." A poor choice of words for the translation;
staircase would be better.

35:19 "Death of Rachel." A misunderstanding of terms:
she was buried "on the way to Ephrata" or Bethlehem. The
present tomb is a medieval myth. Her tomb was on the southern
border of Benjamin, which is north of Jerusalem (1 Sm 10:2).
Also the term "Rachel weeping for her children" in Jeremiah
31:15, in Ramah, which is north of Jerusalem, is the place where
the Babylonians put to death the old and infirm that could not
make the trip to Babylon. Thus, Rachel is pictured as weeping,
from her tomb, for her Israelite children, as the spiritual mother
near the place where they died.

50:10 A historical fact often overlooked where "beyond
Jordan" means west. You must first know where the writer is, which
in this case would be on the east side. (See also Nm 32:19, Dt 3:20
and 25, Jos 9:1—a possible exception—and Is 9:1). Since most
of the Bible books using this term were written later in Israel, the
term usually means "on the east side" of the Jordan.

Exodus is connected to Leviticus and Numbers, which start,
"And the Lord . . ." as a direct continuation.

Deuteronomy, chapter 34 is a postscript by Joshua.

Joshua was partly written by him as shown in 18:9 and
24:26, an eyewitness account (5:1, 6). The Jebusites were still

in Jerusalem (15:63), thus pre-Davidic (996 BC). Jezer was not taken (16:10), thus pre-Solomonic. Ba'alah (15:9) the name was later changed to Kiriath-jearim and a possible redactor had supplied the new name. Gibeonites (9:27), thus pre 1010 BC under Saul (2 Sm 21:1–9) while they were still slaves. See the reference to Israel in 11:21, but the term was used in Exodus 16:31 and 40:38.

Judges: No king is mentioned thus before 1000 BC. See the first and last verse, but especially 18:30b, which would have been added after 586 BC.

15:1 Samson "visited" his wife. There are different types of marriage; this is *Sadiqa* where the wife lives at her father's house and the husband has visiting privileges. *Beena* is the type where the husband goes to live with the wife's family; the children are named after the wife (see 2 Sm 17:25 for an example).

Ruth 1:1 In the time of the Judges 1375–1075 BC.

1 Sam. 1:3 Shiloh was destroyed about 1050 BC by the Philistines (see 7:1).

1 Kings. 22:48 "Ships of Tarshish." These are large merchant or ore carriers. Tarshish is used in the Nora inscription from Sardinia (which may actually be Tarshish) and dates to 825 BC (see the discussion in BAR 16[1]: 58 [90]).

2 Kings. 25:27 Evil-Merodack (Amel-Marduk) reigned from 561–560 BC.

2 Chronicles. 36:22 Cyrus II reigned from 559–529 BC. Part was written before the fall of Jerusalem (5:9; see also 1 Kgs 8:8; note: verses 22 and 23 are copied from Ezr 1:1–2). This is an old archive devise to indicate the next scroll to follow. There are several examples of this in the Torah. There were other Chronicles used in 1 Chronicles 29:29 from the time of David: Samuel the seer (possible the same as the book of Samuel), Nathan the prophet, and Gad the seer. From the time of Solomon in 2 Chronicles 8:29: Book of Nathan, Prophesy of Ahijah the Shilonite, and Visions of Iddo the seer. See also

Numbers 21:14. From king Rehoboam in 12:15 the Genealogies of Shemaiah and Iddo are mentioned. From king Abijah in 13:22 is mentioned the Midrash (story or interpretation) of Iddo. In (2 Chr 25: 26, 27:7, 32:32 and 33:18) the Book of the Kings of Israel and Judah. From Manasseh in 33:19 we have the sayings of the seers or Chozai. Nehemiah 12:23 records a public national record available in the archives.

Ezra. There is a 50-year lapse between Chapter 6 and 7. Events in the book of Esther occurred here. Chapter 4:7–23 should follow chapter 10. From 4:23–24 Ezra's mission ended in failure.

7:8 The 7th year of Artaxerxes I (464–424) would be 458 BC. Critics have suggested that the chronology of Ezra and Nehemiah should be reversed. Actually more problems are created by doing this (HJP p. 174).

Esther 1:1 Ahasuerus is the same as Xerxes 485–465; his third year would be 483 BC v. 3. The battle of Salamis occurred on Sept. 29, 480 BC. The battle of Thermopylae was earlier in the same year. In 2:16, the 7th year was 479. Herodotus says during this time, Xerxes paid attention to his harem.

1:9 Vashti. Herodotus (Book VII Par. 61) says that Amestris was his queen. Persian kings had many concubines but only one queen. Both Vashti and Esther were probably subsidiary queens that ranked above concubines.

Job. Reasons for dating the writing about 2000 BC: extensive ownership of cattle 1:3 and 42:12; head of family offers sacrifice, not priest (1:5); Job's great age (42:16); and no allusions to the Mosaic law, thus before 1400 BC. Albright shows the forms of names date to about 2000 BC. In 2:11 Eliphaz the Temanite, was from Tema in NW Saudi Arabia. Bildad the Shuhite, a tribe descended from Abraham by Keturah, Zophar the Na'amathite a tribe of Arabia, and Uz see (Jer 25:20; Lam 4:21). Reason for a late date: Highly developed poetry, but Ugarit epic poetry is early and dates to 1400 BC.

39:9–10 Unicorn. The Hebrew is re'em and the horns are plural (Dt 33:17 and Ps 22:21). Not the mythical medieval one horned animal but the "auerochs" or wild ox, extinct now but described by Julius Caesar and pictured on relief's by Tiglath-pileser I (1115–1077 BC) and in Akkadian is the rimu. For this and the next, two see NUBD p. 66–79.

40:15 Behemoth is the hippopotamus. V. 23 indicates at one time it was present in the Jordan River thickets.

41:1 Leviathan is the crocodile, but Isaiah 27:1 may use the term for the Canaanite monster Lotan, described in the Ugaritic literature from Ras Shamra, Syria.

Psalms. Seventy-three are said to be by David (1004–965 BC), although the DSS heading superscriptions lists several others by David. Solomon wrote Psalms 72 and 127 and Heman wrote Psalm 88. Asaph wrote Psalms 50, 73–83, while 74 and 79 speak of the destruction of Jerusalem in 587 BC. Sons of Korah wrote Psalms 42, 44–49, 84, 85 and 87. Forty-nine are anonymous according to the Hebrew. Psalm 137 was written during the Babylonian captivity 587–538 BC. Psalm 96 in the LXX superscription adds, "When the house was being built," thus after the captivity or 536–520 BC. The LXX divides Psalm 116 into two parts at v. 10. Moses wrote Psalm 90.

Proverbs. Mostly by Solomon (965–925 BC; see 1 Kings 4:32; see also the comment to 25–29 of the men of Hezekiah). Agur wrote 30 and Lemuel wrote 31; vs. 10–31 comprise an acrostic. The strikingly similar Proverbs of Amen-en-Opet of Egypt date from 1000–600 BC and were probably derived from contact with Israel, since Solomon's fame was wide spread. See ANE Vol. I p.237 where parallel verses exist in 22:17–23:14 for all but five verses. See DSS for additional information.

Ecclesiastes. This and the next book had a large discussion in the Mishnah as to Canonicity.

Song of Songs. Does not mention God. "Mare in Pharaoh's chariots" (1:9), only because the subject is a woman. Mares were never used in the chariot corps anywhere in the near east. In fact a way to disrupt a chariot charge was to loose a mare in heat into the battle. See the account of Thutmose III at the second battle of Kadesh (WERE p. 59).

Isaiah 1:1 During the time of Uzziah (769–733 BC), Jotham, Ahaz, and Hezekiah (727–698 BC). Isaiah is quoted 20 times in the New Testament; total of all other prophets combined is not this large. In 6:1, the date is 733 BC and in 7:1, 14:28, 20:1 and 36:1 the dates are chronological.

7:10–16 The sign of Immanuel. This is a case where prophecy carries a present and future implication, the present quite clear but the future quite obscure. These verses cannot be separated at this time, but v. 14 carries the double meaning. In v. 10 Ahaz, about 733 BC, had taken a new wife (see Prophesy and Current Events for the discussion of virgin) who may already be pregnant. By age two or later he would be weaned, and could eat butter and honey. Verse 16 indicates that before the boy knows to refuse evil and choose good[34] (or before the age of accountability at 13) both kings that threaten you will be dead. The reference is to Rezin of Damascus and Pekah of Israel, both of which were dead by 728. If the reference can be stretched to the fall of Samaria in 721 BC, the boy would only be 11 years old. The kings of Assyria would be a threat to Judah also at this time.

7:22–25 "butter/curds/milk and honey." All 19 times, that this or any combination of these words are used in the Pentateuch, the terms are used to signify abundance. But as is here emphasized it refers to an area that is uncultivated and left desolate such that cattle can have their fill and bees will nest in various places. The Canaanites, at the time of Moses, had done little to cultivate the land except for olive oil and wine, which was exported. This looks to the time after the Captivity when the land will revert to a briar patch. This thought is a horror to the Israelis.

9:6 "A child is born—a son is given." This is poor rendering of the Hebrew. The correct form is "unto us a child has been born—unto us a son has been given." The reference may be to Hezekiah rather than the Messiah (Hertz p. 305).

'Wonderful, Counselor, Mighty God, Everlasting Father, Prince of Peace." —All scholars realize that the comma after Wonderful should be removed. There are only four titles and qualities of the king listed. The Hebrew would never be read this way, rather: Wonderful of council is God the mighty, the Everlasting Father, the Ruler of Peace (IB Vol. 5, p. 233).

44:28 Cyrus. As in 1 Kings 13:2 where Josiah is mentioned by name 300 years before his birth. Here Cyrus is mentioned about 139 years before the death of Isaiah in 698 BC, a startling prophecy.

Jeremiah 1:2 Josiah's (639–609) 13th year was 626 BC; covers up to Nebuchadrezzar and the fall of Jerusalem in 587 BC. Jeremiah died about 580 BC in either Egypt or when Nebuchadrezzar overran Egypt, but a Jewish statement in the Talmud and Apocrypha says he escaped and died in Babylon. Chapter 52 is recopied from 2 Kings 24:18–25:30. A contemporary prophet was Uriah ben Shemaiah (25:30).

Lamentations 5:7 "fathers." If one generation is meant, then the date is about 570 BC.

5:18 Temple not yet rebuilt.

Ezekiel 1:1 The 30th year refers to the beginning of the Babylonian kingdom of Nabopolassar (625–605 BC).

1:2 The 5th year of exile of Jehoiachin (597) is 592 BC and 29:17, the last date is 27th year of captivity, or April 26, 571; the spring New Year.

10:15 and 20 Cherubim. The same creature as mentioned in 1:5. Known in Assyria as *Karibu* and *Lamassu* (see ARAB Vol. II # 711) the winged bull, is described as such, from the palace of Sargon III at Khorsabad now displayed in the Oriental Institute at the Univ. of Chicago; others are in the British Museum and the Louvre. An ivory from Megiddo and the throne of king Hiram of Byblos also depict winged creatures.

Daniel 1:1 From the 3rd year of Jehoiakim (608–598 BC) to the 3rd year of Cyrus (559–529 BC) in verse 10:1.

5:1 Belshazzar. Known as Bel-sharusur (Bel has protected the king) the eldest son of Nabonidus who is not mentioned in the Bible; was in self-imposed exile (?) at Tema in NW Arabia. As such he was coregent with his father, and able to confer on Daniel only the position of third ruler (v. 29).

Hosea 1:1 Uzziah (769–733) through Hezekiah (727–698). Jeroboam II (784–748) through the fall of Samaria in 721 BC. The book is largely poetry. He is the only prophet who came from Israel itself.

Joel 3:4 and 19. No king mentioned. Enemies are Philistines and Egyptians, etc., not Assyria or Babylon. Compare Amos 1:2a with Joel 3:16a and Amos 9:13b with Joel 3:18a. This was probably during the reign of Joash (836–798 BC), as a minor Joash was under the guardianship of Jehoida the high priest. Nothing is known of Joel. This and the next two are poetry.

Amos 1:1 In days of Uzziah of Judah (769–733 BC) and Jeroboam II of Israel (784–748 BC). This was two years before the earthquake, about 763 BC (see Zech 14:5). Evidence of this earthquake damage was found at Hazor.

1:6–8 Note the omission of Gath, which was destroyed by Sargon III in 711 BC; compare 6:2 and 2 Chronicles 26:6.

7:14 "sycamore." This is the sycamine fig, which must be punctured to ripen, thus Amos was a small sheepherder who needed a second summer job.

8:9 This partial eclipse of the sun is the same one mentioned in the Assyrian eponym list of Bur-Sagale for the 9th year of Ashur-Dan III 6-15-763 BC. See ARAB Vol. II p. 435 and Menzel p. 173. This is the start of recorded history on Earth and established the dates of all the kings by synchronizations both backward and forward for 1000 years each way. Earthquakes and eclipses of the sun or moon were strong harbingers of disaster and feared all over the Near East. In Assyria, an eclipse was thought to foreshadow the death of the king. An ingenious solution was to have the king step down and a surrogate ruler takes his place for 100 days. The substitute was then killed, which fulfilled the astrologers' predictions while the true king escaped unharmed (TLBM p. 68).

Obadiah. The shortest book in the Old Testament. Nothing is known of him, and dating is uncertain; verse 11 may refer to 587 BC. Compare Amos 9:2 with Obadiah 1:4 and Jeremiah 49:7–22 with Obadiah 1:1–6. It is before the captivity. The king of Nineveh is either Adad-Nirari III (810–783 BC) or Ashur-Dan III (772–755 BC). Compare 2 Kings 14:25 in the reign of Jeroboam II (784–748 BC), a prophesy not otherwise recorded.

Micah 1:1. Before the captivity. This and the next three are poetry. Jotham (758–743 BC) to Hezekiah (727–698 BC).

Nahum. Nothing known of him. Wrote between the destruction of No-Amon (Thebes) in 661 and 612 BC when Nineveh was captured by the Meads and Babylonians (3:7–8). His village was Elkosh; Jerome says it was in the Galilee. Note: Capernaum means the village of Nahum. However, it may not refer to the prophet.

1:12 "Quite and likewise many." Schofield (p. 950) shows this is a transliteration of an Assyrian legal formula meaning a joint venture and several responsibilities for carrying out an obligation. Dozens of Assyrian tablets have been found at Nineveh using this phrase. An example is how the scribes would copy manuscripts carefully, even when they didn't quite understand them.

Habakkuk. Little is know of him. Apparently a Levitical member of the Temple choir (3:19). Probably written during the reign of Josiah (639–609 BC) or Jehoiakim (608–598 BC). In the DSS Habakkuk Commentary, Chapter 3 is omitted. Burrows p. 321 says "the last column has only four lines, showing the end of the commentary had been reached." Scholars had long believed that the third chapter was not part of the original book.

"Its absence is consistent with this theory but does not prove it. Being a psalm, it does not lend itself to the same use. It is even possible the commentary was never finished. The LXX has all three chapters, but whether this particular part of the LXX is older than the Habakkuk Commentary is another matter."

3:5 "Pestilence and burning coals." These are the names of Canaanite gods Deber (the god of plagues) and Reshep (the god of pestilence and lord of the underworld). Yahweh was known to appropriate these gods' names unto Himself. Similarly with Baal, "the Rider of the Clouds" in Psalms 68:4. See the excellent discussion in Wright (p. 106).

Zephaniah 1:1. Great great grandson of Hezekiah in the days of Josiah (639–609 BC) and prior to the destruction of Nineveh in 612 BC (2:13).

1:14b The Hebrew is literally, "The sound of the day of the Lord is bitter; a warrior is crying there." "There" is without a proper antecedent and the word order is unusual. By omission of one letter from "sound" read "swifter" and by transposing one letter from cries to the preceding word we obtain "than a runner," rendering it: Swifter than a runner the day of the Lord and speedier than a warrior. The original manuscripts had no vowels and were without spaces between words. For instance, there is a great difference how GODISNOWHERE is read: either it is "God is now here" or "God is nowhere."

2:4 Gath is again omitted, for it had already been destroyed by Uzziah in 760 BC (2 Chr 26:6). There is a play on words which sound alike, between Gaza and deserted and between Ekron and uprooted.

Haggai. Nothing is known of him. A contemporary of Zechariah (Ezr 5:1–2). Dated from Darius I Hystapis 2nd year, 520 BC, thus after the Captivity, since a Gentile monarch is mentioned. Covered four months from August–December (1:1) 1st day of 6th month; (2:18) the 24th day of 9th month.

Zechariah 1:1 A grandson of Iddo. Covers two years. Dated from Darius I Hystapis 2nd year Oct–Nov 520 BC to Nov–Dec 518 BC (7:1). Compare 4:9 when Zerubbable builds the Temple with Ezra 3:8–11. Starts two months after Haggai. Chapters 9–14 are undated, probably about 480 BC. Chapters 9, 10 and 13 are largely poetry.

7:2 "House of God" or Bethel. Actually Bethel sent a delegation consisting of [El]Sherezer, (the god's name has been lost) and Regem-meleck. The Babylonian name of Nergal-Sharezer is known, but the god could be El, Bel or Bethel (an ancient Canaanite deity), the names Bethel-Nathan and Bethel-Akab are known from the 5th century Aramaic papyri from Elephantine in Egypt (see IB Vol. 6, p. 1082).

9:5 Gath is not mentioned because it was already destroyed.

9:13 "Greece." One of the reasons cited for a late date of 333 BC from Alexander the Great.

11:13 "A goodly price"—Is actually the price of a slave. Matthew 27:9 has this from Jeremiah, but some scrolls had Jeremiah as the first book in the prophetic section.

14:21 "Canaanite." In this case the name means "trader or merchant," since this was their specialty.

Malachi. His name (if this is a proper name) means my messenger (see 3:1). The theme covers corruption of Priests and miserliness. The Temple had been completed for some time or about 520 BC (see 1:7). Ritual had been long practiced (1:7–10 and 3:8). Priestly piety had degenerated (1:6–8). Foreign marriages had flourished (2:10–12). Tithes had been neglected (3:8). A Persian governor was in authority in Jerusalem (1:8).

2:11 "Profaned the holiness." The Hebrew is *qodhesh*, where the meaning is better understood as "the sanctuary."

4:4–6 An editorial summary probably added by a later scribe.

CHAPTER 10

APOCRYPHA

Secret

THE WORD MEANS ("secret,") from II Esdras, which is an apocalypse; these 15 books were excluded from the Hebrew Bible and include:

I and II Esdras (Ezra), Tobit, Judith, Esther (additional chapters), The Wisdom of Solomon, Ecclesiasticus (Wisdom of Jesus the Son of Sirach), Baruch (sometimes the last chapter is The Letter of Jeremiah), Letter of Jeremiah, The Prayer of Azariah, and the Song of the Three Young Men, Susanna, Bell and the Dragon (the above three are often additional chapters in Daniel), The Prayer of Manasseh and I and II Maccabees.

These were probably written in Hebrew originally; only fragments exist now. Tobit in Aramaic and Hebrew and Sirach were found in Cave Four at Qumran, among the Dead Sea Scrolls. The Greek Septuagint (LXX) was translated from the Hebrew under Ptolomy II Philadelphus (285–246 BC). The Law was translated about 275 BC, and the rest of the Old Testament from 250–200 BC is our main source of information and included all but II Esdras, which had not been written yet. The Academy of

Jamina in 90 AD did not include them in the Old Testament, since it was known that they were later than Malachi.

Jerome in 404 included the Apocrypha in his Latin Vulgate, and the Council of Trent in 1546 accepted all except I and II Esdras and the Prayer of Manasseh.

Martin Luther in 1534 placed these books between the Old Testament and New Testament since they contain useful material reflecting conditions, which occurred between the 400-year period of the Old Testament and New Testament.

The Geneva Bible of 1560 was the first to exclude them due to its Calvinistic and anti-ecclesiastical feelings expressed in the marginal notes.

The Bishops Bible of 1568, representing the Anglican Church view, included them. Their heritage was derived from the Roman Catholics, and some quotations were already established in their prayer book.

In general Protestants "allowed" them only "for example of life and instruction of manners" and not as spiritually authoritative.

The KJV of 1611 AD, first edition, included them between the Old Testament and New Testament. The Puritans strongly objected and later editions omitted them. The KJV in England (published only by a firm holding a Royal Patent) and in America can be obtained with or without them.

Those who wrestled with this problem in countless hours of prayer for divine guidance, and in study and discussion, were used by God to put aside those books, which lacked authenticity. So only the present 66 books are essential to the full revelation of the Gospel. These 66 have been found "profitable for doctrine, for reproof, for correction and instruction in righteousness" (2 Tm 3:16), and they are indeed the Holy Scriptures, the Word of God, given by inspiration.

Description of the Books

I Esdras—Written about 120 BC, it includes 2 Chronicles 35–36:23, all of Ezra and Nehemiah 7:38–8:12. Josephus followed II Esdras rather than the LXX. It is a rehash of reform of Israelite worship by Ezra, Josiah, and Zerubbabel.

II Esdras—Written about 50 AD in chapters 3–14. Some unknown Christian added chapters 1–2 about 150 AD, and another Christian added chapters 15–16 about 250 AD. The latter is an apocalypse on aftermath of destruction of Jerusalem in 70 AD. In 4:1, the Angel Uriel instructs Ezra if he can weigh the weight of fire, or measure a measure of wind or call back yesterday. In 6:42, which states on the 3rd day God dried up six parts of the water; was used as an argument by Columbus before Ferdinand and Isabella of Spain, that the ocean was not very wide. The funds for the expedition were provided by confiscating the property and expelling to Portugal the Sephardi Jews of Spain. The Vulgate and KJV do not contain 7:36–105. It contains an emphatic denial of the value of prayers for the dead. However, it is present in Syriac, Ethiopic, Arabic, Armenian and two Latin manuscripts (compare II Mac. 12:43–45). The statement in 14:42 says that Ezra rewrote the 24 books of the Hebrew canon in the new square Hebrew script, along with 70 esoteric apocalyptic books.

Tobit—Written about 170 BC. The Aramaic and Hebrew version were found at Qumran. It is a blend of Scheherazade romance, Jewish piety, and sound moral teachings. It includes the blinding of Tobit, and Tobias's search for a deposit of money, as well as the deliverance and love for the demon-haunted Sarah, accompanied by the Archangel Raphael.

Judith—Written about 150 BC. Judith, a beautiful pious widow delivers herself and her people from Nebuchadrezzar's general Holofernes, an Assyrian who marched his army from Nineveh to Damascus in three days (which is impossible). Nebuchadrezzar was Babylonian and no general named Holofernes is known at this time. Holofernes reaches Bethulia (an unknown city) near Dothan, where she gets the general drunk and decapitates him. All kinds of historical errors of fact mark the story as fiction. The geographical boundaries of Judah given in the story were present only from 108–107 BC, during the Hasmonean period under John Hyrcanus, during the siege of the region of Samaria and prior to the capture of Scythopolis (Beth-shean); this may provide a better date (MBA p. 132).

Esther Additions—Written about 114 BC, it adds 107 extra verses. Written by Lysimachus, an Alexandrian Jew living in Jerusalem, it supplies the religious element missing from Esther. Haman is called a Macedonian in 16:10.

Wisdom of Solomon—Written about 75 BC, it recalls and amplifies Solomon's prayer in 1 Kings. 3:6–9. It contains the phrase on which "It Came Upon the Midnight Clear" is based in 18:14. Only here it refers to the night of the first Passover when the Logos leaped from heaven to deliver God's people.

Sirach—Written about 180 BC. The only book whose author is known (Yeshua ben Sirach), it was translated by his grandson from Hebrew to Greek about 132 BC. It is the last great example of Jewish wisdom literature. Chapter 44–50:24 contain the Praise of Famous Men.

Baruch—Written about 150 to 60 BC; several authors had a hand before the final redaction. It furnished the missing letter of Jeremiah 36:4–6.

Letter of Jeremiah—Written about 317–165 BC. For v. 70 compare Jeremiah 10:5. It furnished the missing letter of Jeremiah. 29:1.

Prayer of Azariah and Song of the Three Young Men— Written about 190–90 BC. Placed between Daniel 3:23–24. It gives the words and prayer of Daniel 3:23.

Susanna—Written about 190–90 B.C, it was placed after Daniel Chapter 12. It shows Daniel's wisdom in clearing Susanna of false charges of adultery by two lustful elders. A model of artistic fiction.

Bel and the Dragon—Written about 190–90 BC. It was placed after Daniel Chapter 12. It describes Daniel's wisdom in unmasking the chicanery of the priests of Bel by showing their tracks left in flour sprinkled on the temple floor, not to mention killing a dragon god by feeding him cakes of fat, pitch, and hair.

Prayer of Manasseh—Written about 200 BC (some date it between 190–10 BC). It provides the missing prayer in 2 Chronicles 33:11–13 and 18–19.

I Maccabees—Written about 100 BC. It covers the period from Alexander the Great (336–323 BC) to the establishment of the Seleucid Empire (175–130 BC). It describes the struggle for Jewish independence from Antiochus IV Epiphanes to John Hyrcanus I. This is a very good historical account of the rise of the Hasmoneans or Maccabees. (Arguably, this background should be included in our Bibles.) It mentions Daniel and the three young men (3:59–60). In addition, it contains a letter stating that the Spartans were related to the Jews through Abraham (12:21). Some of the historical information was taken from a book of the chronicles of the high priests, which is now lost (16:24).

II Maccabees—Written about 50 BC. Covers the period 180–161 BC. Based on a lost five volume history of Jason of Cyrene, the author interprets history theologically; he is less trustworthy than I Maccabees. It contains the statement in 2:5 that Jeremiah hid the Ark of the Covenant in a cave on Mt. Nebo. The eternal death of sinners is taught in 7:9 and 14 and in 7:11; and in 14:46, the resurrection of the flesh. A woman and her seven sons, before they are killed, makes the statement that she nursed her last son three years (7:27); also in the Koran 2:233 two years are proscribed. In 7:28, she makes the clear statement that the world was created out of nothing. In 8:7, the practice of night attacks and guerrilla raids are mentioned. The Catholics picked up the statements in 12:43–45 that the living might pray and offer sacrifices for the dead who would rise again from Purgatory; and in 15:11–16, that the saints in heaven interceded for men on earth and were alive before the resurrection. The doctrine of Angels is taught in 3:24–28, 10: 29–30, and 11:8. In 15:37 the statement is made that Jerusalem is still in Jewish hands; thus it was definitely written before 70 AD. In 15:39, he makes the statement that he hopes the style of the story will delight the ears of those who read it. The custom in antiquity was to read aloud to oneself.

Influence of the Apocrypha

Many of our present names or derivations came from the Apocrypha: Edna, Susanna, Suzan, Sue, Judith, Judy, Raphael, Tobias, Toby and Macabre. Several operas, oratorios and anthems including Longfellow's New England Tragedies, Handel's Susanna, Judas Maccabaeus, and Alexander Balus draw upon the Apocrypha. Many classic paintings feature characters from the Apocrypha. For those who have been to the Church of the Dormition (Rest of Mary) in Jerusalem, her crypt in the basement has a mosaic that she can gaze at, in the ceiling, showing famous women of the Bible; one is Judith holding the head of Holofernes.

Some of our popular sayings originating in the Apocrypha include: A good name endures forever (Sir. 41:13); you can't touch pitch without being defiled (Sir. 13:1); great is truth and mighty above all things (I Esd. 4:41), or the Latin version, *Magna est veritas, et praevalet.*

Ecclesiasticus—Sirach is quoted three times in the Talmud as scripture. Josephus regards I Esdras, I Maccabees, and the Esther additions as canonical. However, the Midrash Qoheleth 12:12 has, "Whoever brings together in his house more than 24 books [the Hebrew Bible] brings confusion." Rabbi Akiba (d. 132 AD) is quoted in Sanhedrin 100b: "Readers of Apocrypha literature had no part in the future world."

Some 80% of Old Testament quotations in the New Testament are from LXX, there are allusions to certain passages in the Apocrypha; but there are no direct quotes. However there are direct references to some of the Pseudepigrapha: The Assumption of Moses in Jude 9, Book of Jannes and Jambres in 2 Timothy 3:8, The Martyrdom of Isaiah in Hebrews 11:37 and Enoch in Jude 14–15. The survival of the Apocrypha and the Pseudepigrapha is due entirely to the early Christian Church.

Further information can be found in the IB articles by Robert H. Pfeiffer (pp. 391 and 421). The best version of the Apocrypha is the Oxford Annotated Apocrypha RSV edited by Bruce M. Metzger, Oxford Univ. Press 1965. Some information is contained in the section on the Dead Sea Scrolls.

Pseudepigrapha

This includes an expanded group of writings, some added quite late. The term means pseudo-authors, or persons writing in the name of some well-known person. All are fictitious. There is no standard order. The two main groups are the Palestinian written in Hebrew or Aramaic, and the Alexandrian written in Greek.

Palestinian

Legends: Testament of the Twelve Patriarchs (ca. 140–110 BC); each gives details about their life.

Book of Jubilees (ca. 104 BC) supplies most of the missing material in Genesis such as Adam and Eve had nine sons and daughters, so that Cain married Awam, and Seth, Azura; the angels were created circumcised; Satan is called Mastema in Aramaic: "the enmity or enemy."

Martyrdom of Isaiah—Several Christian writers had a hand in 4:2–5:1a; the Antichrist or incarnation of Beliar is identified as Nero (54–68 AD). The Jewish parts may date to 50 BC.

Paralipomena (remaining words) of Jeremiah (or Baruch)— the reference to Agrippa places it after 50 AD, but probably around 136 AD.

Lives of the Prophets (ca. 80 AD) details the lives and deaths of the prophets. It also contains the account of the Ark of the Covenant being hid at Mt. Nebo by Jeremiah.

Testament of Job (ca. 50 BC). Some of the material made its way into the LXX of the canonical Job. Job's first wife was Sitidos (the woman of Ausitis or Uz). After her death, he marries Dinah; this is where the Greek and Egyptian names of the seven sons are given.

Life of Adam and Eve (Apocalypse of Moses; ca. 60 AD). Eve relates in detail the story of her fall and that they had 33 sons and 30 daughters.

Hymns and Psalms: Cantica (noncanonical hymns and psalms; see Dead Sea Scrolls).

Odes of Solomon—ca. 80 AD. This reflects the Pharisees' hostility toward the Hasmonaeans, and refers to the death of Pompey in Egypt after 48 BC. J Rendel Harris in 1909, in some papers he bought in Syria, found a 16th century Syrian manuscript with 42 Odes of Solomon. Nine were included in the October 1975 copy of Decision Magazine. The complete series was published by James H. Charlesworth (Oxford Univ. Press 1973).

Apocalypses: Book of Enoch (ca. 163–80 BC). Composed of several parts of various dates. It is known as the Ethiopian Enoch or I Enoch. Parts of eight manuscripts were found at Qumran, but lacking chapters 37–71. 1:9 or 60:8 is quoted in Jude 14–15.

Assumption of Moses—ca. 2 BC–28 AD, since several of Herod's children are alluded to. Book is badly fragmented but quoted in Jude 9. In the Latin manuscripts, chapters 8–9 have been displaced and should be restored between chapters 5–6, the chronology will then be correct.

Apocalypse of Baruch (II) (ca. 90–100 AD) is concerned with the misfortunes of Israel and the unanswered question: Why are so few people to be saved?

Alexandrian

Jewish Propaganda Attributed to Gentiles: Letter of Aristeas (ca. 100 BC). It contains the account of the translation of the Pentateuch into Greek, the LXX, by 72 Hebrew scholars in 72 days (each of the 72 were said to be identical translations).

Sibylline Oracles—Jewish Book III (ca. 140 BC); Book IV (ca. 80 AD), which refers to the eruption of Vesuvius; and Book V (ca. 125 AD, since Hadrian is mentioned). Originally, 15 books, Book IX, X and XV are lost. Several of the books are of Christian origin. The official collection in Rome was lost by fire in 82 BC, but a new collection was prepared [only to be burned under Honorius in 401 AD by instigation of Augustine and the Bishops (Grant p. 285)] in Greek hexameter as in the Iliad and Odyssey, some of the early oracles Homer (ca. 1000 BC) even plagiarized. In the colophon of Book III the Sibyl is said to come from Babylon and married to Noah's son, her name as the first Sibyl was Sambethe. The Greeks call her the Erythaean, which is west of Smyrna in Turkey; she was the fifth Sibyl. Ten Sibyls were said to have uttered oracles from different regions. The main information comes from Firmianus Lactantius in his *Divine Institutes,* Book 1, and chap. 6. Justin Martyr (155 AD) remarks on her in his *Hortatory Address to the Greeks.* All were said to have proclaimed only one God. Augustine (354–430 AD) remarks on the acrostic in Book 7 lines 284–330 (Greek text 17–250) where the letters ΙΗΕΟΨΣΧΡΕΙΣΤΟΣ ΦΕΟΨ ΨΙΟΣ ΣΩΤΗΡ stand for Jesus Christ the Son of God, Savior.

One of the Sibyls was the Delphi Oracle of Apollo, who continued to be consulted up to 390 AD. Her prophecies were famous throughout the Mediterranean.

Two faults run through the travertine of the spring at Adyton, site of the Pythian Sibyl. Gases released from the fault contain ethylene and ethane. The ethylene is 2.4 times better than nitrous oxide (laughing gas) as an anesthetic, which results in light-headedness and euphoria, producing the effects needed for the visions. The earthquake of 373 BC released such a quantity of gas that the oracles declined. Josephus mentions her oracle on the Tower of Babel in *Antiquities* 1.4.3. The most famous one was when Croesus asked her if he should invade Persia. She responded that if he did, "he would destroy a great empire." Only it was his own that was destroyed in 546 BC. Other oracle centers were also built over springs such as at Clarya and Didyma Turkey. The one at Siwa Egypt to Zeus Ammon, visited by Alexander the Great, relied on a secret chamber from which the priests gave the replies to questions. Alexander's answer shook him; he promised to tell his mother all about it, but died before getting back home. Cambyses, in 525 BC, lost 50,000 men in a sandstorm; on their way to punish the oracle for an unfavorable prophesy (the bodies have never been found).

Legendary History: III Maccabees (ca. 1 AD). A misnomer about Ptolemy IV (221–204 BC); completely mythological in tone.

Popular Philosophy: IV Maccabees (ca. 30 BC–30 AD) before Philo of Alexandria (d. 45 AD); better than II Maccabees. A devout Jew but not a Pharisee.

Apocalypses: Slavonic Enoch (II) (ca. 50 AD): written in Greek as shown by the statement that the first letter of the cardinal points spells out ADAM. It describes Enoch's vision of the seven heavens and mentions the eighth, ninth, and tenth. Satan is in the fifth; their fallen brothers are chained in the second. Angels, archangels, and others are in the sixth. Archangels, cherubim, seraphim; the enthroned Lord are in the seventh.

Greek Baruch (III) (ca. 150 AD) was known to Origen. A Christian added 4:9–15 and edited chapters 11–17, where the Church is mentioned in 13:4, and Matthew 25:21 is quoted at 15:4. Five of the seven heavens are described and the other two are lost. An editor omitted the original ending.

Information on the Sibylline Oracles can be found in R. H. Charles, Vol. II Pseudepigraphia (Oxford 1913; Milton S. Terry, *The Sibylline Oracles*, AMS Press Edition of 1973, ISBN 0-404-06362-4).

CHAPTER 11

NEW TESTAMENT CANON

THE NEW TESTAMENT was designed for public use (see Col 4:16, 1 Thes 5:27 and Rev 22:18a). The apostles quote the work of others in the New Testament, as in: Luke 1:1; 1 Timothy 5:18b quotes Luke 10:7 or some Gospel collection containing it; 2 Peter 3:15–16 mentions the epistles of Paul; and Jude 17–18 quotes 2 Peter 3:3. Note Acts 20:35 is not found in the Gospels. The Apostolic Fathers (70–120 AD), such as of Rome in 95, quote from 18 New Testament books. Nine books including Jude, 2 Peter, and 2 and 3 John are not quoted; 1 and 2 Thessalonians, Colossians, Titus and Philemon are questionable. The Apologists (120–170 AD) had the Gospels separated from the other "sayings of Jesus" in oral tradition. By the end of the 2nd century AD, the four Gospels and all 13 of Paul's Epistles were known.

An interesting statement by the martyrs at Scili in North Africa in 180 AD said they kept the letters of Paul in their church chest with their church "books or Bible." Thus, we can see the process by which a book would later become part of the Bible. The Old Testament and the Gospels were included; Paul's letters were not, but were in the chest that contained the books.

The Muratonian Canon of ca. 195 AD (found in Milan, published in 1740) is a mutilated list that does not contain Hebrews, 1 and 2 Peter, James or 3 John. These may have been listed on missing parts, or the missing books may not have been collected in some churches yet. It did list the Revelation of Peter, but admits that some will not have it read in church. Iranaeus of Lyons 189, Clement of Alexandria and Tertullian of Carthage all wrote between 170–350 AD and knew the Gospels, Acts and all 13 of Paul's Epistles, 1 Peter, 1 John and Revelation (which was questioned at times).

Eusebius who wrote the *Church History* in 397 AD lists all 27 books as known and accepted the disputed James, Jude, 2 Peter, 2 and 3 John and Revelation. He and all others proficient in Greek realized the different style of Hebrews from Paul's other books and said, "The diction in Hebrews does not have the rough quality the apostle himself admitted having, and its syntax is better Greek. The content of the epistle is excellent, and not inferior to the authentic writings of the apostle . . . If I were to venture my own opinion, I would say that the thoughts are the apostle's but the style and construction reflect someone who recalled the apostle's teachings and interpreted them. If any church, then, regards this epistle as Paul's, it should be commended, since men of old had good reason to hand it down as his. However, who wrote the epistle only God knows. Traditions reaching us claim it was Clement, Bishop of Rome, or Luke" (Mayer p. 227). Athanasius, Bishop of Alexandria in 367 listed all 27 New Testament books.

The Council of Laodicea in 363 AD accepted all but Revelation. The Council of Hippo in Africa in 393 AD lists all 27 books as Scripture. The III Council of Carthage in 397 AD confirmed them. Hebrews was still somewhat questionable. In Asia Minor only Revelation was excluded, in fact ca. 394–403 AD the Eastern Church was divided when two of the four "doctors" rejected it; it is not used in the Greek Church today. The Council of Trent during the Reformation in 1546 AD confirmed all, plus the Apocrypha except for I and II Esdras and the Prayer of Manasseh in the Old Testament.

Erasmus wrote what became the Textus Receptus of 1516 AD, in Greek, based on 10th century manuscripts. He denied Hebrews, 2 Peter and Revelation having apostolic origin but did not question their Canon authority.

Martin Luther in 1534 set Hebrews, Jude, James, and Revelation at the end of his version and spoke of them with varying degrees of disrespect.

Calvin (ca. 1560) denied Paul as the author of Hebrews and questioned the authenticity of 2 Peter; he noted the doubts of James and Jude but did not set any aside as noncanonical.

The Articles of the Church of England in 1552 did not list the Books of Scripture. The Elizabethan Articles of 1562 and 1571 lists Old Testament and Apocrypha books and "all the books of the New Testament as they are commonly received, we do receive and account them Canonical." However, they did not name them.

Further information on the development of the New Testament canon can be found in the article in the IB by Edgar J. Goodspeed (p. 63).

New Testament

Book	Author	Place of Writing	Theme	#Date (AD)	Critics Date (AD)
Mt	Mt	Judea	Christ-King	65–68	66–130
Mk	Mk	Rome	Christ-Servant	60–65	58–150
Lk	Lk	Caesarea	Christ-Man	58–65	70–140
Jn	Jn	Ephesus	Christ-Deity	90–95	95–160
Acts	Lk	Rome	History of Early Church	58–65	70–140
Rom	Paul	Corinth	Gospel of God	58	58–60

1 Cor	Paul	Ephesus	Christian Conduct	57	58
2 Cor	Paul	Macedonia	Paul's Authority	57	58
Gal	Paul	Cor-Eph	Salvation by Grace	48 or 52	52–59
Eph +	Paul	Rome	Church-Christ's Body	62–63	61–64
Phil +	Paul	Caes.-Rome	Christian Experience	58–60	61–63
Col +	Paul	Rome	Christ's Pre-Eminence	61–63	61–63
1 Thes	Paul	Corinth	Christ's Return	52	52–54
2 Thes	Paul	Corinth	Day of the Lord	53	52–54
1 Tm	Paul	Macedonia	Church Order	62–65	64–68
2 Tm	Paul	Rome	Holding the Truth	67–68	66–68
Ti	Paul	Mac-Gr Church	Order	65	64–68
Phlm +	Paul	Rome	Love Exemplified	65	61–64
Heb	?	Judea-Italy	Christ-High Priest **	63–64	63–90
Jas	James	Jerusalem	Practical Church Living	45–61	44–150
1 Pt	Peter	Bab-Rome	Suffering and Glory	65 . . .	
2 Pt	Peter ?		Last Days **	66–67	170
1 Jn	John	Judea	Fellowship	90–95	95–160
2 Jn	John	Ephesus	Christ's Commandment	90–95	95–160
3 Jn	John	Ephesus	Walking in Truth	90–95	95–160
Jude	Jude	?	Contending for the Faith **	66–80 or 75	. . .
Rv	John	Patmos	Consummation ***	96–98	68–Sept. 30 395

James and Galatians were probably the earliest books written, followed by the rest of Paul's letters, then the Gospels, Hebrews, Jude and John's writings last.

Generally accepted date. New evidence allows some refinement

* The only Gentile author see Col. 4:11 and 14

** Accepted late

*** Least accepted

+ 1st Imprisonment

o 2nd Imprisonment

Chester Beatty (p^{46} [Set II] page 53) is the center; thus the folio had 104 pages originally, has the order: seven leaves lost, Romans 5:17, Hebrews, 1 and 2 Corinthians, Ephesians, Galatians, Philippians, Colossians, 1 Thessalonians to end, seven leaves lost (two for 2 Thes and five blank since 1 and 2 Tm, Ti and Phlm would require 10).

Internal indications of date when the books were written and other information explaining and bearing on the times at hand are shown below for each book:

Matthew—Written before the fall of Jerusalem in 70 AD. His interest in money marks him as a CPA type. The 2nd oldest manuscript known is p^{64} a papyrus manuscript which dates to ca. 175, it covers part of chapter 26 (see Bible and Spade 9: 59 (80). The German Journal for Papyrology and Epigraphics now dates it to 75–100 AD or within a generation of Jesus probably written as an eyewitness account, Bible and Spade 8: 61 (95). Numbering system changed when Bible and Spade changed to ABR and back again.

16:13 Caesarea Philippi. On the way to the Transfiguration (17:1), Jesus and the three apostles were in, or near, this city of Herod Philip. This also had a pagan temple dedicated to the god Pan. The massive rock cliff or Petra would have been a perfect place for the play on words directed to Peter or Petros (a small stone). Thus, the declaration of Christ as the rock or

Petra of Peter's statement, 'the Church would be built and not on Peter himself'.

17:27 "fish." This fish that is caught by a hook is not the St. Peter's fish, Tilapia Galilea, which is caught by net as in Luke 5:1–7; the fish in question is the Barbus Longiceps or Long-headed Barbel, a member of the Carp family (see BAR 19[6]: 46 [93]).

18:6 "millstone." The type Jesus refers to was the upper stone driven by donkeys and weighing over 400 pounds (see EHB p. 487).

25:1 "lamps." This would be the small Herodian spatula shaped nozzle lamp that held about four ounces of olive oil and would burn about six hours.

26:73 Galilean speech. Galileans were famous for their accent. In the Talmud 'Erubin 53b we find this statement: A Galilean enquired "who has amar?' "Foolish Galilean do you mean "amar (wool), "imar (a lamb), hamor (an ass) or hamar (wine)?'

Mark—Also known as John Mark, John, his Jewish name, and Mark, his Latin. Tradition states that Mark wrote from Peter's notes, after his death in 67–69 AD. Only four paragraphs are unique to Mark, the rest of the 16 chapters are covered also in Matthew or Luke.

16:9–20. These verses are not contained in the oldest manuscripts, Codex Vaticanus and Sinaiticus. Although Irenaeus 202 AD and the Diatessaron of the second century AD knew of it.

9:2 "the Transfiguration." The high mountain is either Mt. Tabor or somewhere near Mt. Hermon, since they had just left Caesarea Philippi (8:27). One of the mountains of Hermon is the better choice, especially since there was a settlement from the Iron I, Hasmonean and Herodian periods on the top of Tabor. One cannot picture Jesus and the three trying to hold a meeting with villagers coming and going all around them. Tabor was well known and could have been identified, if it was the mountain in question (see SMM Section 15-2 San-The).

Luke—Although not named, the author shows a keen interest in diseases, treatment and diagnoses. As a historian, he is first rate. Both Luke-Acts were dedicated to Theophilus, a Roman, but nothing else is known of him.

1:5 Zacharias. Was of the eighth course of Abijah, 1 Chronicles 24:10. As a priest, his wife Elizabeth was a Levite.

1:36 "thy cousin." Mary's mother would also be a Levite, see above. From other sources, her name was Anna. Levite women could marry outside the tribe. In her case to a Judahite.

2:24 "a pair of turtledoves." It is interesting how we can fill in details or read between the lines. The poorness of Joseph and Mary was obviously before the visit of the Magi; afterward they were well off and by law would offer a lamb. By the time the Magi arrived, they were in a house. Thus some time had passed.

4:2 "ate nothing." This was a fast of food only since drink is not mentioned. Medically, it has been shown that the appetite will decrease until the fat supply is exhausted; after about 40 days, it then returns. Water cannot be done without for more than three days.

8:32 "swine." Unclean to Jews, but here on the east side, the area of Gergesa was non-Jewish. There is some confusion on the location, but the best choice is either Kursi or Tel Samra. The later is more likely for there are no Herodian or Iron Age tombs at Kursi for Legion to live in.

10:30–37 "the Jericho road." This old Roman road from Jerusalem to Jericho via Herod's winter palace clings to the walls of wadi Kelt, which is also known as "the valley of the shadow of death" in the 23rd Psalm; until the early 20th century this road was a haven for bandits and solitary travelers took their lives in their hands to travel it alone. Trucks can still use it today.

John—The oldest New Testament codex fragment known is John 18:31–33 and 37–38 and was found at a trash dump in Oxyrhynchus Egypt and dates from 100–150. This is p^{52} or the Rylands 457 John. Deissmann dates it to the reign of Hadrian (117–138) or possibly Trajan (98–117). The original copy was thus composed before 125 and within a generation of John's death. This could be copied from the original manuscript. However, what was it doing in such an out of the way place off the beaten track? The Bodmer Papyrus II dates from about 200 and does not contain John 7:53–8:11 or 5:3b–4.

1:1 "was God." Jehovah's Witnesses have missed a crucial Greek lexical meaning. It has been shown (the Granville Sharp Rule); an absent article "a" stresses quality rather than identity. To insert the "a" here would require it to be added in 1 Thessalonians 4:15 "a Lord" or Titus 2:13 where the great [God and our Savior Jesus Christ] are one and the same and not separate beings.

1:18 reads God (*Theos*) rather than Son (*Huios*).

2:10 "good wine." Again, the Greek *oinos* does not distinguish between wine and grape juice, but must be determined by the context. Only here the context is neutral. However, from v. 13 the Passover was at hand so the marriage was probably near the first of Nissan. The grape harvest was from July-September. Any juice prepared then would already ferment to wine since no pasteurization was known. Left over grapes would not be available this late, from anywhere. The 2–3 firkins would be from 18–27 gallons, if the average were 20, then 120 gallons of wine were prepared. From the stewards comment only a superior vintage was prepared or if grape juice, then an even greater miracle was evident, since no one in the crowd or anywhere else in Israel would have ever seen juice in March-April.

2:15 "a scourge of small cords." If one did not intend to lay it on someone's back, you would not make one in the first place.

5:2 "Bethesda." Bethesda, which means House of Mercy, is another topic, which escapes full meaning. Archaeology has shown that this site was actually the Temple of Asclepius (there was another at the hot springs south of Tiberias); see ABR 2:24 (89). The two large sheep pools were too large and deep to get into and the water surface would not have been noticeably disturbed in the spring season by the freshening of the spring that fed it, with clay-tainted water. However, the Temple that was outside the sheep pools to the east fits the description. Part of the votive statuary with the serpent of Asclepius or Eshmun has been found here along with several votive plaques presented by those who had various parts of the body healed. The Byzantine church central apse was built over the healing cave into which the water from the spring was led. The Jews could not admit to the pagan shrine by its name and so called it Bethesda. The construction of the Pool of Israel at the NE corner of the Temple Mount, by Herod, caused the twin pools at Bethesda to go out of use, lending further support that these were not the place of the healing.

5:3 "waiting for. . ." and all of vs. 4 are missing from the oldest Vaticanus and Siniaticus manuscripts

10:22 "feast of the dedication." This marks the feast of rededication of the Temple by Judas Maccabeus in 165 BC after the desecration by Antiochus Epiphanes IV on the same date in 166 BC, the 25th of Chislev.

11:16 "Thomas Didymus." This means that Thomas was a twin.

12:1 "six days before the Passover." Since Ephraim in 11:54 was 19 miles from Bethany by road, Jesus would have arrived late in the day as v. 2 indicates. This would have been Sunday, since as an observant Jew he would not travel on the Sabbath, so he could not have left Ephraim on Saturday. Then six days before would have been Sunday. The Triumphal Entry would have been on the next day (v. 12) or Monday. So much for Palm Sunday. Those that follow "types and examples" will recall that the Passover lamb was selected and set aside for a four-day examination period four days before Passover. Thus, Jesus presented himself as the "lamb" for examination by the priests four days before, or on Monday.

12:10 "put Lazarus to death." Lazarus's resurrection after four days, when putrefaction would have started, was a greater feat that that of Jesus. No wonder he was included in the hit list.

18:28 "Praetorium." Another controversy is over where Jesus was tried by Pilate. Either the palace of Herod the Great at Joppa gate, or the Antonia Fortress at the NW corner of the Temple mount is meant. Since Herod Antipas was in town for the Passover (Lk 23:7) both could not use the Palace at the same time, as it probably belonged to Antipas (there is strong evidence that he stayed in the old Hasmonean palace just south of Wilson's arch; it was used by Agrippa II and Bernice in 66, where he gave a long speech on the strength of the Roman Army throughout the empire). Antipas was not summoned to see Pilate, which would be possible if both were close by in the same building. Since all riots started near the Temple, it was imperative that Pilate be near the action to direct things and bring order. A full cohort of 400–600 soldiers was stationed here and would be expected to be the place where prisoners were jailed and tried in the courtyard or Gabbatha in Hebrew or Lithostroton in Greek. For anyone who has been to Jerusalem and traveled the narrow streets (probably no wider in the time of Jesus, the Via Dolorosa or Street of the Chain is a good example) crowded with people at Passover (and similar to today when the services at the Dome of the Rock lets out on Friday), even a squad of Roman troops trying to travel from the Palace to the Antonia would have had to run down everyone in their path to make any time. Even for them this would present obstacles of the first order (see MBA map 236).

19:14 "the 6th hour." The difference in hours in the Gospels has caused all kinds of concern. John is the only one to use Roman time the same as we do now. John had lived too long out of Judea that he was probably acclimated to the Roman system. This is especially true if this is compared with Matthew 27:1–2 where "when morning was come" would make this 6 A.M. and not 12 noon. Everything will fall into place if this is kept in mind.

19:29 "hyssop." Matthew and Mark mention reed. The Greek word *hyssos* for the Roman pilium or javelin, and hyssop is only two letters shorter. One 11th century manuscript (476) uses *hyssos*.

19:30 "It is finished." Greek *Telelestai*, stamped on every contract to proclaim completion of all the terms. Time had been rushing headlong to this conclusion since Daniel 9:25–6. The illegal trials at Annas, Caiaphas, Pilate, Herod Antipas, and Satan's efforts at Luke 4:13 (for a season) all took part in the Father's timing; it was indeed *Tetelestai*. See the chapter on the Talmud.

20:5 "stooped down." Tombs in various ages are very distinctive. This description fits a Herodian tomb in every detail. A rolling stone to close it, while possible, is not as likely as a stone plug. The rolling stones are small and placed in a narrow opening with no room above them and only about six to twelve inches thick, very hard to sit on (Mt 28:2, rolled back can also simply mean moved), EHB p. 46.

Large rolling stones like the one at "Herod's family tomb" behind the King David Hotel, are very rare and does not remove the difficulty of sitting on such a narrow ledge, EHB p. 528. John had to bend down probably on his hands and knees (the openings are only about 2.5 ft high) and could see the principal burial bench directly in back of the door, with angels sitting on either side, v. 12. There would be three benches, one on each side of the opening, with a pit between them (the maneuvering pit for those bringing the body inside). Behind the benches and carved into the wall were usually chambers called *kokhs* to hold extra bodies, and the benches frequently had arches carved above called *archosolia*. The angels sat on either side of the center bench with their feet in the pit. Now you know what to look for, not the type of tomb at the Garden Tomb, which is an IA tomb (at least three IA lamps were found near the door when it was excavated) in an Iron Age cemetery (there are at least twelve IA tombs in this vicinity); reworked in the Byzantine period where at least two burial benches were removed from the entrance chamber. The Garden Tomb entrance is large, no bending required, but the burial slots are in another chamber that runs off at 90° to the right and could not be seen easily from the doorway. Further evidence that it isn't the right type as well as it isn't a new, unused tomb.

Acts 1:6 "language." The Greek word is actually *dialectos* or dialect, which is even more specific. As an illustration with tongue in cheek: south Galilean would be spoken with a "you-all" at the end of most statements.

2:13 "new/sweet wine." The Greek is *gleuchos* from which we get glucose. This is a case where the context only can tell you about it. For Peter's comment in verse 15 would be the height of irony if it were not actually intoxicating, seeing it was only 9 A.M. This is the type of wine called "fruit of the vine" in Luke 22:18, or "pure wine" in Revelation 14:10, and produced from the purest juice of the grape.

3:2 "Beautiful gate." This was the east gate into the Court of Women. Those diseased such as a leper could go no further, until cured. Often mistakenly confused with the Nicanor gate, which separated the Court of Women from the Court of Israel, Mazar p. 116.

11:28 "famine." This occurred in the reign of Claudius in 46 AD, so the time of the prophecy was in 45; 12:2 then occurred in 44 AD.

18:2. The banishing of the Jews from Rome occurred in 49 AD.

18:12. Gallio became proconsul on July 1, 51 AD and lasted one year. Thus from 18:1 and 11, Paul came to Corinth ca. 50 AD after the Jerusalem Council.

19:24 "Diana." Luke uses the Roman name throughout this chapter for the Greek Artemis; in v. 35, Jupiter should be Zeus.

27:14 "Euroclydon." Means east wave; we would call it the typical "noreaster." The book ends rather abruptly. There is an 11-page conclusion dated to 300 AD, in the Hamburg museum.

Romans—Written from Corinth (Acts 20:2–3), after taking the collection to Jerusalem (1 Cor 16:1–4 and 2 Cor 8 and 9). Paul was about to leave for Jerusalem (15:25). Since 2 Corinthians was written from Macedonia, from there he went to Greece. Thus, Romans was written after 1 and 2 Corinthians. The letter was delivered by Phoebe (16:1–2) a servant or probably a deaconess.

16:7. Apostles. The Jewish woman Junias—the Latin name may be the same as the Hebrew Joanna, the wife of Chuza Herod Antipas's steward (Lk 8:3). Because of her Christian connections, Chuza may have divorced her and she later married Andronicus. A witness of the resurrection of Jesus, who ministered to Him from her wealth, was jailed at one point and could be called an apostle. The term notable can also mean prominent or outstanding. A rare term given to a woman, BR Spring 2005 p. 14.

1 Corinthians—Probably written in the spring of 54–5 AD from Ephesus (16:8–9) during the later half of the 27 month ministry (Acts 19:8 and 10). Another letter is apparently lost (5:9 and 16:1).

7:18 "become uncircumcised." Many Jews did this by a painful operation; see Josephus and Michener.

8:5 "to lead about a wife." We hear of Peter's mother-in-law, but all of the apostles and the Lord's brothers were probably married, except John. By age 30, Jewish men were expected to be married according to the Talmud.

9:24 "run in a race." The reference is to the Isthmuthean Olympic Games held in Corinth every two years. Paul was very good at bringing current events into his letters.

2 Corinthians. Written possibly from Philippi in fall of 54 or 55.

2:14 "triumph." The allusion is to the Roman Triumphal Procession, of a general or emperor, familiar to everyone.

4:7 "treasure in earthen vessels." It was quite common to store money or other valuables in pottery jars (compare the DSS).

11:32 "Aretas, the king." This is Aretas IV (ca. 35 AD), the first king of Damascus under decentralized Roman rule from 37 AD. No Roman coins have been found at Damascus from 34–62 AD.

Galatians—These people were actually Celts who entered this area as mercenaries from Europe about 278 BC. King Nicomedes of Bithynia invited them into the area in his struggles with Antiochus I (TLLC p. 68). The place of writing is uncertain, either at Antioch at the end of the first missionary journey (Acts 14:26–28) or at Ephesus at the end of the third MJ in 52 AD (Acts 19:10). See comments on James. If after the Jerusalem Council in 48 AD (Acts 15), then why was their decision on circumcision not mentioned (2:3 is only a statement)?

2:1 "fourteen years." After Paul's conversion? Was this the famine relief journey? The famine, known from Roman records and Josephus, occurred in 46 AD; it was predicted by Agabus in 44 AD (Acts 11:28). The relief may not have been sent until it was already underway, probably in 47 AD; if so then his conversion was probably in 33 AD, or about three years after Christ's death.

Ephesians—A circulating letter sent from Rome while he was in prison 3:1 and 6:20, probably in 61 AD. No personal greetings listed. Written before 1 Peter (Acts 20–27), Hebrews or Revelation, since expressions from Ephesians appear in these. Letter carried by Tychicus (6:21) along with Colossians and Philemon.

1:1 "to the Ephesians." Not included in the best manuscripts, see Colossians 4:16 where this may be the unknown Laodicean letter.

1:3–14 and 15–23. Are both one sentence in the Greek, showing why Peter thought Paul's letters were sometimes hard to understand.

2:18. Another verse where the Trinity is present.

Philippians—Probably the last of the Prison Epistles. Written before Epaphroditus returned to Philippi, probably in 61 AD (2:25 and 28).

1:13 "the palace." Is actually "in the whole praetorium" (see also 4:22).

3:17 "have us for an example." This was necessary, since the New Testament was not yet available.

3:20 "for your citizenship." This contrasts Phillipi's colonial status, which granted Roman citizenship to all citizens.

4:3 "true yokefellow." Syzygos is a proper name, which means the above, but the name should be substituted. "Those women" are the Euodia and Syntyche of vs. 2, two women with an official position in this church who did not get along well together.

Colossians—Sent along with Philemon by Onessimus (4:7–9) along with Tychicus, probably in 61.

2:14 "Blotting out the handwriting of ordinances." Another example where Telelestai was written across it, "it is finished" (see Jn 9:30).

3:5 "Mortify." Simply means to bury.

4:10. John Mark was back in good stead (Acts 15:37–38).

1 Thessalonians—Silas and Timothy (1:1) joined Paul at Corinth (Acts 18:1 and 5). Probably written in 51.

1:9–10 "turned to, to serve, to wait." Covers their past, present and future.

4:16 "shout." A Greek term used only here, is a military term of orders such as "Attention" or "Fall Out."

5:14 "unruly." Is also a military term. These types of words carry an emphasis lost in the English but the Greeks would be fully aware of the implied meanings.

2 Thessalonians—Also about 51 AD.

2:2 "the day of Christ is at hand." The KJV mistranslates it; it should read, "the day of the Lord is now present."

1 Timothy—Written to Ephesus 1:3 after Paul's 1st release in 64–5, at the same time Titus was written.

3:11 A good case can be made that the subject of wives between vs. 10 and 12 may be that they are deaconesses.

2 Timothy—Written just before his death, to Timothy at Ephesus in 67, who was to stop at Troas 4:13 and Corinth 4:19 on his way to Rome 4:21.

4:20 "sick." The gift of healing Acts 19:12, was apparently drying up, for Trophimus was not healed.

Titus—Titus was in Crete 1:5, and Paul was not in prison (3:12) the date is around 65.

3:12 "Nicopolis." There are three known: Thrace, Cilicia, and Epirus four miles from Actium near Dalmatia (1 Tm 4:10), which is probably the one meant.

Philemon—Written to Philemon at Colossae from Rome 1:1 about 61.

1:18 "If." In the KJV "if" at the start of a sentence is the Greek first class conditional and should be translated with the sense of "since" or "and it has."

Hebrews—The Temple was still in existence 13:10 and all the other references to the Temple are in the present tense, thus before 70 probably 66. All Old Testament quotes except possible

10:30 are from the LXX. Whereas Paul quotes from both the Hebrew and LXX. Apollos is an author that could fit the bill. See also the introduction to this chapter.

12:2 "finisher of faith." The "our" in italic should be removed; it detracts from the full meaning.

13:5 "never leave thee." The Greek is even more emphatic in that three negatives precede the verb "I will not."

James—The Temple had not fallen. James was martyred about 62, maybe the 1st New Testament book written. Probably before the Jerusalem Council of Acts 15 in 48, since Paul's arguments are not stressed. The book is highly Jewish in tone.

2:24 "justified by works." Much confusion over this verse. The whole argument is that salvation is by a faith that works and not through works alone. James uses the word "faith" in the sense of intellectual orthodoxy, Ephesians 2:8–10 puts both ideas together.

1 Peter—Indicates knowledge of James, 1 Thessalonians, Romans, Colossians and Philippians, thus written after the Prison Epistles ca. 64. Mark and Silas were present in Rome 5:12.

1:2 "Elect." In the Greek, this is a modifier of sojourners, so the letter is to the elect sojourners of the Dispersion, all those in western Turkey 1:1.

3:19 "spirits in prison." The Greek literally means that Noah preached to the unsaved, their spirits are now in Sheol. Not that Christ gave them a second chance.

5:13 "Babylon." It is thought that this is a code word for Rome. The Jewish community in Babylon was scattered in 41 under Caligula 37–41 or Claudius 41–54, thus making it less likely that the city still contained Jews. One of the earliest references to the books existence is 2 Peter 3: 1.

2 Peter—Differences in vocabulary may mean that he wrote it himself without a secretary or amanuensis as in 1 Peter 5:12 where he had Silvanus or Silas also 2 Corinthians 1:19.

No particular group is addressed. He was awaiting death under Nero who died in 68. The book is referred to in Jude 17, by quoting 3:2–3.

1 John—Author is not named but is similar in style to the Gospel.1 John contains no salutation or benediction. All three letters may date to 85–95.

3:9 "is born." The Greek perfect participle of past action with results continuing to the present, literally means, "has been and remains born."

4:2. Can Jehovah's Witnesses claim this statement?

5:7 This is the only known forgery in the Bible and has been eliminated in the NIV, RSV, and NAS. See Minor Bible Errors for more details. The only Greek New Testament to contain it is Codex Montfortianus MS 61, a minuscule, which is written on "paper" and not parchment; it has the articles, which shows it was translated from the Latin.

2 John. The elect lady and her children of verse 1 and her elect sister of verse 13 may be the local church, the children would be the members, and the elect sister would be John's own church.

Jude—Written by Jude, the brother of James and Christ (Mt 13:55 and Mk 6:3) about 65. He refers to his brother rather than his father probably because James was so well known. He was not an apostle but the book met less resistance than 2 Peter. Quotes the Assumption of Moses v. 9, which was written before the destruction of Jerusalem in 70 and the Book of Enoch v. 14.

Revelation—Eusebius says John was exiled to Patmos in the 15th year of Domitian or 96. Grammar differences such as 14:19 "great" is feminine gender and "winepress" is masculine gender, has been shown to be everyday usage, other blunders and solecisms were common in the 1st century. Eusebius termed the Greek barbaric and ungrammatical (Maier p. 274). An amanuensis was probably used for the Gospel, whereas Revelation was probably written by John's own hand (see Acts 4:13). The definitive date in the introduction is due to Nikolaus Morosow in 1912 who claimed that Revelation was an astrological exercise by John Chrysostom a church father who died shortly after 404 (Free p. 334).

1:4 "washed." Here is a case where one of the early manuscripts was probably produced by dictation, since the Greek *lousanti* is pronounced the same as *lusanti*, "released." One scribe probably supplied the wrong word, although no real damage is produced.

3:15–16 "lukewarm." The allusions to the situations present in each of the Seven Cities of Asia is full of accurate information, which would be well known to the residents. Laodicea was famous for the hot springs of nearby Hierapolis and other sources, some of which were tapped by a six-mile aqueduct which brought cooler or lukewarm water to the city; which did not satisfy the thirst in that condition. (See New Testament Archaeology.)

5:9–10. Most older manuscripts leave out "us" in v. 9 and read "them or they" instead of "us and we" in v. 10.

7:4–8 The tribe of Dan is omitted, Irenaeus (ca. 190) said a belief was current that the Antichrist was to come from this tribe. Ephraim is also omitted unless Joseph is equivalent to Ephraim.

11:1 "the angel stood." This is lacking in the older manuscripts. Read "and one said, Rise etc."

22:16–21 This was missing from all the Greek manuscripts. Erasmus used it to prepare his Greek New Testament in 1516. He translated these missing verses from a Latin manuscript, back into Greek. However, in this badly flawed manuscript (he was using Codex 1) a cursive of the 12–13 century and contains defective and inaccurate passages. Unfortunately, this was the version, which was eventually used by the KJV. For example, 22:19 "book of life" should now be read as "tree of life."

Manufacture of Manuscripts

While early copies of texts were written on clay tablets, we have no Bible texts written on clay. Although there is a poor mans Gospel written on 20 potsherds, ten of those in Luke are numbered (see Coburn p. 165). Some non-Biblical manuscripts from Egypt are on papyrus (ca. 2850 BC) or animal skin scrolls (ca. 2550 BC). Clay is bulky and unwieldy; and papyrus, because of the direction the fibers run can only be written on one side easily. There are some texts on lead, gold, silver, or copper, usually religious in nature or for permanence (for example, the silver scrolls from St. Andrews, and the copper scroll from Cave Three at Qumran).

Some are on linen by the Romans, Egyptians, and Etuscans. Vellum or parchment made from animal skins was refined in Pergamun by Eumenes II (ca. 182 BC), to break the embargo placed on the export of papyrus by Ptolemy V Epiphanes in the rivalry between the two libraries. The result was pergamena, which later became parchment in English. Scrolls were easily made in great lengths and could be written occasionally on both sides, as in Revelation 5:1 where it is called an opisthograph. In about 85 AD, books began to appear in the form of a codex or leaf style, where several layers of parchment were folded over and sewn together. This actually derived from the Latin term *caudex*, as thin sheets of wood covered with wax. One example of eight pages is known. Most of the oldest forms are from Egypt and made of papyrus. This is an easier form to carry and read from, or to turn to a specific passage without the trouble of rolling and unrolling a scroll. It became the dominant form of the early Bible by 100. At present there are 88 papyrus manuscripts or fragments, 274 parchment uncials (written in Greek capital letters), 2,795 minuscules on parchment (although two are on paper), and 2,209 lectionaries. There are 1,348 manuscripts of Luke alone. Some 24,900 New Testament manuscripts or fragments are known.

Of the 476 second-century, non-Christian manuscripts from Egypt, some 465 (more than 97%) are scrolls; but of the eight Biblical manuscripts known from this period, all are codices. By the end of the 4th century some 111 Biblical manuscripts are from Egypt, and 99 are codices (89%). *Biblia,* originally meaning papyrus rolls, was the root for the name "Bible." (See Finegan and Metzger for additional details.)

Technical Details about Manuscripts

1. **Quire and Folio**—Usually four sheets were folded to give a *quattuor* (or "quire") of eight leaves (16 pages). A single folded sheet gave a *folium* (leaf of four pages). In the case of **P⁴⁶** 52 sheets were folded giving 104 folios. Many books are still made this way. (One need only examine the spine.)

2. **Recto and Verso**—Recto is the front side, verso is the back. For papyrus, the recto side has the fiber running horizontally for easy writing; and for verso, the fibers run vertically. For a codex, the parchment was often placed so that the flesh side, which was lighter, faced a flesh side and the hair side, which was darker, faced a hair side. The same could be done for papyrus. Both types were done just for aesthetics.

3. **Pen and Ink**—Pens were made by splitting a reed, sharpening it, and splitting the point. Black ink (melan) was made from soot, gum, and water. Brown was made from oak gall or tannin. Red ocher or iron oxide furnished red (from the Latin, *ruber*). It was mainly used for titles, headings, initial letters, or the name of God. Other colors mentioned by Josephus are blue, purple, gold, and silver. Some pages were stained with these colors.

4. **Columns and Rulings**—Guide lines were placed by pinpricks and sharp impressions pressed into the parchment,

whereas the fiber strips on papyrus furnished the guides. There is even a science of pinpricks for this area. Frequently several columns might be found on the same page two or three inches wide. Strange to us, the scribes wrote beneath the lines rather than on the lines.

5. **Opisthograph and Palimpsest**—On a scroll, the back carried only an address, title, or other material such as a list of witnesses. Scrolls written fully on the back and front are opisthographs. Due to the expense or limited availability, some parchments were recycled by erasing the old text and rewriting over it, known as a palimpset or "scraped again." Of 250 New Testament uncial manuscripts, 52 are palimpsets. In 692, the Council of Trullo (or the Quinisext Council) condemned the practice of reusing Scripture manuscripts for other purposes. The penalty was excommunication for one year. However, the practice apparently continued. (See Metzger p. 12 for a complete list.) Use of chemical reagents or ultraviolet light helps to read some of these.

6. **Uncial and Minuscule**—Uncials are essentially capital letters, first used for inscriptions, from the Latin *uncia*, which means the twelfth part. Exactly what "part" is uncertain, but many manuscripts have only 12 letters on a line, as in Codex Sinaiticus; Codex Vaticanus, however, has 16–18. By the 9th century, the script of smaller letters similar to lower case, with frequently connected letters, was in vogue. The minuscules could be written a little faster, took up less space, and soon surpassed in number the uncials. Thus, the older manuscripts are usually uncials.

7. **Punctuation and Abbreviation**—As previously mentioned, little spacing was used with little or no punctuation. In the oldest New Testament fragment (P^{52}) there is slight spacing with dots over Iota to indicate that it is pronounced as a separate syllable from Omicron and Upsilon following it. Later the period is placed high or middle, at the end of a

line, and sometimes between words. Sacred names are often abbreviated, sometimes in color and with a line above the letters.

8. **Sections, Canons and Lections**—Words were often written in the margin, or a space was left (as in Mt 26:31 of **P**[64] and Codex Vaticanus). This method of calling attention to the beginning of a section goes back to the 2nd century. At this same point in Codex Vaticanus Greek numbers appear in the margin showing that Matthew was divided into 170 sections (Mark, 62; Luke, 152; and John, 80; as were other books). In Codex Alexandrinus, a different system is used, along with the Latin *titlus* giving a concise summary of the contents. Thus Mark 1:23 is titled, "Concerning the man possessed by a demon"; and 1:29 has, "Concerning the mother-in-law of Peter."

These were forerunners of the Chapter divisions of Stephen Langton (see Chapter 1). Eusebius used a different system of sections with 355 in Matthew, 233 in Mark, 342 in Luke and 232 in John, which he called canons. These were cross-referenced for each Gospel with the canon numbers for the same text in the other Gospels as well as all combinations. These became so popular that many Byzantine manuscripts contain them, as well as Nestle-Aland and the American Bible Society. Other sections of scripture to be read at Saturday and Sunday services, feast days or other weekends are called lections. These were placed in the margins or between the lines with "arc" abbreviated for "beginning" and "tel" for "end" of each section. These were frequently written in the margin in red ink, giving the day of the week for the reading. Some manuscripts were prepared with several such readings arranged in the order they would come up for reading. These are called lectionary manuscripts: those for the Gospels are called *Evangelion;* those for the Acts and Letters are called *Apostolos;* those for the church year starting with Easter are

Synaxarion; and those for saints' days and festivals starting with the civil year in September are *Menologion.* Some 2,000, starting in the 6th century, are known.

9. **Prologues and Colophons**—The prologues derive from Marcion (ca. 144 AD); he used mostly Luke's Gospel and the ten Pauline letters. He calls Ephesians Laodiceans, in different order: Galatians, 1 and 2 Corinthians, Romans, 1 and 2 Thessalonians, Laodiceans, Colossians, Philippians, and Philemon. The prologues to the personal letters of 1 and 2 Timothy, Titus, and Philemon are briefer. These contain the information of who received the letter and their nationality (e.g., the Galatians are called Greeks, whether they adhered to or fell away from the faith; the place where the letter was written ex. Galatians from Ephesus, and the person who wrote it or delivered it ex. Romans written from Corinth (by Tertius in 16:22) and carried by Phoebe the deaconess. Tertullian wrote extensively against Maricon and his system in 207. (For additional background on Maricon and this material, see Finegan p. 36.) The colophon is placed at the end of a book, giving the name of the scribe who copied it, other information about the book, information on his labor or a prayer, or warning about altering the book. In essence, Revelation 22:16–19 is a colophon. Eusebius gives this colophon to Irenaeus's *The Ogdoad,* which we no longer have: "I adjure you who shall copy out this book, by our Lord Jesus Christ and by his glorious advent when he comes to judge the living and the dead, that you compare what you copy, and correct it carefully by this transcript from which you copy, and that you likewise copy this adjuration and put it in the transcript." Some call this a Coronis or crown as a finisher.

10. **Stichometry and Euthaliana**—Greek letters in the margin are also numbers which correspond to a line of hexameter verse (such as in Homer or Virgil), of 34–38

letters, corresponding to 15–16 syllables, the amount that could be read in one breath (since everyone read aloud even to oneself). The number of stichoi was probably used also to pay the professional scribe a set price per stichoi. In 301 AD Diocletian set the wages of scribes at 25 denarii per 100 lines of the first quality and 20 denarii for 100 lines of the 2nd quality (the difference was not defined). At these prices Codex Sinaiticus, would cost ca. 30,000 denarii. Under Caracalla (211–17), a legionary was paid 750 denarii per year. This would be 40 years wages, although inflation is not taken into account. Manuscripts produced in monasteries were thus free from the cost factor.

In Codex Sinaiticus these are given for Paul's letters, but nowhere else. A particular scribe probably copied this section. Texts usually were copied in units of sense or space-lines called a comma or colon, thus colometry. The scribe Hermas says he copied a little scroll of heavenly origin "letter by letter, for I could not make out the syllables." The Euthaliana is associated with the name of Euthalius who wrote about Maris and Cyril both of whom were condemned at the 2nd Council of Constantinople in 553; he had been dated to about 650 AD. He collected much information on the life of Paul, the date of his memorial feast at Rome (June 29), a chronology of the life of Paul, short summaries of the Pauline letters, and the statement that Onesimus in Philemon underwent martyrdom at Rome under Tertullus by breaking his legs.

11. **Paleography**—Deals with handwriting and covers everything discussed herein, as to the date for a particular manuscript. Handwriting tends to change over narrow periods of time. Old Hebrew is different from Modern Hebrew, or Iron Age inscriptions from Persian, Hellenistic, or Herodian. Types of abbreviations are introduced or change with time.

After all, even an individual's handwriting changes. In fact, I recently realized that I have changed my signature four times already, or about once every 15 years. The differences in scribes writing helps identify how many scribes worked on any particular manuscript. This was even used by the scholars working on the DSS, who with small scraps were able to match up disconnected pieces by the handwriting characteristics. Eventually the numerous pieces could be fitted together like a jigsaw puzzle.

We have already seen that the Uncial manuscripts tend to be the oldest. The contents also help date a document when a date is given (such as the earliest dated copy of the Gospels in minuscule Greek in the Public Library of Leningrad May 7, 6343 (in the year of the world = 835); or a historical situation is mentioned, such as the battle of Actium on September 2, 31 BC; or Issus on November 333 BC; or some historical person is mentioned as having just died. Finding a fragment in a tightly controlled archaeological excavation also narrows the time period.

This is a brief summary of this subject (for information that is more complete see Finegan or Metzger).

One could reasonably ask, is there an original manuscript I could photograph? Unfortunately the answer is no—all have been destroyed. In fact, a case could be made that the original of Jeremiah was the first to be destroyed (see Jer 36:1–32;) v. 28 represents the 2nd edition (composed ca. 606 BC).

Most churches will have a doctrinal statement such as this: We believe that the Bible is the word of God, consisting of the 66 books of the Old and New Testament, is verbally inspired of God, and inerrant in the original writings and that they are the supreme and final authority in faith and life (2 Tm 3:16; 2 Pt 1:19–21).

Since we have no originals and the ones we do have consist of variant readings, the quest has always been to restore the text to as close to the original as possible. Thus, the search is on for the oldest text available. The thought being that the oldest will have fewer errors due to its being copied less often. (See the section on Masoretic text copying errors and the Dead Sea Scrolls.) The DSS pushed the age of copies of the Old Testament back from their discovery in 1947 to the oldest Old Testament text of 1008, or 939 years, and for the oldest fragments back to 280 BC, or 1,227 years. Moreover, many original readings and better readings were found. Overall, they showed that even this degree of copying produced a text little changed from the one we are all accustomed to read.

The New Testament is closer in time but suffers from the same problems of copying. The Textus Receptus or Received Text derives mostly from the Syriac Peshitta (simple or common) of 380 AD. The oldest example is Codex Alexandrinus (A) in the Gospels and most of the minuscules are the Syrian text. The Coptic version of Egypt is also an early translation using Greek and seven demotic characters, previously copied in hieroglyphics of demotic and hieratic until Christian times. By 405 AD, the Peshitta did not contain 2 Peter, 2 and 3 John, Jude or Revelation.

The Samaritan Pentateuch, closely related to Hebrew, developed from 432 BC when Manasseh, the son-in-law of Sanballat took a Torah copy with him when he was forced to leave Jerusalem (Neh 13:28). He built the sanctuary on Mt. Gerizim (Josephus Ant. 11.8). Continued Hebrew copying resulted in the Talmud Mishna of 180–200 AD, which has no quotes from Nehemiah, Daniel, Obadiah, Nahum, Habakkuk, or Zephaniah. By the time the Greek LXX was translated from the Hebrew (ca. 250 BC), this became the copy most used in New Testament times. In fact, most New Testament quotes are from the LXX rather than the Hebrew. Our two oldest copies of the LXX are the Codex Vaticanus and Codex Sinaiticus.

Important Witnesses to the New Testament

The parchment uncials are identified or indexed by English capital letters or numbers, generally in the order found. When

Sinaiticus was found all the letters had been assigned, so it was given the first letter of the Hebrew alphabet.

Codex Vaticanus—(known as B or 03). Dates to ca. 340 AD. It first appeared in the Vatican library catalogue of 1475. Neglected until the 19th century, library officials placed continued obstacles in the way of scholars wishing to study it. Dr. Constantin von Tischendorf (finder of Sinaiticus) in 1843 could not take notes with pen and ink or have any paper on him (he was searched both before and after a visit) and was forced to memorize the entire 759 leaves, eight leaves at a time.

Originally a complete Bible in Greek, the pages are 11 x 11 inches with three columns per page and written in brown ink with 40–44 lines per column. The Old Testament on 617 leaves is missing Genesis 1–46 and 30 Psalms, but contains the Apocrypha, except for I and II Maccabes (possibly an oversight) and Psalm 151. The New Testament on 142 leaves is missing Hebrews 9:14 to the end, 1 and 2 Timothy, Titus, Philemon, and Revelation. It has primitive chapter divisions: the end of Galatians is #58, Ephesians has #70, Philippians, Colossians, 1 and 2 Thessalonians were grouped together with #93, followed by Hebrews #59. This shows that in a previous manuscript ancestor Hebrews followed Galatians. And 2 Peter had no chapter divisions, indicating that it was still not considered canonical. The lack of ornamentation was the basis for dating it slightly older than Sinaiticus.

The New Testament book order agrees with that of Athanasius' 39th Festal Letter written in 367, probably by Alexandrian scribes during his stay in Rome in 340 AD, by order of the Emperor Constans. One school of thought holds that this and Sinaiticus were two of the 50 books ordered by Constantine from Eusebius in 331 AD. Another holds that this is a reject copy due to the missing Maccabees, the lack of Eusebian canon tables, and the many corrections by different scribes. One scribe wrote the Old Testament and another wrote the New Testament.

Codex Sinaiticus—(known as Aleph or 01) dates to 350 AD. Part was discovered in 1844 by Dr. Tischendorf when he saw a basket of scraps to be burned in the monastery oven and was told that two baskets had already been burned; the rest in 1859 by Dr. Tischendorf, when he visited Mt. Sinai again. It contains the complete New Testament. John 21:24 ended the book; later the Coronis was erased and v. 25 added. It contains I and IV Maccabees, II Esdras, Tobit, Judith, Wisdom, and Sirach; the Epistle of Barnabas and the Shepherd of Hermas are both appended at the end of the New Testament. Originally a complete Bible of 730 leaves; only 405.5 plus 14 fragments survive today [BAR 33(6): 41 (07)], 267.5 of the Old Testament and Apocrypha, and 148 in the New Testament.

The pages are 15 by 13.5 inches with four columns per page in pale brown ink. It has 48 lines to the column written on the lines, 12–16 letters per line. Three scribes worked on it, one doing most of the New Testament from a written exemplar; a part of the Old Testament was copied by dictation due to phonetic errors. A later scribe added the Eusebian canon tables in the New Testament. Tischendorf noted some 14,800 corrections. A colophon at the end of Esdras and Esther has this statement: that the manuscript was corrected from "a very ancient manuscript by the hand of the holy martyr Pamphilus" of Caesarea (Eusebius's teacher, who died in 310). After the Russian revolution, the British Museum purchased it for $500,000; it arrived December 25, 1933. (The fascinating details of the discovery and other information are found in Finegan, Metzger, and Cobern.)

Codex Alexandrinus—(known as A or 02) dates to 400–450 AD. A 17th century note in the flyleaf says it was a gift to the Patriarchal Library of Alexandria in 1098. A 13th or 14th century note in Arabic on the first leaf of Genesis says the manuscript belonged to the Patriarchal Library in Cairo. The ornamentation at the beginning of books is in red, and panel-shaped tailpieces or colophons are at the end with inclusion of material, from Eusebius d. 339 and Athanasius d. 373, before the Psalms would require a date later than 373.

Originally 822 leaves, there are now only 773 leaves measuring 13 by 10.5 inches. Each contains two columns of text with 46–52 lines per column and 20–25 letters per line. The Old Testament is on 630 leaves and the New Testament on 143. Several mutilations of the Old Testament exist. Of the New Testament, Matthew 1–25:6, John 6:50–8:52, 2 Corinthians 4:13–12:6, and I and II Clement are missing. It was sent to King Charles I in 1627 by Cyril Lucar Patriarch of Constantinople and missed being included in the KJV of 1611. Two scribes wrote the Old Testament with the first writing the New Testament also. The original scribes and others made several corrections. Mostly it is Alexandrian in text, but the Gospels are the oldest Byzantine type text.

Codex Bezea Cantabrigiensis—(known as D or 05). It dates to the 4th century. A bilingual text, in Greek on the left and Latin on the right, on 409 leaves, in a single column, on ten by eight inch leaves. It contains the Gospels (with some gaps) and Acts, plus one leaf of 3 John v. 11–15. The Gospels are in the Western order: Matthew, John, Luke, and Mark. Written in brown ink in cola-lines with the first three lines in red, it has more remarkable variations and unique readings than any other text. (See Luke 6:4 for a verse added extra.) This was probably a private Bible and did not contain the Old Testament; some nine different hands corrected it. It was presented to Cambridge in 1581 by Theodore Beza, Calvin's successor. It contained the statement at Luke 23:53 that Joseph of Arimathea "put before the tomb a [great] stone which twenty men could scarcely move." It is the principal authority for the verse inserted after Matthew 20:28; found only in one other uncial F, the Old Latin, Curetonian Syriac and several Vulgate, similar to the passage in Luke 14:8–10, except the emphasis is on dining (Metzger p. 50).

Codex Ephraemi Rescriptus—(known as C or 04). It dates to 345 AD. It is a palimpsest of the Bible, which was erased in the 12th century and its sheets printed with 38 sermons of St. Ephraem, a Syrian Church Father of the 4th century. Only 145 leaves of the New Testament are extant, about 5/8 of the original (only 2 Thessalonians and 2 John are missing). The Old Testament has 64 left. Two correctors worked on it, one in Palestine in the 6th century, and the other in Constantinople in the 9th century.

Codex Washingtonensis—(known as W or 032) dates to 390–410 AD. It has 187 leaves of very mixed text types, apparently because its ancestor was pieced together from fragments after Diocletian's attempt to crush Christianity. It contains the only known reference mentioned by Jerome at the end of Mark 16:14: "And they excused themselves, saying, 'This age of lawlessness and unbelief is under Satan, who does not allow the truth and power of God to prevail over the unclean things of the spirits. Therefore reveal thy righteousness now.' Thus they spoke to Christ. Moreover, Christ replied to them, 'The term of years for Satan's power has been fulfilled, but other terrible things draw near. And for those who have sinned I was delivered over to death, that they may return to the truth and sin no more; that they may inherit the spiritual and incorruptible glory of righteousness which is in heaven.'"

The first five above constitute the oldest and most important of the uncials. The papyri uncials give us the next most important class of witnesses to the original text. Most date from the 2nd–5th century, and the latest in the group dates to the 7th century. These are identified by **P**, usually in Old German, and a superscript number, as these are discovered they are published and new numbers given in Zeitschrift fur die neutestamentliche

Wissenschaft or ZNW, all are codices except for **P**[12,13,18 and 43]; these include:

P[52]—The Rylands John fragment, our oldest piece of the New Testament, dated 125 AD. Discovered at Oxyrynchus Egypt by Grenfell and Hunt expedition in 1920, but not identified until 1934 by C.H. Roberts. Contains John 18:31–33 and on verso side vs. 37–38.

P[77]—Oxyrhynchus 2683, ca. 190 AD. Contains Matthew 23:30–39 one of the oldest known.

P[64]—Ca. 180–200 AD. Contains Matthew 26:7, 10, 14–15, 22–23 and 31–33.

P[66]—Bodmer II in Geneva from 150–200 AD. Consists of six quires, of which 104 pp remain. Contains John 1–6:11 and 35b; an additional 46 leaves of 14:15, 26, 29–21:9 were found later. A space shows that it did not contain 7:53–8:11 (woman taken in adultery) or 5:3b–4 (moving of the water at Bethesda); 1:16 reads God (Theos) rather than Son (huios). 7:52 reads "the" prophet.

P[46]—Chester Beatty II in Dublin from 200 AD; has 86 of 104 leaves (folio p. 52 is the center); has order in decreasing length: seven leaves lost, Romans 5:17–Chap. 27 with gaps, Heb., 1 and 2 Corinthians, Ephesians, Galatians, Philippians, Colossians, 1 Thessalonians to its end, seven leaves lost (two for 2 Thessalonians, and five blank (?), since 1 and 2 Timothy, Titus, and Philemon would require 10). The Doxology in Romans 14 is placed at the end of chapter 15.

P[72]—A Bodmer Papyri of 210 AD. Contains the oldest copy of Jude and 1 and 2 Peter, along with a miscellaneous assortment in the order: The Nativity of Mary, apocryphal correspondence of Paul to the Corinthians, 11th Ode of Solomon, Jude, Malito's Homily on the Passover, a Hymn fragment, the Apology of Phileas, Psalm 33 and 34, and 1 and 2 Peter. It appears to be a personal collection written by four scribes.

P[75]—A Bodmer Papyri of 175–225 AD. Contains 102 of 144 leaves of Luke and John. Those of Luke are the oldest known.

P[45]—Chester Beatty I of 250 AD. Has two leaf quires, 31 of 220 leaves preserved. Has two fragmentary leaves of Matthew and John, six leaves of Mark, seven leaves of Luke, 13 leaves of Acts with one leaf of Matthew in Vienna.

P[47]—Chester Beatty III of ca. 265 AD. Has ten damaged leaves out of 32 of Revelation 9:10–17:2 (middle portion of book).

With the bewildering assortment of variant texts, it became necessary to establish "canons" or rules in order to make selections; these include:

1. No reading is preferable unless some ancient witness supports it. Older is better.
2. The shorter reading is preferred. Assumes nothing has been added to improve or change the reading. No extra details have been added.
3. The harder reading is preferred. Assumes that changes have smoothed out the reading.
4. Choose the one from which the others could have developed.
5. Choose the one most characteristic of the author of the document. The style of writing should be consistent throughout.

New Testament Apocrypha and Pseudepigraphia

Just as additional literature developed to fill the voids in the Old Testament, the same occurred for the New Testament. A more thorough discussion can be found in the IB articles of E.J. Goodspeed Vol. I p. 63 and H. J. Cadbury Vol. VII, p. 32. These include:

Sayings of Jesus found at Oxyrhynchus in Egypt, many of which are probably original and fit John 21:25.

Seven Epistles of Ignatius (115 AD), Bishop of Antioch.

Protoevangelism of James (ca. 150 AD). Legendary account of Mary; the oldest is Papyrus Bodmer VII $\mathbf{P}^{72}$ of the 3rd century.

Shepherd of Hermas (ca. 140 AD). A brother of Pius, Bishop of Rome (140–150 AD), mentions Clement. Considered to be scripture by many, it is found in Codex Siniaticus.

The Didache (Teachings of the 12 Apostles; ca. 150 AD).

Epistle of Barnabas (80–150 AD) found in Codex Siniaticus. Mentions the destruction of Herod's temple in 70 AD.

I Epistle of Clement to the Corinthians (ca. 95 AD). Written from Rome.

II Clement (ca. 150 AD): an anonymous sermon.

Epistle of Polycarp (155 AD) Bishop of Smyrna.

Epistles to Diognetus (250 AD author's name lost).

Martyrdom of Polycarp.

Acts of Peter.

Acts of John.

Acts of Paul and Thekla (150 AD), known to Tertullian (160–228 AD). Thekla is now known to be real, as an inscription in remembrance of her martyrdom was found in the church of St. Menas in N. Cyprus (Coburn p. 237).

Gospel of Mary contains missing material from the childhood of Jesus. Includes the story of Jesus making a sparrow out of clay (also quoted in the Koran, The Table 5:110, and The Imrans 3:49) and stretching wood to size so it doesn't need to be cut.

Gospel of Judas, recently found in Coptic, dates to about 400 AD. This could not be by Judas, as he died the same day as Jesus and it would not occur to him to write a Gospel this early. Originally composed 130–170 AD.

Gospel of Peter.

Gospel of Thomas, the most famous found at Nag Hammadi Egypt in Coptic and dates from 340 AD. A Gnostic work, same as the Gospel of Judas (original composed from 50–140 AD). Four fragments in Greek were found at Oxryhynchus Egypt dating from 190 AD.

Gospel according to the Hebrews dates to 80–150 AD.

Gospel according to the Egyptians dates to 80–150 AD.

Revelation of Peter (ca. 150 AD).

The Unknown Gospel (ca. 150 AD).

Acts of Andrew.

Acts of John.

Tradition of Matthias.

Nazarene Gospel.

Laodiceans.

III Corinthians.

Information on Clement and the Church fathers are mentioned and discussed in Eusebius.

CHAPTER 12

ARCHAEOLOGY OF THE OLD TESTAMENT

MODERN ARCHAEOLOGY BEGAN with Napoleons Nile Valley expedition of 1798. For those interested in this subject, the major discoveries are listed below with a short description of its importance, in the order of the discoveries. While palaces, gates and shrines or the everyday homes of ancient people shed light on the culture, inscriptional material is the prize that all archaeologists yearn for.

It is only through texts written near the time of the Biblical events that many of the strange customs of their day can be understood. Otherwise, the implications of the laws of hospitality of Lot and Jael to protect a guest at the expense of everyone in the household would escape us. The laws of seducing a virgin, the giving of a handmaid as a secondary wife, levirate marriage, and all types of covenants would leave us in the dark.

Rosetta Stone (1799): Deciphered by the brilliant work of Jean Francois Champollion in 1818. Originally thought to be comprised of black basalt, when recently cleaned in 1999, its restored pristine state revealed it to be grey granodiorite with pink veining (Fagan p. 260); the stela contained a trilingual inscription in Greek, Egyptian demotic. and Egyptian hieroglyphics. The Greek could be easily read and soon the other scripts were cracked. The missing hieroglyphics were found on a stela at Hermopolis Parva in the Delta in 1898 and at the Temple of Isis at Philae near Aswan. Duplicate copies were often made.

Behistun Inscription (1835): An inscription of Darius I (who fought the Battle of Marathon in 490 BC) written on a cliff face, 225 feet up, at the sacred mountain of Semiramis in three languages: Old Persian (vaguely similar to Aramaic) in the center with 515 lines in four columns, plus an appendix (an alphabetic script invented [?] by Darius); Elamite in 650 lines; and Akkadian in 112 lines: both lack the appendix (Cook p. 100; FRB p. 70; Time Life Books Cradle of Civilization p. 136; AO Sept/Oct 2005 p. 30; www//livius.org/be-bm/behistun/behistun0.1html). The Old Persian was read with difficulty in 1847 by Henry Rawlinson, who first studied it in 1844, and the other two soon followed, the last the Akkadian or Babylonian in 1850. The monument was restudied in 1857, 1903–4 and completed by George C. Cameron of the U. of Michigan in 1948. (See J. of Cuneiform Studies 10: 1 [56].)

Some doubted that the chicken scratch cuneiform could actually be read, so an interesting test was devised. On May 29, 1857, a four-way translation of a newly found tablet of Tiglath-Pileser I was proposed. When compared, the results were beyond doubt. All the old Babylonian and Assyrian tablets, which had been piling up (some 500,000 are now known, only a small part of those still awaiting to be found), could now be read, (BAR 31(2): 39 (05); Wellard p. 72–81). An Aramaic papyrus copy of the Inscription was found at Elephantine (Aswan) Egypt and a black diorite copy was found at Babylon (Wycliffe p. 271–3). The Oriental Institute of the U. of Chicago now has the task of editing the Assyrian Dictionary, as new tablets are found and word meanings are clarified. Scholars have become so proficient, that grammar mistakes in Egyptian, Assyrian, and Babylonian can now be corrected.

Sargon's Palace (1843): At Khorsabad (Dur-Sharrukin or Sargonsburg). The local Arabs knew the site as Sar'un, a corruption of the name (Gadd p. 17). The only reference in the Bible is Isaiah 20:1. We knew nothing of him until this discovery. Some thought he was fictitious. He now should be identified as Sargon III rather than the usual Sargon II (Free p. 195).

Black Obelisk of Shalmaneser III (1846): Found in a courtyard at Calah by Austin Henry Layard (see part of the account in RPNF pp. 36–44; FRB p. 108). The Citadel contained the palaces of Shalmaneser I and II as well as Ashurnasirpal II, whose palace covered 4000 ft². It dates from 841 BC, has carvings on all four sides, and 210 lines of cuneiform inscriptions: shows Jehu, or more likely his emissary, of the House of Omri, [BAR 21(1): 26 (95); 29(5): 50 (03)]. A second fragment covering the 2nd year was found at Assur (the old city from which Assyria gets its name, Kalah Sherkat).

Moabite Stone (1868): Found at Dibon (Arabic Dhiban) Jordan in Moab by F. Klein, a French missionary from Alsace (his nationality was involuntarily changed to German when they took over the region). A paper squeeze was made but soon after, Arabs in 1873 destroyed the stone to increase its value and hid the pieces in their granaries as a good luck charm. Its 34 lines of Moabite (Hebrew) script tell of the liberation of Moab by Mesha from Ahab of Israel. The men of Gad are mentioned, but Reuben, who lived in this area, is the first tribe to disappear. The House of David and YHWH are also mentioned for the first time—dates to around 830 BC. As many of the pieces as could be, were recovered (some 67.3%) and taken to the Louvre in 1873. The squeeze provided the full translation (BAR 28[1]: 38 [02]); some of the conflicting accounts of events are corrected in TWLSGF p. 497.

Tell El Amarna Letters (1887): Found by a peasant woman at the Royal Archives of Akhenaton's capital. Since the definitive count by J.A. Knudtzon of 382, some 24 others have now been identified. Many show the unrest in Palestine due to the Habiru (the dusty ones or those who cross a boundary also "bandits"; HJP p. 17–19; Frank p. 74 or Kitchen p. 69). Unfortunately, some 150–200 others were completely destroyed by poor handling or packing and a like amount broken or seriously damaged (Campbell p. 33). At least five kings are mentioned. In letter EA 289 Lab'ayu is accused by Abdu-Heba of Jerusalem (Urusalim) of turning Shechem over to the 'Apiru (Shechem was not captured by Joshua). Letter EA 287 says the same thing only Shechem is not mentioned by name. (For the relationship between the Habiru and 'Apiru see HJP p. 41.)

Merneptah Stela (1897): Found by William M. Flinders Petrie in Merneptah's mortuary temple at Thebes. A fragmentary duplicate is in the temple at Karnak. The original Hymn of Amenhotep III is on the back before Merneptah usurped it; it stood originally behind the Colossi of Memmon at Thebes. The 28 lines commemorate a victory over the Libyans in his fifth regnal year of 1231 or 1207 BC, depending on which chronology of the 18th Dynasty is used. Israel is mentioned for the first time in the penultimate line: "Plundered is the Canaan with every evil; Carried off is Ashkelon; seized upon is Gezer; Yanoam (near the Sea of Galilee) is made as that which does not exist; Israel is laid waste, his seed is not." The hieroglyph determinative before Israel is for a people, not a country or nation. This would place it in the period of the Judges before consolidation of Israel under Saul, (BAR 19[5]: 50 [93]; Kitchen p. 59).

Oxryhynchus Papyri (1897–1907): Contains over 2,506 manuscripts and fragments covering letters, legal contracts, poems, sermons and hymns as well as the oldest fragment of John. Found in a trash dump and crocodile cemetery; published in 29 volumes. They shed light on Koine Greek of the 1–3rd centuries.

Code of Hammurapi (more correct 'Ammurapi; 1901): Found by Morgan at Suza. It had been carried there from the Esagila (the lofty house) temple of Marduk in Babylon by an Elamite raider as a trophy of war. Its 3,964 lines is a book written on black diorite. The law was commissioned in his second year or 1726 (or 1758) BC, but it contains material in the prologue from later in his reign. Some 282 laws are covered and 35 crimes are punishable by death. The last 35 lines were erased, but the Elamite king's inscription was never cut. The missing lines are restored from a fragmentary law court copy. At present, of the preserved words, only one word in par.137 is uncertain. A statement is made on the stone: "The oppressed . . . shall (have) read the writing . . . and he shall find his right," which indicates that the common citizen was able to read (or have it read to him; ANE Vol. I, p. 138). There are six older law codes than Moses, the oldest is from Ebla 2500 BC, [Wiseman p. 27, Finigan p. 53–5; BAR 28(5): 29 (02)], next is Urukagina of Lagash 2378 BC, next is Ur-Nammu of Ur ca 2100 BC in two damaged copies, next is Bilalama of Eshnunna 1919 BC, in Akkadian there are two copies on two tablets broken at par. 60 preserving 48 sections, next is Lipit-Ishtar of Isin 1868–1857 BC with 38 regulations in the existing half or several fragments that remains followed by Hammurabi, then Moses of ca. 1400 BC.

Elephantine Papyri (1903): Found at Aswan Egypt. The documents are in Aramaic from the Jewish colony stationed there and covers the period 500–400 BC. They are mostly marriage and divorce contracts. Several people are mentioned here and in Nehemiah, including Sanballat and Johanan the High Priest; date the monarch Nehemiah served under as Artaxerxes I, (UOT pp. 306 and 310 and ANE p. 278).

Hittite Monuments at Boghazkeui (gorge village; 1906): Found by Sayce in 1880, who identified the Hatti as occupying central Turkey. Their language was an early form of Indo-European (Scientific American March 1990 p. 110). Before this, these people were mentioned only in the Bible (Gn 10:15; 23:3 [Kitchen p. 154; Time/Life Books *The Emergence of Man: The Empire Builders* 1974; *Lost Civilizations: Anatolia* 1995; Bible; and Spade 8: 10 (95)].

Tutankhamun's Tomb (1922): Found by Howard Carter. Although the tomb was plundered of about 10% of its gold, silver and precious oils (60% of the jewelry in the treasury) on at least two occasions after 1352 or 1327 BC, the fabulous artifacts found here for a relatively nobody king still cause the mouth to drool. What would an unplundered tomb of a Thutmose III or a Ramses II hold? Noblecourt p. 61. A new CAT scan led to the conclusion that Tut didn't have a skull fracture, but did have a broken leg that may have led to gangrene.

Ur-Nammu Stela (1922–34): Discovered by C. L. Woolley in over 100 fragments around the Ziggurat. It dates to 2112 BC. The reassembled 10.5 x 5 foot stele shows Ur-Nammu starting construction on the Ziggurat in five registers of pictures and text. Actually, not all fragments were added, one is in the British Museum. A disconnected pair of woman's feet and others of goat's hoof, wrestlers, chariots, angels and a god (from the Univ. of Penn. storerooms) indicated the reconstruction was incorrect. In 1987, the stela was taken apart at the suggestion of Dr. Jeanny V. Canby (deceased in 2007), but problems and her death prevented a timely reconstruction. Some two-thirds of the stela are now known. The first register shows the earliest representation of flying angels (Woolley p. 159).

Sarcophagus of Ahiram of Gebal (Byblos; 1923): Discovered by Montet, dates to 975 BC. Has five lines of Phoenician-Hebrew script and shows a cherub.

Nuzi Tablets (1925–31): Southwest of Kirkuk Iraq, about 12 miles. Excavated by Edward Chiera. The several thousand tablets shed light on the Hurrians or Horites of 1400–1300 BC.

Another group of people resurrected from the ash dump of history. The older name of the city was Gasur. Mainly they illuminate the period of Abraham and the Patriarchs. Childless states, transference of the birthright, marriage customs and the teraphim or household gods are now fully understood [HJP p. 39; New Bible; and Spade 10: 65 (81); Bible; and Spade 7: 27 (94). An early double accounting method using tokens was also found (Scientific American June 1978 p. 50).

Ras Shamra (Hill of Fennel) Texts (1929–50): Several hundred clay tablets were found between the Temples of Baal and Dagon in the city of Ugarit by C.F.A. Schaeffer. A peasant's plow broke into a tomb in 1928. They date to 1400–1300 BC. Cyrus Gordon worked out the script for the Canaanite alphabetic cuneiform related to Hebrew, many lost words, grammatical forms and syntactical usages previously unrecognized were found (Kitchen p. 160–5 and Wycliffe p. 229–31). From these we learn of the Canaanite pantheon of El, his consort Asherah and his son Baal the god of storms and fertility, with his brother Mot(h) the god of death and the underworld and their sister Anath the war goddess; allied to these was Kothar the god of crafts and equivalent to the Greek Hephaestus (HJP p. 11).

Mari Letters and Lachish Ostraca (1934–38): Some 25,000 cuneiform tablets (5000 were written to Zimri-Lim) found at Mari in East Syria just inside the Iraq border by Andre Parrot after Bedouins found a headless stone statue in 1933. Excavated from 1933–39 and 1951–56. The palace of Zimri-Lim had 300 rooms and covers over 15 acres including correspondence to Hammurabi of 1760 BC and covers the period of Genesis 26–34 or the 19–17 century BC. He sent five kg of tin to Wari-Taldu of Laish (Dan) and 35 kg to Ibni-Adad king of Hazor in three shipments. Even these small shipments, to make bronze, were diplomatically important. A people known as Mari-Yamina (Binu-Yamina sons of the South) is similar to Benjamin, [Kitchen p. 43–50, Wycliffe p. 40–1; ABR 5: 105 (92)].

One letter decrees a census of nomads within his territory. The first written record of the term "Canaanite" appears in these records, Mazar p. 189.

J.L. Starkey found eighteen of the twenty-one Lachish Ostraca in a gate guardroom in 1935. Written by Hoshaiah, an outpost commander in the hills to the East, to Yaush the commander at Lachish. They describe the advance of the Babylonian army toward Jerusalem. One says the signal fires of Azekah (to the North) could no longer be seen, indicating Lachish (Jer 34: 7) was the next target. One starts "in the 9th year." It was in the 9th year of Zedekiah that the siege of Jerusalem started in 588 BC.

Dead Sea Scrolls (1947–56): Old Testament scrolls 1000–1250 years older than any previous. See the separate chapter.

Jarmo (1948): Excavated by R.J. and Linda Braidwood in Iraq 30 mi West of Kirkuk. Stone house foundations dated to 6500 BC. One of the early sites for development of village life. Obsidian was imported from Lake Van 250 mi away. Sheep, goat, pig and oxen bones show animal domestication, but grain was gathered wild; no hoes were found (Wycliffe p. 8–9).

Derbe (1956 and 62): This site on Paul's first missionary journey was identified and confirmed by inscriptions on the dates shown. Since it is 60 mi from Lystra in Acts 14:20, this verse should now be read with the understanding of "for or toward" Derbe.

Ebla (Tell Mardika; 1975): A name known only from some cuneiform documents until the site was identified by Paolo Matthiae and Alfonso Archi, South of Aleppo, Syria. It is a site of 2300 acres. Some 20,000 tablets covers the period of Sargon I 2350–2295 BC who is mentioned during the reign of Ebrum=Eber (Gn 10:24–5 and 11:14–7). The country flourished from 2400–2250 BC and was destroyed by Naram-Sin of Akkad=Agade, in 2250 BC. Many Biblical type names are known such as Ab-ra-mu, E-sa-u, Da-u-dum, Sa-u-lum=Saul,

Mi-ka-ilu=Michael, Hazor, Kish and Gaza, (BAR 18(3): 4 (92); 9(6): 74 (83), BA 39: 94 (76), Arch. 24(1): 55 (71), TWLSGF p. 589 and CBMW).

It is unfortunate that the politics of Syria entered into the archaeological results. Anything related to Israel had to be suppressed and the Italian team was essentially blackmailed if they wanted to continue digging. Name endings IL or YA points to a "god" Ya at Ebla. This is one they had to retract [see BAR 6(5): 42 (80), 8(1): 54 (82); BR 8(2): 24 (92)]. Some 100 gods are known; if divine epithets are eliminated about forty gods and goddesses are left, about the same as in Akkadian, Ugaritic and Canaanite, Eblaitica Vol. 2 p. 80, 1990. The patron god of Ebla was DA BI IR (Pestilence) = Hebrew DEBER [Bible and Spade 9: 71 (80)], also known as Rasap or in the Bible as Reshef. The goddess of new wine was TE RI ISH TU= Hebrew TIROSH. E DA BAR (KI) = Temple of the Word. Nimrod, the etymology now appears to be an animal name plus a god, as Ebalite DA SI MA AD the He goat of the Grand or Ugaritic NI MI RI YA the Panther of YA, thus Nimrod is Panther of Hadd= Hadad or Baal. The goddess Adum (meaning red or earth), a consort of Reshef, is found in Obed Adom (2 Sm 6:10) as Servant of the goddess Adom, rather than the Masoretic form Edom. Astar (grammatically masculine) has its Akkadian counterpart Ishtar, Summerian Inanna and the Canaanite Athtar identified with Venus as the morning star. Astapil, a counterpart to Astarte (a second aspect of Venus as the evening star). Kabkab (the Star) is actually found in Amos 5:26 along with Sakkuth and Kokab as other gods. Lahmu appears in a Cannanite name Bethlehem (meaning the House/Temple (of the god) Lahmu) that means "hairy" a Canaanite god of war, Eblatica Vol. II, p. 79. Did Ebalites originate from the Tigris? NI DA KUL= I DA QUL= Hebrew Hiddeqel=Tigris. The Hebrew root HMT generally means Wrath or Fury but on occasion, this context does not fit. Ebalite I MA TU has a meaning wife also Egyptian

HM T and Ugaritic HM HM T (pregnancy or impregnation). In Proverbs 6:34, "fury" becomes the subject of the sentence and the verb QIN e AH now means "incite jealousy", read vs. 32–33, He who commits adultery lacks sense; he who violates a woman destroys himself. Blows and shame will he find, and his disgrace will never be wiped away. vs. 34–35, If a woman incites her husband to jealousy, he will not spare ... on the day of vengeance. No payment will placate him, nor will he accept though she offer an enormous bribe. Psalm 76:11 has two "wraths". Read: Indeed women, men will praise you, the offspring of women will surround you.

Khirbet el-Kom Aramaic hoard: About 1000 ostraca began to show up on the antiquities market beginning in 1970–1983. Many are dated between 362–312 BC. Mentioned are Artaxerses I and II, Alexander the Great and his general Philip Antigonus. #3 is dated the 6th year the 12th of Tammuz, probably of Ptolemy II Philadelphus or July 25, 277 BC. A name Maqqedah occurs several times and is likely el-Kom itself; it is mentioned in Joshua 10, about 15 miles West of Hebron. Several temples are mentioned including a new one to Yahweh called Beth Yaho. The same name is used for the Temple at Elephantine, Egypt, destroyed in a an anti-Jewish riot in 410 BC and finally disappeared in 398 BC, a Temple of Uzza (known from Nabatean inscriptions) and the Temple of Nabu of Mesopotamian origin. Two names are interesting: the father is Hananyah (the Yah is a theophoric element) and his son is Qoshanah (Qos is an Edomite diety), indicating a mixture of ethnic/religious communities, (BAR 30(4): 38 (04); TWLSGF p. 545).

Tel Dan stela (1994): Three fragments have been found which mention "the House of David', BAR 20(5): 22 (94).

The pictures drawn on tombs or walls in Egypt, Etruscan, Syria, Hittite and Assyrian or Babylonian and Persian palaces or cylinder seals; Greek vases, and a myriad other artifacts convey a wealth of information on how things work (such as the small model scenes of weaving, butchering, brewing, etc., placed in Egyptian tombs) clothing, jewelry, weapons and battle tactics are shown. Truly, pictures are worth more than 10,000 words. For more on annals, treaties, war reliefs, tablets and text cashes see ECIAT pp. 144–6.

Tell—This word means a mound (Jos 11:13; Jer 30:18); many Arabic place names in Egypt, Israel and Mesopotamia still use this word; in Turkey Huyuk= mound. The KJV before archaeology translated "stood in their strength," rather than "on their mounds." A recent survey completed in 1952 in Iraq found over 5000 tells (FRB p. 280).

History Corrected—The votive Stele of Benhadad I of Aram, 850 BC, was discovered at Aleppo in Syria in 1941. The Aramaic royal inscription identifies that he (contemporary of Asa and Baasha) was the same individual as the so-called Benhadad II (contemporary of Elijah and Elisha). This clears up the whole period of the Northern Kingdom from the division of the Monarchy (922 BC) to the rise of Jehu (842 BC) and authenticates the dynasty of the Aramean kings at Damascus in 1 Kings 15:18.

History Discovered—The recovery of the Hittites and now the Ebla kingdom has and will do much to further our understanding of the contributions of these kingdoms in the Biblical period.

The Alphabet—The oldest examples are: the Cuneiform "ABC" tablet from Ugarit of 1400 BC, the Ebenezer (Izbet Sartah) abecedary of 1200 BC, see BAR 4(3): 23 (78), the Tel Zayit abecedary (BAR 32(1): (06), the Gezer Calendar of 925 BC, and the Lachish bowl and jar contained Canaanite script identical to the Sinai Serabit el-Khadim (turquoise mines) of 1500 BC. Eighteen Proto-Canaanite signs from store jars of 1525 BC or during MB IIC/LB I were found at Gezer in 1973 (TWLSGF p. 477).

Language—It is interesting that from the study of Ebalite, Ugaritic, Akkadian, Aramaic, Minoan, Syriac and others the scribes tended to turn diphthongs into monophthongs as an aid to pronunciation, which tends to preserve some foreign accents (Eblaitica Vol. II, pp. 18, 91, 127).

Ras Shamra Tablets—Canaanite Culture versus God. The first reference to Canaan is Genesis 10:6 and 15–19. The chief god was El (Father of Years), whose wife was Asherah (pl. Asherim ex. Ex 34:13). Most frequently mentioned was Baal (god of thunder and rain), the son of El. By 900 BC, Asherah was regarded as the wife of Baal. Compare Elijah "there shall not be dew or rain" (1 Kgs 17:1); "fire from heaven" (1 Kgs 18:38). Baal often took long journeys and slept (1 Kgs 18:27). It seems God was the one in charge of the elements.

Critics have stated that the Levitical Code (P) in the Book of Leviticus was written about 500 BC by priests, and that the ceremonial laws of the Old Testament were produced later than the writings of the Prophets. These tablets date from ca. 1400 BC (near the time of Moses" death) and report:

A trespass offering (compare Lev 5:15)
A peace offering (7:37)
A burnt offering (6:9)
A wave offering (23:15)
Oblation of the 1st fruits (2:12)
New moon offering (23:23–4)
Bread of the gods (21:6)
Courtyard of the tent (6:16, 26)
Holy Place of the Holy Places (16:2)

These similarities suggest that the Ugarites and Israelites, both of Semitic stock, had received these laws and ceremonies from God in purity, but the Canaanites corrupted them. Wight p. 101 quotes: One university professor made the statement that because of the discovery of the Ras Shamra tablets, the date of the Book of Leviticus would doubtless be considered one thousand years earlier that many critics formerly allowed. The silver scroll from St. Andrews in Jerusalem dates to about 605 BC; contains the Priestly Benediction from Numbers 6:24–6, which is also said to date to the (P) redactor but was actually known before the Babylonian Captivity. So much for (P).

Canaanites practiced sacred prostitution, both male (Kedishim) and female (Kedeshoth) as a cult of fertility to (the Great Mother Goddess) insure good harvests (1 Kgs 14:23–4 and 2 Kgs 23:7). Hosea probably had this in mind (2:5, 8). Part of this cult proscribed "Thou shalt boil a kid in its mothers milk," whereas Mosaic Law stated the Israelites should not do this (Ex 23:19; 34:26; Dt 14:21). Some of the Ugaritic words have been challenged, but the principal of separating life from death is still valid [see BR 1(3): 48, 56 (85)].

The Ammonites (descendants of Lot's youngest daughter) worshiped Molock. The Moabites (descendants of Lot's eldest daughter) worshiped Chemosh (connected with Astral divination 2 Kgs 21:3, 5), parents sacrificed their children in furnaces (Lev 18:21; 20:1–5; 2 Kgs 21:6) as their highest possessions (their children) were not withheld. Even Solomon fell into this (1 Kgs 11:5).

Important Events. Abu Hureyra, Syria, near a bend of the Euphrates (now underwater from a dam), was found to be a settlement of the Natufian period, hunter-gatherers who used sickles to gather wild grain. While in the upper-most village, the change to plowing and selection of a more hardy grain type was being cultivated. Charcoal C-14 placed the age at 11,000–9,500 BC near the end of the Younger Dryas Ice Age, RPNF pp. 172–176.

Jericho. Kathleen Kenyon found the oldest walled town so far discovered (the oldest C-14 date is 9687 BC + or -107 years). Carbon-14 dated a burned house at 7800 BC. A stone defense tower buried to 30 feet had a burned house on the surviving top dated to 6800 BC, indicating the first defense's date at a minimum to 7000 BC. This was the pre-pottery Neolithic, (ADHL p. 19; EAEHL Vol. II p. 550).

Honshu. Japan has the oldest pottery from 10,000 BC, the Joman (coiled clay) culture, WBF p. 97 ref 5.

Malta and Gozo. There are some thirty megalithic stone temples dating to ca. 5000–3500 BC built partly below ground with roofs of corbelled style, containing disarticulated bones of some 7000 people. The walls of many are painted red. These buildings are older than the pyramids.

Jarmo Iraq. Stone foundations of a house in the pre-pottery Neolithic, dated by C-14 of snail shells to 6500 BC. Bones of sheep, goats, pigs and oxen indicate that animals were domesticated. Wheat was ground on grindstones, but no evidence of the hoe was found, indicating that the grain was gathered wild. Obsidian for tools was obtained from Lake Van about 250 miles away (Wycliffe p. 8). Pottery was in use from 5800 BC (Lloyd p. 34).

Tell Hassuna. NW of ancient Ashur, dates to ca. 6500 BC; this and several of the sites to follow is the region of the Garden of Eden. Much of the early development of technology occurred here. Infants were buried in clay jars with other jars nearby for food and water in the afterlife. Much of the pottery was over-fired and dates to 4200 BC (Lloyd p. 66, Wycliffe p. 9).

Catal Huyuk. (The mound at the road-fork) in Turkey is a large Neolithic village of 32 acres, dating from the 8–7 century BC. Linen dates from 5900 BC, thread died red and the oldest murals on walls date to 5850 BC. The oldest piece of linen (dated to 7000 BC) was found wrapped around an antler at Cayonu Turkey, (BAR 20(1): 24 (94); (Macqueen p. 13; Time/Life Anatolia p. 26–28, 35. Barber pp. 10, 223; WBF pp. 91, 108). By contrast the oldest silk dates to 2700 BC, and by 300 BC they were able to hit 569 x 132, or 701 threads per in² [Archaeology 39: 64 (86)].

Tell Halef (Gozan) E of Haran. Pottery, dating to 5000 BC, was fired in intense heat of a closed kiln to a porcelain-like finish. One vase shows the oldest representation of a man riding in a two wheel 8-spoked chariot. Flat stone stamp seals were in use (Wycliffe p. 10).

Tell 'Obeid, also known as Uba(e)id. Located above Ur on the Euphrates River. Discovered in 1919, excavated in 1923–4 and 37 by Leonard Woolley. The pottery wheel was in use, and closed kilns for better heat control was an important technical advance. Dome stamp seals were in use by 4000 BC. A copper panel from a Sumerian temple of 2600 BC shows the god Im-du-gud (Wycliffe p. 10). These people are older than the Sumerians and appear to have come from the east side of the Black Sea around 5000 BC, bringing an early version of the flood story with them, as well as farming and metallurgy. Many of their polysyllabic words having to do with agriculture and crafts are non-Sumerian such as: engar=farmer, udul=herdsman, shuhudak=fisherman, apin=plow, apsin=furrow, nimbar=palm, sulumb=date, tibira=metalworker, simug= smith, nangar= carpenter, addub=basket maker, ishbar=weaver, ashgab=leatherworker, pahar=potter, shidim=mason and damgar=merchant. Their obsidian came from Turkey and they tattooed their bodies like the Catal Huyuk people (WBF p. 139; RPNF p. 200).

Tepe Gawra (Great Mound), 15 mi NW of Nineveh. The oldest known bronze axe was found in the "Obeid levels. The vaulted arch found in level eight dates to ca. 3000 BC. Oldest pottery was of Halef type. A bone-playing pipe was found in the right hand of a boy's grave (Boyd p. 30).

Eridu, south of Ur in Iraq. Site of first kingdom before the flood (Sumerian King List). Eridu was dated to around 5300 BC as one of the oldest cities of the world, as the Sumerians believed in their early myths. Lowest level ca. 4500 BC contained

14 shrines built one above the other on the same site. Pottery was older than the 'Obeid ware (Wycliffe p. 11).

Erech (Ureck or Uruk), north of 'Obeid about 35 miles on the Euphrates (Gn10:10). Virgin soil was found 70 ft down, revealing 18 levels of occupation. Founded by 'Obeid people ca. 4000 BC. Originally called Kullab. It was founded by Meskiaggasher ca. 3000 BC; its fifth king was Gilgamesh, the same as in the Gilgamesh legend (he was probably a real person). Pottery was made on a spinning wheel, baked in a smothered down kiln for smoke penetration, polished, but unpainted. Rough limestone blocks formed the oldest stone pavement known. The Ziggurat (two are present) is the oldest staged temple tower found. Cylinder seals were in use for the first time. A crude pictographic script, the earliest known, comes from level IV about 3300 BC, on flat clay tablets in Sumerian (Wycliffe p. 11, Lloyd p. 55).

Jemdet Nasr, near Babylon. Bronze and stone sculpture developed to a fine art. Trade was highly developed. An advanced pictographic cuneiform script was developed, and the full light of history entered for the first time ca. 3000 BC (Wycliffe p. 12).

Advance of Knowledge

Sumerians of lower Euphrates (Ur 2800–2400 BC). Developed:

1. The first literature from a script, the origin of which is not known (ca. 2800 BC). It was still used in writing until 76 AD on an astrological text (Saggs p. 378; CBMW p. 122; Oats p. 189). Discontinued as a spoken language ca. 1800 BC.
2. By 2180 BC, the Babylonians had driven a tunnel under the Euphrates River.

3. An afterlife was known, since sacrificed victims, tools, musical instruments, jewelry, wagons, animals, etc., were buried with the bodies.

4. They kept commercial accounts, inventories and a forerunner of the double entry accounting method.

5. Chariots were used in battle as a platform for javelin throwers. Hittites had three men per chariot. The oldest scene of chariots in battle is from Thutmose II, ECIAT p. 154.

6. The phalanx was used in battle long before Alexander the Great.

7. The arch of 2500 BC was first found at Tepe Gawra and other methods of construction including vertical sewers were known from Ur.

8. Gold work with soldered granulation and gem cutting was excellent; the helmet was in use at Ur.

9. School children studied verb declension; multiplication up to 12 x 90; square and cube roots were worked out.

10. At Mashkan-shapir 200 mi NE of Damascus was found a six-inch clay model of a domesticated horse dating to 2300 BC, pushing back the role of the horse another 300 years (BAR 19[4]: 16 [93]). The provincial governor of Terqa wrote to Zimrilim of Mari in the 18th century BC, advising the king to "give dignity to his kingship" by foregoing horses in favor of the socially acceptable chariot and mules (TLBM p. 34).

Egypt. The Hebrew name Mizraim is a dual ending reflecting the two kingdoms of Upper and Lower Egypt:

1. Hieroglyphics with 24 consonants plus groups, but no vowels, was known by the III Dynasty (2700 BC); probably known in the I Dynasty (3100 BC), the Narmer Palette contains 15 true individual hieroglyphic symbols, but none were in sentences at this time. The last known inscription is

dated Aug. 24, 394 AD in the reign of the Christian Emperor Theodosius, on the Temple of Isis at Philae.

2. Step Pyramid at Saqqara of the III Dynasty is the oldest stone structure in Egypt (2686 BC) and required extensive knowledge of mathematics and stone working. It is 412 x 358 ft and ca. 200 ft tall.

3. Senferu the first king of the IV Dynasty 2600 BC. His Northern Bent Pyramid of 621.3 x 621.3 feet has one casing block at NE corner dated in the 21st year of his reign; another half way up is dated in the 22nd year, thus it took only three years to construct one of three pyramids he built. The Great Pyramid is only 1/3 larger. Herodotus states it took 20 years to construct it. This may be conjecture. He actually built four pyramids, and as such is the greatest pyramid builder.

4. Cheops/Khufu's Great Pyramid ca. 2500 BC is 755.8 x 755.8 feet and has casing joints, which average only 1/50-inch clearance. The pyramid orientation error in the four sides: N 2'28" S of W, S 1'57" S of W, E 5' 30" W of N, W 2'30" W of N. One minute is the area subtended by a dime at one mile (Tompkins p. 99). The SE corner is ½ inch higher than the NW due to wind effect on the water level used in the leveling process.

5. Chephern/Kafre's Second Pyramid valley building contained 23 larger-than-life statues of the king in diorite, schist, and alabaster, a total of 100–200 separate statues, based on fragments, were used in the complex. For all three Pyramids, a total near 500 is possible. The burial chamber roof consists of 20-ton limestone slabs set in gable fashion at the same pitch as the pyramids' sides. There is no relieving chamber above them; they carry the full weight of the core stones. The first few courses are cut from stone that protrudes above ground at the SW corner.

6. Mycerinus/MenKaure's Third Pyramid contained granite slabs weighing 220 tons. The roof of the burial chamber is carved completely out of the bedrock limestone and has a roof made of 18 slabs of granite. These would have been raised from the floor by some unknown method and set in place in gable fashion. There was no ceiling room to use block and tackle. Maneuvering space is very limited for any manhandling. Near the ends, the crews could work only from one side. The basalt sarcophagus (thought to be from a later date) was lost at sea when the Beatrice went down in 1838 between Malta and Spain.

All three of the Giza pyramids are now known to have been built (at least the ground plan and maybe the first few courses) following a layout of the three belt stars of the Orion constellation. However, the only time the overhead stars would match this orientation on the ground was in 10,450 BC (Hancock p. 356). This same date was suggested for the carving of the Sphinx, based on water erosion around the Sphinx and the trench. This occurred when the climate was considerably wetter. Since then the Sphinx was buried up to its neck in sand off and on for over 2500 years, and erosion could not occur (Hancock p. 423; HBMS p. 74).

The Valley Temple of Khafre and the Osireion (of Seti I) at Abydos contains some of the most massive stonework and strange construction methods, not used in any other structure in Egypt. The core limestone (taken from the trench around the Sphinx) megaliths, some 40 feet off the ground, weigh over 200 tons. In America, there are only two land cranes that could lift and set this size stone. The stones are badly weathered (indicating they had been there for a long time), but the granite casing stones on each side have been carved to fit the bumps and valleys, rather than just evening up the slabs.

Many of these casing stones are cut as polygons with corner angles wrapped around and set into re-entering angles on the adjacent blocks. The Osireion contains three cartouches of Seti I (it is suggested that Seti added these for a renovation project); the huge stones used in the building were not the type of stonework used by anyone in the Nineteenth Dynasty. The function of the building, which is actually a water installation, is not known. It is set 50 feet below the level of Seti's Temple, which is directly to the NE. Both structures are aligned the same and skewed to the Ramses II Temple nearby (Hancock pp. 341, 400; HBMS pp. 26–32). The problem of moving and setting such large stones with the precision shown and tolerances used is mainly a problem of logistics: how to get enough workers around them in confining spaces to set them in place. Even levitation by an advanced civilization before the Egyptians has been proposed (Hancock p. 310). There is no getting around the fact that pyramid construction seemed rather hit or miss and learn as you go, beginning with the step pyramid of Djoser, Snefru's pyramid at Medium, the bent pyramid as well as its cult pyramid through the three pyramids at Giza (Verner p. 458).

There is no consensus on methods of lifting the core stones for the pyramids. The forth Dynasty pyramid at Sinki, five miles S of Abydos still has the remains of four ramps. It is thought that the gravel mound around the Meidum pyramid is a ramp. Other ramps are known from the unfinished first pylon at Karnak (now removed), the pyramid of Neferirkare, the pyramid of Ammenemes I at Lisht and the unfinished mortuary temple of Mycerinu (Verner pp. 95; 169, Edwards p. 205). Recently Zahi Hawass found two parts of the ramp for the pyramid of Khufu at the SW corner; he proposed a spiral ramp continued up the pyramid as it rose (Hawass p. 62).

7. Sahure's complex ca. 2470 BC in the V Dynasty used copper drainage pipe more than 1000 feet long, connected to five copper-lined stone basins fitted with lead plugs.

8. Senwosret I of the XII Dynasty of 1990 BC had six statues found in a pit near the pyramid, with ten of 24 Tura limestone statues found in a pit near the court complex.

9. Senwosret II or Sesostris's sarcophagus of red granite in the XII Dynasty was almost perfect in regularity; the error was 1/100 in. per cubit of 20.62 inches.

10. Amenemhet or Ammenemes III of the XII Dynasty ruled for 46 years. He built the Labyrinth on the SE side of his pyramid (which covered 28,000 m² and according to Strabo contained 42 halls, one for each province in Egypt [Verner p. 431]) and Lake Moeris; it was 3600 stades by 50 fathoms deep or 413.7 mi by 300 ft. Diodorus Siculus in 57 BC said it cost 50 talents to open or close it. It is still in use and is 147 ft below sea level. His burial chamber, in the pyramid at Hawara, was a single block of yellow quartzite 22 x 8 x 6 feet and weighed 110 tons without the lid. The inner corners were cut so sharp Petrie thought they were jointed. Again, the technology to do this is unknown.

11. Khendjer (Boar) of the XIII Dynasty of 1777 BC, whose burial chamber, sarcophagus and Canoptic chest were carved from one piece of granite of 150 tons. The lid in this case was set on granite posts over narrow sand-filled chambers. The sand was allowed to drain away, lowering the lid into place. This was the first time this method had been used (Verner p. 440; Edwards p. 184).

12. Hatshepsut of the XVIII Dynasty of 1490 BC had two red granite obelisks 97½ ft high, each weighing 350 tons, which were constructed in seven months. Her temple at Deir el-Bahri had over 190 statues and relief carvings. She had linen cloth of 540 threads per in²; the best modern linen

has only 180 threads per in². For other examples on textiles, see Barber p. 148.

13. Amenhotep III of the XVIII Dynasty (1412–1375 BC). He built the Colossus of Memnon, originally nearly 47 ft high and weighing over 792 tons; brought from Heliopolis near Cairo, 420 mi away by barge.

14. Akhenaten of the XVIII Dynasty (1387–1366 BC). His new capital of Akhetaton was 8 x 3 mi. The most humble houses had bathrooms with lavatories fed by running water.

15. Ramses II of the XIX Dynasty (1279–1212 BC). The first court of the Ramesseum at Thebes has a statue in red granite of approximately 1000 tons.

Egypt took delight in working in the hardest stone, with great precision, and in setting them in narrow places with close tolerances, using methods still not understood. In the early dynasties, the wheel was not known, although log rollers were probably used. For example, in Abusir, the intact tomb of Iuf-aa of the 26th Dynasty had a sixty ton sarcophagus lowered down a sixty foot shaft (Hawass p. 143). For additional details, see Edwards.

Syria—Baalbek about 200 AD has three stones 68 x 14 x 14 ft, each weighing 1780 tons; these were the largest cut blocks ever used in a building. In a nearby quarry, a 2,000-ton stone never made it out of the quarry. This was man's swan song.

The following observations are the type of information that can be gleaned from a typical excavation. This is from the Tomb of Tutankhamen by Howard Carter:

1. The third coffin is solid gold 6'1 3/4" long and 1/8" thick; it weighed 296 lb troy. He died at about 18 years of age, based on the epiphyses of the leg bones (Reeves pp.110, 116).

2. A folding camp bed was used in the field and shows portable camping equipment (Carter p. 198).

3. King's ears were pierced. He probably wore earrings up to age 7–12 (Carter p. 181).
4. The crook (Hekat) and flail (Nekhekhw) represents the insignia of Osiris and authority over the two principle factions in Egypt, the herdsman (Upper Egypt) and shepherd of (Lower Egypt).
5. An iron-bladed dagger and two other iron items, the Sacred Eye bracelet found on the mummy and the headrest, which was usually in hematite. In the tomb were found 16 model implements for the Ushabtis, also in iron. This is near the beginning of the Iron Age and Iron was still rare and more valuable than gold (Carter p. 189).
6. A scarlet tinted gold, produced by an unknown method, was found on some of the jewelry (Carter p. 180).
7. One inlayed box has 45,000 pieces of inlay in ivory and ebony (Carter p. 177).
8. An heirloom lock of auburn hair of Queen Tyi wife of Amenhotep III (possibly his grandmother) was given a royal burial in a nest of four coffins (Carter p. 187).
9. A stillborn mummy and a premature-born mummy, both daugthers of 17 yr old Tut and 19 yr old Ankesenamen (Akhenaten's third daughter, who was married both to Akhenaton [incest was common and she bore him a daughter Ankhesenpaaten Tashere (or Jr.)] and Tut. She was married to her father about age 10 (Carter pp. 108,188).
10. From a bow case, animals were bred and game reserves were used to hunt in (Carter p. 191).
11. A knob, when turned, locked a lid on a box, the earliest automatic fastening device (Carter p. 203).
12. A bow drill was used for making fire (Carter p. 203).
13. Four royal cubits of 19½ inches were found; several others were stolen since their cases were empty. In the Pyramid Age, the cubit was 20.61 inch (Verner p. 451).

14. A game resembling chess was played on 10 x 3 squares of five pieces black and white per side. One called senet the other side for a game called *tjau* (thieves) (Carter p. 209: ET).
15. Boomerangs, both return and non-return types were known (Carter p. 213).
16. Jars marked at 14½ and 16 ¾ hin, shows that a hin=460 cc (Carter p. 216).
17. Wine jars record that the vineyards were in the Delta region. Aten worship lasted for at least 17 years and changed to Amen in the third year of Tut's reign, which lasted for at least nine years. The Aten wine estates were productive for at least 21 years (Carter p. 11).

The season of his death can be determined by the flowers on the body and in the casket. Mandrake is the love apple of Genesis 30:14 and Song of Songs 7:13. The fruit was and still is in the Near East, considered to possess aphrodisiac powers and to promote conception. It ripens during wheat harvest in Mar-May. The blue water lily, or Lotus, is in flower July-Nov. Probably cultivated in garden pools and available earlier in the year. Olive and Willow leaves are indeterminate and available all year. Picris flowers in Mar-April. Woody nightshade, only the berries were used, ripen Mar-April. Cornflower flowers in Mar-April. Thus, King Tut was buried from the middle of March to the end of April. He died 70 days before, or in early January to late February. A possible skull fracture was reexamined in 2005; it was felt this did not lead to his death.

A listing of the objects found in the tomb, which had about 10% of the smaller gold, silver objects and valuable perfumes and oils stolen from two early break-ins include:

- Annex—300 including 116 baskets of fruit and seeds
- 278 arrows

- 2 Sickle swords known as the khepesh, or in Canaan the kidon (Jos 8:18), for ceremonial use only as it was obsolete and had not been sharpened—the smaller one was for a child. These are hacking weapons;
- 36 wine jars, 26" high—The wine was not touched by the thieves—it was not valuable enough. One jar carries the docket—year one of the domain of Amen, indicating he changed his name from Amum in the third year of his reign
- 50 Alabaster jars containing 400 liters of oils, resins, etc. Some had the ancestral name of Thutmose III going back some 85 years from presses of vintage unguents, although some will become rancid in time. The contents were stolen, except for one
- 1 serpentine jar
- 2 four legged cabinets
- 4 beds
- a throne and stool
- 2 chairs, one made of reeds
- 1 three-legged stool
- Antechamber—6–700 includes four chariots
- 2 beds; the one nearest the guard statues is a lioness, but the goddess named is Mehturt, who is a cow goddess; Isis-Meht, who is mentioned on the cow bed, was a lioness; the names were probably transposed by the engraver, ET
- 10 alabaster jars (originally from the Annex) from 7–26½ inches high; one has the partially erased prenomen and nomen of both Amenhotep III and IV probably indicating a co-regency
- 4 cubits
- 1 throne
- 1 folding couch
- 2 guard statues of Tut painted black

- Burial chamber—194 including two wooden caskets
- 1 brown quartzite sarcophagus, the lid, of pink granite was painted brown and was probably appropriated from somewhere else; it had also been broken and the crack cemented and painted. A hurried up job due to the king's death
- 1 solid gold casket weighing 296 pounds troy, or 110.4 kg
- 1 solid gold face mask weighing 10.23 kg
- 4 gold covered shrines: first is 16'6" x 10'9" x 9"; surrounded the sarcophagus; between the third and forth shrine an ostrich fan shows attendants carrying off the dead birds—this species Struthio Camelus would weigh ca 345 pounds, thus a flight of imagination to think that one man could carry one. Some of the scenes written on the walls of the shrines are normal hieroglyphics and parts are in an enigmatic script still undeciphered. Parts of the scenes depicted are also strange and not understood, ET
- Jewelry on body—194 objects in 101 separate groups 143 within the bandages
- Treasury—about 200 including two chariots
- 2 stillborn children 6–7 mo of age
- 1 anubis jackal shrine; one pendant found below the shrine shows Nut as a vulture with the king's names inverted and written in reverse order within the cartouche and with the epithet "Ruler of Heliopolis of Upper Egypt" placed in the wrong order, ET
- 1 alabaster Canopic chest; the four goddesses were carved on the corners
- 1 wooden canopic cover with four gilded statues of goddesses; Serket, with a scorpion on her head, was placed on the S side and should have been on the E; Nephthys

on the E side wearing a castle tower on her head should have been on the S; shows carelessness of details

- 4 Solid gold coffins for the internal organs; Smenkhkara's name was erased on these; the face is also not that of Tutankhamun but similar; each weighed 30 pounds
- 10 shawabti (answerers) figures. They worked for the King in the afterlife
- 22 shrines of gods and king, two statues in each shrine or 44 total; the one of the king on the back of a leopard (painted black because the scene is in the underworld) shows him with distinctive breasts of a woman (?); there were several with this feature including the "harpooner," the significance is unknown
- 20 model boats
- 413 figures in kiosks
- 1,866 model implements
- 27 chests of jewelry, etc.

Several of these are probably grouped together. The total is about five thousand. The estimated value of the raw objects in 1925 was $50,000,000. The number of objects buried can be mind-boggling. King Djoser's Step Pyramid of 2686 BC contained 40,000 alabaster and other stone jars (in two of the underground storerooms) after numerous objects had been looted, (National Geographic Nov. 1955 p. 643; Carter pp. 52, 85, 155, 179, 193; RW pp. 122–127).

Old Testament Archaeology

Genesis 8:4. The Ark rests on the mountains of Ararat. This double volcano has been extinct since June 20–23, 1840 when 17 mi^3 blew out, forming the Ahora gorge. It is one of the largest above-ground mountains, covering some 550 mi^2. It is extremely dangerous to climb due to the pulverized basalt and hydrogen sulfide being given off. It is known that reports of the Ark being near a lake on Mt. Ararat have been circulating since 1018 to 1049 AD. The wood brought back by Fernand Navarra in 1955 was dated in Paris and Madrid (by examination of the cell structure) to be 5000 years old. Carbon-fourteen examination in 1966 at the U. of Pennsylvania and in the British National Physical Laboratory, Teddington gave dates of only 650 and 760 respectively. An expedition in 1969 brought back several new pieces of White Oak, dated at the U. of California at Los Angeles, La Jolla and Riverside, gave reading of 1200 BP or 700 AD, from above timberline and several hundred miles from the nearest source. This sample was reexamined in 1970 at UCLA to extract out tar and pitch to give a date of 1230 (+/- 60 years, BP) or 740 (+/- 60 years). Hans Seuss of La Jolla crosschecked the sample with a bristlecone pine sample from 10,000 feet and a Danube River sample near sea level (both 2,000 years old) to determine if higher cosmic rays with elevation would change the result. No effect was found. This may be from a shrine constructed on the mountain in the Byzantine period. This expedition was continued in 1971 (Moody Monthly Apr. 1970; Bible and Spade 6: 95 [77]; WBF p. 35).

New evidence by Dr. Robert Ballard has confirmed that the Black Sea was a lake ca 5600 BC, with sand dunes and beaches and with a collapsed house lying 311 feet down in the water. The lake level at this time was 520–550 ft lower than today (RPBF p. 138). The wood dated to 5600 BC (the wood was preserved by the hydrogen sulfide content in the water, this layer extends from 200 feet to the deepest bottom of 7000 feet). Fresh water mussels dated from 13,500–5500 BC and none of the salt-water mussels was earlier than 5500 BC. This was the date the Bosporus was breached, killing off the fresh water mussels and giving rise to many myths about the great flood (WBF p. 41, 63). Diodorus Siculus, who researched the library at Alexandria from 60–57 BC, knew of the lake and flood from these now lost records.

Philo Judaeus 20 BC–50 AD (the Jew) writing in Greek; also using the Alexandria material reports that before the sea level rose from melting ice. Sicily had been joined to the mainland of Italy. It is also reported in Eusebius that Philo went to Rome and spoke with Peter (Maier p. 73; WBF pp. 58; 153; 320).

Genesis 10:11 and Jonah 3:3, Nineveh. By 750 BC Nineveh and the suburbs was approximately 60 mi in circumference and contained 120,000 people (children). Yet by 612 BC its location (by outsiders) was forgotten (Xenophon in his retreat in 401/400 BC passed by the location without knowing it; so also did Herodotus) until excavation in 1847. Among the natives the name Ninaway, where the tomb of Jonah (Nebi Yunas) was venerated, was known by Ibn Hawkal, an Arab geographer of the 10th cent., who was born in Mosul. In 1173 the Spanish Jew, Benjamin of Tudela, says that Mosul was formerly called "the great Assur" and is divided by a bridge across the river from ancient Nineveh (Gadd pp. 6–7).

Nimrud or Calah, where the Black Obelisk of Shalmaneser III was found, was also the site where in April 1988, Muzahim M. Hussein found the tombs of Yabaya, the wife of Tiglath Pileser III and daughter of Sargon III; Banitu, wife of Shalmaneser V; and Talya, wife of Sargon III. The kings had ruled in succession from 744–705 BC. Some 80 gold objects weighed 35 kg. The tomb of Yabaya came with an inscribed curse: "If anyone lays hands on my tomb let the ghost of insomnia take hold of him forever and ever". Hussein didn't say he lost any sleep! In June 1988 the tomb of Queen Mulisu-Shumi-Marmani, wife of Ashurnasirpal II (883–859 BC) was found, but the stone sarcophagus was empty. Three unidentified bronze sarcophagi (probably of concubines) were also present, holding 440 gold objects weighing 22 kg plus a horde of cuneiform tablets. Others may be present, but the first Gulf War caused the dig to stop in 1991. These tombs were located under the floor of the harem near the throne room and reception rooms behind an extremely thick wall; the area above had been repeatedly excavated. They were found only when an air vent showed they had been digging the roof and not the supposed floor. This find was said to rival King Tut's tomb [TLBM pp. 79–81; Time Oct. 30 1989; Archaeology 43(2): 20 (90)]. After the second Gulf War, all ancient sites have been looted on a daily basis, since they are not guarded. The objects stolen will appear on the black market.

10:2. The Table of Nations. Mescheck is the earlier peoples known as the Moschians (calf-men, worshipers of the bull cult) later known as the Phrygians. They regarded themselves as an ancient race, older than the Egyptians as reported in Herodotus. Tubal was an ancestor of the copper and ironworkers of the southern Black Sea area. All the sons of Japheth appear in this region and out into the Aegean Sea (WBF p. 177).

10:25. Peleg . . . the earth was divided. May refer to the separation of languages (Josephus 1, 6, 4). In Assyrian Peleg is Palgu and means canal; may refer to the introduction of irrigation canals (Hertz p. 38; Sci. Amer. June 78 p. 50).

11:3–4. Tower of Babel. The ziggurat (lit. mountain peak) temple towers of Babylonia are thought to be models for the Tower of Babel (or visa versa). At present there are 33 known in 27 cities; texts mention others not yet found (Baumann p. 80). The oldest known is that of Urek the Erech of Genesis 10:10 (modern Warka) ca. 3800 BC. It is made of stamped clay, buttressed with brick and asphalt. In Babylon, the Etemenanki (the House of the Foundation of Heaven and Earth) was of seven stages. Alexander the Great kept 10,000 men busy for two months clearing away some of the rubble (Oats p. 157; NUD p. 133). Nearby was the Temple of Marduk, Esagila (the temple that raises its head) where the 12 cubits high statue (18 feet) of 22 tons of gold stood, and to which was burned 2.5 tons of frankincense each year (as reported by Herodotus, TLBM p. 139).

11:31. Ur of the Chaldees. This old city had a very advanced civilization, including sewers made of vertical clay pipes. This was the city of Ur-Nammu (2112–2095 BC) the Third Dynasty of Ur (Oats p. 42), although another Ur (Urfa) near Haran has become known from tablets at Ebla, Ugarit, Alalakh and Hattusha. If so, then this city was near the destination of Abraham and Terah to begin with. The term "of the Chaldeans" is a later scribal gloss to locate a city where the term Chaldeans was no longer known. It refers only to the Southern Babylonia region (FLAP p. 70). Before 1000 BC the entire territory as far as Armenia, or Urartu in Kurdistan, was their original home and would include the Northern site as well (NUD p. 217). In both Ur and Haran the moon god Nannar was worshiped, so for Terah, no break in his local pagan gods were involved (Jos 24:2). Terah's homeland of Padan-aram (Gn 25:20 [the Plain or field of Aram, i.e. Syria]) in Assyrian Padanu Harranu means "a way." Aram Naharim of Genesis 24:10 means Aram of the (Two) Rivers, indicating the area of the Tigris and Euphrates, but the Euphrates and Habur in the area of Haran would also suffice.

12:16. Abraham's camels. Critics contend the camel was not domesticated until about 1200–1000 BC, whereas this account dates ca. 2000 BC. This story, as well as that of the Queen of Sheba (950 BC) in 1 Kings 10:1, 2, are considered in error. J. P. Free has shown the knowledge of camels in Egypt even before the time of Abraham. Statuettes, figurines, rock carvings and drawings, bones, a skull, and a camel hair rope; over 20 objects range from 3000–600 BC. A sculptured stone relief from Tell Halaf 1000 BC shows a Dromedary camel and rider sitting on a camel saddle [Free p. 170; Bible and Spade 13: 77 (00)].

Abraham was from Ur in Babylon; he might have brought the camels with him to Egypt. W. F. Albright indicates that sporadic, partial domestication of the camel may go back several centuries before 1100 BC.

14:14. "trained servant." The Hebrew Hanikim is used only here in the Bible. Such words were a headache to the KJV translators, who made an intelligent guess, which has turned out to be correct. The word is now known to mean retainers and is used in the Egyptian execration (cursing) texts against opposing Hittite princes and their retainers. The word has also been found at Ashkelon. These 318 men were a part of Abraham's caravanier network that moved his donkey caravans to Haran and other places from trade carried out with the Canaanite merchants.

19:24 and 26. The Dead Sea area is an old fault line that runs through the Arabah, the Gulf of Aqaba, and the Red Sea, into the African Great Rift Valley ending near Lake Chad. The area in the Dead Sea is a large natural gas area with the gas deposits capped with sulfur and salt. The destruction of Sodom and Gomarrah was probably the result of a gas blowout, which was set on fire by the cooking fires in the kitchens of the cities. Sulfur melting in the heat, and salt covering the molten sulfur raining down, could have caused Lot's wife to look like a pillar of salt. The ruins of Sodom, Gomorrah, Admah and Zeboiim (Dt 29:23), have probably been found 300 ft above the Dead Sea (the area where springs debouch from the mountains and where the first breezes for comfort can be felt) at Bab edh-Dhra (Gate of the Arm [the area into the Lisan]), Numeira, Feifa and Khanazar respectively (Bible and Spade 6: 25 [77]). In fact Gomorrah in Hebrew is 'MR; the ' is a guttural Ayin, Numeira is NMR, Nasalization in time would turn the Ayin into the Arabic N. The original name may be preserved in this case only. These are the only cities in the area which could fit the location and in fact Zoar (Safi) is still located here as well (ABR 1: 12 [88]).

23:9. Cave at Machpelah. The name means "double or fold" (Talmud 'Erubin 53a). The site was sanctified in the Hasmonean period, and Herod the Great built the present building over the cave in 10 BC. This is very likely the oldest authentic site in Israel, with Jacob's well at Shechem the second oldest. It was purchased from Ephron (the Hittite) at Hebron (20 mi S of Jerusalem). In a bargaining tactic still used today, by insisting on paying for the cave, Abraham was obligated to buy it (at the offered price, 400 shekels of silver ca. 300 troy oz.). The Code of Hammurabi lists the wages of a workingman at 8–11 shekels per year—Law 274, or a cost of 36 years' wages. A high price indeed.

During WW I Col. Richard Meinertzhagen, of Gen. Allenby's staff (his Intelligence Officer), went into the Moslem mosque (which stands over the cave) seeking the Turkish officials of Hebron who were supposed to have fled there. Passing through a door inside Abraham's cenotaph, he slid down a steep incline into a cave about 20 ft². In the cave was a block of stone ca. 6 x 3 x 3 ft. Not realizing the significance, he left without investigation. A later effort to visit the cave was refused by the Moslem guardians of the mosque who had returned. Does anything remain in Machpelah from ancient times ca 2000 BC? Machpelah means a fold, or double, indicating there may be two chambers present. Col. Meinertzhagen later had a chance to kill both Ribbentrop and Hitler in Berlin (he carried a loaded pistol to the meeting for this very purpose but let the opportunity slip by). Additional details are in his book *Mideast Diary* 1917–1956 published in 1960 and Peter H. Capstick's book *Warrior*, New York 1998. The cave incident is found only in Free p. 67.

A non-Arab has not entered the cave again until Oct. 9, 1968 when Gen. M. Dayen had a 12-year-old Jewish girl, Michal, lowered through the 11-inch hole by the mosque door. Photographs, notes, and measurements were made. She found 15 steps, three tombstones, burial niches, and a blocked door, but no sealed entrance from the outside. Details are in his book *Living With the Bible,* p. 45. The photographs have not been published. Col. Meinertzhagen apparently slid down a ramp and the description does not match his. This may have been the second cave. This is the oldest site definitely known from Bible times.

46:18. Sons of Zilpah. These are actually her grandsons. It says she "bore them or begat them." Begot may be used in the sense of "to have as a descendant." Genesis 11:26 says that Terah lived 70 years and begot Abram, Nahor and Haran. Not all three were born near the same time since Genesis 11:32 and 12:4 show that Abram was born 60 years later, when Terah was 130. This simply says that Terah first became a father at 70 with Haran as the eldest son (v. 28); also it explains why Abram took Lot, Haran's son with him as his heir apparent.

Exodus 1:11. Pithom and Rameses. Have now been identified with Tel el-Dab'a the old Hyksos capital of Avaris. Qantir, near by, seems to represent Rameses (BASOR 281: 27, 73 [91]).

2:3. Ark of papyrus. The Egyptian myth of Isis has her recovering the body of Osiris in a papyrus boat, since crocodiles abhorred papyrus. Moses was protected in the same way.

5:13–18. Straw in brick making. The Anastasi Papyrus records the lament of an Egyptian officer: "I am without equipment. There are no people to make bricks, and there is no straw in the district" (Free p. 92). At Tell el-Mashkuta near the site of Pithom of Exodus 1:11, storerooms with no doors were found, the bricks in the lowest level contained chopped straw, further up only reeds were found, and at the top no binding substances at all (Wycliffe p. 58). The tomb of Rekhmire, the vizier of Thutmose III, shows Semites and other captives making bricks: The brick layers say, "He supplies us with bread, beer and every good thing." A task master with a rod says, "The rod is in my hand, be not idle" (WERE p. 86; KOROT pp. 247–8).

7:10–12. Serpents. This was directed against the serpent goddess of the Delta Wadjet of Buto, or Apep (also known as Apophis [fans of Stargate SG1 take note]), the demon serpent of the underworld, who was never worshiped and had no temples. Psalm 78:43 specifically refers to the Delta area around Goshen (Zoan), although after the first three plagues there is a demarcation between the Egyptians and Goshen.

7:20–11:6. The Plagues of Egypt. From 12:12, the plagues were directed specifically against the gods of Egypt. The Nile, whose god was Hapi. The Nile flood at Memphis is in November. In v. 21 the fish died, whose goddess was Hatmehyt, whose symbol was a fish. Only open streams and reservoirs are affected, but not wells. For a list of the gods of Egypt and their characteristics see BER p. 108, or www.touregypt.net. This reference, which is very good, also gives information on the pyramids, Pharaohs and religion of ancient Egypt (KOROT pp. 249–53).

8:5. Frogs, whose goddess was Hekt (power of creation).

8:16. Gnats or No-see ums. Aimed at Priests who wore only linen and no wool, to avoid vermin. Dust was against the god Seb (Earth god).

8:21. Flies, or insects. Could represent the dung beetle Khepri, a creation god that could not control this creation. Alternatively, Uatchit the fly god.

9:3. Cattle god was Apis (of Memphis), Mnevis (of Heliopolis) and the goddess Hator (of Dendera).

9:9. Boils. Against the god of healing Imhotep and against the magicians or Priests who may have tried to protect the King.

9:24. Hail and fire. The gods Reshpu and Qetesn, who controlled natural elements except light. Hail occurs in Jan.-Feb. 15th. Flax is in flower at the end of Jan., barley ripens end of Feb. or early March, wheat ripens end of Mar. or early April. The seventh plague then occurred at the end of Jan. to the middle of Feb. There are eight weeks between the seventh and tenth plague to Nissan 14th. All the plagues took about six months from Nov.-Apr. The fire mentioned here can also mean lightning.

10:13. Locust god was Senehem, whose symbol was a locust. Also all the gods of harvest and crops ex. Geb (god of vegetation) and Min (a fertility god of growth and ripening of grain). They were brought by the East wind and destroyed by a West wind. Set was in charge of winds and storms. *Ripley's Believe it or Not* records the locust swarm of 1784 in South Africa, and the one of 1889 crossing the Red Sea, covering 2000 mi², containing ca 250,000,000,000 and weighing 508,000 tons. These are the Desert locust (Schistocera gregaria). People of the near east take some vengeance on them by boiling them in oil and eating them as a delicacy.

10:21. Darkness for three days was against the Sun god Amen-Ra. The Hamsin is a wind that blows for 50 days in March-May in Nubia, before and after the vernal equinox where the day and night are equal. A thick dust is stirred up so that people cannot see to move about. Some have tried to equate the darkness with the explosion of the volcano on the island of Thera (Santorini), which has been dated to 1626 BC using the new AMS C-14 method on seeds buried under the ash at Akrotiri Thera (Encarta encyclopedia 2000; RPNF p. 145). This would be 188 years before the Exodus, by the conservative date. Another view equates this with the eclipse on March 13, 1335 BC, where the three days applies to the effects of the dread which paralyzed the people for three days, whereas the eclipse lasted only for the usual seven minutes (Goshen did not have a total eclipse) (Hertz p. 251). An interesting theory but appears to be 70 years late. This would date the Exodus to March 27, 1335 BC.

12:29. The first-born was against Pharaoh himself, the first born of the incarnation of Ra. Except for some details of the plagues, most of these would all naturally follow one upon another: fish dying, which brings gnats, frogs, flies, and boils or disease. What caused the fish to die is harder to explain. Blood itself ordinarily would not cause this, but something like a Pyrrophyta algae of dinoflagellates, which are responsible for the red tide, these are not associated with the yearly flooding of the Nile, at least not on this scale, and would not appear in reservoirs at the same time, although a heavier reddish silt load does occur in the Nile. The fire running along the ground is also not the usual behavior of lightning. The death of the first-born is, however, the direct hand of God, for which no explanation will suffice (KOROT note 13 p. 553).

14:21. Sea parted by a strong East wind. Gen. Tulloch in Jan-Feb of 1882 reported a strong East wind drove back the waters of Lake Menzaleh seven mi (Free p. 100). The route taken out of Egypt is given in ABR 3: 98 (90); Bible and Spade 7: 97 (78). Psalms 77:16–18 also reports a storm at the same time. Josephus in *Antiquities of the Jews* Book II, Chapter XVI, par. 3 also knew of this storm, showing that there were some manuscripts that contained it.

Exodus 26:7. Weaving. One of the first industries particularly for women, although first mentioned here in the Bible, linen cloth had been available much earlier; in fact it goes back to the Upper Paleolithic Venus figures. These are shown wearing the original micro miniskirt, known as a string skirt. Several examples were found in Middle Bronze graves in Denmark and other Scandinavian countries. Thus for 20,000 years since the clay Venus statues of the upper Palaeolithic (they are still worn in Mordvin, Romania, Macadonia and Albania today); these have been used to call attention to a woman quite visually as available for marriage. From the waist, some are only six, and much later, fifteen inches long. They are also described in Book 14 of the Illiad, Barber pp. 255–258; WW, pp. 58–66. The Dorak (near Troy) queen's tomb contained one six-inch high electrum figurine wearing one, possibly as the Great Mother Goddess. The textiles on and below the skeleton disintegrated upon exposure to the air (WBF p. 165).

Leviticus 15:1–33. Mikveh or Jewish Baptism. Contact with semen, blood, or contact with the dead rendered one unclean until the evening. The washing usually referred to in the Bible is not the type of bath we take. Rather, the person would simply immerse in enough water to cover the body, usually by bending and spreading the knees and arms so that water can reach every hair of the body.

Numbers 22–24. Balaam. At Tel Deir Alla (now thought to be Penuel) on the Jabboc River in Jordan, on a wall of a house was found inscribed in red and black ink within a frame of red lines, an Aramaic version of the story in 16 preserved lines. Dated to about 750 BC, the house was destroyed by earthquake, probably the same one referred to in Amos 1:1 and Zechariah 14:4–5. Only one and a half frames out of the four were filled before the building was destroyed. A second text is present in the first frame not relating to Balaam, but the context is not known. These were probably drawn from old edited manuscripts in conjunction with a religious school, BAR 11(5): 26 (85).

Numbers 6:3. Nazarite vow. The prohibition against wine and strong drink makes some sense. But why that against juice, grapes, raisins, and vinegar? Actually, the injunction is against yeast or leaven, since every one of these products contains yeast. Even freshly pressed grape juice will begin to ferment, almost immediately, and will contain about 1% by volume of alcohol after standing three days at 50°F. Each percent of sugar fermented will give 0.55% alcohol. Nine percent alcohol is necessary to prevent vinegar formation. All the sugar will be fermented within 10–14 days depending on the temperature.

Deuteronomy 8:9. A land of iron and copper. The use of copper as far back as 4000 BC is known. The old copper mines (used in the Chalcolithic period) in the Arabah North of Elath were used by Solomon to cast the bronze sea in the clay of the Jordan valley North of the Jabboc river at Succoth and Zarethan (1 Kgs 7:46). These mines are being reworked by Israel today. The old slag heaps are still to be found from Solomon's day.

At Tell Asmar 50 miles North of Baghdad, an iron blade was found in the level of 2700 BC. A steel axe from Ur and other objects have also been found. Iron ore is found in the Arabah, in Genesis 4:22. Tubal-cain, a smith, was a descendant of Cain.

Joshua 1:4 Hittites. The descendants of Heth (Gn 10:15). These people were unknown except for the Bible references, until 1880 when A.H. Sayce identified the Hittites with the Hatti inscriptions on the monuments; in 1906, Hugo Winchler excavated the old Hittite capital of Hattusa at Boghazkoi (Gorge village) in central Turkey. The over 30,000 tables found there are written in an Indo-European language. Details are found in the Time/Life Books *Lost Civilizations*: Anatolia: *Cauldron of Cultures* and *The Emergence of Man: The Empire Builders*.

A peace treaty between Ramses II in his 21st year, or 1284 BC, with Hattushilish III was sealed by the marriage of his daughter to Ramses. This is the second oldest peace treaty known. The oldest is the Stele of the Vultures.

14:6 Caleb the Kenizzite. In Numbers 13:6 and later he is simply called a leader from the tribe of Judah. Actually, he was a proselyte (in Hebrew a *ger*) from the Kenizzites, which were related to the Kenites (Hobab the son of Reuel or Jethro [Moses's father in law], Heber and Jael as well as the ascetic Rechabites were all Kenites). These were coppersmiths par excellence from the Wadi Arabah related to the Midianites. In many cases these proselytes were devoted Jews extremely zealous for the law as in all those above (also compare Othniel, Caleb's younger brother, Urriah the Hittite, Obed-Edom the Gittite, Ruth the Moabitess, Rahab the Cannanitess, Ittai of Gath [HJP p. 97, 2 Sm 15:19–22], and the Gibeonites [were actually slaves]).

15:15 and 48. Location of Debir in the highlands. Albright in 1926–32 excavated Tell Beit Mirsim (probably Ashan) as Debir in the lowlands 13 mi SW of Hebron that included underground water basins.

In Oct. 1967–69 an Israeli, M. Kochavi, found at Khirbet Rabud in the hills nine mi SW of Hebron, an old Canaanite city of 15 acres: less than two miles away two subterranean chambers called the "Upper and Lower Well of the Leach" (leaches are found in stagnant water). This site satisfies all of the conditions for Debir's identification (see v. 19), and this site is now accepted as the correct location. In Hebrew Debir is spelled DBR, Rabud is RBD or Debir spelled backwards. In Arabic many names have retained the memory of Biblical names; this may be one (BAR 1(1): 5 [75]).

Joshua 24:26. Massebot at Shechem. Joshua's stone (about half of it still exists) containing the law at Shechem was found and reset up in front of the altar (which was removed) at the Migdol Temple 2a. Its original site was about three feet to the N; placed here for safety reasons.

Judges 1:16. Kenites of Arad. Arad 12 mi SW of Masada is a dual site of 25 acres; the name was later used for another site (Tell Malhatah) 12 mi to the SW, as shown from Shishak's Karnak Temple inscription dual listing of 924 BC. At Tell Arad a bowl with 'RD inscribed seven times in ancient Hebrew letters is one of the few sites where the name has been found in situ. An Israelite sanctuary with Holy of Holies and two incense altars, one on each side of the doorway, dates from 900–850 BC; it is the earliest known. In the court is a five-cubit^2 altar built of unhewn stones. The LXX states that the Hobab Kenite family of priests, related to Moses, settled here (see above, BAR 24[6]: 56 [98]).

7:1. Ein Harod. The spring (trembling) where Gideon had his army whittled down to 300 men can be seen about 1.75 mi E.S.E. of Jezreel. Saul's army also camped here (1 Sm 29:1).

18:30. Captivity of the land. This verse was changed after the Babylonian captivity. But how priests became attached to the tribe of Dan is not clear. The verse probably originally read "the son of Moses" instead of the son of Manasseh.

1 Samuel 17:49. Sling of David. Goliath may have been a professional soldier, but he was completely outgunned in this battle and should have known it. Depending on whether Goliath was a troop commander, the commander's first law of combat is, "know your enemy." The sling was the primary weapon of the shepherd, to defend against predators. The Philistines didn't use slings. The effective range for a bow was about 300–400 yards. The sling and bow are primarily saturation weapons—put enough in the air and you are bound to hit something. The heavy spear could be thrown about 50 feet, but was primarily a thrusting weapon. All David had to do was stay back about seventy feet and pick Goliath off at leisure. Did Goliath know David was a shepherd? If so, as soon as the sling came into view Goliath should have known he was in big trouble. The sling could fire at ease over 900 feet (the record for a 51-inch sling and a 2-ounce stone is 1434 feet two inches), Ripley's *Believe it or Not* Aug. 21, 1981. Whether one could hit a target at that range is another matter. The Assyrian sculptures always show the slingers behind the bowmen as having a greater range (Yadin p. 430, Scientific American Oct. 72, p. 35).

2 Samuel 2:13. Pool of Gibeon. The pool at El-Jib is 37 ft in diameter and 35 ft deep and was excavated by Pritchard in 1957; it is the actual site of the military contest between the men of Ishbosheth and David. Some 56 inscribed jar handles were found in the debris of the pool, inscribed "GB'N GDR" (vineyard of Gibeon) followed by one of several personal names. Cisterns for holding over 25,000 gal. of wine in 9 3/4 gal. jars were found, indicating that wine exporting was the principal occupation at Gibeon (BAR 6(2): 28 (80), ADHL p. 139).

11:5. Bathsheba's children. It is obvious that Bathsheba had been married for more than a year (if the provision of Dt 24:5 was being observed, as Uriah was a military man). Any woman not pregnant during this time would have been extremely rare, but no children are mentioned. The same is true in the case of Abigail and Nabal (1 Sm 25:3). The story does not indicate they were newlyweds, yet no children are mentioned. One could read between the lines and suppose that Nabal's character and possibly Uriah's many absences on the battlefield caused the women not to have relations with their husbands. The home life of each was probably not very happy. Bathsheba could have politely refused the offer.

11:11. Uriah the Hittite. As a Jewish proselyte, he was acting as a better Jew than David. David was trying to cover up his adultery with Bathsheba by suggesting that Uriah should visit his wife and have relations. The Jewish military were obliged to forego sexual relations with wives, concubines or captives while the army was engaged in the field, as shown in the DSS (almost all wars were dedicated to the glory of God and therefore Holy). See the similar case for David himself in 1 Samuel 21:4–5.

18:18. Absalom's pillar. This monument, the northernmost of three, shown in the Kidron has nothing to do with Absalom. A recent faint inscription in two lines four feet long was found that reads, "This is the tomb of Zachariah, martyr, very pious priest, father of John [the Baptist]." It dates to the 4–5 century AD (and has nothing to do with John or his father). Also present is the name Simon and others (BAR 29[6]: 19 [03]). These three tombs actually date to ca 50 AD and show Greek influence. All are Herodian type tombs. The top represents the nefesh for the soul, and below it is an arcosolia for a burial. This is probably a high priest's tomb, or a member of the Sanhedrin. Behind it and connected to it is the "Tomb of Jehosaphat" with eight chambers of arcosolia and kokhim not completely excavated and cannot now be entered. The middle tomb is that of the family of Beni Hezir, known from an inscription above the columns in three lines, naming six brothers and two sons of one of the brothers. This is also known as the "Tomb of St. James." It dates to ca 37 BC. The family belongs to the 17th course of priests in 1 Chronicles 24:15. It contains three unfinished chambers, a 3-bench arcosolia and several kokhim. This is a good example of the type of tomb of Christ, although more elaborate. The third monument, a pyramid-topped nefesh, also belongs to Beni Hezir's tomb as stated in the inscription. They are connected by a short tunnel and stairs. It is popularly known as the "Tomb of Zechariah." The tomb chamber at the bottom is a secondary late addition.

1 Kings 9:15. Millo, Hazor, Megiddo and Gezer. The remains of some of Solomon's building activities have been identified. The Millo in Jerusalem is thought to be the "stone stepped structure" or glacis near the Nehemiah Wall of Yigal Shiloh's excavation in the City of David (O'Connor p. 108). The gates and casemate walls attached to them, in the three cities above, are essentially made from the same "blueprints." Some controversy over these gates had developed. W.G. Dever, who dug out the eastern half of the gate at Gezer, returned in 1984 and 1990 to rework the western gate and wall area and determined that his original date for Solomon was correct (BAR 20(3): 75 (94). Gezer had been destroyed by an unnamed Pharaoh of Egypt, who gave it to Solomon as a wedding gift. Solomon built his gate to block a 600 feet gap in the wall destroyed by Pharaoh. Usually gates and temples were rebuilt in the same areas, one on top of another. The Megiddo gate is just to the NW of the LB Gate, which had no wall. The Hazor gate seems to be in a new location.

12:28. The Golden Calf Temple. Built by Jeroboam I at the northern border at Dan; it has been found. The other at Bethel has not been found, probably because Bethel (presently identified with Betein) itself has not been positively identified, BAR 24(5): 38 (98).

14:25–28. Shishak I. His triumphal inscription at Karnak lists 156 Judean towns that he conquered (Megiddo, Beth-Shemesh, Gibeon, Taanach and Jerusalem), which were probably mentioned, but the damaged inscription does not contain them. Montet says Jerusalem was found in the part that was lost (p. 242). A part of his Stela was found at Megiddo, which proves he took this city as his inscription states. He is the first Pharaoh mentioned by name in the Bible. He ruled 935–914 BC. He is also known as Sheshonk I and started the XXII Libyan Dynasty. The gold-masked mummy of Shishonk II (no relation) was found at Tanis in 1938–9.

15:13. Idol in a grove. The Hebrew is "mifletzeth of Asherah." The only four times this word is used is in reference to the Queen mother Maacah, Asa's grandmother (see v. 2). The word means terror and is used derogatorily. A "Queen mother" held considerable influence at court, and to be deposed by a son or grandson was a severe loss of face (HJP p. 118).

15:18. Benhadad (of Syria) I and II same? It is known from the Benhadad stela (ANE Vol 1, p. 219) that the previous two Benhadads (1 Kgs 20:1 contemporary to Asa and Baasha 896 BC and 2 Kgs 8:7, contemporary to Elijah and Elisha 843 BC) are the same (UOT p. 240). Albright's reading of the Melqart stela (same as above) is questioned as not referring to Aram Damascus (KOROT p. 12).

20:16. Drinking himself drunk in the pavilions (Succoth). This is the second place where Succoth should be a place name. The LXX also translates it this way. The battle makes sense, in that the Syrians were trapped in the Wadi Fara on their way to Samaria by the small Israelite force of 7,000, while the leaders remained in Succoth. The Turks were trapped, and two divisions annihilated, in this same valley by Field-Marshal Lord Waverly (Yadin pp. 305–310).

2 Kings 8:15. Hazael. In the Annals of the 14th year of Shalmaneser III is the statement that "Hazael son of a nobody (no royal birth) seized the throne" (ARAB I # 681).

13:10. Jehoash of Israel. This 18th king of Israel ruled from 800–784 BC. Joash of Judah the 7th king ruled 836–798 BC. In the spring of 1967, the British School of Archaeology found a marble stela at Tell al-Rimah 50 mi West of Nineveh. The eighth line states that Adad-Nirari III of Assyria 810–783 BC received the tribute of Jehoash of Samaria. This is the first known mention of Jehoash from outside the Bible (Bible and Spade 1: 20 [72]).

17:4. So. This Egyptian General of the XXIV Dyan. was depended upon by Hoshea in 724 BC for protection after the fall of Samaria. In the Assyrian records, he is known as Sib'e (the Hebrew is Sewe), and Sargon III says that he did appear to fight about a year later when the Assyrians moved south along the coast to retake the areas of Philistia. "Sib'e, *turtan* (not called a king) of Egypt, who had come out against me at Rapihu (south of Khan Yunus) to offer battle and fight, I defeated. Sib'e became frightened at the clangor of my weapons and fled, to be seen no more." A great ally indeed (ARAB II p. 26).

20:20 and 2 Chronicles 32:30. Hezekiah's Tunnel ca. 701 BC. In 1880, 19 ft from the end of the tunnel before it enters the Pool of Siloam, a small boy wading in the water slipped and fell. As he was getting up he noted letters carved on the wall. The remaining inscription of six lines was cut from the end and the beginning was not finished, which would probably have listed Hezekiah as the builder. It describes the tunnel as 1200 cubits long, the tunnel is 1777–1707 ft long (depending on who measures it and from what point). This makes the cubit 18 inches long. The tunnel was carved from both ends at the same time in a zigzag manner, apparently following a natural crack in the rock. The western end is much higher, showing that the floor had to be lowered for the water to flow properly, BAR 11(6): 33 (85); 34(5): 50 (08). Two other prepared places for inscriptions are further inside but more inaccessible and would be therefore harder to read; the inscriptions were never cut. Another is present in a round chamber between corridors III and IV at the Gihon end; this inscription was also never cut (Simons p. 183). The inscription is now in the Istanbul museum in a storeroom and not on display, except by special permission. Israel wants it back.

23:29. In his (Josiah's) day Pharaoh Necho King of Egypt went up against the King of Assyria (AV and ARV). The Hebrew *al* usually means against, but can have more specialized meanings. The Babylonian Chronicle indicates why Josiah attacked the Pharaoh, who appeared to be going to battle against Ashuruballit, in that Necho was actually going to his aid. Thus "went up to" is more accurate (UOT p. 282).

2 Chronicles 26:21–23. Uzziah a leper. On the grounds, in the cemetery of the Russian church of Mary Magdalene at the foot of the Mt. of Olives, was found in 1931, an ossuary (now in the Israel Museum) with the inscription, "Hither were brought the bones of Uzziah king of Judah. Do not open." His tomb was originally located in "the burial field of the kings" and not in the royal Tomb of the Kings in the City of David, because he was a leper. When this graveyard (probably the one near the SW corner of the Temple Mount) was relocated, his bones, and all the others, were moved so the area could be purified and made a part of the city (Mazar p. 187).

32:5. Part of this 23-feet thick "broad wall" built by Hezekiah ca 701 BC to enclose the new Mishneh and Makhtesh quarters with the refugees, following the fall of Samaria, can be seen in the Jewish Quarter of Jerusalem.

Isaiah 20:1. In the year, Tartan came unto Ashdod. The Assyrian Eponym Chronicles state that in the year 711 BC Sargon stayed in Assyria. His turtanu, or commander-in-chief actually captured the city. The Annals of Sargon boasts that he took the city, since everything that happened the king could take credit for. The Eponym list is unimpeachable and agrees with the Bible. Sargon died in battle in 705 BC in the Taurus Mountains, and his body was not recovered.

Jeremiah 22:30. None of Jehoiachin's children to sit on the throne of David. In 95 AD, two of Jude's grandchildren were brought before Domitian. He asked about their connection to the house of David, their wealth, and was told it consisted of 39 plethora of land (ca 20 acres) worth 9,000 denarii, of which each owned half. Domitian was convinced they were rustic farmers that posed no threat to the Empire and released them (Maier p. 109). Until ca 420 AD members of the House of David (of which there were six families) had the title of exiliarch in Babylonia (these were descendants of the five sons of Jehoiachin that were exiled to Babylon). Bustenai, the first exiliarch under Islam, was later disqualified because of his marriage to the recently defeated Persian emperor's daughter. There was also a branch in Israel at Jabneh known as *nasi*, of which Hiller was one. This office of Patriarchate (which functioned as the Sanhedrin) was abolished by Theodosius II in 429 AD. Even the Arabs, until 825 AD recognized the exiliarch as the only recognized Jewish authority (HJP pp. 310, 355, 421). Both positions were held in high honor, but only about internal Jewish matters.

Ezekiel 8:1. Sitting in my house with the elders. This reference may be to the start of the synagogue system. This assembly known in Babylonian by an Aramaic loanword as *kinishtu* or in Mishnaic Hebrew as *Knesset*. Thus the synagogue goes back to the time of Ezra, HJP p. 173.

30:10–12. Nebuchadrezzar to invade Egypt from Migdol (near Suez) to Syene (Aswan) in v. 6. Near Syene, an inscription, now in the Louvre, records a claim of an Egyptian prince that he drove back the Babylonian army so that they did not succeed in getting beyond the 1st cataract of the Nile, which is at Syene (Wright p. 88).

Daniel 3:19. Fiery furnace of ca. 600 BC. Excavations at Babylon found what looked like a brick kiln; however, an inscription reads "This is the place of burning where men who blasphemed the gods of Chaldea died by fire." An inscription of Ashurbanipal 668–627 BC reads, "Saulmagina my rebellious brother, who made war with me, they threw into a burning fiery furnace, and destroyed his life."

A king of Larsa (N. of Ur) a contemporary of King Hammurabi 1728–1686 BC (or 1792–1750; there is a high, low and middle chronology) gave sentence for a slave to be thrown into a furnace (Wight p. 65).

4:30. Babylon built by Nebuchadrezzar. Critics such as R.H. Pfeiffer contend that Daniel was written ca. 167 BC. If this is so, how did the writer know that the glories of Babylon were built by Nebuchadrezzar (UOT p. 295; Boyd pp. 151–53)?

4:33. Nebuchadrezzar's madness. Rawlinson found a mutilated inscription (the king's name is not given) that may refer to this event, which reads: "For four years the seat of my kingdom in the city . . . which . . . did not rejoice my heart. In all my dominions I did not build a high place of power; the precious treasures of my kingdom I did not lay out, in the worship of Merodach, my lord, the joy of my heart, in Babylon the city of my sovereignty and the seat of my empire I did not sing his praises, and I did not furnish his altars: nor did I clear out the canals." The "seven times" of Daniel may refer to periods of summer and winter, the only seasons counted by the Babylonians (Wight p. 65). This period does fit quite well with the reign of Nabonidus, whose name may have been left out. He left Babylon in self-exile to Tema in Saudi Arabia and during his absence, the New Year festival to Marduk could not be held. For details, see Oppenheim p. 122.

6:16. Den of lions ca. 538 BC. The excavator, Dieulafoy, at Babylon, fell into what looked like a well, but upon examination found an inscription, "The place of execution where men who angered the king died torn by wild animals."

At the palace in Shushan (Suza), a record list was found of 484 men of high rank who had died in a lion's den.

One of Ashurbanipal's inscriptions reads, "The rest of the people who had rebelled they threw alive among bulls and lions, as Sennacherib my father (grandfather) used to do, Lo, again following his footsteps, those men I threw into the midst of them."

Many other authentic sites than those listed here can be seen in Israel, especially in Jerusalem and Shechem, both for the Old and New Testaments.

Israel personages recovered from seals, bullae and inscriptions

Most of the seals and bullae are in Robert Deutsch's Messages from the past Hebrew bulla from the time of Isaiah through the destruction of the first temple. See also KOROT pp. 16–21.

House of David from the stela at Tel Dan (fits only 2 Kgs 9:14–29 where Hazael killed both Johoram son of Ahab and Ahaziah son of Joram [KOROT p. 17]) and the Moabite stone, BAR 21(2): 78 (95). Thus, David is real.

Uzziah from an ossuary in the Israel Museum. "Hither were brought the bones of Uzziah; do not open." Shown in most books. Also the Tiglath-pileser III tribute list as Azriau (aka Uzziah). An account not mentioned in the Bible.

Seal of Jotham son of Uzziah (MBA p. 91).

Seal of Abiyah and Shebnaiah servant of Uzziah (KOROT p. 604).

Seal of Ahaz and Ushna servant of Ahaz (ibid. p. 604).

Seal of Queen Jezebel (872 BC) BAR 34(2): 32 (08).

Seal of Hezekiah (ibid p. 604).

Stela of Adad-Nirari III which mentions Jehoash of Israel.

Inscription above the tomb of Shebnayahu or Shebna in the Silwan village

Seal of Shebnayahu Servant of the king (Hezekiah) BAR 35(3): 45 (09).

Menahem King of Israel from the Iran stela of Tiglath-pileser's 9th year (737 BC) in the Israel museum. Also mentioned is the tribute paid in the 8th year. An event not recorded in the Bible (Bible and Spade 14(1): 23 [01]).

Seal of Manasseh (KOROT p. 604).

Seal of Josiah (ibid. p. 604).

Seal of Johoiakim (ibid p. 504).

Seal of Jehoiachin (ibid p. 604). Ration list from his captivity at Babylon.

Seal of Shema servant of Jeroboam II (ibid. p. 604). Shema is not mentioned in the Bible.

Hezir from the architrave above his Kidron family tomb. (1 Chr 24:15). Shown in most books.

Seal of Abdi servant of Hoshea (king of Israel dates to 732-722 BC), BAR 21(6): 49 (95).

Seal of Pequa King of Israel (1 Kgs 15:25; Bible and Spade 14(1): 24 [1]).

Ahaz King of Judah on a clay tablet of Tiglath-pileser III giving his full name as Jehoahaz (Ibid).

Bulla of Ahaz son of Yehotam (spelled Jotham in the Bible) King of Judah (BAR 24(3): 54 [98]).

Seal of Ushna servant of Ahaz. Not mentioned in the Bible (Ibid 56).

Bulla of Gemariah (Gemaryahu) son of Shaphan. Scribe of Josiah (BAR 17(4): 29 [91]).

Bulla of Berechiah (Baruch) son of Neriah the scribe showing his fingerprint [shown in BAR 22(2): 36 (96)]; (Ibid above p. 27).

Bulla of Yerahme'el (Jerahmeel) (Jer 36:26) the king's son (can be a title for an office) (Ibid above p. 29). He may be the one sent to arrest Jerahmeel and Baruch the scribe.

Seal of Seraiah son of Neriah. Brother to Baruch (Ibid above p. 30).

Seal of Azaliahu son of Meshullam. These are Shaphan's (see above) father and grandfather, four generations are thus represented (Ibid above p. 30).

Ring of Hanan son of Hilq'yahu (Hilkiah) the priest. Finder of the book of Deuteronomy in 622 BC (2 Kgs 22:8; Ibid above p. 31).

Bulla of Azaryahu son of Hilkiyahu, (1 Chr 6:13) grandfather and great-grandfather of Ezra (Ezr 7:1; Ibid above p. 33).

Inscription of Tobiah the Ammonite at Araq el-Emir, Jordan (BAR 19(6): 33 [93]).

Seal of Ma'adanah the King's daughter (which king is unknown) from Jerusalem 7th century BC (BAR 12(6): 66 [86]). Seals for women are rare.

Seal of 'Elishama servant of the king (Jer 36:12; 41:1; BASOR 290–291:109–14 [93]).

Seal of 'Asayahu (Asaiah) servant of the king (2 Kgs 22:12; BAR 22(2): 38 [96]).

Bulla of Yehuchal (Jehucal) son of Shelemiyahu (Shelemiah) son of Shovi (Jer 37:3; BAR 32(1): 26 [06]). The grandfather was not known before.

Seal of Palta (Pelatyahu or Pelatiah) a high government official under King Zedekiah ca. 596 BC (Eze 11:1; BAR 35: 30 [09]).

Babylonian cuneiform tablet in British Museum of Nebo-Sarsekim (Nabu-sharrussu-ukin) in Jeremiah 39:3 (BAR 33(6): 18 [07]).

Narmer (Menes) Palette from Hierkonpolis Egypt ca. 3060 BC. Contains 15 true hieroglyph symbols but before sentences were written. The only sign that can be read as a sentence is the Horus- falcon holding the nose rope. Read as: "The Horus-falcon (the divine king) overcame six thousand enemy from the papyrus land (lower Egypt)". Slate 24.5 inches high, Cairo Museum, Courtesy Jurgen Liepe.

Ur-Nammu Stela from Ur Iraq 2112 BC. Ur-Nammu being given instructions to build the ziggurat by the god Nanna. The top register shows the earliest representatives of flying angels. Limestone 10.5x5 feet, University of Pennsylvania Museum, Philadelphia, Paul McCoy.

Law Code of Hammarapi ca. 1726 BC from Sippar Iraq originally, but taken to Susa by Elamite raiders. A book written on stone, its 282 laws cover 35 crimes punishable by death. The sixth oldest known. Black diorite 7 feet 4 inches tall, Copy courtesy University of Chicago Oriental Institute, Paul McCoy

Tell el-Amarna letters, left EA 147 from Abi-Milik prince of Tyre ca. 1370 BC, asking help from invaders. Right EA 15, from Ashur-Uballit I, king of Assyria ca. 1352 BC who wrote two. This one asks for much gold in exchange for the gifts he sends. Burnaburiash II the Kassite king of Babylon got wind of it and wrote to King Tut, outraged at the presumption of the Assyrian ruler, whom he considered his vassal. He demanded the envoys be sent home empty-handed. Metropolitan Museum of Art, New York, Paul McCoy.

Merneptah Stela from Thebes 1209/8 BC. Israel is mentioned in the penultimate line (the dark area) for the first time as a people and not yet a nation. Black granite 7.5 feet tall, Cairo Museum, Courtesy Jurgen Liepe.

Tel Dan Stela from 841 BC probably of Hazael, mentions Jehoram king of Israel, Ahaziah king of Judah and the earliest reference to the House of David in the white area in the middle of the fifth line from the bottom. Basalt, © The Israel Museum, Jerusalem.

Black Obelisk of Shalmaneser III from Calah (Nimrud) Iraq to his 31st year. In his 18th year or 841 BC Shows Jehu (spelt in a shortened form Yah) or more likely Joram (Jehu was not a son of Omri, Jehu would be Yah-hu and Joram would be Yah-ram) or his emissary offering tribute. Alabaster 6 foot 7.5 inch, Copy courtesy University of Chicago Oriental Institute, Paul McCoy.

Moabite Stone from Dhiban Jordan from 838 BC, mentions YHWH, the revolt against Jehoram and the House of David. The tribe of Gad is mentioned in line 10. Black basalt 44 inches high by 27 inches wide and 13.8 inches thick, Louvre, Paris, Zev Radovan.

Winged Bull or Lamassu (Cherub) from the palace of Sargon III (II) at Khorsabad 711 BC. The three sets of horns indicate an "archangel". An inscription on the back was never intended to be seen. Gypsum (alabaster) 16 feet tall weighing 40 tons in 16 pieces, Courtesy University of Chicago Oriental Institute, Paul McCoy.

Annals of Sennachrib, 689 BC. The final account of eight campaigns in which Hezekiah (in the 3 rd campaign of 701 BC) was shut up inside Jerusalem. The Taylor prism, a duplicate in the British Museum, dates to 691 BC. Clay, Courtesy University of Chicago Oriental Institute, Paul McCoy.

Ketef Hinnom Silver Amulet from 605 BC, one of two, both contain YHWH, first time found in Jerusalem. Both contain the priestly blessing from Numbers 6:24–26 as the oldest OT scripture known, and before the P redactor and the Babylonian captivity. © The Israel museum, Jerusalem.

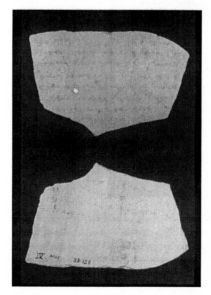

Lachish Ostracon # IV from 589 BC to Yaosh commander at Lachish mentions the Babylonian advance from Azekah where the signal fires can no longer be seen. YHWH is mentioned at the beginning. Courtesy Rockefeller Museum, Jerusalem, Paul McCoy.

Behistun Inscription Iran. Set up by Darius III in 520 BC, 225 feet above the road. This trilingual inscription on a cliff face in Old Persian, Elamite and Akkadian allowed cuneiform Akkadian or Babylonian to be deciphered for the first time. © Department of Archaeology, Boston University #29066. Used by permission.

Rosetta Stone set up by Ptolemy Epiphanes V in 196 BC. The three script inscription in hieroglyphics, demotic and Greek allowed hieroglyphics to be deciphered for the first time. Grey grano-diorite, 3 feet 10 inches by 2.4 feet by 11 inches, thick weight 1676.5 pounds, originally about 6 feet high, Metropolitan Museum of Art copy, Paul McCoy.

Dead Sea Scroll of Isaiah 1QIsaᴬ,100 BC. The only complete Bible text from the Dead Sea, composed of 17 sheets some 23.5 feet long overall, this is column 32 Isa 38:8–40:2, © John C. Trever, Ph.D. courtesy of the Trever family.

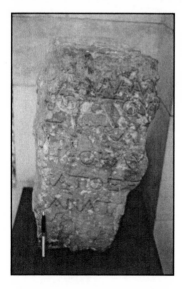

Balustrade (Soreg) warning Inscription from 13 BC. One of two known to have stood on the Temple Mount of Herod and seen by Jesus. The translated text comes from the complete stone in the Istanbul Museum. Both are in Greek but originally they alternated in Latin and Greek, the main gentile languages. Paul in Acts 21:28–29 was accused of taking Trophimus past these. Mizzi limestone, Courtesy Rockefeller Museum Jerusalem, Paul McCoy.

Pinnacle of the Temple Stone. From 12 BC, 8 feet long by 3.4 feet high and 3.3 feet thick pried off the top by Titus's troops in 70 AD, it fell 130 feet to the pavement below. The inscription reads "To the place of trumpeting to" [distinguish between the sacred and the profane]. Very likely the stone Jesus stood on when tempted by Satan. Limestone. © The Israel Museum, Jerusalem.

Rylands 459 John P^{52} 100–125 AD. Papyrus codex contains John 18:31–33 and on the back (not shown) 37–38. The oldest NT fragment known copied from the original (?) within a generation of John's death. © Rylands Library, Manchester, England.

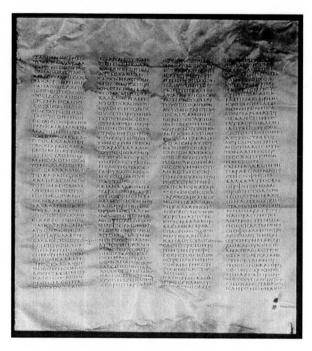

Codex Sinaticus of 350 AD, the oldest complete NT known. Shown is Numbers 23:23–24:18. © British Library Board. All Rights Reserved 1023910.282.

CHAPTER 13

ARCHAEOLOGY UNSOLVED AREAS

GENESIS 1:2. Prehistoric man and dinosaurs. This is the only place they can be inserted. Otherwise, the Bible is silent on this area. Evidence exists that the dinosaur age ended about 65 million years ago, when a 10-mile wide asteroid hit off the coast of Yucatan leaving a 110-mile wide crater. Our latest near miss was the 30-feet-across asteroid (1994 XL1) that missed us by 52 minutes. Any asteroid over one mile in diameter that hits us is a "nuclear winter killer." This will bring on winter around the world and kill off crops, as well as some species. That great time gaps are included, is to be found in 4:14 where "whoever finds me will kill me" must allow for many other sons and daughters or grandsons and great-grandsons not named. In 4:17, Cain's wife must have been a sister at least 15 years old.

There are reports of human and dinosaur tracks in the Cretaceous limestone (others say the deposit is volcanic ash) of the Paluxy River in Texas. Dr. Carl Baugh had TV and media coverage from the Dallas-Fort Worth Star Telegram and others present when some new tracks were excavated with cameras rolling. More sensational items were a fossil human finger, a human child's tooth (later discredited) found with some of the tracks and a steel hammer with wooden handle encased in Ordovician limestone, although neither of the last two were documented as found *in situ*. Some of the detached tracks are known to be forged by locals (ABR 1: 18 [88]). If dinosaurs and man were wiped out in the Flood, one would expect to find human and dinosaur fossils intermingled in deposits or at least an occasional arm, leg or other part of humans in the belly of a flesh-eating dinosaur. However, alas, such is not the case. Irrespective of whether Nessie lives in Lock Ness, (the famous photograph was declared faked by the owner before he died), there are reports of a sauropod dinosaur creature alive in the Congo. (Called Mokele-Mbembe by the natives, and sighted as recently as 1980, November 1980 issue of Science; C&EN Nov.3, 1980 p. 64; see also the internet, mokelembembe.com.)

The coelacanth, thought to be extinct for 70 million years in the cretaceous period, was first found alive in 1938, since then over 100 have been found. Their home is around the Comoros islands off Madagascar.

The extinction of the mastodons in Siberia and Alaska appeared suddenly around 13,000–11,000 years ago when they were frozen and preserved, such that mammoth steaks were served in restaurants in Fairbanks, or decayed meat fed to sled dogs. In Siberia ivory from frozen mammoth graveyards has been mined since the Roman period and since the 1900's have produced 20,000 pairs of tusks every decade. Some of the New Siberian Islands were made up almost entirely of tusks and mammoth bones; remains of a fruit tree some 90 feet tall were found with the roots, seeds, leaves and fruit still preserved. Stomach contents of mammoths showed grass, bluebells, buttercups, sedges and wild beans; such do not grow there now. The volcanic ash present speaks of violent volcano activity; several Krakatoas must have gone off nearly at the same time, such that the ash thrown into the atmosphere resulted in a vast cooling followed later by a global warming due to the large amounts of carbon dioxide, a greenhouse gas, injected into the atmosphere.

The rise in sea levels was such that whalebones have been found north of Lake Ontario 440 feet above sea level, a skeleton in Vermont was 500 feet above sea level, and another in Montreal-Quebec was 600 feet above sea level.

The darkening of the skies and the black rain (dust and smoke being washed from the air), spoken of by the Aztecs and the many accounts around the world of a world flood, may be a darkly remembered era at the close of the Ice Age, in which man was almost wiped out.

The Basques of the Pyrenees have their own language not related to any other Indo-European type. Their isolation in the mountains and their twice as high Rh-negative blood factor relative to the rest of Europe, indicate they may be direct descendants of Ice Age Cro-Magnons (RPNF p. 206).

Genesis 1:3. Creation account. The Sumerian creation account on six tablets known as the *Enuma elish* "when on high" dates to about 2500 BC. In Babylon it was recited on the fourth day of the New Year's festival. Creation is described *ex nihilo*. The first tablet describes the time when heaven and earth did not exist, Two and three describe the birth of the gods who spring from the primordial Apsu and Tiamat. Four describes how Marduk was chosen to defeat Tiamat, splitting her in half, and forming the sky and the land. The fifth describes creation of the stars to mark time and the moon to regulate the days before the creation of plant and animal life. The sixth describes the creation of man (note the similar Bible account, versus days). A seventh tablet was added much later to extol Marduk's role. A Sumerian prism from Kish dating to 1820 BC names the ten kings who ruled before the flood with reigns from 21,000 to 10,800 years, with the tenth one surviving the flood. One tablet describes the creation of woman who is named *Nin ti,* in Sumerian translated as "the lady of the rib" and "the lady who makes live." Thus, well before Moses these concepts were known, but badly garbled, with accounts of gods and goddesses fighting for control. Many seals from 2000 BC show a sacred tree and a serpent, but no text reports the Temptation of Eve. The earliest Sumerian pictograph script dates to 3300 BC (Wiseman pp. 7–15).

Genesis 3:14. Serpent to crawl on its belly. A remnant of this may be found in the anaconda, boa constrictor, python and the worm snakes (family Typhlopidae) that have a pelvis and vestigial hind legs. The ajolote is a worm lizard with only two front legs. Whales, porpoises (the hind legs have been lost) and sea lions all have vestigial limbs and hands from their days on land. If evolutionists are looking for a missing link, I can't thing of a better candidate than the platypus. Unless God is showing a sense of humor and made him out of left over parts.

4:14. Cain is afraid that others may kill him. 1. According to the Bible account, Adam was the only other male mentioned as being alive at this point. 2. Great gaps in time would be needed for many unnamed males to be a threat. However, there is no indication of any other births to Eve at this point. Eve must have had other unnamed daughters, since Cain married one in v. 17. Josephus in *Antiquities of the Jews* 1.2.3. says plainly, there were other sons and daughters. 3. Is this an indication of the existence of some prehistoric men still being around? Only #2 seems to have any credence to it.

Genesis 7:17. Noah's flood. Young Earth Creationists try to explain the Grand Canyon formation and other points as being a result of the flood. However, many facts cannot be squeezed into this mold. No large lake east of the Grand Canyon could hold enough water to scour out and remove the rock deposits by a sudden burst. Removal of silt and clay in canyon formation is one thing, but not the solid rock found here. Neither Niagara Falls nor Victoria Falls nor any other, cut back their rock formations very fast. Niagara Falls has only cut back seven miles in its entire history, which (by C-14 of mussel and clam shells) is estimated to be 12,500 years. The mini canyon formed by Mount St. Helens was in unconsolidated sediments, not the limestone, schist, basalt lava, granite, and shale of the Grand Canyon. Some of the pre-Cambrian formations near the bottom are tilted, whereas recent sedimentary formations would be level. The limestone and shale were formed at sea level, as were much of the sandstones at or near sea level. But such is not the case now or when the down cutting of the canyon began with the slow uplift of the Colorado plateau. The formations of the Grand Canyon are stratified with small worms and crustaceans in the lower older levels, and the larger dinosaurs in the upper levels. Flood deposits would not do this. In addition, floods do most of their work in the first fifty feet of depth. After this the currents do little shifting of deposits, as witnessed by the ocean floors.

Large limestone deposits over 10,000 feet thick required untold years for the creatures to form shells, die and accumulate to form the depths that are found (compare the 600-foot high and 300 additional feet below sea level at the chalk cliffs of Dover). Shale and sandstone deposits interspersed with the limestone and basalt flows all require enormous time to form (not the 10,000 years usually allowed for creation). Coal deposits of 120 seams in West Virginia are known to be interspersed with sand and clay or shale layers. This again requires time for trees to grow to maturity, die, be buried in shallow water, and the whole process repeated 120 times with the intervening sterile deposits laid down.

In the Pennsylvanian Period a slow subsidence of 2,000 to 4,000 feet was required for the deposits to be laid down (Moore p. 211). Some coal seams are up to 400 feet thick in China (it requires up to 20 feet of vegetable matter as peat to produce one foot of coal). Stumps up to ten feet high have been found standing upright in some coal beds, with the roots still in place (Ries and Watson p. 599; Life Nature Library: *The Forest* p. 43). Coal has been in use since 1000 BC. Aristotle knew it as "the stone that burns" around 330 BC. The Amethyst Cliff in Yellowstone Park on the East fork of the Yellowstone River shows 18 separate petrified forests of Tertiary Age (just before our own Quaternary Age), still standing, some trunks still 20 feet tall, covered by volcanic ash and lavas over 2000 feet thick. Again, time to grow mature trees, time to be covered up, and more time to have the cellulose eventually replaced by silica from the volcanic ash. Moreover, the whole process repeated 18 times. Although the total silicification could have been a one-time process for all, this is not very likely (Dunbar pp. 426–7).

The basalt flows of the Columbia River canyons are from 50 to 400 feet thick. The flow near Yakima, Washington has two layers of petrified logs and some stumps still upright growing into the decomposed surface of the basalt layer below, enough to form soil for growth. Further up are layers of silt, clay and pumiceous ash and a diatomite layer (which can only be laid down in water). All this is now folded at an angle of 20 degrees. All layers when formed were level, since sand, gravel, and liquid lava would not be of uniform thickness on a slope (Gilluly pp. 184–5). For some on the Grand Canyon problem see ABR 2: 77 (89); ABR 4: 16 (91).

Their way out of this dilemma is to assert that God formed these deposits without the usual deposition processes. Yet the age of the deposits have not been found to be young. This has never been considered. The coal of the world has no residual C-14 left, showing it is more than 45,000 years old. It may be argued that the trees of the Garden of Eden (which were fully-grown) were created with the growth rings in place (Gn 1:12).

The Copts traditions, for example, place the flood at about 10,300 BC (HBMS p. 242).

Other evidences for a young earth are: no loss of radiogenic lead derived from uranium decay, and retention of helium from alpha particles in the same decay. The results are from core samples of 3–15,000 ft in granites from New Mexico (ABR Supplement to 2: 4 (89) published 1990).

Genesis 37:28. Price of a slave. If Genesis was written late, how did the writer know the correct price of a slave? During the exile, the price had risen to 90-100 shekels. A chart on slave prices through the ages can be found in BAR 21(2): 53 (1995).

Genesis 39–50. Pharaoh of Joseph. The chariot in 41:43 was not said to be available in Egypt until the Hyksos Period, starting in 1725–1550 BC. They may have known of it from their contacts in southern Palestine. However, it is not mentioned or shown on monuments until the time of Thutmose I, ca. 1493 BC. Thutmose III at the battle of Megiddo in 1457 BC says he mounted his golden chariot and captured 924 chariots in all. Joseph, in 41:46, about 1883 BC, was about the age of thirty and he later died at the age of 110 (Gn 50:26), about 1803 BC. It should be easy to look back into the Egyptian Dynasties and find the corresponding Pharaoh who was on the throne in the strong 12th Dynasty; this would be Senuseret I (1917–1872 BC).

The recent book by David M. Rohl has thrown things into a quagmire. Based on an eclipse at Ugarit on May 9, 1012 BC, and correlated with the death of Amenhotep III by the El-Amarna letters, this would place the Amarna period in the late 11th century and not the mid-14th century, as is now the case. This throws the 18th Dynasty of 1570 BC, 377 years later to 1194 BC. (See also Redford, p. 215.)

Joseph's name of Zaphenath-Paneah has been shown by Kenneth Kitchen in 1993 to be "zat-en-aph", or in Egyptian *Djed(u)-en-ef,* which means "he who is called" *Pa'aneah.* The Pa or Pi in Egyptian is Ipi, Ipu, or Ipiankh (u). Ipi is given life. This name is common in the Middle Kingdom but not later. Ishpi is also Yaseph or Joseph and could be read (Ish) pi-ankhu or "Joseph lives' (Rohl p. 351).

Exodus 1:8. Pharaoh of the Oppression. The sojourn was for 430 years (Ex 12:40–41) or 1871–1441 BC. The Hyksos were finally driven out of Egypt in 1570 BC by Ahmose I (1570–1546 BC) (Johnson p. 73). The birth of Moses would be about 1520 BC during the reign of Thutmose I, 1525–1512 BC; his daughter, the later Queen Hatshepsut (1503–1482 BC) probably found him in the Ark on the Nile. She was married to her half brother Thutmose II; her only daughter (Nefrure) was married to Thutmose III. At least these were the old conventions. Rohl's book shot all this out of the water.

Exodus 12:37. Date of the Exodus ca. 1441 BC. Calculated from the 4th year of Solomon's reign (961 BC), 480 years after the Exodus (1 Kgs 6:1). Study of the King lists should make it easy to pick out who was on the throne during this time. The Pharaoh of the Exodus was probably Amenhotep II, or Amenophis (alternate spelling) 1450–1425 BC, the son of Thutmose III who reigned for 54 years 1504–1450 BC. Based on the Sphinx Dream Inscription (the stela between the paws), of Thutmose IV, 1425–1417 BC, he was not the oldest son of Amenhotep II. (Bryan, p. 40 claims that the inscription only says he had not been appointed as heir apparent; it is from an inscription of Thutmose III that Amenhotep II is called "his eldest son") However, does eldest son = first-born son? His first-born son would have died in the 10th plague. Eldest could mean eldest surviving son.

Either Amenhotep II or Thutmose IV could be a candidate. After excluding those Pharaohs whose first born sons actually succeeded them, or those not connected to the previous ruler, the list of possible candidates shrinks. Unfortunately, there is still room for doubt, as there is still some uncertainty as to the correct date of the kings. The Pharaoh of the Exodus could not have been a first-born son, for he too would have died in the 10th plague.

On the boundary stela at Akhenaten's new capital of Amarna, he wrote that he had been "forced to listen to terrible things, worse even than his father (Amenhotep III) and his grandfather (Thutmose IV) had been forced to hear." This may be a veiled reference to the disaster of the Exodus and Conquest for Egypt (Johnson p. 85).

Information on all the kings buried in the Valley of the Kings for the 18–20th Dynasties, their tombs, mummies and the grave goods found, will be found in RW up to 1996. The newly relocated tomb of Ramses II sons (KV 5) in 1985, had as recently as 1995 been discovered to have four additional descending stairways still being excavated to add to the 95 chambers so far found, bringing the present total to about 150 (Weeks p. 197).

One confirmation of the 1400 BC date crops up in a strange place. Fiber-wetting bowls to prepare flax for spinning occur in late-bronze-period sites in Israel. Based on Egyptian prototypes which were in use from 1500–1450 BC, only by women during this period when they had just arrived from Egypt in considerable numbers. This is the only period where they occur. Take a bow ladies (WW p. 254).

Seti I lost his first-born son in infancy, and then a girl was born, followed by Ramses II. There is a popular view that Ramses II was the Pharaoh of the Exodus. We know that his first-born son by Nefertiry, Amenhirkhopshef, died at the advanced age of 50 in Ramses' 40th year. By the conventional dating this would be 1238 BC (Weeks p. 276), and it was his 13th son Merenptah who succeeded him in 1236 BC. This date appears to be too late (the first 16 sons of Ramses II and their fate are listed in Weeks pp. 252–3). Everything made sense until Rohl. Rohl would make Dudimose the last king of the 13th Dynasty in 1448 BC, as the Pharaoh of the Exodus. However, we know nothing of him, and very little about the 13th Dynasty (ECIAT p. 104).

For more confusion, we know that the calculated date of about 1400 BC leaves many unanswered archaeological questions at all the sites listed in the conquest narrative, especially Jericho, Bethel and Ai. Dr. Gerald E. Aardsma has proposed (Biblical Archaeologist Vol. II, No. 3 1990) that 1 Kings 6:1 should read 1480 years, since the 1000 symbol is easy to lose. This would place the Exodus at 2450 BC, and most of the problems would disappear.

Joshua 6:1. Jericho was excavated in 1930–36 by John Garstang, who showed that the destruction and fire was dated ca 1400 BC and that the latest Bronze Age pottery dated no later than 1385 BC. Kathleen Kenyon in a 1952–56 excavation, dates this pottery at 1350–1325 BC.

Garstang found no evidence of Amenhotep III (1417–1379 or 1390–1352) in the Jericho IV ruins. Above this, evidence of Akhenaten (1379–1362 or 1352–1336 BC) is plentiful, distinctive, and well established. In addition Jericho is not mentioned in the Amarna Letters of 1382–1361 BC (the capital of Akhenaton), whereas other great cities of S. Canaan are. Abdu-Heba, the governor of Jerusalem, mentions the Habiru invading the land and that Lab'ayu of Shechem had turned his city over to the Apiru (same as the Habiru). Note: Joshua did not capture Shechem in battle (Wycliffe p. 137). While some Hebrews may have been Habiru (those who cross a boundary), not all Habiru were Hebrews.

Joshua 7and 8. Location of Ai. This site has a bearing on the conquest problem in general. These conditions must be met: (1) Ai is beside or near Bethel (12:9), whereas the traditional site of Et Tell is 1.5 miles from Bethel (Beitin); (2) the site is small (12:9), whereas Et Tell is a large site of 27.5 acres; (3) after the conquest, Ai remained a ruin for a long time (8:28), And Et Tell was unoccupied from 2400–1220 BC, which includes both dates for Joshua's conquest, but was resettled from 1220–1050 BC; (4) a broad valley is north of Ai (8:11), but at

Et Tell no valley, which could be called such, is present; (5) Ai was occupied during the Exodus (1400–1200 BC dates cover the range), But Et Tell was not occupied between 2400–1220 BC. As shown in the excavation by Judith Marquet-Krause in 1960 (EAEHL Vol. I, p. 49); no Canaanite pottery from the period of the conquest has been found at Et Tell.

Our site of Khirbet Nisya has attempted to propose a new and better location for Ai. The only factor missing is the wall or gate, which was present (Jos 9:29). Our site has been dug to bedrock four times in the Iron II, Persian, Hasmonean-Herodian, and Byzantine ages. So wall evidence is lacking at this small site of six acres, which was probably only an observation post, for the valley route coming up from Jericho to Bethel (el-Bireh), to give advance warning. Between Kh Nisya and el-Bireh is a tall mountain, Jebel et-Tawil, on which the present west bank settlement of Psagot has been established. Canaanite pottery at this site is abundant (Livingston p. 12).

Joshua 7:4. 3,000 men sent and 36 killed. Another place where 'elep and 'alep were confused. Actually three squads (rather than 3,000 men) of about 20 men each (although records can list these as small as 7–12 men each), and with 36 killed, almost the entire force was wiped out. Otherwise 36 out of 3000 is insignificant and would not cause a rout (TWLSGF p. 253).

Joshua 8:18. The kidon. This word is not the javelin but rather the sickle sword (a hacking weapon and not for thrusting) used in the MB period and already obsolete by this time. However, it was used as an emblem of divine authority. Ishtar is shown holding one on a wall painting at Mari, and Nergal is shown with one on a cylinder seal from Larsa (Yadin pp. 172–3). Several were found in King Tut's tomb, known as a khepesh (RW p. 43).

Joshua 8:30. The altar on Ebal. There is nothing said about any fighting for Shechem or its capture. The Israelites just appear there and hold an antiphonal reading of the blessing, and curses from the law, and place their inscription on the altar. Abraham (Gn 12:6) and Jacob (Gn 33:18) especially spent time in Shechem. Joseph was to be buried there (Jos 24:32) in land bought from the sons of Hamor. Although we are not told, apparently some of the descendants of Jacob still lived there and did not make the trip to Egypt. In the Tel el-Amarna letters EA 287 and especially EA 289, Lab'ayu is accused of giving Shechem to the 'Apiru. These letters to Amenhotep III date to ca. 1370 BC and may reflect the time of Joshua when the 'Apiru may have included the Hebrews. No direct proof equates these two, but the 'Apiru and Habiru as "dusty ones or those that cross a boundary or immigrants" does fit the bill.

Joshua 24:12. The sir'a or hornet. This may be symbolic as a reference for Thutmose III, who for 19 years raided into Canaan on seventeen separate occasions and softened it up for the Israelis. One of his symbols was the hornet (TWLSGF pp. 315–16; J. Garstang, *Joshua and Judges* London 1931).

The stele of Merneptah (1236–1223 or 1213–1203) mentions, in his 5th regnal year, a raid into Canaan where Israel is mentioned for the first time as being in Canaan as a "people" suggesting they were not yet a nation. This fits the time of the Judges, since Joshua did not fight against Egypt (ANE p.231). This may be Egyptian hyperbole, except for an inscription at the temple of Amada in Nubia where one small campaign into Palestine is recorded for him (Kitchen p. 60).

1 Kings 10. Queen of Sheba. The name Sheba has not been found in South Arabian inscriptions from Yemen. The oldest inscriptions of Saba (Sheba) date only to the 7–8th century BC, and Assyrian inscriptions do not mention Sabaean kings until the end of the 8th century BC. Queens are known to rule large tribal confederacies in N. Arabia from 9–7th century BC as cuneiform inscriptions relate (Phillips p. 106). In Matthew 12:24 Jesus called her the "Queen of the South." In 1950–51, Wendel Phillips found at Mareb Yemen, the Temple Bilqis (the name the Arabs call the Queen of Sheba). The origin of Bilqis is unknown. Thus, the home of the Queen of Sheba was in South Arabia and coexisted with the empire of Solomon (Wight p. 208, and Phillips p. 212).

1 Kings 11:23–25. Who was Rezon? The stele of Benhadad I discovered in North Syria in 1940, through Albright's translation, confirms the list of Syrian kings in 1 Kings 15:18. Rezon may be a secondary form of Hezion (the names are similar in Hebrew); otherwise his identification is unknown at this time. He lived about 984 BC (NUD p. 1080). Not to be confused with Rezin (2 Kgs 15:37 and 16:9) who lived about 750–732 BC.

2 Kings 18:14. Hezekiah's tribute was 300 talents of silver. Whereas Sennacherib, as recorded on the Taylor prism in the Oriental Institute, claims 800 talents of silver as tribute. It has since been found that one Assyrian weight would have been 800 talents = 300 Hebrew talents. However, both accounts record 30 talents of gold. Would the silver talent differ from the gold? This may be a textural corruption.

2 Kings 18:17. The Tartan, Rab-saris and Rab-shakeh. Tartan was known to mean the "Commander-in-chief" or second-in-command if the king himself was present. The Rab-saris has been convincingly shown to mean Chief eunuch, and Rab-shakeh means field marshal or chief-officer (TWLSGF p. 279). Any beardless face shown on the Assyrian palace sculptures is a eunuch. They are also somewhat chubby, as is true of eunuchs.

Acts 15:2 and Galatians 2. Paul's itinerary and the Jerusalem Council. There has been considerable confusion in this area in relation to the famine relief journey. Josephus states that when Queen Helena of Adibene visited Jerusalem during the procuratorship of Cuspius Fadus (44–46) and his successor Tiberius Alexander (46–48), she found the population starving and purchased wheat from Egypt and figs from Cyprus to provide food. This would place the relief visit probably in 46 AD. Acts 12:25 reads "from" Jerusalem in numerous manuscripts and "to" in others. Whether they were going or coming makes some difference (Tenney p. 208). After this, the first Missionary Journey occurred from 46–48 AD. This would place the Council in 48–50 AD.

Galatians does not seem to mention the Council; it seems it was written before the event. The visit in 1:18 was only a fifteen-day stay where he saw only James and Peter. In 2:1–20 there is no mention of a relief journey but "by revelation." The crux of the problem surfaces in 2:3, but the results of the Council are not stated. The visit to Jerusalem was to clear up this point on circumcision of Gentiles. The differences are summed up thus: Galatians 2:2 is a private conference to authenticate Paul's gospel message, versus Acts 15 as a public council to correct misunderstandings. In Galatians 2:3, Titus is cited as an example versus Acts, where he is not mentioned. In Galatians 2:4, the friction was due to "false brethren" claiming authority, versus Acts 15:24 where James disavowed the legalists. Galatians 2:7–9 was a personal agreement, versus Acts as a public letter.

CHAPTER 14

SCIENCE AND THE BIBLE

MUCH OF THIS is for general information, and includes some material on the humanities. Many points are interesting from a creation standpoint and would need to be considered as to timing, versus the first week of creation.

Agriculture—The use of the scarecrow is mentioned in Jeremiah 10:5 about 626 BC and the Letter of Jeremiah 6:70. The egg is mentioned in Job 6:6. The Hebrew is juice of purslain, which is uncertain. Not related to the Bible is the discovery of seed of the eight-petal magnolia on 4-6-93 in a tomb 6.5 feet underground at Yamaguchi 490 miles SW of Tokyo, from the 7th century BC, which germinated after three months soaking. Seeds of the pink Lotus found in a Manchurian lake, dated to 958 AD, can be seen at the Kenilworth Aquatic Garden in Washington D.C. But the record for germinating lotus seed found near Tokyo was dated to 2075 BC (Nat. Geo. Vol. 114, Aug. 1958 p. 250).

A variety of evidence now indicates that the area around the Black Sea was the home of some of the earliest agriculture including einkorn wheat, barley, lentils, chickpeas, rye, broad beans, flax, and the grape vine. Cultivation to select the stronger rachis (which may have survived the harvesting process) from the wild wheat and grapes with hermaphrodite qualities were the first advances. Animal husbandry was next, by selective breeding animals of superior quality for meat, wool, and milk, and for their being easier to control (more docile, compared to the ferocious aurochs). Breadmaking, weaving, house building, town planning, carpentry, pottery, metallurgy and decorative arts on stone or walls all were used early in this area as a "cradle of civilization" (WBF pp. 84, 180, 181; 270). The oldest wall painting, a geometric design, was found at the Neolithic site of Djade al-Mughara on the Euphrates in Syria and dates to ca 9000 BC (BAR 34(4): 22 [08]).

Architecture—The first prefab is the Tabernacle of Exodus 36, probably based on the Egyptian Holy of Holies. King Tut's was a portable shrine.

Genesis 6:15. The Ark was 450 feet long, 75 feet wide, and 45 feet deep (the standard proportions to an ocean liner in length, and 1/6 the width). The displacement would be about 43,000 tons. The Babylonian myth has one as a six-story cube of 180 feet with a mast and pilothouse. The side planks were sewn together. The Ark may also have been built this way (BAR 31(3): 18 [05]). The Greek Berosus legend has it 3,000 feet long and 1,200 feet wide.

Genesis 11:4. The Tower of Babel of about 5000 BC is the first skyscraper, patterned similar to the later Ziggurats of 3–7 stories.

Deuteronomy 22:8. Building codes or OSHA type regulations.

1 Kings 5:13 and 1 Chronicles 22:14. The Temple cost has been calculated at over five billion dollars. Based on 1500 troy oz/talent. David provided 100,000 talents of gold and a million talents of silver, plus other materials not specified in amount.

1 Kings 7:23. The Molten Sea or Laver. It was 5 x 10 cubits, hemispherical in shape, holding 2,000 baths, or about 10,000 gallons. It was cast in the clay ground east of the Jordan in Succoth (v. 46).

2 Chronicles 26:15. Large machines for defense to hurl stones and bolts from catapults in 750 BC.

Job 3:14 Waste places may also be rendered pyramids or tombs, since Job speaks of wishing to be in the land of the dead with kings and counselors of the earth.

Astronomy—The constellations Arcturus (the Bear), Orion, and the Pleiades are mentioned in Job 9:9, and the constellations in 38:32. The constellations (Hebrew *Mazzaroth*) were known to the Hebrews, but not studied as in Babylon, due to the command against Astrologers (Dt 18:10–11). In the Herodian period in Galilee, the Zodiac is found on several Synagogue floors, along with Helios the Sun god and human representations (EAEHL Vol. I, p. 188). The eclipse observed in Anyang China in 1302 BC has been used to calculate how much the earth's rotation has slowed since that time. This is due to the tides, which results in the Moon moving away from us by 3.82 centimeters per year. This has been confirmed by lasers bounced off mirrors left on the Moon by Apollo 11 in 1969. Several computer programs are now available, which you can use to make the same calculations. One is called Superstar from Picoscience of Fremont, California, and Dance of the Planets by A.R.C. Software of Loveland, Colorado. Josephus *War* 5.5.5 says the seven lamps on the lampstand represent the seven planets, and the 12 loaves of the showbread represent the 12 months of the zodiac, or year.

The Sumerians' and Babylonians' studies of the Sun, Moon, and Venus (in Babylon the star studies were recorded starting in 750 BC for over 350 years) allowed eclipses and time markers that could be used to establish dates of the early kings of Babylon.

One piece of fallout from the Hubble telescope was the study of Cepheid stars in the M100 galaxy in the Virgo cluster.

These were 56 million light years away with a Hubble constant of 80, which said the Universe was only 12 billion years old. Yet some stars gave an age of 14–16 billion years. Astronomers are uncomfortable to explain how stars would have formed before the universe began. The problem results from not knowing how tightly packed the universe is with matter. The higher gravity from a higher density could have slowed the expansion of the universe in the Big Bang, giving an age closer to eight billion years. Theories suggest the density of matter was high, but they haven't been able to find it yet. In fact, Drs. Phillip Crane and Alan Hoffman of Princeton University have calculated that there is only one particle of intergalactic dust for every 60 cubic feet; this calculates to 98% still missing (C&EN April 30, p. 16, 1973). Einstein had postulated a cosmological constant (a universal antigravity force) making the universe appear younger than it actually is. He then retracted it as the greatest blunder of his life. They may now start looking for it again, or the Big Bang may be in trouble, if eight billion years is correct (Time Nov 7, p. 69 [94]).

Confirmation of our 10th planet (depending on where you put Pluto) was made on 1-5-05 at the Palomar Observatory and given credit to Spanish astronomer J.L. Ortiz. Called 2003 UB 313 (discovered Oct. 21, 2004, now called Eris), it is ten billion miles from the Sun and orbits at a 44° angle. This is why it took so long to find it. In Oct. 2005 its moon, Dysnomia (also first named Gabriella) was announced. It has now been placed in the same class as Pluto.

If the Sphinx is older than we imagine, having a lion's body, it may have pointed to the constellation of Leo at the vernal equinox in 10,450 BC. The epoch of Leo ran from 10,970 to 8810 BC. Each Age lasts 2160 years, but some constellations are wider than others are. By using the computer program Skyglobe 3.6, you can run these for yourself. The Age of Taurus the Bull ran from 4380–2200 BC. In this period the Minoans of Crete and Egyptian Apis and Mnevis Bull cults flourished. The next Age of Aries the Ram 2200–40 BC found Abraham offering a ram and the Egyptians involved with Amun the ram-headed god (Hancock pp. 240, 455; HBMS p. 74). We now reside in the no-man's land between Pices and Aquarius, thus the refrain from the musical *Hair*, "the Age of Aquarius."

Everything about the Egyptian religion points to the fact that the Heliopolis priest's title was "Chief of the Astronomers'; the Pyramid Texts, the Shabaka Texts (HBMS p.143), and the Building Texts (HBMS p.199) all speak of the Zep Tepi "First Time" of the gods, as the origins of their civilization (HBMS pp. 200–206). These ancestor-gods of the circle of the sky were the "Followers of Horus" who started everything off (Tompkins p. 147).

The oldest meteorite impact has now been dated to the Barberton Greenstone belt tektite spherules containing iridium in South Africa. Radioactive dating of trace elements gave ages of 3.45-3.25 billion years ago from four separate impacts imbedded in sedimentary rock (see Discover, p. 22, April 1990).

The extinction of the dinosaurs is now dated to the Cretaceous-Tertiary boundary of 65 million years ago, when an asteroid crashed into the Yucatan peninsula offshore. The resultant clay layer 0.1 inches thick, traced around the world, contained 200,000 tons of iridium, an element that is otherwise rare on earth. Bolder fields and tektite deposits helped locate the impact site (Discover, p. 32, Sept. 1990).

Job 26:7. Except by inspiration of God, how could Job at least 3,000 years ago know that nothing holds the Earth up? Compare this with the Hindu version of elephants standing on a turtle that stands on a serpent. The movement of the serpent caused the earthquakes. In Egypt, heaven and earth are made from pulp (or a large egg in another version). In China, the god Pwangu carved heaven out of granite.

Chemistry—Gold is first mentioned in Genesis 2:11–12 and Iron in Genesis 4:22, which was probably of meteoric origin as in Acts 19:35. It requires a temperature of 2300°F to make cast iron. This knowledge was lost and rediscovered several times in history, since the Iron Age did not begin until about 1200 BC with the monopoly of the Hittites, and later by the Philistines who held this secret, but which was broken by Saul and David about 1000 BC. Although the Pyramid Texts from the tomb of Unas date to 2400 BC, they mention a ladder hung from an iron plate suspended in the sky that Osiris climbed; an iron throne is mentioned three times, as well as an iron scepter. R.J. Hill, working with Colonel Howard Vyse in 1837, blasted a gash in the south face of the Great Pyramid, and behind two layers of stone found an iron plate (previously covered with gold) 12 x 4 inches and 1/8 inch thick. Analysis showed the nickel content to be low and therefore not meteoric in origin (usually 7% or more). If original, this would date to about 2500 BC (the British Museum's position is that it may have been planted by Vyse, just as he may have planted the Khufu cartouche in the relieving chambers above the kings tomb chamber in the Great Pyramid (HBMS pp. 104–108). In Egyptian, iron is *'b'ja'* (Hancock p. 368; HBMS p. 108). At Tel Asmar (Eshnunna) evidence of an iron blade from 2700 BC was found. Eleven swords were found in a tomb at Dorak (dated to ca 2500 BC) 100 km from Troy. One was of silver showing seventeen oared ships (with up to 30 rowers); five have a sail, and one sword was of iron (Yadin pp. 144–5). A piece of gold from a throne had the hieroglyphs of King Sahure, the second king of the Fifth Dynasty (ca. 2458–2446 BC). Indications of ocean-going ships and knowledge of iron thus extend back this far (WBF p. 162–3). The Kultepe tablets (1950 BC) describe mining of a meteor; another that was known to have been mined is at Erzurum, Turkey. The iron was worth eight times the price of gold in the Bronze Age. A steel battle-axe from Ras Shamra dates to 1400 BC. Magnetite (Fe_3O_4, 72.36% iron) sands from the Black Sea coast contain olivine (a self-flux), which can be melted at 900° C to a sinter sponge (Science 182: 885 [73]). This probably accounts for the early smelting in this region. In Deuteronomy 8:9 "Stones are iron." Dr. Ammon Ben-Tor found near Beersheba some 15 million tons of low-grade ore in a one-mile long outcrop containing 60–65% iron. Hematite (Fe_2O_3) is 69.9% iron.

Electrum is an alloy of 75% gold 22% silver and 3% copper. Hatshepsut wanted to set up two electrum obelisks at Karnak, but didn't have enough. She had them plated instead; the grooves are still there to be seen. Thutmose III, in his Asiatic campaigns in Palestine, took out enough gold and silver to make two solid electrum obelisks of 2,500 talents total weight, or 166,650 lbs. Ashurbanipal, in the reign of Tanoutamon, took them to Nineveh as tribute to avoid the sack of Karnak.

Alexander the Great captured large quantities of gold and silver. At Suza 40,000 talents of silver and 9,000 talents of gold; at Persepolis 120,000 talents of silver, 8,000 talents of gold plus jewels and gold objects, the amounts captured at Dascylium and Sardus in Turkey, Darius's personal treasury captured at Issus, as well as the amounts captured at Damascus, Pasargadae, and Babylon are not recorded (Wilber p. 14).

Silver is mentioned in Genesis 44:2. It was first mined at Beycesultan in Turkey and Sialk in Iran about 4000 BC. Lead is mentioned in Exodus 15:10 and the oldest piece comes from Catal Huyuk Turkey, Level nine of 6400 BC, along with the oldest piece of copper slag from Level six of 5850 BC. Tin and copper for bronze are mentioned in Numbers 31:22. Tin replaced Arsenic in bronze by 2000 BC. The Assyrian word *annaku* is thought to be tin. The source was in the Elburz Mountains of Iran, as there are no known ores in Asia Minor or Mesopotamia. There were very few sources known at this time, except for Cornwall, England (which was developed late), so almost all came from the former.

Copper came from several areas usually associated with smelters called *tarshish*. When the Hittites controlled Cyprus (Kittum), the large amount of copper removed was priced at four minas (240 shekels per silver shekel). In Babylon, trade between Ur and Dilmun around 1900 BC was valued at four minas (240 shekels [the Hittite mina was lighter than the Babylonian]) of copper per silver shekel. There were 60 shekels per mina, and in Israel there were 50 shekels per mina (Saggs p. 215). The oldest use of hammered native copper was at Cayonu, Turkey dating to 7500–6500 BC (Lloyd p. 30).

Anion exchange is described in Ex 15:25, where a tree cast into bitter water made it sweet. Some types of highly oxidized cellulose can act by ion exchange to remove the chloride ion (Kunin p. 1).

The production of carbon dioxide gas is described in Proverbs 25:20 (although not called such). The pouring of acetic acid or vinegar on soda or sodium carbonate or bicarbonate produces a violent foaming.

Malachite and chrysocolla, when finely ground, gave the lovely blue-green Egyptian eye makeup, which is an antibiotic, and the copper content will kill eggs of eye parasites, as does ground stibnite (antimony trisulfide), the black eye paint. Cosmetics were not the only purpose in its use.

The oldest battery is the Baghdad battery, dated to 250 BC–250 AD, based on the pottery jars containing the copper cylinder. When tested at the General Electric High Voltage Laboratory at Pittsfield, Massachusetts using an iron rod and filled with lemon juice (citric acid), it produced 1.5-2.75 volts, enough to gold plate objects (Kenyon p. 203).

Chronology—Trying to put firm dates on kings of the Bible has always caused a problem. Now thanks to the discovery of the Assyrian eponym lists with the eclipse of the sun on 6-15-763 BC during the eponym of Bur Sagale in the 9th year of Assur Dan III (history is said to start with this date), all the dates can be placed for + or - 1000 years. Minor differences, such as whether a regnal or ascension year system was in use, and whether any co-regency was in force, allows a one-year spread for the first two, and as much as ten years for the third. Since then several other eclipses are known, which further tighten the calculations. E.R. Thiele is the final authority in this area.

Family Planning—Or lack of same. The average Jewish husband and wife spent almost half of their married life, during his wife's fertile period, in abstinence (Lev 18:19). The 5–7 days of her period (*niddah*) and the next seven days of separation (*taharah*) would almost guarantee that at the next union she was at the time of ovulation. Compare the situation of Bathsheba in 2 Samuel 11:2, 4 where the bathing was the *miqveh* purification from her period; the second purification in v. 4 followed intercourse, where a person was unclean until evening. As a result, large families were the norm. (See the comments in Hertz pp. 491–2). In Israel a child was not considered to have an independent existence until the eighth day (see Ex 21:22: the harm described is to the woman; the child could die from the miscarriage, but only a fine is exacted, as the woman could have other children (Riedel p. 172).

The ancients used several forms of birth control. By the 7th century BC, Greek colonists from Thera founded the city of Cyrene in Libya and discovered a plant called silphion (Latinized to silphium), a member of the genus Ferula or giant fennel. It grew in a narrow band 125 miles long by 35 miles wide facing the Mediterranean Sea. It could not be grown in Greece or Syria. Overharvested by the 1st century AD, it was extinct by the third or fourth century AD. A related plant, but less effective, was asafoetida (also used in Worcestershire Sauce).

Also used were Queen Anne's lace (which blocks the production of progesterone), pennyroyal, that is somewhat toxic (contains pulegone), artemisia, myrrh, and rue. Willow, date palm, and pomegranate all stimulate the production of female sex hormones, as do modern contraceptive pills. Acacia gum is a spermatocide producing lactic acid anhydride, used in contraceptive jellies and also bonded to the edges of vaginal diaphragms.

Between 1–1000 AD the population of Europe, Egypt, and the Roman Empire actually declined by use of contraception and infanticide (plague pandemics also took a toll, especially the one under Lucius Verus in 166–169 [GRE p. 94]). Much of this knowledge was confined and passed down by the women, especially midwives, and today's healers or homeopaths. The Renaissance mostly confined the medical profession to men in the new medical schools, and the knowledge was no longer stressed or available to them (Archaeology p. 29 Mar/April 1994).

Genetics—Described in Genesis 30:32–43 and 31:11–12. Jacob tried to influence the breeding process, but the angel of the Lord showed him the real reason through the laws of heredity. The mule is mentioned in 2 Samuel 13:29, but Leviticus 19:19 said the Hebrews were not to have them. They were first imported from Togarmah in East Cappodocia (see Eze 27:14).

Mutants have never been shown to be beneficial, and evolutionary natural selection could not use them to improve the species. This would also be a direct violation of the second law of thermodynamics. You cannot pull the species up to higher ground by its bootstraps.

Recent work by Svante Paabo in Germany, on a limited amount of 38,000 year old Neanderthal DNA, has shown that there was little interbreeding with modern humans, as was suspected.

Geology—Oil and gas is indicated in Genesis 19:24–28, where a gas blowout is the probable cause. Surface asphalt-seeps and asphalt-blocks floating on the Dead Sea (the latest was in the 1950s) have been known since about 2000 BC, when the Egyptians used asphalt from the Dead Sea. Asphalt for the Ark in Genesis 6:14 or the tower of Babel in Genesis 11:3 comes from the oil seeps near Kirkuk or Hit in Iraq. Israel drilled its first well on the West side of the Dead Sea on 11-3-53, a small amount of noncommercial oil was found at the Masada 1 well after deepening in 1980. A total of 300 wells have been drilled. The Herletz-1 well near Ashkelon has produced 18 million barrels of oil, and still produces some today. Three small gas fields are in operation ten km west of the Dead Sea and South of Masada (DSLS p. 58).

Job 28:5 indicate volcanic origin is deep underground. Job 28:1–2, 6 indicates metal is dug out of the earth. Earthquakes are mentioned in Amos 1:1 and Isaiah 24:19–20, as well as Matthew 27:51–54; 28:2 and Acts 16:26.

Minerals are described in Revelation 21:19–21, where the colors of the foundation stones cover the spectrum. Gold will be so common it will be used for paving.

History—The Assyrians and Babylonians were able to keep detailed accounts of events in archives and the Assyrian King Lists. Tiglath-pileser I (1114–1076 BC) said that the temple of Anu and Adad, built by Samsi-Addu I, had become dilapidated after 641 years. Shalmaneser I (1263–1234 BC) said that 159 years had passed between the repair of Assur's temple by Erishu and that done by Samsi-Addu I, and that an additional 580 years had elapsed until his own reign. A boundary stone of Enlil-nadin-apli (the 5th king of the Second Dynasty of Isin) says that 696 years from his 4th year had elapsed from his father Nebuchadrezzar I and Gulkisar, the 6th king of the First Dynasty of the Sealand. From this information, the chronological data for the beginning of the Kassite Dynasty at 1660 BC, as well as the dates for Hammurabi (1760 BC) and Samsi-Addu I who died between years 11–14 of Hammurabi, can be reasonably established. Thus occasional gaps in the Assyrian and Babylonian

King Lists can be closed up (Iraq 46: 115 [1984]). We think we are doing well to remember events from the time of George Washington.

Literature—Paul quotes Greek poets in Acts 17:28a; Epimenides, 28b; Aratus in the "Phagnomena," or from Cleanthes "Hymn to Zeus." In 1 Corinthians 15:33 he mentions Menander's play "Thais," and in Titus 1:12 Epimenides' "Minos." Jude quotes the Assumption of Moses in v. 9 and the Book of Enoch 60:8 in v. 14/15.

Mathematics—The Pyramid of the Sun at Teotichuacan in Mexico has a ratio of the height of 233.5 feet to the perimeter of the base of 2932.76 feet, which is a relationship of four pi. The Great Pyramid's original height of 481.3949 feet and the perimeter of its base of 3023.16 feet give a ratio of two pi. Yet pi was only crudely known to the Greeks (Hancock p. 319). The King's Chamber of the Great Pyramid also incorporates phi (or the "golden section") when the 10 x 20 royal cubit measurements are realized and used. The Greeks also used it in the Parthenon construction (Hancock p. 336; Tompkins p.189).

Medicine—The need to isolate an infected person was known to Zimrilim of Mari, where a letter to his wife gave instructions concerning a woman with a contagious unnamed disease: He gave strict orders, no one is to drink from the cup she uses; no one is to sit on the seat she takes; no one is to lie on the bed she uses, lest it infect the many women who are with her (TLBM p.14).

Pliny reported that there was a plant, the juice of which could stanch bleeding and cure cough; it was called ephedrine. A purer and stronger form has been known since the 1880s, but it killed the dogs it was tested on because it was too strong.

The Bactrians near the Afghanistan-USSR border used a water extract with poppy to produce a hallucinogenic brew. The Zoroastrians picked it up from the Bactrians and used it as well. Hashish, obtained from the tops of marijuana plants, was used by the Assassins (the name is derived from hashish) founded in Qazvin (Kazvin), Iraq by the Shiite sect in 1090. In their drug-induced state, they murdered many Crusaders. Myrrh was used by the ancients to fill gashes in plants and was used as a wound drug, not knowing that it is a bactericide (research at Rutgers University shows it to contain furanosesquiterpenoid, a compound toxic to cancer cells of leukemia, breast, prostate, ovary and lung by deactivating a protein in cancer cells that resists chemotherapy). Its soothing smell also covers the stench of infected wounds, and the resin never decays in nature (Scientific American p. 126 June 1976; TFFK p. 209).

Jewish women who practice the laws of niddah and taharah (see family planning above) were found to suffer uterine cancer only one to fifteen that of Gentile women in the same social and economic class. This study on 80,000 Jewish women was done at Mount Sinai Hospital, New York (Hertz p. 492).

Attempts to contact the spirit world were common, by use of severed or shrunken heads in Ecuador or Peru. The use of hallucinogens, by healers or shamans among some North American Indians continues today, such as coca for its cocaine (in the eastern Andes and has been in use since 2500 BC). Datura (contained in jimson weed), wilka, the fruit known as espingo, or the San Pedro cactus which contains 2% mescaline (the highest known) also sends the user into never-never land (Hadingham pp. 7; 171). Some ceremonies are still conducted today along the straight-line paths at some Bolivian and probably Nazca lines. Particularly in areas where water was scarce, the ceremonies would invoke a plea for water (Hadingham p. 256).

Summer rye is easily affected with ergot, from which lysergic acid amide is obtained; it only has 10% of the activity of D-LSD or lysergic acid diethylamide. It is also found in morning glory seeds (ololiuqui) used by the Aztecs. Convulsive ergotism produces hallucination, crawling sensations of the skin, vertigo (see the symptoms of Mt 17:15), tinnitus aurium, epileptiform convulsions, tingling of the fingers, delirium, mania and psychosis among others. Women and children are affected more than men are. The symptoms were often associated with women, in witchcraft or demon possession. Many of the Bible cases may be of this type (although the cases where the demons speak may be different); the Salem witch trials are of the same type (Science 192: 21 [1976]). Marijuana as a legal drug in California is supposed to give relief to many that cannot get pain relief in other ways. However, the smoke, contains some of the same tars present in tobacco smoke, including the potent carcinogen benzopyrene. Therefore, realize that users are still at risk for lung cancer.

Metallurgy—In Deuteronomy 8:9 the copper from the hills was the basis for Solomon's wealth and was used for barter (1 Kgs 9:26 and 2 Chr 8:17–18). Dr. Ammon Ben-Tor studied this area in 1949. As much as 100,000 tons of metallic copper is estimated to have been removed from the Timna mines, and by extension of the deposits; at least 200,000 tons can still be mined. Israel has since reopened the mines. Refining of ore is mentioned in Job 28:1, 2, 6; Isaiah 1:25; and Ezekiel 22:16, 20.

Fired bricks in Genesis 11:3 require a temperature of 1900–2200° F. Glass requires only 2012° F and was known in Egypt by 3000 BC. Enamels require 1300° F.

Mental Health—In Job 5:2, physicians and psychiatrists recognize the principle of hate and anger in emotional instability (Prv 22:24).

Physics—In Job 38:19 light does not dwell in a place; indeed, it travels at 186,281 mi/sec (Boyd p. 42). Why a child's Crayola picture is held to the fridge by a magnet is still not understood.

Publics Works—How to take an island. In Ezekiel (26:3, 7, 15) he prophesied that Tyre would be destroyed. Nebuchadrezzar destroyed the land city after a 13-year siege in 587–573 BC. The record probably belongs to Egypt's Psamtik I; his siege of Ashdod lasted 29 years before the city fell, ca 610 BC (Herodotus II 157). Nebuchadrezzar could not take the island city since he had no navy; the population simply moved lock stock and barrel from the mainland. The island city was not taken until Alexander the Great constructed a 650-foot land bridge (mole) using the debris from the old land city in 332 BC. Fishermen nets are still dried in the old land city today, which has several good fresh water springs, but the old city has never been rebuilt except for some population pressures within the last few years in this area.

The oldest known dam was built by Khufu in Wadi Gerawi (Verner p. 155).

Religion—The oldest version of the Book of the Dead is the Pyramid Texts (inscribed on the walls) from the 5th and 6th Dynasties at Saqqara, known as the Heliopolitan version edited by the priests of the college of Annu (On of the Bible). Next is the Theban version written on papyrus used in the 18th to the 20th Dynasties. This is the famous Papyrus of Ani. The next version also used in the 20th Dynasty is sometimes written in hieratic. The final version known as the Saite was used from the 26th Dynasty to the end of the Ptolemaic period 330 BC. The purpose of the texts were to assist the passage of the newly departed to heaven, by knowing the names of the gods and spells to reanimate the body. Some of the earliest chapters are older than the 1st Dynasty. Please note some of the Dynasty dates in Burge have been lowered. Chapter 64 is the only one roughly dated. A rubric on the coffin of Queen Menthu-hetep of the 11th Dynasty says it was found in the foundations beneath the hennu (solar) boat in the time of the king of the north and south, Hesep-ti the fifth king of the 1st Dynasty (Budge p. xiii; Tompkins calls him Udimu p. 369, and Verner lists him as Den p.18; Rohl p. 15). This chapter was said to be the most important, and its recitation was as effective as reciting the entire book (it is not contained in the Papyrus of Ani). It also contained information on the size and shape of the earth and that the spirits of those in the Nether World are 12 cubits high (20.6 ft). Many parts were already ancient and scribes had trouble copying or understanding them even as early as the 6th Dynasty. The Papyrus of Ani has two copies of chapter 18; apparently the scribes lost count. A Berlin papyrus of the 19th Dynasty has chapter 77 starting from the wrong end, although the title is given (Budge p. xxix).

Statistics—Some 332 prophecies in the Old Testament refer to and were fulfilled by Christ. This probability being fulfilled by one man is $1/84 \times 10^{97}$. For anyone who appreciates these kinds of calculations, there can be no room for doubt. The details of Tyre above show that some 25 details were cited. The Law of Compound Probabilities states that if a prophesy concerning a person, place or event has 25 details beyond the possibility of human calculation, collusion, collaboration, comprehension and coincidence, there is only one chance in 33.55 MM of its accidental fulfillment. In Zephaniah there are again 25 prophecies directed against the land of Palestine, and all have come about; the probability function would be the same.

The Law of Chance states, "events whose probability is extremely small will *never occur*." The range is $1/10^{15}$ or 10^{-15} as negligible on the terrestrial scale. On the cosmic scale any probability of 10^{-50} will not occur. The probability of one gene occurring by chance is 10^{-236}. Thus, evolution will never occur and our galaxy has not been around for a long enough time for it to occur. So why do we insist on keeping this disproved theory (Coppedge pp. 166–7)? Statistics also says that if one foot is on a hot plate at 172° C and the other in liquid air at -147° C, then on average you are comfortable at 25° C or room temperature. Try telling either foot that. Evolution ignores these laws, but they do open the door to Intelligent Design. Statistics is the one discipline that can destroy evolution theory. Remember that these are large numbers such that the age of the universe of 12 billion years expressed in seconds is only 3.787×10^{17} seconds.

You have probably heard this story. What would you rather have: a billion dollars, or one grain of wheat doubled for each square on a chessboard? The sum of all the grains on the squares is 1.843×10^{19} or more than all the wheat produced in the world. Please take the wheat. You will be rich beyond your wildest dreams.

In Revelation 21:16, how many people will a city of 1379 mi^3 hold (12,000 stadia in the Greek at 606.75 feet per stadia)? Tongue in cheek that will be your homework assignment for today.

Textiles. The best percale today runs only 100 warp threads per inch. Whereas, a 1st Dynasty sample has 200 warp threads per inch (Barber p. 148). The Inca of Nazca had burial cloth 20 feet wide and 80 feet long and another of 160–200 feet long. None of these large looms has been found. A tremendous amount of cloth has been consigned to burials. Weaving done by women was the most labor intensive and resulted in the most time spent in yearly activities, with grinding of grain second on the list.

Urban Renewal—In Ezra 3:10 and 6:1, 13, the Temple was rebuilt by Zerubbabel in 520 BC and was about 1/3 larger than Solomon's, which took 7.5 years to build. Herod essentially tore Zerubbabel's down and expanded the temple proper in 1.5 years (20–19 BC); the courts took eight years, but continued work was still in progress 46 years later (John 2:20) and was not completed until 64 AD, and was finally destroyed again by Titus in 70 AD.

The oldest city found so far with a street network is Sha'ar Hagolan, a pottery Neolithic Yarmukian settlement at the south end of the Sea of Galilee (see Garfinkel). A site known as Poliochni on Lemnos (also mentioned in Jason and the Argonauts as being a home of Amazon women warriors) at the Dardanelles Strait revealed two Stone Age Neolithic settlements with streets at right angels (WBF p. 159). The oldest town of 32 acres is Catal Huyuk south of the Hasan Dag volcano, which is shown erupting on a wall painting. The city dates from the 8–7 century BC, with evidence of cattle farming, bread making, stamps for making patterns on cloth and some of the oldest pottery known as well as evidence of early metallurgy from slag dumps. Metal tubes for a woman's string skirt as well as pictorial representations are present (WBF p. 108).

Writing—Before the alphabet, as man started to produce crops, herds and goods, a method of counting was developed in Turkey, Iraq, Syria, Jordan (at "Ain Ghazal) and Israel using miniature clay cones, spheres, disks, tetrahedrons, cylinders, ovoids, rectangles, and odd shapes for animals. Some were pierced; the oldest date to ca 8000 BC. This was five thousand years before Egyptian hieroglyphics or Mesopotamian cuneiform. One from Nuzi found in 1928 was found inside a clay envelope inscribed in cuneiform: "Counters representing small cattle 21 ewes that lamb; six female lambs, eight grown male sheep, four male lambs, six she-goats that kid, one he-goat, three female kids. The seal of Ziqarru the shepherd." Inside were exactly 49 counters (WBF p. 99). The worlds oldest language, Sumerian, is now being put in dictionary form by the Univ. of Pennsylvania. Completion is expected (they have completed A and B) by 2137 (BAR 19(5): 27 [93]).

The oldest pictographic writing comes from two of three clay tablets found at Tartaria, near Turda in Romania in a pit containing an adult male dating from 4500–4000 BC and 1000 years older than similar tablets found at Uruk Iraq. Once they were recognized for what they were, other similar signs were recognized on pottery fragments found as early as 1872 in the same area (WBF p. 142).

The World—How much did God reveal about the earth? In Job 26:7; 38:12–14; 28:25; 38:35, God hangs the earth upon nothing and the earth turns (changed) in its rotation. The air has weight and messages are sent by lightening or electricity. In Proverbs 8:27, God set a compass (circle) upon the face of the deep (ocean). Moreover, in Isaiah 40:22, it is God who sits upon the circle of the earth. In spite of the Flat Earth Society, the Earth doesn't have any edges or boundaries. As Hawking observes, "reports of people falling off the edge are thought to be highly exaggerated" (SHUN p. 83). In Ecclesiastes 1:6–7, winds have circuits. Water evaporates and precipitates. In Luke 17:31–36, Jesus taught that the earth rotates for the events described, "In that day and in that night" the same event is taking place.

Communication—In Revelations 11:3–12, v. 9 indicates, "all the world shall see them." Some 1900 years ago instant, communication as by TV satellite is predicted. Christ's second coming in Revelation 1:7 where "every eye shall see him" is of the same type.

Public Banquet—At the entrance to the throne room in the new palace of Ashurnasirpal II (883–859 BC) at Nimrud or Calah in 869 BC, on a sandstone slab was carved in 154 lines, the intricate details for a ten day banquet (for 47,074 men and women of his country, plus 5,000 foreign dignitaries, 1,500 court officials and 16,000 local townspeople who consumed 2,200 oxen, 16,000 sheep, 1000 calves, 33,000 game birds, 1,000 stags and gazelles, plus innumerable condiments and vegetables, plus 10,000 skins of wine and 10,000 barrels of beer) (ANE Vol. II p. 99; BAR 16(5): 63 [90]).

Additional Unsolved Areas

These are not mentioned in the Bible, but relate to overall problems involving creation or the flood.

Age of pre-Cambrian Deposits. Coppedge visited the Schefferville Mine of Iron Ore Company of Canada, and was shown several fossil wood specimens from depths of several hundred feet. The company geologist said no overturns of strata or fissures that would catch material in crevices were present in the ore body. Carbon -14 dates of only 4,000 years were obtained. The ligno-cellulose structure was well preserved (Coppedge pp. 184–5).

Pollen from pine trees and flowering plants has been found in pre-Cambrian strata in the Grand Canyon. Evolutionists were caught off guard, as algae and mosses were only supposed to exist then, and had to suppose that such advanced development had to occur earlier than was expected, Coppedge pp. 194–5.

Amino Acids. The Murcheson meteorite from Australia was found to contain six protein type amino acids (adenine, guanine, thymine, cytosine, and uracil) in both L and D forms in essentially equal amounts. These would be of inorganic origin, as no selectivity of forms is found as in living systems (Scientific AmericanVol. 226, June 1972, p. 42; C&EN Sept. 5, 1983 p. 4).

A number of organic molecules have been found in space. Hydrogen atoms with the high kinetic energy of space has been termed "hot" and will react to form free radicals at temperatures as low as 50°C. These hot hydrogen atoms can exist for about 100 years. Ammonia, methane, water, methanol, formaldehyde, carbon monoxide, formic acid, aspartic acid, serine, threonine, glutamic acid, proline, alanine, leucine, and isoleucine have been detected in space (C&EN June 3, 1974 p. 17). In addition silicon monosulfide, dimethyl ether, and hydrogen deuterium oxide have been found (C&EN Nov. 4, 1974 p. 4). Now sulfur dioxide, cyanodiacetylene (HC_5N) were added in (C&EN Dec.15, 1975 p. 19). The largest molecule to be detected is a porphyry, bispyridylmagnesiumtetrabenzoporphine ($MgC_{46}H_3ON_6$). These are important to life processes such as photosynthesis (chlorophyll) and respiration (cytochrome) (C&EN Nov. 1, 1971 pp. 5–6; Aug. 27, 1984 p. 22).

Early analysis of moon rocks found amino acid precursors of glycine, alanine, glutamic acid, aspartic acid, serine, threonine, and others in ranges of 7–40 ppb. Absence of water stopped the process at this point from giving the amino acids. The low concentrations have prevented identification of the precursors at this point. One of the moon rocks from Apollo 16 gave a date of 4.47 + or - 0.02 billion years for the age of the moon (C&EN March 19, 1973 p. 35).

The oldest life on Earth is now thought to be the ancestral forms of cyan bacteria, a type of blue-green algae, 3.5 billion years old from Warrawoona, Western Australia. J. William Schoph has found six different species of filamentous fossils. These Precambrian rocks from the Archean period had escaped the 500°C temperatures that defaced and destroyed the early records elsewhere of Earth's history (Discover Oct. 1990 p. 98).

In 1953 Stanley Miller, a student of Harold Urey at the Univ. of Chicago proposed passing an electric discharge through an early earth atmosphere of methane, ammonia, hydrogen, and water vapor in a reducing atmosphere to produce amino acids; again a D, L mixture (C&EN Aug. 27, 1984). Since 1966, it is now known that this gas mixture for the early earth was in error and was not hydrogen rich. Rather it contained carbon dioxide, nitrogen, methane, ammonia and water vapor. Under these same conditions, the products will be formaldehyde and cyanides. Remember your high school embalming fluids! Not very conductive to preserving life (Strobel p. 37). In fact water vapor and oxygen (needed at some point in life processes) in this mixture will result in the amino acids being destroyed, thus excess time will work against the process.

In nature, we find only the L form of amino acids used in proteins. All amino acids have the structure $H_2NCHRCO_2H$, where the difference occurs only in the R group. Of the twenty-five amino acids, only glycine is not optically active (in the above case R is H). Usual lists have only twenty or twenty-one, sometimes found are cystine, a disulfide of cysteine, hydroxy-lysine, hydroxyproline, thyroxin (a tetra iodide), asparagine and glutamine. When a carbon atom is joined to four different groups it becomes asymmetrical or optically active, by twisting of the plane of polarized light to the left or right known as L or D. Two such carbon atoms with identical groups give a third form, by internal compensation; the meso form may be present, which is not optically active due to a plane of symmetry. The D and L forms are mirror images of each other, as is the right and left hand (except for scars or other defects). Everything has a mirror image (except a vampire). Similarly, the vitamins such as L ascorbic acid (vitamin C), are the only ones the body can use. In the sugars, the D form is the only one used. This convention for sugars has nothing to do with the rotation observed; most of the sugars used are dextrorotatory (+). All sugars are optically active; glucose for example has four centers. Optical activity is also possible in other atoms such as nitrogen, which can hold three different groups; silicon, which can hold four; or phosphorus, which can hold five. Some D-amino acids are found in bacteria cell walls and in some polypeptide antibiotics such as bacitracin A, which has three; and polymyxin B, which has one. Some hallucinogens are also the D form.

The D-isomers can be used to some extent but are less effective. D-Adrenaline is 1/12 as active, D-hyoscyamine (the L form is atropine) has no physiological effect. D-Thyroxine is 1/3 as active. D-Ascorbic acid is much less active. Only one stereoisomer of Chloromycetin is an antibiotic. D-Ephedrine has no action as a drug and interferes with the L-form. (-) Glucose cannot be metabolized by animals or fermented by yeast. Cocaine has three asymmetric atoms, but study of the molecule showed that only some of the groups were necessary for activity. Stovane and Alypin have only one and Novocain has none. Each would be easier to synthesize. A slight alteration in the position of a group or a slightly different group can alter the activity of a drug, especially the antibiotics, where the D and L forms are again quite different in action. Among some poisons such as nicotine, the L-isomer is more toxic.

Evolution would have to explain this to produce life, but there is no known mechanism to account for it or allow it to happen. Thus, we, our food and enzymes necessary for life processes, are all optically active. Several theories have been proposed to show how it could happen: Spontaneous crystallization. Special temperatures are often needed (Pasture found the D and L-tartaric acids, as the sodium ammonium salt, which crystallizes only below 28°C this way), but it will not work for proteins. Formation of amino acids does occur under the influence of circularly polarized light: the best result gave only 0.7% of one enantiomer. Formation on quartz crystals: quartz is SiO_2 and is not optically active as a liquid or in solution; but quartz crystals, composed of the same SiO_2 are. In nature, the D-quartz (left hand) predominates to less than 1% over the L-quartz. In fact, optical activity was first discovered by examination of quartz crystals. Joining of L amino acids in definite sequences to form a protein results in an alpha spiral, which would be needed at the same time as the duplication process for any meaningful life to form. Incorporation of even a few D amino acids will terminate RNA replication by disrupting the alpha spiral.

No actual results have been reported when either of the above methods were tried. Asymmetric polymerization has been proposed but no results have ever shown it to work. Another was irradiation with chiral electrons. Asymmetric electrons from beta decay of strontium-90 will destroy the D form of tryptophan at a lower dose than for the L form, but after a few months the solution was not significantly more left handed (radiation is also destructive for both forms). The Earth's magnetic field was proposed, but there was no way to test it by magnets due to the perpendicular lines of force. In fact, no natural solution has been found which could account for the exclusive use of L amino acids in naturally occurring proteins (Coppedge pp. 243–247).

Intelligent Design. The code of life is bound up in the genetic code. The double helix of DNA (deoxyribonucleic acid) along with RNA (ribonucleic acid) determines how L amino acids are formed into proteins. Geneticists are convinced that RNA came into being first, since it takes RNA to produce proteins (with oxygen at the right amounts necessary to process life). All the parts (DNA, RNA, D-ribose, phosphate [as a tri phosphate] and L amino acids) must be available at the same time and within the right temperatures to prevent the early precursors from being degraded before they can be used (Ashton pp. 26; 209). Ribose is a five carbon cyclic sugar, the only one used.

The code only has four letters: A, G, T and C from adenine, guanine, thymine and cytosine, and occasionally 5-methyl cytosine for DNA; RNA has A, G, C and U where U is uracil. Adenine and guanine are purines (a condensed six on five-member ring), while cytosine, thymine and uracil are pyrimidines (one six-member ring). With the unwinding of the helix of DNA, the RNA matches up with it in a specific way. Adenine of DNA pairs with uracil of RNA, guanine with cytosine, thymine with adenine and cytosine with guanine. Thus, AATCTTAG on DNA becomes UUAGAAUC for RNA. Of the twenty amino acids used in proteins, a three-letter code stands for and causes a particular amino acid to be incorporated into the growing protein chain. This was first proved by Nirenburg and Matthaei who placed each amino acid (only one of which was radioactive), with E. coli extracts, ribosomes, ATP (adenosine triphosphate an energy transfer source), and t (transfer) RNA containing only uracil in each of twenty test tubes. Only one was found to contain radioactive polypeptides consisting of phenylalanine. Thus, some combination of only Us was responsible. The code said U; the answer came back as phenylalanine. All the others have been found by the same procedure. However, several three-letter codes (or codons) can code for the same amino acid. Proteins are built from the RNA side only by splitting out a molecule of water from the carboxylic acid group of one amino acid and the amine group of another. Thus, GUA codes for valine; AAA codes for lysine; GGG codes for glycine. There are 4^3 (or 64) combinations for the twenty common amino acids leaving three stop signals to halt chain growth: UAA, UAG, and UGA. The synonyms occur on the third letter such that UUU, and UUC code for phenalanine but UUA, UUG, CUU, CUC, CUA and CUG all code for leucine. Only methonine AUG and tryptophane UGG have only one codon; all the others have at least two. The reason or significance for this is not known. God still retains some secrets.

In sickle cell anemia, normal hemoglobin contains glutamic acid (coded by GAA or GAG), but sickle cell hemoglobin contains valine (coded by GUU, GUC, GUA, or GUG). Thus, the replacing of one adenine for a uracil in 450 nucleotides results in a life or death situation. Not all is bad, though, since antibiotics alter the ribosome RNA, causing misreading of the code and death of the offending organism. The recent determination of the human genome will allow all genetic diseases to be determined as to where the defect occurs in each chromosome (Curtis p. 257). At present, the genetic code of mice, rats, chimps, chickens, dogs (with 19,300 genes) and humans (with 22,300 genes) have been worked out.

This short diversion should show that *chance* is not operating here, especially if coupled with the use of only the L amino acids. Consult the above reference by Curtis or any college biology or chemistry textbook for additional information or formulas. Biologists who still allow for evolution have to sweep a lot of stuff under the rug and play the part of the ostrich with head in the sand routine. Such denial of alternate sources of information is not the true scientific method. Nobel Laureate Francis Crick even proposed panspermia, the idea that earth was seeded by life from other planetary systems in order to avoid the time problem. How convoluted can this get? Consider that the enzymes that make the amino acid histidine themselves contain histidine, a classic "which came first, the chicken or the egg" question. Also females use testosterone in their bodies to produce the female sex hormone estradiol.

Dating Methods. Several methods are available to date organic and inorganic objects. Carbon-fourteen relies on cosmic rays, which are actually high speed protons (as shown by the greater number coming from the West and having a positive charge of average 10^8 electron volts) with a smaller number from helium nuclei or alpha particles from the sun and a smaller number of higher energy 10^{18} electron volts galactic cosmic rays (VSE p. 447). These react in the upper atmosphere to produce neutrons, which react with nitrogen-fourteen to produce a radioactive carbon-fourteen by ejection of a proton. Since capture of a neutron and ejection of a proton decreases the atomic number by one, nitrogen is changed to carbon. The carbon-fourteen is then oxidized in the air to carbon-fourteen dioxide, where it is absorbed by plants and then eaten by animals. When the plant or animal dies, the uptake is stopped and the radioactive carbon-fourteen begins to disintegrate back to nitrogen-fourteen (with the emission of a 0.155 Mev beta particle, which is what is actually measured). The rate for half to disappear is 5730 years (the rate was adjusted from 5568 years in 1973). Older dates obtained before 1973 can be recalibrated by multiplying by 1.03. After seven half lives, the remaining carbon-fourteen is too low for accuracy and dates of 45,000 BP (before the present) are the maximum obtainable. The natural isotopes, 99% carbon-twelve and 1% carbon-thirteen, play no part in the processes. At present, there is no known way to change the decomposition rate (based on processes naturally occurring on earth). No current book even mentions any method to change the decomposition rate (www.iem-inc.com/ph rlfr.html).

It is known that if the cosmic ray flux rate in the upper atmosphere changes, or if carbon dioxide from fossil fuels from oil or coal (which has already decayed to zero and thus is over 45,000 years old, and contains no carbon-fourteen) is injected into the atmosphere, there can be a distortion on the dates obtained (Time June 11, p. 55 [1990]). Reports of residual carbon-fourteen in coal or oil is thought to come from radioactive decay in the absorbed Uranium Thorium series, which produces new C-14. Bacteria and fungi growth can also distort C-14 values on samples kept wet (see internet Carbon-14 in coal deposits or Dr. Harry Gove). In fact, the burning of coal and atmospheric nuclear testing (the neutrons produced result in carbon-fourteen being formed from nitrogen-fourteen) caused a doubling of atmospheric carbon-fourteen production that was first detected in 1950. These large atmospheric burst effects were put to use, in that the mixing rates in various carbon reservoirs, such that once laid down a tree ring, does not exchange carbon-fourteen with other tree rings. In fact, all samples are computed using 1950 as the zero reference point with an oxalic acid standard stocked by the US National Bureau of Standards. The older Libby half-life of 5568 was also retained, because many of the early results used this value. Therefore, BP (before the present) also means 1950. Calibrated dates can be adjusted from these data (Bowman pp. 19; 42).

In addition the effects of a change in the earth's magnetic field (which has been decreasing since first measured in 1835) including field reversals and colder temperatures during the ice ages, which cause carbon dioxide to dissolve more in cold water and ice and to be released as the temperatures rise world wide (Barnes p. 33). It was recently announced that the earth's magnetic pole is sliding off to the west and will soon be located in Siberia. The strength of the earth's magnetic field shields us from most of the effects of cosmic rays. It had been determined that the half-life for the rate of decay is 1,400 years. Since the decay rate is exponential, the field will reach zero in 11,000 AD. There are very serious implications in these results, including more cosmic rays reaching earth and more genetic damage down the pike, which may be showing up even now (Barnes pp. 23,25).

Field reversals have not occurred in the timescale of radiocarbon. This old carbon dioxide effect has not been established. (See Bowman for the discussion.) The eleven-year and two-hundred-year sun spot cycles both cause cosmic rays to be deflected, resulting in lower carbon-fourteen production. The effect of the eleven-year cycle appears to cause no more than a twenty-year variation in age. The greater ocean surface area in the southern hemisphere leads to an increased carbon-fourteen dioxide removal, in that radiocarbon dates are about 30 years older than normal.

A cross correlation was made with sequoias and bristlecone pine (in Ireland the Oak Quercus has been used for up to 7000 years, also the German Oak) samples of known date (in ten year increments), which at present can be dated to 8000 years (BP, FLIA, p. 54). Good correlation was obtained up to 550 BC; then divergence up to the last dated sample of 5350 BC (not enough wood was available for the older samples but could now be redated by the newer AMS method below) gave a carbon-fourteen date of only 4760 BC, or 11% low. Major spikes and broad divergent areas were found for 1700 AD, 1540, 1460, 350 BC, 650, 1850, 2200, 3405, 3750–4100, 4500–4800, and 5100–5300. The tables can be used to correct the apparent dates. The MASCA Newsletter published by the University Museum of the University of Pennsylvania correlates all methods of dating with other laboratories. Vol. IX (1) for August 1973 contains the needed information. The method has been correlated with samples as old as 40,000 BP.

Intolerable variations are obtained with older samples, as the fraction of carbon-fourteen left is too low. Sample purity is the hardest factor to control (see the bitumen problem from wood taken from Mt. Ararat on the Noah's Ark problem); also recent mold, fungus and penetration of the sample by young rootlets (will introduce younger C-14) or salts absorbed and included in the sample will through off the true weight of the sample, if not removed (see also above).

The preferred method in use today is Accelerator Mass Spectrometry (AMS): the carbon atoms in the sample are turned into plasma by stripping off the electrons. The nuclei are then propelled to 10,000 miles per second by 2.5 million volts of electricity; the C-12, C-13, and C-14 are then bent into arcs (due to their positive charge) and separated. The amounts of each are read and calculated, the C-12 and C-13 provide the ratios and allow evaluation of the fractionation. Less than 0.03g of sample is needed (RPNF p. 144; Bowman p. 34). The Journal *Radiocarbon* lists the latest data for all types of dating methods. AMS was used to recheck the acacia wooden beam found in the Step Pyramid, which placed it in the first Dynasty (RPNF p. 145).

Plant and animal remains contain only L amino acids. After death, these will start to racemize to produce some of the D form. Moisture and heat are the only variables to affect the rate. If both are fairly constant then the method can be used to date samples. Aspartic acid, alanine, and isoleucine have the slowest racemization rates so that samples of bone of 40,000 BP can be cross dated by carbon-fourteen for aspartic acid, 100,000-150,000 yr and + 150,000 yr respectively for the last two amino acids above. The method is very sensitive to temperature changes. Ocean sediments or bones near hot springs where the temperature has been fairly constant give good correlation. Remains found in caves can be used to determine past climate and temperature changes from those available at present. For bones, the collagen fraction is used. Samples from the Pleistocene and Tertiary periods are ideal for the method. Bones from Olduvai Gorge in Africa have been dated to 56,000 (+ or - 3,500 years) (MASCA 9(2): 6, (73); 10(1): 4, [74]). Racemization rates are derived from the Arrhenius reversible first order reactions for the relationship between T1/e and temperature. The equation is: $k=Ae^{-EA/RT}$ where k is the specific reaction rate constant, EA is the energy of activation, R is the gas constant of 1.987 calories per degree per mole, T is the absolute temperature, and A is the frequency factor constant. One plots log k against 1/T the straight-line slope is -EA/2.303 R. The activation energy EA = slope X 2.303 R.

Electron spin resonance (ESR) has been used to date bone up to several hundred of millions of years. Natural radiation from uranium, thorium, potassium, and their daughter elements produce lattice defects in bone that can be detected by ESR. A natural radiation of one rad (100 ergs of deposited energy per gram of matter approximately equal to the absorbed dose delivered when soft tissue is exposed to one roentgen of medium voltage X-rays) per year in an open site and 0.1-0.2 rad in a limestone cave are expected. The bones have a low concentration of radioactive elements and the lattice defects have a high stability (C&EN March 3, 1980 p. 20).

Neutron activation analysis is accomplished by irradiation of a sample in a nuclear reactor, particle accelerator, or an isotopic source emitting alpha rays, which then react with beryllium, which in turn emits neutrons. These neutrons react with stable nuclides producing radioactive ones. When applied to pottery and clay the identification of the source can be determined since various clays contain different amounts of trace elements. The method is also used to differentiate imports from locally produced pottery. It is one of the most powerful tools used by the archaeologist (BAR 2(1): 30 [1976]), but not strictly a dating method.

Thermoluminescent Dating (TL) is used to date pottery, metal slag, and even burnt soil. This method is used when bone or carbon sources are lacking. If the artifact has been heated high enough to remove the geologically accumulated thermo luminescence, thus starting the sample from zero, the TL signal is measured to give a low natural signal. The sample is then irradiated with alpha particles (Po-210) or X-rays to a dose of about 100 (1,000 rads to give an artificial TL signal) the comparison will give a date for the sample. The measured age = true age since firing + residual geological age (which must be zero). The method can also be used in conjunction with Differential Thermal Analysis DTA and Thermogravimetric Analysis TGA to determine the actual temperature of annealing or firing temperatures for the object. This last is an interesting development relating to advances in metallurgy or pottery and brick baking down through time (MASCA Newsletter 10(1): 1, 3 (74); 11(1): 1 [75]). Polonium-210 was the material used to assassinate the former Russian spy Alexander Litvinenko in London (Time Dec.4, p 45, 2006). What an exotic way to assassinate someone, since everyone exposed to this will also die of radiation poisoning when the vial is opened.

Other radioactive series can be used to date rocks. These include potassium-forty to argon-forty with a half-life of 1.27 x 10^{10} years (C&EN Sept 24, 1984 p. 32). A more accurate refinement, developed at Berkley in the 1960s, is to irradiate the P-40 with neutrons to Ar-39 (which is not present in nature). The A-40/ Ar-39 ratios are then read. Thorium-232 to lead-208 with nine alpha particles emitted which form helium. If the right amount of helium is found indicating that none has been lost, the age of the sample can be found: the half life is 1.39 x 10^{10} years, rubidium-87 to strontium-87 has a half life of 4.7 x 10^{10} years, and uranium-238 to lead-206 with eight alpha particles emitted to form helium with a half life of 4.51 x 10^{9} years. In the earth's crust the amount of U-238 and Pb-206 are approximately equal, indicating one-half life has passed or an age of the earth of 4.5 billion years, assuming all the Pb-206 originally came from U-238 (Menzel p. 82). If the sample contains both thorium and uranium the lead isotopes can be determined by mass spectroscopy from the natural lead-204 (which has no natural radioactive precursors) to date the sample (VSE p. 1463). Lead from Katanga, Africa can be shown to come from radioactive decay since the Pb-206 isotope is much larger than the Pb-208 isotope in natural lead. Any attempt to challenge ages based on any radiochemical series is actually a challenge of the accuracy of the half-life involved. Since no valid results have shown that the half-life can be changed, a date—say of ten million years old—would need to be challenged on some other basis or the date stands. Sample preparation and purity tend to cause the most problems.

The oldest rocks on earth are found at Great Slave Lake in Canada; the zircon crystals uranium lead ratios indicate 3.96 billion years, the western Greenland samples date to 3.86 billion years, and the pegmatites from the south rim of the Bridger Mountains near the Wind River Canyon of Wyoming are of 3.5 billion years (which also intrude through older sedimentary and volcanic rocks). The meteorites from the Apollo moon mission were found to be 4.5–4.8 billion years old (Science News 136: 228 (89); VSE p. 1463; Menzel p. 218).

Geography. Accurate knowledge of longitude was not available until the development of the Harrison Chronometer in 1761. However, many ancient maps such as the Piri Reis Map of 1513, the Dulcert Portolano of 1339, the Zeno Map of 1380, the Oronteus Finaeus World Map of 1531, and the Portolano of Iehudi Ibn Ben Zara from 1487 are based on longitudes and latitudes accurate to within half a degree or less. The Dulcert has longitudes from Galaway Ireland to the east bend of the Don in Russia accurately placed. A Chinese map copied from an earlier one on a pillar dates to 1137, which required spherical trigonometry. Were such accurate clocks already known, as well as the knowledge that the earth is curved, requiring advanced mathematics and geometry for the calculations (Hancock pp. 24–32)?

Lost Civilizations. In 2001, 25 miles off the coast of Gujurat, India in the Gulf of Cambay was found a five-mile-long section of a lost city with drains running along the streets; complete with artifacts including a proto-Tamil Indus Valley script. One was carbon dated to 8,500–9,500 years old, which would make it the oldest city known (Kenyon pp. 78–80).

The case for Atlantis is confused. It was first published by Solon ca. 570 BC. The unfinished manuscript was given to Plato ca. 410 BC. Solon had visited Egypt and the Temple of Neith at Sais, the Nile Delta capital of the 26th Dynasty. The high priest Sonchis translated the hieroglyphs written on select columns for him. Plato may have changed or misunderstood some terms, such as the location of Atlantis (Kenyon pp. 145, 152; RD pp. 11–27).

An inscribed stone found at Maikop some 56 miles east of the Black Sea commemorates the Argonauts' expedition to Colchis in search of the Golden Fleece—perhaps suggesting that the fable had some basis in reality (RD p. 318).

Lost Knowledge. The Nazca lines of Peru were dated from 350 BC to 600 AD based on pottery and C-14 of organic remains embedded in the lines. One of the spiders has been shown to be genus Ricinulei found only in remote parts of the Amazon rainforest. The reproductive organ on the end of the right leg is shown, which can usually be seen only under a microscope. The monkey is also out of place in this dry area. The size of the specimens would have required accurate surveying. Some lines are straight for more than five miles. The true form of many can only be discerned from several hundred feet up. No nearby elevation offers a vantage point for observation (Hancock pp. 35–41; Hadingham p. 5). It has been proposed that man-carrying balloons were used for perspective (Kenyon p. 203). One experiment created a primitive balloon using native materials and carrying several passengers, reaching a height of 600 feet before being blown back to earth by a wind gust (RD pp. 283–4). The Greek Archytas of Tarentum was reported to have invented a leather kite to carry a young boy for aerial reconnaissance in the fifth century BC (Kenyon p. 204). Some fourteen-model airplane type gliders have been found in Egypt, the oldest from a tomb at Saqqara of the first Dynasty (ibid).

The Inca said their civilization was founded by the Viracochas (the same that produced the Nazca lines; whose name means "the foam of the sea') and said to be a blue-eyed white man. How could they carve and move stones or raise them high off the ground, often weighing 361 tons, when they did not have the wheel or machinery capable of such fetes? The Incas living the furthest south and presumably arriving last never had a written language but did have an intricate counting system.

This same Viracochas is known as the Aztec Quetzalcoatl, the Quiche Maya know him as Gucumatz, and at Chichen Itza as Kulkulkan. All names apparently mean the same thing: Plumed (or Feathered) Serpent. Other names are the Maya Votan. His name meaning is not known, but his symbol was a serpent. Itzmana was a Mayan god of healing, also a robed and bearded individual whose symbol was a rattlesnake. All these were wise men (originally probably the same man) who introduced writing, the calendar, architecture, introduced corn, medicine, could raise the dead, gave laws and knew the properties of plants.

He disappeared to the East but said he would return in the year 1 Reed (the very year of Cortez's arrival in 1519 at Veracruz by ship from the East). The appearance of Hernan Cortez, pale skinned, bearded and in shinning armor with his followers, was looked upon as the fulfilled prophesy and the end of Aztec rule.

The destruction, by Catholic friars, of thousands of Aztec codices, temples and inscriptions wiped out some 99 plus percent of their accumulated knowledge. Only twenty codices and scrolls remain (Hancock pp. 109–114). Only five codices of the Maya remain (a History Channel program).

The Aztec pyramid at Chulula, whose base sides are 1,500 feet long and originally some 200 ft high has a volume of some three million cubic meters. It is the largest ancient building ever erected on earth (Hancock p. 116).

One of the Aztec kings, Nezahualcoyotl, built a temple without idols dedicated to a single deity, "the unknown god," and banned human sacrifice. A strange practice for an Aztec ruler. Where and how did he come up with this idea?

The temple pyramid at Mexico City is partly covered on three sides by lava; Bryan Cummings for the National Geographic Society has dated the lava in 1933 as 8,500 years old. The structure would be even older. Historians and archaeologists of course discount such an early date (Hancock p. 115).

The oldest culture in America are the Olmec (rubber people) who also used the bar and dot cylindrical code (one stela gave a date of Sept. 3, 32 BC, far older that the oldest Maya date of 228 AD [although one is now known from Belize dated 146 BC]). They may actually have invented this system. The recently discovered Cascajal Block contains an undeciphered Olmec inscription dated to ca 900 BC, the oldest found in the Americas (Archaeology 60(1) p. 72, 2007). The huge stone heads of the Olmec have distinctively Negroid features. One stela at La Venta shows two figures; one face is mutilated, the other is a bearded Caucasian with high-bridged nose, and both wear pointed shoes and long robes. Two other monuments here show the same type: Anglo-Saxon pointed beards and a curiously floppy hat and flamboyant sash. Were these representations of Phoenicians? One similar stela was found at Monte Alban (Hancock pp. 132–134). Remember, the Asiatic people that came across the Bering Sea land bridge during the Ice Ages, and became the North and South American Indians, have little or no beards. Why did not the North American Indians learn to build in stone, and only the Aztec, Olmec, Maya and Inca who developed in Central and South America were able to do this? The Mississippian culture of the Cahokia of 700–1100 AD, built an earthen platform city of some 50,000 people 8mi E of

St. Louis. This was the largest city in North America. Of the 120 mounds, Monks Mound is the largest covering 14 acres, (AO 8(5): 52 (05); History Channel).

At the Kalasasaya (Place of the Upright Standing Stones) at Tiahuanaco on Lake Titicaca in Bolivia, the date of the building by astronomical alignments based on the earth's obliquity of the ecliptic (it takes the Earth 41,000 years for one cycle) was found to be 15,000 BC. Whereas the precession takes 25,776 years to complete one wobble; this is the basis of the Zodiac. Historians found this hard to believe, but the calculations were checked by four astronomers and found to be correct (Hancock pp. 79, 237). In fact, Lake Titicaca was once at sea level and filled with salt water. There are fossilized seashells and many marine ichyofauna present, including the seahorse and Alloroquestes. The lake is now at 12,500 feet, as the area was raised above the seabed. The ancient strandline is not level but is 295 feet higher in the north but 274 feet lower in the south of the present lake level. The lake level has also dropped about 100 feet as shown by ancient docks at the city of Tiahuanaco, which was on the lakeshore then, but is now 12 miles inland.

At Teotihuacan the Pyramid of the Sun in the two upper levels were found sandwiched a thick and extensive layer of mica, which was stolen and sold for its value in 1906. Later at the Mica Temple located in a patio 1000 feet south of the west face of the Temple of the Sun, were found under a floor and out of sight, paved with large slabs of mica, some 90 ft^2, in two layers on top of each other. Trace mineral analysis indicated this mica came from pegmatites in Brazil, some 2000 miles away. Mica has few uses, such as thermal and electrical insulation, opaque to fast neutrons, and a moderator in nuclear reactors. Local supplies are nearby, but why was such labor expended to bring it to this site and for what purpose (Hancock p. 174)?

The Aztecs believed the universe operated in great cycles, where the earth's people had been wiped out on four such cycles or Suns (depicted on the Stone of the Sun at Izapa in Chipas Mexico). The First Sun (Matlacli Atl—Ten Water) lasted 4,008 years where seven couples hid in a cave to escape the flood that wiped out humanity. The Second Sun (Ehecoatl—Wind Serpent) lasted 4,010 years when men were turned into monkeys; only one couple was saved, standing on a rock. The Third Sun (Tleyquiyahuillo) lasted 4,081 years and was destroyed by fire. The Fourth Sun (Tzontlilic) lasted 5,026 years after a deluge of rains and floods (this seems to correlate with the flood of Noah). The present Fifth Sun, depicted by Tonatiuh the Sun god as a wrinkled old man, is already very old and near the end of its cycle. "The Sun of Movement" will be destroyed by earthquake. This cycle started on 4 Ahau 8 Cumku, or Aug. 13, 3114 BC (RD p. 270 gives Aug. 11) and will end 4 Ahau 3 Kankin, or Dec. 23, 2012 (see the earlier quote where a date of Dec. 24, 2011 is calculated (Kenyon p. 124 gives Dec. 21, 2012). The Aztecs had forgotten how to calculate the end (having reverted to the Short Count), but the Maya dot and dash method gave the date. The total age of man is thus some 22,251 years to the end, by their reckoning, (Hancock pp. 98–100; 122). See Time Life *Lost Civilizations* Aztecs, Incas, and Maya volumes for additional information.

The Maya calendar was able to calculate the solar year as 365.2420 days, versus our now known 365.2422 days. They are off only 0.0002 days, an accuracy better than the Gregorian calendar of 365.2425 days. Their time for the moon to orbit the earth was 29.528395 days; we know it as 29.530588 days. They also could predict solar and lunar eclipses, knowing they occur within + or - eighteen days of the node. The famous Long Count helped them establish the time cycles. One stela at Quiriga Guatemala gives the day and month positions for a date over 90 million years ago, and another has a date over 300 million years before that (Hancock pp. 158–162). Yet with all this at their disposal, they failed to invent the wheel, convert from a corbelled to a true arch, or develop a system of weights. However, they did invent zero.

Lost Technology. When Petrie examined the granite sarcophagus in the king's chamber of the Great Pyramid, he found that it must have been cut from the surrounding block with straight saws at least eight feet long, probably of bronze, with cutting points of hard jewels (diamonds?). However, none is known in Egypt at this age and no jeweled saws are known. The inside was probably cut out as described below. Others propose sand as the cutting material.

The Egyptians had a method of drilling (one drill hole is still preserved in the sarcophagus in the Great Pyramid) with tubular drills, none of which has been found, but the cores are numerous, some as much as five inches in diameter. The spiral of the cut of granite in core #7 sinks one inch in the circumference of six inches. The pressure needed for this cut is estimated as about four tons (Hancock pp. 331–332; see Kenyon p. 236 who examined core #7 and has some different conclusions; see also www.gizapower.com).

Petrie found some diorite, slate, basalt, and metamorphic schist bowls with hieroglyphs incised 1/150 inch wide by a drill 1/200 inch wide and parallel lines only 1/30 inch apart on their centers. Diorite is one of the hardest stones known, even harder than iron. Pounding stones, such as granite, schist and others to rough shape was usually done with diorite. Some diorite vases with narrow thin necks have the inside shoulders fully hollowed out. No instruments known today can do this. They would need to be narrow enough to pass through the neck, of the right shape, often at right angles, and strong enough to scour out the shoulders and rounded interiors. No stone carver today could match this work, nor would anyone in his right mind attempt it. Limestone or calcite vessels, on the other hand, can be hollowed out by hot vinegar, but the procedure would be tricky, requiring almost constant turning of the object. So how was it accomplished (Hancock pp. 333–334)? There are some 40,000 of these vessels in chambers six and seven under Djoser's step pyramid (although most are alabaster [calcium sulfate], which is softer to carve). Some are from zero dynasty kings Narmer, first dynasty Djer (13 jars), Den, Adjib, Semerkhet, Kaa, second dynasty Hetepsekhemwy, Ninetjer (13 jars), Sekhemibi and Khasekhemwy. No one knows for sure why these older vessels were stored here (ancestor respect was proposed; Verner p. 120–122). Some similar bowls, found elsewhere date to predynastic times of 4000 BC or earlier.

On the base of two granite obelisks at Karnak, Queen Hatshepsut says they were cut from the quarries at Aswan, moved and set up in seven months. A foremost stonemason, Denys Stocks, calculated using modern time management studies that to cut the 440-ton stones using the trenching and undercutting method visible on an unfinished obelisk still there, using the diorite pounding balls and flint chisels, allowed the granite to be removed at a rate of 30 cm^3 per hour. Workers spaced at two feet by two-and-a-half feet wide around the stone (no more workers could work on the stone until it is removed) would require 15.7 years to cut the sides and 34.3 years to do the undercutting at five cm^3 per hour for a total of 50 years. This allows no time for chip removal, or replacement of tools. The above space is for a kneeling worker. The undercut would require the worker to be lying down and assumes that a diminutive worker can cut stone in the same space. The stone must be removed, dressed, transported, the inscription cut and raised, all of which we have allowed no time for (Kenyon p. 256). In addition, she did it in seven months? However, not by these methods.

Other artifacts little explored are the rough stone sphere, a two-pronged hook in metal shaped like a swallow's tail, and a piece of cedar wood about 12 cm long with notches cut in it, all of which were found sealed in the northern vent (?) shaft of the Queen's chamber of the Great Pyramid in 1872 by the Dixon brothers. A chimney sweep type tool used by them became lodged behind a door, which was pushed partly open and remains there to this day. These objects were misplaced in the British Museum and not found until 1993 (the piece of wood was missing and could have been C-14 dated).

When Rudolf Gantenbrink examined the southern shaft in the queen's chamber with a robot TV camera, a metallic hook and a wood baton were seen at a higher level than the Dixons could explore; the wood is still there. It needs to be removed and carbon dated. Some 15 samples of organic material from the mortar in the great pyramid were dated by the AMS method and gave dates of 3809–2869 BC. These dates are not in question but are from 200 to 1200 years older than they should be, thus the great pyramid is at least 400 years older than originally thought. Egyptologists and others have simply ignored this result (HBMS p. 302). At 200 feet into the shaft, a sealed door was found. A piece of the copper bolt from one of the two sealed holes broke off in antiquity and is lying further down the shaft next to the two-pronged hook object. Zahi Hawass allowed a hole to be drilled through the door for a National Geographic documentary, only to find a second door further inside blocking the shaft (HBMS p. 112; Verner p. 200). See www. cheops. org for additional interesting details of Gantenbrink's work (although he has been excluded from continuing his work by Hawass); also see Kenyon p. 263.

The quartz crystal skull found by Anna Mitchel Hedges in 1924 in Belize was estimated to take 300 years for one man to carve by the use of sand on leather strips.

Probably the world's first computer is the Antikythera mechanism found on a Roman shipwreck on the island off the NW tip of Crete. It dates to about 80 BC and although badly corroded has been shown to contain from 29–70 gears, the most complex one known. Also found were a number of marble heads and bronze statues. This was presented on the History Channel (and TLBG p. 112).

Lost Literature. Ancient writing in Greek in the library at Alexandria contained the Hermetic (Thoth) Texts. Where Thoth says to his disciple Asclepius: "Do you not know, Asclepius, that Egypt is an image of heaven" (the operations of the powers which rule and work in heaven have been transferred down to earth below). This may be a reference to the pyramids being constructed according to the pattern of Orion's belt.

The Pyramid Texts appear for the first time in the Pyramid of Unas, the last king of the Fifth Dynasty ca 2510 BC, and continue from Teti, Pepi I, Merenre, Pepi II and his three queens, all of the Sixth Dynasty and the tomb of Ibi, whose date is uncertain but probably the last of ca 2180 BC (the text is already full blown; which contains a hieroglyphic text difficult to translate, as it relates to concepts as old as the First Dynasty; there are some 700 "utterances" total; the text in the pyramid of Unis contains only 228 [which can be read at www.pyramidtextsonline.com], Edwards p. 139). In the Shat Ent Am Duat—the Book of What is in the Duat, instructions are given to build a replica on the ground of a special area of the sky known as the "hidden circle of the Duat" and in the body of Nut (the sky). The Zep Tepi "First Time" relates to the remote time when the gods came to earth and established their kingdom in Egypt (HBMS p. 78).

Manetho's *History of Egypt*, which later commentators said was in three parts, deals with the gods, demigods, the Spirits of the Dead, and the mortal kings who ruled Egypt. "The gods" ruled for 13,900 years, "the demigods and Spirits of the Dead" (epithets for the "Followers of Horus") ruled for 11,025 years, and the mortal kings in 31 Dynasties who ruled Egypt for 5,000 years. Fragment three preserved in the works of George Syncellus says the gods ruled for 11,985 years and the total for all was 36,525 years. Diodorus Siculus ca. 20 BC was told by the priests of Egypt that the gods and Heroes ruled for a little less than 18,000 years and the kings for a little less than 5,000 years. Obviously long histories of chronologies were kept. The Turin papyrus, although badly damaged originally, contained a summery of the Akhu (which means "those who recite formulae") with Thoth ruling for 3,126 years and Horus for 300; the followers of Horus (the Shemu Hor) ruling for 13,420 years and those before the Shemu Hor for 23,200 for a total of 36,620 years (HBMS pp. 209, 211).

Orthodox Egyptologists recognize that all aspects of Egyptian knowledge and culture seem to be in place from the Zero Dynasty, with little process of development being apparent. The implications for this often go unmentioned, and any Egyptologist who ventures into this area will have his career quickly curtailed, publications stopped, and funds cut off. Academic infighting among archaeologists can be brutal, witness the ongoing debates in BAR.

The Problem of Dolomite. Geology describes the formation of Dolomite from limestone by immersion in seawater, which contains 3.69% Magnesium to 1.15% Calcium (Gilluly p. 379, 603). Limestone consists of almost 100% Calcium Carbonate, whereas Dolomite will contain up to 45.65 % Magnesium Carbonate. Yet a core hole drilled in the Bikini atoll to a depth of 2,200 feet found no Dolomite or increase of Magnesium content with depth, even though the bottom deposits had shells of Miocene age. All had been in contact with seawater for 15 million years. Dolomite is usually found in Mesozoic and older rocks (Gilluly p. 427).

Shale. Mud and clay has covered thousands of square miles forming in shallow water with fossils accumulating (in shale the limestone shells have actually dissolved leaving only perfectly formed casts). There is no comparable area on Earth today where future limestone is forming. The shells for limestone formation can only form in clear water up to several hundred feet deep before growth is cut off due to lack of sunlight. Consider the Cretaceous chalk of the Dover cliffs of England and France. The Green River oil shale in Utah, Wyoming and Colorado was laid down in a huge Eocene lake covering 50,000 square miles; it is 2,000 ft thick and has shown layers of 6.5 million years of annual deposition (another dating method). It is estimated that 100 billion barrels of oil could be extracted (Dunbar p. 415; Moore p. 412).

Oil. In the 30s, porphyrins related to chlorophyll were found in petroleum indicating a plant origin. Now steroid carboxylic acids, structurally related to bile acids, have been found in ten million-year-old California petroleum as a result of diagenesis (gradual chemical change taking place in sediments). Identified so far are 5b-cholanic acid (cis-C_{24}) 5a-bis-norcholanic acid (trans C_{22}), and 5a-cholanic acid (trans C_{24}). The 5b-cholanic acid is thermodynamically the less stable isomer: the A and B rings being cis indicates they are derived from bile acids. Isomerization from plant-derived 5a-cholanic acid cannot explain the occurance of 5b-cholanic acid since the same thing would be expected for the trans-C_{22} acid. Only traces of cis-C_{22} acid are found. Petroleum is thus plant and animal derived (C&EN June 25, 1973 p. 13).

Ocean levels. Each spring the ocean levels in the Northern Hemisphere drop eight inches with no corresponding rise south of the equator. There is no explanation as to where the water goes. The oxygen content of the oceans has dropped 12% since 1920 (Life Nature Library: *The Earth* p. 160).

Ice Caps. The Canadian Shield ice cap known as the Laurentide is thought to be of such thickness (between 8–10,000 feet) as to force the earth's crust downward 1,000 feet. Without a driving force such as a slope, the ice will not move much. If no mountains or other barriers are present, it will flow, due to the weight, in all directions. During the Wisconsin stage of 55–25,000 years ago in the recent Pleistocene epoch, there was no driving force to move the ice to the north and few or no moraines in the south, showing the elevation was not high enough. The very last ice advance known as the Mankato, covered tree trunks with an age by C-14 of 11,400 years; however, this is less than half the age expected by geologists (Dunbar pp. 443, 450–51; Rapport p. 51; Life Nature Library: *The Earth* p. 108). The Greenland ice cores taken totaled 3,053 meters, covering the 160,000 years of the ice (each year's ice could be counted and the trapped gas bubbles analyzed), which dated the Younger Dryas (named for an artic member of the Rose family) mini Ice Age 10,500–9,400 BC with a accuracy better than carbon-14 dating (WBF p. 130; RPNF pp. 172, 184).

The mini-Ice-Age of 1560–1850 has even impacted our own history. For instance, Washington crossed a frozen Delaware in 1776 (it has not frozen to this extent since). Part of the reason for the French revolution in 1789 was the resulting famines. The extreme cold led to the defeat of Napoleon in 1812 at Moscow and the following retreat, where out of 600,000 troops only 1,000 remained. It was reported that snow hovered in the air and would not settle to the ground due to the colder air near the ground. The Irish potato famine of 1845–1849 was a result of the excessive cold; the effects were felt until 1851. Over a million died in the famine. The Tambora volcano explosion on April 5, 1815, added to the problems, giving snow and frost in June in the NE U.S., resulting in "the year without a summer." The result was the world's first pandemic of cholera (History Channel 2006).

About five million years ago the Mediterranean, which was blocked at Gibraltar, dried up, as shown by some five feet of salt cores brought up from the bottom by the Glomar Challenger in 1970. This resulted in the Nile cutting a gorge deeper than the Grand Canyon. When cores were drilled for the Aswan High Dam, the channel was still 930 feet to bedrock. The entire area under Cairo had been scoured away all the way from Alexandria to some 600 miles inland (RPNF pp. 86–92).

There is evidence that maps such as the Admiral Piri Reis made in Constantinople in 1513 (from many older source maps, some from Alexandria) show an ice-free Antarctica, which was not even discovered until 1818. There is some evidence that Antarctica may have been further north and shifted to the South Pole later due to continental drift. Other maps by Oronteus Finaeus of 1531, Mercator in 1569, and Philippe Buache in 1737 show Antarctica separated by a waterway across the Ross, Weddell, and Bellinghausen Seas, something that was not known until the 1958 IGY Seismic Survey (Hancock pp. 4–25).

There are fossilized tree stumps at 7,000 ft on Mt. Achernar in Antarctica, as well as coal beds within 200 mi of the South Pole and fossils of leaf and fossilized wood on Mt. Weaver, showing that at some point the climate was sub-tropical. In fact, Antarctica may have moved south some 2,000 miles to its present location (Hancock pp. 471–6). Evidence also exists that areas of Spitzbergen, Baffin Island, and Greenland were also subtropical at some time in the Miocene, since water lilies and fossil swamp cypress and palm leaves 10–12 feet long have been found along with birch and alder found in peat. These cannot grow in a polar climate exposed to six months of darkness per year and must have been further south. There is also palaeomagnetic evidence for the earth's poles having flipped some 170 times in the last 80 million years; the next reversal is expected in 2030. The North Pole has moved toward Greenland some ten feet from 1900–1960 and another ten feet from 1960–68. Likewise, the South Pole marker was moved on Jan. 10 1995 by a 17-year-old student, Elizabeth Felton. These data may indeed imply the crust is moving around (Hancock pp. 484–486). In fact, the Earth's N pole is in the south; it is the compass magnet's N pole that is attracted to the Earth's S pole.

In the Mississippi Valley there is a driftless area—two hundred by 100 miles, in SE Minnesota, SW Wisconsin and the NE corner of Iowa—that is free of glacial evidence. All around this area shows glaciation. A similar area is present near Orel, Russia. No evidence is offered to explain this. The gray gneiss boulders on the summit of Mt. Washington are known to come from a source 3–4,000 ft lower. Glaciers do not move rocks uphill.

Time Travel or Extraterrestrial Visits. Hawking thinks that nature abhors time machines in that the laws of physics do not allow time machines and will keep the world safe for historians. The answers lie in the laws of quantum gravity; not completely understood at this time (Thorne pp. 498–521). The probability that Kip Thorne could go back in time and kill his grandfather is $1/10 \times 10^{60}$, SHUN p. 153. Hawking also believes that UFOs are not a government cover-up. With his usual wit, he declares that its record for cover-ups is not that good (SHUN p. 142).

For those into parallel universes, consider that most objects are only 10% matter, thus nine other objects could occupy the same space at the same time. Is this how Christ could pass through solid doors?

Life in the Universe. The famous equation of Frank Drake in 1961 and made popular by Carl Sagan on the Nova series is: $N = N^* f_p \, n_e \, f_l \, f_i \, f_c \, f_L$, the first and last terms in the original equation were R and L.

Where N is the number of civilizations capable of communicating. N^* is the number of stars in our Milky Way Galaxy (estimates range from 200–400 billion). f_p is the fraction of stars with planets around them (Drake used 20%). n_e is the number of planets per star capable of sustaining life (a typical answer is from 3–5, for Earth, Mars and Venus and a couple of Jupiter's moons); f_l is the fraction of planets where life evolves (the ranges are from 100%-to near 0%); f_i is the fraction where intelligent life evolves (the ranges are from 100%-to near 0%, there is some reason to doubt that intelligent life exists even on Earth); f_c is the fraction that can communicate with us (ranges are from 10–20%, but we have been able to communicate by radio etc. for only 100 years); f_L is the fraction where the planet can sustain life long enough for their signals to reach us (this is the hardest to estimate—the Earth and Sun have been around for about ten billion years): if we are to destroy ourselves tomorrow the answer is 1/100,000,000th. If we survive for another 10,000 years, the answer is 1/1,000,000th. If we supply the estimates 200 billion, 20%, 3, 50%, 20%, 20% and 1/1,000,000th above, the answer is 2,400 galaxies able to communicate. Changing the estimates to 200 billion, 5%, 1, 5%, .05%, 5% and 1/1,000,000th will give 0.0075 galaxies. Thus, very open ended and essentially eliminating Earth as having intelligent life (a thought that is gaining support every day).

Almost everything is open and any good numbers can be inserted. If you chose large numbers then the possibilities are large (example going from 200 to 400 billion galaxies). This is the approach of the liberal school looking to support evolution. Some figures are reasonably known and are included in the best guess above. See www.activemind.com/Mysterious Topics/ SETI/drake_equation.html. Or check SETI Institute on the internet.

As of February 22, 2008, some 277 exo-planets have been found (History channel 3-22-08). However, see Astronomy section above for the discovery of our 10th planet. The first exo-planet was found in October 1995 in 51 Pegasi (which is similar to the Sun in mass and temperature) the velocity of the star changed by +/- 50 m/sec over four days. A four-day orbital period shows it is very close to the star, but massive (Mercury for example orbits in 66 days). The mass is about half Jupiter's but the temperature is 1500 F°. 70 Virginis has six times the mass of Jupiter and 47 Ursa Majoris is two times the mass. Tau Bootes (HD 120136) is three times Jupiter and orbits in 3.3 d and has

8.3 stellar radii. Upsilon Andromeda's planet has a multiple mass of a Jupiter planet. HD 114762 discovered in 1989 is ten times Jupiter. Lalande 21185 (BD +362147) has two planets, both about the mass of Jupiter. The star is much cooler than the Sun of Type M2 and much smaller. Neptune's moons require liquid water, thus both mass and orbit are needed. Too small an atmosphere and the water will evaporate; too large, the water will be very hot. It is thought Europa of Jupiter may have liquid water. Life, as we know it, would depend on conditions necessary for a habatible zone. Including radiation from its sun of about one kilowatt per square meter at the surface (Menzel p. 152), within plus or minus 1% to prevent freezing or boiling of water which would also be necessary. Planets with larger or hotter suns would need to be located at distances to give these conditions. The National Geograpic Discover on 6-18-02 reported the 90th planet in Cancer, a gas giant similar to Jupiter. Some of these discoveries are found indirectly (such as a dimming of a sun as the planet passes in front of it) and usually are very large planets necessary to cause orbit changes, which we can observe; they are closer to their suns and have temperatures above 1500° F, not conductive to life, (Strobel p. 172; National Geographic Dec. 2004 p. 72). The recently discovered Hat-P-1b orbits a star 450 light years away at a speed, which would cover Earths orbit in 75 days. It is 1.4 times the size of Jupiter but has only half the mass (about the same density as cork. Present theories can't account for it (Smithsonian Dec. 2006 p.35). Sara Seeger in the Popular Science article above has charted twelve separate atmospheres for some of these planets.

CHAPTER 15

BIBLE MYSTERIES

IN THIS SECTION, we will look at some unexplained "mysteries." The insight of many of these will depend much on outside sources.

Genesis 1:1 In the beginning. Some Cosmologists such as Stephen Hawking would put the "Big Bang" here. For some problems with this, see Bible and Spade 6: 1 (93); Coppedge pp. 197, 207. In 1923 Edwin Hubble discovered that light from distant galaxies is red shifted, indicating they are moving away from us. In 1925, 43 were red shifted to only two blue shifted. This is the familiar Doppler effect used in weather prediction. Thus if you run this backward there must have been a beginning or singularity to produce the "Big Bang" (SHUN p. 76). Einstein's equation $E=MC^2$ when rearranged to $M=E/C^2$ shows that if E increases, M increases slightly. However, as matter approaches the speed of light the mass becomes infinitely large and prevents speeds faster than light (Magueijo pp. 36–7). In fact, the energy in one gram of matter equals 20,000 kg of TNT. The Large Hadron Collider outside Geneva is expected to propel protons to within 99.999999% of the speed of light. They will be looking for the Higgs particle as well as some new ones.

1:2. Why was it necessary for the Spirit of God (Holy Spirit) to move over and search out the face of the water? Was it to make sure the earth controlled by Satan, which included the dinosaurs and prehistoric man, had been destroyed? The Talmud also mentions Adam's first wife Lilith. This missing information would provide a place for the Age Gap theory.

1:26. Who was God talking to? God is the Hebrew word Elohim and means Mighty One, and is plural "let us. . . ." This is the first reference to the three-fold nature of God. In 1:1 God created; in John 1:1–4 Christ created; and Genesis 1:2 God and the Holy Spirit, or Job 26:13 and John 3:6.

2:8. Eden. Which means "plain" in Sumerian. A Sumerian poem eulogized the Paradise of the gods of Sumer. A place where there is no preying of beast on beast, where no one ever grew old or was sick (TLBCC p. 103; Bibby p. 80): "The land of Dilmun is holy, the land of Dilmun is pure, the land of Dilmun is clean, the land of Dilmun is holy." Said to be the home of the only survivor of the flood who was given immortality, Ziusudra the Babylonian Utnapishtim. Dilmun is mentioned three times on the pavement inscriptions of Sargon III palace at Khorsabad (ARAB Vol. II Par. 96, 98 and 99). The myth of Enki and Ninhursag takes place in Dilmun (Bibby p. 79). One other fragment links the land of Dilmun to the god Inzak, the Sumerian god of Dilmun with the present island of Bahrain (Arabic for two seas). This may be the ancient Eden. In fact, today on the island, tourists are shown "The Tree of Life" standing in a desert area with no other plants around. Aerial photos show at least 100,000 burial mounds. A Ubiad plaster fragment found inland in Saudi Arabia and across from Bahrain (Bibby pp. 314; 376) and 12 feet above water was covered with barnacles, which suggests the Ubiad culture may have come from Iraq, since neutron activation analysis of the pottery in

Saudi Arabia shows it was imported from Sumer (Lloyd p. 64). The Arabian plate has been rising for the last 2,500 years, which may have caused it to lose its water and become a desert. The Gulf of Bahrain may have been dry and joined to Arabia at this time. Dilmun is also known as Tilman (Saggs p. 15).

2:24. and they shall be one flesh. This phrase gets little comment in commentaries. From the Talmud, and probably also in the Kabbalah, is the concept that this does not take place until after the couple has intercourse. The depositing of semen in the woman was thought to be absorbed throughout the woman so that they literally were now of "one flesh." That there is some absorption of seminal fluid that contains estrogen, testosterone, follicular stimulating hormone, luteinizing hormone, prolactin and prostaglandins have been shown medically. Some of these show up in a woman's blood hours after intercourse. Is this why some long-time married people come to resemble each other in facial features? This would find its outlet in levirate marriage, in that the first-born son of the union was thought to be derived from the first husband (the Talmud doesn't explain how this would work if x number of daughters were born before a son). The levirate semen would then displace the first husband's and all other children would be by the second husband (thus the abhorrence of taking a woman as a wife who had been with someone else.) The same thought is present in 1 Samuel 25:44. When Michal was given to Paltiel, the law required that the first husband could never take her back. Nevertheless, David demanded this (Chouraqui p. 129). See also DDS 4Q397 fr.5, Vermes p. 224.

3:15. Who is God talking about? Who will be enmity between the woman's child and the followers of Satan? Who will deliver a killing blow to the serpent's head but only bruise his heal in the process? Jesus Christ accomplished this when he said in John 19:30 "It is finished" (a shout of victory). John was the only apostle present when this was said, thus the statement is only found in his account.

3:20. Adam and Eve. Our Creationist brothers have had a hard time finding a place for the first man and woman along with prehistoric man, as to who came first. With Neanderthal man placed about 110,000–30,000 BC capable of making sophisticated tools and weapons, burying their dead with a sense of an afterlife, graves oriented East-West in a fetal position and in the case of "The Woman of Tabun', at Mt. Carmel, Israel, buried with a jewelry headdress of dentalia. Her cranial capacity was 1271 cm³. She dates to the Mousterian period of 55,000–35,000 BC.

By the time of Cro-Magnon man 50,000–10,000 BC, the graves were dug into lower older occupation levels, covered with stones or shoulder blades of mammoths and the bodies covered with red ocher to give a semblance of life to the pallid skin. The Clovis point, from New Mexico, for spears were more finely made. Moreover, an arrow point has been found imbedded in one of 50 extinct Bison taylori bones (Dunbar p. 516, Moore p. 505, Time-Life Nature Library *Early Man*; EAEHL p. 290).

Geneticists have traced the DNA trail of women back to a single woman from whom we are all descended, the ancestral Eve. The same was found for man, that there was an ancestral Adam whose genetic material on the chromosome is common to every man now on earth (Nat. Geo. Program; Cross p. 69 and references therein).

3:22. This is not a complete sentence in the Hebrew, known as an ellipsis. God did not wish for man to live forever in a state of sin, so he quickly drove him away from the tree of life as an act of love. From this, note, that man was not created immortal in the Garden of Eden. These usually mark passages where the results are too terrible to contemplate. Others are to be found at

Genesis 35:22, Israel heard . . .; Genesis 49:4, defileast thou . . . he went; and Exodus 30:32, forgive their sin. . . .

7:11 and 8:2. Where did all the water come from during the flood? A recent Science Channel has shown that if all the moisture were wrung out of the clouds and atmosphere, rain would add only one inch worldwide. The torrents of rain were apparently from the ice canopy above the earth's atmosphere, which broke up and collapsed. (This same canopy was apparently responsible for diffusing the light of the sun and producing a greenhouse effect; some shielding from cosmic rays may be responsible for the long ages of man, producing a superior gene pool.) From 7:11–8:14 the water was upon the earth for 370 days. Where did the excess water go? Its still here: the land rose, as Psalm 104:6–8 indicates, forming submarine valleys for the water to pool or drain into.

Behind many of the ancient flood "myths" and other myths of Norse, Maya, Homer's Odyssey, the Egyptian Osiris and Indian Puranas tend to have similar elements involving a dog/jackal, mill, whirlpool and numerous sets of interrelated numbers (the numbers appear to be out of place and unnecessary for the telling of the stories as such). The encoded information tends to relate to the earth's precessional cycle leading to Ice Ages and rapid melting, both disasters for ancient man. Mathematics is the only thing that can show up as a hidden code. The full tale is too long for telling here, but I recommend Hancock pp. 242–272 for a fascinating *tour de force*.

The Sumerian tradition of the flood has five cities in the King List—Eridu, Bad-tibiri, Larak, Sipper, and Shuruppak—that existed before the flood. Eight kings reigned for 241,200 years. Dumuzi (Biblical Tammuz) of Bad-tibiri was said to rule for 36,000 years. When Eridu was destroyed and the next post-diluvial dynasty of Kish was established, this allows a calculated date for the Sumerian flood. Archaeology has shown that Eridu had no important occupation after the Uruk period by 3000 BC, and Kish did not emerge until the Jemdet Nasr period of 2900 BC (Saggs p. 27).

The interesting Sumerian Gilgamesh Epic (He is shown on the Lyre of Abargi of Ur dating to 2500 BC) and Utnapishtim (Noah) and Sumerian Job stories were pieced together from fragments brought back from the Library of Ashurbanipal (the world's first Archaeologist) at Kuyunjik, or Nineveh, by George Smith who studied them in 1872. The Gilgamesh Epic, Tablet XI of a total of XII, was missing about 17 lines and the London Daily Telegraph paid his way to Nineveh to look for them. This was the proverbial needle in the haystack search, but lo and behold and wonder of wonders, he actually found them, including some 384 other fragments. Also included was the sixth tablet of the deluge account, as well as the Sargon III expedition against Ashdod in Isaiah 20 (FRB pp. 167–174; WBF p. 19; TLBCC pp. 103–117; ABR 3: 66 (90), Baumann pp. 57–60; Bible and Spade 12: 57 [83]). The whole story can be found in Jacobsen pp. 195–208. From the Utnapishtim story of the Ark, a boat in which the planks were sewn together was apparently made; as possibly was Noah's Ark (BAR 30(3): 18 [05]).

15:9–18. "Covenant." This is the first time the formalities are listed. An interesting covenant ceremony is given in the Covenant Treaty between Ashurnirari V of Assyria (754–745 BC) and Mati'ilu of Arphad: This spring lamb has been brought from its fold not for sacrifice, not for a banquet, not for a purchase, not for (divination concerning) a sick man, not to be slaughtered for [. . .] it has been brought to sanction the treaty between Ashurnirari and Mati'ilu. If Mati'ilu sins against (this) treaty made under oath by the gods, then, just as this spring lamb, brought from its fold, will not return to its fold, will not behold its fold again, alas Mati'ilu, together with his sons, daughters, officials, and the people of his land [will be ousted] from his country, will not return to his country, and not behold his country again. This head is not the head of a lamb, it is the head of Mati'ilu, it is the head of his sons, his officials, and the people of his land. If Mati'ilu sins against this treaty, so may, just as the head of this spring lamb is torn off, and its knuckle placed in its mouth,[. . .], the head of Mati'ilu be torn off, and his sons [. . .]. This shoulder is not the shoulder of a spring lamb, it is the shoulder of Mati'ilu, it is the shoulder of his sons, his officials, and the people of his land. If Mati'ilu sins against this treaty, so may, just as the shoulder of this lamb is torn out, and [. . .], the shoulder of Mati'ilu, of his sons, his officials, and the people of his land be torn out and [. . .] (ANET Vol. II, p. 49).

Then follows the conditions of the treaty, the return of runaway slaves, and the furnishing of troops for war. Failure to abide was "to result in leprosy, famine, and drought so that only one in 1,000 is left, may he and his soldiers become public prostitutes, his seed be that of a mule (which is sterile), his wives barren and Ishtar cause sterility." Then at least (the tablet is broken at this point) 36 goddesses and gods are called as witnesses. The parties to ratify the covenant then passed between the pieces (see Jer. 34:18). These covenants were of three types. This one, between a king and his vassals; between kings of equal rank and between high-ranking equals, such as Genesis 31:44–55 where each person swears by his own god.

In Abraham's case, only God himself pledged to keep the provisions by passing between the pieces. Saying in effect, if I do not do these things, may I be cut into pieces (wow!). Several others with somewhat different conditions are also known, such as the one dated ca. 750 BC between Barga'yah, king of KTK (location unknown) and Matti'el king of Arpad. It again mentions a cut-up calf, and sets up the treaty in the bethels (the house of god or local temple). Note the names ending in yah or el, which are theophoric. (See ANE Vol. II, p. 42–69 and 221.) Other covenants are mentioned as in Joshua 24:25, 2 Kings 23:3; in the Dictys Cretensis De Bello Trojano I 15, that the Greeks before setting out for Troy cut up a boar and passed between the pieces in that they "stood in the covenant"; also in Pausanias' *Description of Greece* III 20.9, the suitors of Helen cut up a horse and took an oath standing on the pieces. (See IB Vol. III p. 320.) For other details of Hellenistic religions including miracles, epiphanies and sacred laws see Grant pp. 10–50. For some older Hittite treaties from 1400–1190 BC see Bible and Spade 8:10 (95); Kitchen pp. 92–102. Other Archaeological results for the Israelite cult are summarized in TWLSGF p. 571.

18:20. I will go and see. If the outcry coming up to God was not enough, where was the omniscience or omnipresence of God? Was it necessary for Him and two angels to get the first hand intelligence and look the situation over (BR Spring 2005, p. 22)? Or must God use theophany and anthromorphism to meet finite humans where we are?

20:14. Hagar and Ishmael. When Hagar and Ishmael are sent away, Abraham gives them bread and a skin of water, but no donkey to ride. Why? Abraham was well off and had plenty of donkeys; surely, he could afford to let them depart in some comfort. No explanation is given.

23:1. Sarah died at the age of 127 (the only woman whose age is given in the Bible, why?). The Hebrew says "a hundred years and twenty years and seven years." The Talmud explains this placement of numbers, in that she was "as beautiful at one hundred as she was at twenty and as sinless at twenty as she was at seven." As the mother of the promised seed she became the mother of all believers, in a spiritual sense (see Is 51:2; Matthews and Benjamin p. 30).

31:23. Mt. Gilead (of Syria). In v. 21 Jacob crosses the Euphrates from Haran on the 3rd day. In seven days, you cannot get to Mt. Gilead in the area of Amnon. On camels, at a forced march of 50 miles per day gives 350 miles maximum, thus this Mt. Gilead is in Syria.

32:10. "Passed over this Jordan." Jacob is recounting his first exit from Israel to Laban, since at this time he was in Ammon at the Jabbok, v. 22.

33:14. "Until I come to Seir." There is no indication that Jacob actually met Esau at a particular location in Seir. The region is in Edom and Succoth is located there. So maybe only a general area is specified.

34:1. The missing years. Dinah was Leah's seventh child. She was at least 12, and probably 15 to be desired as a wife. With an unknown gap between the sixth and seventh child, this allows for the birth of the four sons of Bilhah and Zilpah. Children were usually spaced every 2–3 years. Jacob served Laban 20 years—seven before marrying Leah, which leaves only 13 years total for the children to be born (Gn 31:40). Without the gaps and at one child per year for Leah, Dinah would be only age six at Shechem. Thus, there are at least 11–15 years unaccounted for.

35:19. Bethlehem of Judah is only 16 miles from Hebron, where the Patriarchs were buried in the cave in the field of Machpelah. Rachel was his favorite wife; why wasn't she buried with him and Leah (Gn 49:31 and 50:13)? Rachel's tomb has been shown here since about 1020. However, see 1 Samuel 10:2, where it is definitely stated that the tomb was in Benjamin near Ramah, which is north of Jerusalem. Jewish custom required the body to be buried the same day as death. Thus the distance from Ramah to Hebron was over 22 miles; more than a day's travel. She was thus buried "on the way" to Bethlehem.

38:15 and 21–22. Harlot. Two separate words are used in these verses. The first is *zonah*, which is a regular harlot; the second is *qedeshah*, referring to a temple prostitute, although they did not usually practice by the roadside as here, but rather in a temple.

Exodus 4:24. The Lord sought to kill Moses. Why had Moses forgotten to circumcise his son? He knew the requirement but failed to act. Why wait until they arrived at the inn? No answer for this one.

9:6. When all doesn't mean all. We were told that all the cattle of Egypt died, but in vv. 19–26 the hail was directed against the Egyptians' beasts and cattle (there was no hail in Goshen against the Israelis). So where did these cattle come from? In v. 18 only one day had passed. The term means almost all, or an insignificant amount left. Similar to the expression "all the world knows," when really all the world doesn't know.

12:37. Logistics. If 600,000 men left Egypt, and at four minimum per family, this would require a minimum of 2,500,000 people plus cattle and the mixed multitude. In a military formation of four abreast (the maximum number for the roads through the wilderness) and four feet between columns (a modern army allows 11 feet between columns) would mean the four 625,000 person columns of the formation would be strung out for 473.5 miles, with no breaks between columns and an unknown space required for the animals and wagons. If you could get ten abreast, the 250,000 person columns would still cover 189 miles for the people alone. It is about 210 miles from Lake Timsah (the Reed Sea crossing) to Mt Sinai = Horeb by the most direct route. Thus when the head of the column reached Sinai the rear with all the animals would not yet have left Timsah. This little talked about problem would mean that there would be no way for the entire group to get from point A to B in a day's march. The point of designating the stopping places are ludicrous for this number, since the end of the column would still be marching 47 days later at ten miles per day maximum. A gaggle of people, children and animals would not even be able to keep up this pace. Remember an army moves inversely proportional to the number of people and the smallest obstruction on the path such as boulders, width narrowing, streams, cliffs or gullies will result in a funnel effect, slowing down the movement past it. (See also Murnane p. 95; KOROT pp. 263–5).

Herodotus states that the 200,000-man army of Xerxes (Herodotus claimed a larger figure of 1,700,000) required seven days and nights to cross the Hellespont on two bridges. The one on the Black Sea side for the army and cavalry was about 40 feet wide and possibly as much as 90 feet wide. The other on the west was for the beasts of burden and the camp followers. The bridges were made of triremes ca 128 ft long and pentcomers (Herodotus Book VII Sect. 55–6; 60). The Israelites (traveling in tribal groups) would of necessity have to spread out past the roads to graze the flocks and find adequate water. This would make it even harder to keep groups together and to make any real time on the journey. God provided the food, but water was another matter. Even Alexander the Great's army of 65,000 men (small by any standards), 6,100 cavalry horses, 1,300 baggage animals and 8,400 animals carrying provisions required 159,000 gallons of water per day. His army was one of the fastest in the world, with the whole army traveling at 18.5 miles per day over favorable terrain. His speed always caught the Persians off guard. For a thorough account, see Engels pp. 145; 153. Other indications of smaller military forces are the accounts in the Tel el-Amarna letters of requests for reinforcements of 100 men for Megiddo and for 50 men each for Jerusalem and Gezer. Thus it was sufficient to keep the peace, but small by any standards (HJP p. 18). The main striking force of Thutmose III at the battle of Mediddo consisted of three divisions of about 15,000 men total. Ramses II at the battle of Kadesh had only three divisions of 15,000 men present (the division of Seth never arrived in time) plus a support division from the shore of Amuru of another 5,000. The Hittites had 2,500 chariots with three men each and two groups of infantry numbering 18,000 and 19,000 respectively. One of the largest armies assembled by the Hittites (KPT pp. 53, 140)—still modest numbers compared to the Exodus. Even so, the Kalmukes moved a 300,000-man army in one night from Russia toward the Chinese border in

January 1799. Only one third made the five-month journey covering 2,100 miles, fighting the Cossacks all the way (Hertz p. 259: Encarta Encyclopedia).

At the battle of Qarqar SW of Aleppo in 853 BC, Shalmaneser, in his sixth year, lists on the 'Kurkh Monolith inscription, the forces of the 12 kings who opposed him (only 11 are actually recorded, possibly Jehoshaphat of Judah was omitted unless he was counted with Ahab). Ahab of Israel furnished the largest chariot corps of 2,000 with 10,000 infantry. The Arabs are mentioned for the first time furnishing 1,000 camel cavalry. Baasha son of Rehob of Ammon furnished xx, 000 men (the number of thousands has been lost, probably 10,000), this name should be read as "king of Beth-rehob" (a line may be missing at the bottom [from ... from Ammon]), which is in the Anti Lebanon mountains north of Tel Dan. The total chariots, probably containing two men each (the Assyrians used three each) was 3,940, 2,900 cavalry and over 71,900 infantry for a total of 82,680 or more men.

Shalmaneser killed 14,000 (the Black Obelisk lists 20,500; the Bull inscription lists 25,000 but gives 12 kings plus Hadadezer [the Biblical Ben-hadad] and Irhuleni of Hamath), but the battle was not decisive, and was re-fought in 849, 848 and 845. The hot spots in the Assyrian kingdom determined where the next battles would be fought. In the seventh year, he fought Til-abne near the source of the Tigris, in the eighth and ninth years he fought Marduk-zakir-shumi of Babylon, in the tenth year he fought Sangara of Carchemish and Hadadezer of Damascus taking 100 small cities.

In the fourteenth year or 845 a twelve-king coalition again fought him but are not named (as well as in the eleventh year when there were 12 kings plus Hadadezer and Irhuleni); his army is listed as 120,000 men. Ahab was killed in 852 fighting against his old enemy (and ally in the first battle) Hadadezer and it is unknown if Israel was a part of the coalition in the later battles. By the eighteenth year or 841 the Black Obelisk shows Jehu (or his vizier) of Israel paying tribute.

Sennacherib lost 185,000 outside Jerusalem (2 Kgs 19:35). The Hebrew of this verse could be translated "one hundred and eighty and five thousand" meaning 5,180 (see Free and Vos p. 180). The numbers are getting larger, but still small by Exodus standards [ANE Vol. I p. 190; ANET pp. 276–280; HJP p. 121; IEJ 25: 25 (1975)].

The next question is, if the numbers are correct, could the Israelites after 430 years (Ex 12:40) grow to 603,550 (the collection taken in Exodus 39:26 at a bekah per man adds up to 603,550, but doesn't solve the logistics problem) males 20 years old or over (Nm 1:46), starting with the 50 males at the start in Egypt in 1871 BC. Under normal conditions probably, but were these normal conditions? Slaves usually do not fare well, and die off before much of a family has been started. If food is severely rationed young girls and women will cease their period and infant mortality will severely increase due to lack of breast milk. Malnutrition will allow scurvy, beriberi, disease and sickness to multiply. Men worked to exhaustion are probably more in need of rest than sex.

With the real oppression starting about 1550 BC, when the Hyksos had been driven out of Egypt in 1570 BC, any real multiplication was probably confined to this initial 321-year period. The remaining 109 years to 1441 was probably the period when population growth slowed considerably. By assuming the usual 30 years per generation, with 20 years of this to reach adulthood and with two male children born and surviving in the next ten years, we must omit the first starting generation (they already had their children) and any of those who died childless (Serah for one is the only daughter listed by name Genesis 46:17; according to the Zohar she was translated to paradise as the one who told Jacob that Joseph was still alive).

The remaining 50 males in 11 generations would produce only 51,200 males and at four per family about 205,000 for the Exodus. This number is probably still too large based on the logistics above. In fact, any total number above 70,000 will cause large problems in logistics and movement (Riedel p. 276). The statement in Exodus 14:10 and the small number at the Jordan (Jos 4:13), as well as those sent to Ai (Jos 7:3) where 36 were killed; the numbers in Joshua 8:3 and 12 are probably 30 and five rather than 30,000 and 5,000; all points to a smaller total group.

19:16 and 18. Mt. Sinai. Another location not well understood. The Bible account mentions smoke, thunder, and lightning flashes indicating possible volcanic activity. Traditional Mt. Sinai in the Sinai Peninsula has no volcanic strata. There is another location at Jabal al Lawz at 2,580 m high in Saudi Arabia east of the Gulf of Aqaba. This route would require the Exodus from Egypt to use the Darb el Haij route from Lake Timsah to Elath and then south. Volcano or no, the top of al Lawz is blackened and scorched; there is adequate water in the wadi streams; around the base are altars (one altar had about 11 marble columns around it 21 inches in diameter—there is no marble in this area), 12 pillars 18 feet in diameter composed of two rings of stones, with boundary markers around the base of the mountain and outside these a cliff face containing petroglyphs. Saudi archaeologists identified them as of Hator and Apis bulls. Could these be vestiges of a "Golden Calf" shrine? There are no military installations close by, but the Saudi's have built a high security fence around this area (and the petroglyphs) and have established a guardhouse to secure an archaeological site (Williams p. 96 figures; pp. 208–212).

Local Arabs speak of Moses camping in this area. Gordon Franz (Bible and Spade 13[4] 2000 and www//.idolphin.org/ Franz-Sinai.html) has taken issue with this location on several points. A further point is how did the children of Israel get there?

A route down the west side of Sinai and crossing the straits of Tiran (where the depth of the Gulf of Aqaba is 1,062 ft deep at this point) would be a second parting of the sea with impossibly high cliffs to negotiate. The northern route around Elath would be a huge out-of-the-way bypass.

Deuteronomy 1:2 says it is an eleven day journey from Mr. Siani (Horab) to Kadesh-barnea by way of Mt. Seir. This is about 188 miles by the caravan road, or about 17 miles per day. For a small party this is about right. From al Lawz the distance is about 150 miles and thus still fits.

28:30. Urim and Thummim, or lights and perfection. Apparently, these were the two or possibly three stones carried in the high priest's breastplate by which the Lord's will was determined, as is sometimes implied, as in 1 Samuel 14:23–46. The question would be asked such that yes, no, or maybe, or blank would come forth as the answer. See the article on Priestly Divination in Israel in TWLSGF p. 355.

32:28. "3,000 men fell." The Talmud says this occurred on Pentecost (see Lev 23:15). In Acts 2:1 3,000 were saved on the same day.

Leviticus 11:2–31. Kosher foods. Many of the animals cannot be identified but the groups they fall in are. Thus, the carnivores are excluded because of the pain they cause to their victims. All fish are meat eaters, we fish with worms and they eat their own young and the fry of others, the catfish is a bottom feeder, but scales are OK. The ostrich is excluded because of its bad habits toward its young. The swan is a mistranslation—probably an owl is intended. Shrimp and crab can remove cholera bacteria from infected waters, but these and lobsters are carrion feeders. Pork is known to carry toxoplamosis, trichinosis, tapeworm, etc. In general parasites, bacteria, viruses, and toxins were being avoided; but even healthy permitted animals can have these. Much here still remains a mystery.

12:5. "unclean two weeks." The Book of Jubilees explains that Eve was created on the sixth day of the second week, thus the extra week for a girl child. This is the only Jewish writing that attempts an explanation of this strange requirement. This also explains Genesis 1:27 that God created man and woman at the same time, yet Genesis 2:18 indicates some time had elapsed and that "it was not good for man to be alone". How much time does it take to get lonely? (See Brownlee p. 72). For a very good article on other aspects of pollution and purification, including the cases where the person must wait until evening, wash clothes and/or bath in a mikveh (see TWLSGF p. 399), although the author, Tikva Frymer-Kensky was not aware of the Jubilees reference.

23:17. "two loves baked with leaven." A hidden prophesy that the church would be made up of Jews and Gentiles. The "wave sheaf" (Lev 23:10) was offered the day after Passover; then 50 days later on Pentecost, the two wave loaves were presented. Containing leaven (for in the church there is still evil), it was not burned on the altar (2:11) but became the property of the priests. (See Scofield p. 157 and Hertz pp. 520–522.)

Numbers 3:27–28. Numbers of the Kohatites. Amram's family including Izhar, Hebron, and Uzziel in the days when Moses was still alive; and yet they numbered 8,600, which would be quite a feat, unless we admit that Amram was an ancestor of Moses and Aaron, and not his father. His father and mother are not actually named (WMGF p. 481).

19:2–10. The Red Heifer. Described in the Talmud Paran, which says there were only nine prepared up to the destruction of Herod's temple. The first was prepared under Moses, then Ezra, Simon Ha Tzaddik (the Just 219–190 BC Sirach 50:1) prepared two, Yochanan the High Priest prepared two, Eliechonnai ben Hakrot, Hanamell the Egyptian and Ishmael ben Piabi (15–16 AD). The ashes were mixed with the remaining ashes from the predecessor, and divided into three parts, one kept by the Levites, one kept on the Mt. of Olives, and the third placed in the wall Chail, which faced the women's gallery.

Israel is looking for a new red heifer; the ones found in 1997 and 2004 were declared kosher but later found to be unsuitable. In order to be used the ashes would have to be mixed with those from the last candidate, whose location is at present unknown. Some rabbis dispute that the old ashes are needed. Vendel Jones (actually spelled Vendyl) has made several illegal efforts to locate them, but is now barred from further excavations for violations without permits.

35:30. Capital punishment. Once guilt is established through two witnesses (or today we have the final proof through DNA), guilt beyond any reasonable doubt requires the death penalty. Life imprisonment is just as cruel and unusual punishment in the end. Why should society and the state or federal governments bear the high expense for their upkeep? The funds could be better spent for other needed services.

Deuteronomy 6:4. Shema, Israel, Adonai, Elohenu, Adonai, echad. The Shema or "watchword" recited as an article of faith by every Jew. This was actually changed by Rabbi Maimonides to read *yachid* instead of *echad*. The difference is great and persists to the present day, as *echad* means a compound unity, as in Genesis 1:5, Genesis 2:24, Numbers 13:23, Judges 20:1, 8, 11. *Yachid* means an absolute unity, as in Genesis 22:2, 12, 16, Judges 11:34, and Psalm 68:6. It is never used even once in the Bible to describe the oneness of God. Many Rabbis who recognize this difference have accepted a Triune God. What a difference a word makes.

10:17. Lord of Lords and King of Kings. In the Book of the Dead Chapter 185, Osiris is called "the prince of gods and men, the god of gods, king of kings, lord of lords, prince of princes, the governor of the world." Sound familiar (Budge p. liii; 367)? Actually Egyptian religion is a pure monotheism manifested by a symbolic polytheism (Budge p. xcii). See also the short-lived experiment of Akhenaten.

Joshua 3:16. Waters . . . stood and rose up. At Adam, this relates to red or blood. The red silt cliffs here are prone to collapse on each side of the Jordan. Earthquakes have dammed the Jordan here on several occasions (ca. 1400 BC, 1060 AD, 1160, 1267 for sixteen hours, 1534, 1546 for two days, May 23, 1834, 1906 for two days, and June 11, 1927 for twenty-one hours; see DSLS p. 82). Adam (Damiyeh) is about 18 miles from Jericho as the crow flies (the river course in 1980 was about 28 miles); if the river current flowed at five miles per hour, it would take at least five hours for the water to drain away, so that the army could cross on "dry" ground. Note, it does not say the Jordan was parted, as at the Sea of Reeds, there would be no need for this.

10:12–14. The sun stood still for 24 hours. For the earth to stop rotating all at once would cause massive tidal waves and loss of life all over the Mediterranean, since the Earth at the Equator is spinning at 1,000 miles per hour. God formed the laws of nature including Newton's 3rd Law of Motion: For every action there is an equal and opposite reaction. Did he suspend the laws of motion? Obviously some additional factors are involved that we are not told about. Theologians have pondered several theories: 1. Expansion of the rotary motion of the earth. 2. Extraordinary refraction of the light and visible over the whole globe, as if reflected by a mirror. 3. Day merely seemed lengthened due to the great amount of work accomplished (UD p. 715). The poetic expression from the Book of Jashar "Sun stand thou still upon Gibeon and thou, Moon in the valley of Ajalon," describes the natural state following an all night forced march from Gilgal 20 miles away, in the early morning just before the moon sets in the west and the Sun rises in the east (HJP p. 59).

14:7 and 10. Five years for the conquest. Simply put the two verses together. They wandered in the wilderness for 40 of those years.

21:25. Gath-rimmon is recopied from v. 24 by parablepsis. The second city's name is lost.

Judges 1:8. Was Jerusalem captured? According to v. 21, there is indication it was not. If some of the troops of Judah and Simeon managed to set the city on fire during a raid without capturing the defense towers; the city could not be held. At any rate, it was not retaken until David in 2 Samuel 5:7.

11:39. Jephthah's daughter. Was tragically vowed to be burned as a sacrifice, but instead he allowed her to remain unmarried for the rest of her life. The vow as made was not actually fulfilled. One reason vows should not be made lightly, as they can turn and bite you (Matthews and Benjamin p. 19).

15:1. Marriage. The type of marriage where the wife lives at home and the husband has visiting privileges is called *Sadiqa.* Another type is *Beena,* described in 2 Samuel 17:25 where an Ishmaelite (1 Chr 2:17) is named after the Israelite mother.

16:3. Samson's gate at Gaza. The only 11th-century BC gate known from Samson's time is at Ashdod. It is 16.4 ft wide, each leaf about eight ft wide; if only eight ft high and six inches thick this would be 32 ft^3. If made of oak whose density is 44 lbs per ft^3 this would be 1,408 lb per leaf. It says he carried off the doors plus hardware, which could be over 2,816 lbs. The gate at Timnah or Tel Batash (8–7th century) was 13.12 ft wide (see A. Mazar p. 468 or BAR 15[1]: 45 [89] for other IA gates).

1 Samuel 1:1. Elkanah the Ephraimite. In 1 Chronicles 6:27 Zophai is the same as Zuph, and Nahath is the same as Tohu, Eliab is the same as Eliahu; otherwise these would appear to be different genealogies. The problem is the term Ephraimite that describes one from the Tribe of Ephraim. Elkanah was by 1 Chononicles 6:25 of the Tribe of Levi. Since Ramathaim-zophim means the double height, and in v. 19 and elsewhere it is simply called Ramah (the present day Ramallah headquarters of the PLO which has several double heights around it), which is in the Tribe of Benjamin. It seems that Zuph must have moved from his allotted area in Ephraim (these Levites would take on the name of the tribe in whose area they lived). Adding to the complexity, 1 Chronicles 6:28 starts off with the sons of Samuel but makes no mention of Samuel being the son of Elkanah, while v. 33 does (Hertz p. 951).

1 Samuel 1:3. Eli. How Eli became a priest is not known. From 1 Chronicles 24:1 and 3 and 1 Kings 2:27 Eli seems to be descended through Ithamar, but we are not told how this happened (HJP p. 87). Ithamar was Aaron's fourth son (Ex 6:23), rather than Eleazar the third son. Yahweh rewarded Ithamar with a promise that the priesthood should remain in his family forever (Nm 25:13). In the two centuries between Phinehas and Eli, the line of Eleazar fell from power. The reason for this change is unclear. However, the statement remains that Phinehas was the last recorded high priest (Jgs 20:28).

7:1. Ark taken to Kirjath-jearim (city of forests in W. Benjamin at Abu Ghosh) and not back to Shiloh (4:3); why? Excavations indicate that Shiloh was occupied from 1300–1100 BC, but not from 1050–300 BC (see Jer 7:12–15 and 26:6 and 9). The city was probably destroyed by the Philistines during this period of Samuel's judgeship and before Saul was crowned.

14:41. Give a perfect lot. The Hebrew *hava thammin* should probably be amended to *hava thummim*, or "give a yes." Where Saul is inquiring of the Urim and Thummim to discern the Lord's will (BAR 31(2): 34 [05]). Other forms of divination used in Israel, Assyria and Babylonia were: aleuromancy (study of flour offered to deities), astrology (still being used today), belomancy (study of arrows dropped or shot), cledomancy (divination by a chanced word), exispicy (study of sheep entrails), hepatoscopy (study of animal livers), idolomancy (consulting of teraphim) Ezekiel 21:21, lecanomancy (study of oil patterns on water), libanomancy (study of incense burned), necromancy (contacting the dead), use of skulls for the same purpose [Sanhedrin 65b; BAR 35: 16 (09)], oneiromancy (divination based on dreams), ornithomancy (study of the flight of birds), psephomancy (study of pebbles); rabdomancy (divination by rods Hos 4:12), and teratoscopy (study of freak births) (BAR 31(2): 36 [05]). The Chinese as early as 1700 BC in the Shang period used oracle-bones with inscriptions on cow scapulas or tortoiseshells. A shallow hole would be drilled on the opposite side and a hot point applied causing a pattern of fissures to appear, which a diviner read. Only the king himself used the method (Time Life Books Lost Civilizations: *China's Buried Kingdoms* pp. 20; 33 1993).

17:40. Five smooth stones. One for Goliath and one for each of his brothers (or possibly sons, 2 Sm 22:16–22; 1 Chr 20:5), should they come to his aid. Apparently some genetic defect resided in this family, since v. 20 has one with six fingers and toes on each hand and foot. Their great height may also have been a part of this defect. Excess of the pituitary growth hormone somatotropin results in giants, but many are weak in muscle development and have some difficulty moving around, being almost cripples.

2 Samuel 6:6. Death of Uzzah. A confused verse in the Masoretic Text, which can be recovered by careful study: "his hand" is not present. Nor do we know what the oxen did; the verb "to drop" is always used transitively and does not mean stumbled or kicked. Josephus says they shook it. Whatever happened, he was punished in v. 7 "for his (*shal*) slip" for what he did in v. 6. The loss of one letter gives the Hebrew *wayyishal*. He slipped in the oxen droppings, a common euphemism. His death was from a blow to the head on the rocks of the threshing floor (IB Vol. I pp. 1078–9). A statement in the DSS Manual of Discipline says, "But David did not read the sealed book of the law, which was in the ark; for it was not opened from the death of Elazar and Joshua and the elders who served Ashtaroth, but was hidden and not disclosed until Zadok arose. The deeds of David were overlooked, except the blood of Uriah, and God left them to him." If the priests were not consulting the law, it's no wonder the country went downhill.

12:1–23. One of only two times David was punished for breaking the Mosaic Law. The other was for the census in chapter 24.

Other violations not punished are: Eating the showbread in 1 Samuel 21: 4 and 5, versus Leviticus 24: 8 and 9. Had mules 1 Kings 1:33, versus Leviticus 18:19. Multiplies wives, 1 Chronicles 3:1–9, versus Deuteronomy 17:17. Note: a foreign wife per se (Geshur is in Syria, 1 Chr 3:2) is not forbidden until the time of Ezra and Nehemiah. Under Moses only the Canaanites, both male and female, were excluded, Exodus 23:15–16; Deuteronomy7:1–3 (an exception was made for Rahab's family). In Deuteronomy 23:3 only Ammonite and Moabite men were excluded in marriage, 10th generation = forever. Ruth was a Moabite woman, which was legal to marry. Children were counted as the father's.

Took Michal back as his wife after she was married to Paltiel (1 Sm 18:27; 25:44; 2 Sm 3:14). Also he had idols (*teraphim*) in his house (1 Sm 19:13, 16 versus Ex 20:3). Note excavations of early Hebrew homes reveal many fertility figurines in baked clay. It appears that the women made use of these as an aid to conception. Michal was barren (2 Sm 6:23) but later raised the five sons of Adriel (2 Sm 21:8). The teraphim probably belonged to her. Note the LXX and some Hebrew manuscripts read Merab for Michal.

Transport of the Ark (2 Sm 6:3 versus Nm 4:15; 7). The ark was placed in the home of a Ger Obed-edom the Gittite (2 Sm 6:10 versus Nm 3:31). It should have been in the care of the Kohathites. The term Obed-edom the Gittite (from Gath) usually implies a foreigner, as does Caleb the Kenizzite in Numbers

32:12. The person mentioned in 1 Chronicles 15:18; 26:4 may be another person. There is some controversy on this point.

Likewise, David lied (1 Sm 27:10) to Achish about the raids. And he wore an ephod and assumed some priestly duties (2 Sm 6:14; 13:13). If this was carried out it would also be against the Law (compare Dt 27:22). Half sisters are covered under Leviticus 18:9. Why were the rest of these not punished? Unless God spoke to the individual directly or through a prophet, His will as revealed in the Law may not have been known. Questions could be asked by way of the Urim and Thummim. The Law was shut up in the Ark and few priests consulted it, as stated in the Talmud. Apparently, many of the provisions were forgotten with the passage of time (see above). Otherwise this is a flagrant disregard of Scripture, though David was described as a man after God's own heart (1 Sm 13:14; 1 Kgs 15:5).

In contrast, Solomon apparently violated only four. His many wives (1 Kgs 11:3—with 300 wives and 700 concubines he should have had many sons—can you name two?); the sanctity of the altar (1 Kgs 2:28–34 versus Ex 39:37); assumed priestly duties (2 Kgs 8:14–65); and allowed temples to foreign gods and goddesses (1 Kgs 11:5).

12:24. When was Solomon born of Bathsheba? If the list in 1 Chronicles 3:5 and the same list in 2 Samuel 5:15 are chronological (the names in 1 Chr 3:1–3 definitely are), then 8–10 years had passed. Bathshua in 1 Chronicles 3:5 is a variant spelling; her father's name is probably correct since Eliam in 2 Samuel 11:3 is obtained by transposing the first and last syllables. Ammiel means the people of God, and Eliam means God of the people.

1 Kings 1:2. Abishag and David. The context here is learned from Assyrian texts. One of the duties of a king was the procreation of children. If a king could no longer function in this capacity, in the Assyrian realm, he was usually killed and a son would take over. Something more than warmth for the king is implied here, as any of his wives could perform this task. Only a young wife could perform the other role, as he was now quite old and so also were his other wives—probably past child bearing. In Egypt, the 30-year *heb sed* festival required the king to prove his physical strength or be killed and replaced.

18:31–2. Twelve stones for an altar. Another area that slips by us. You can't make much of an altar out of twelve stones (the maximum a man could carry was about 100 pounds). However, this altar had existed here before (v. 30). The minimum size altar was 5 x 5 x 3 cubits or 7.5 x 4.5 feet. The twelve stones set up at Gilgal and the Jordan (Jos 4:8–9) were probably a memorial of standing stones set up as at Gezer (a masseboth of ten huge stones from 10 to 5.5 feet high). These could be in a straight line or a circle. The size or number of stones for the altar on Mt. Ebal (Dt 27:5) are not specified

2 Kings 2:23. Little boys. The Hebrew is *Naar* and means young men or squire. The same word is used in 2 Samuel 18:5 and for Solomon in 1 Chronicles 22:5, yet Solomon already had a son who was about seven years old. The same word is used of Joseph, who was about 17, in Genesis 37:2.

6:6. . . . the iron did swim. A miracle, if the density of iron was made lighter than water. However, this is not what is said. Elisha asked where it fell in the water. He could have said to the axe head, "come up hither" and it would have flopped at his feet. Instead, he cut a branch, fished around in the water until it found the socket, and pulled it out. The miracle is in finding the socket.

20:3. Hezekiah's prayer. The result was ten bad results, vv. 17, 18, 21:1–6, 9, 16 and 19–20. Maybe God does know best! (Compare 2 Sm 12:22). However, Hezekiah had no heir at this time, and without a son, the kingly line from David would have stopped here.

20:11. Sun goes back ten degrees on the sundial of Ahaz! Ahaz was Hezekiah's father; the sundial was probably obtained from Babylonia (Herodotus and Dn 3:6, where hours are mentioned for the first time). There is no consensus for the type of sundial. However, Keil and Delitzsch in the *Biblical Commentary on the Old Testament* (Eerdmans Publishing Co. pp. 464–5 1966) gives a similar account witnessed by the prior and others in the convent at Metz in 1703, where the sundial went back 1.5 hours.

22:20. Josiah to die in peace. Instead, he died in battle at Megiddo 23:30. Although anyone who dies is at peace and cannot see the future evil to come.

23:10. Topheth. This fire altar to Molech was located in the valley of Hinnom or gai ben Hinnom, colloquially known as Gehenna or Hell. The trash fires of the city were always burning in this area, as were many children who were sacrificed to pagan gods. The location would have been in the lower end about 200 yards before it empties into the Kidron. This area has never been excavated and the debris is probably 100 feet deep here.

25:9 and 13–17. What became of the Ark of the Covenant? (See Jer 3:16; Heb 8:5 and 9:23; are these the models for Rev 11:19?) Although *Naus* means sanctuary or shrine, Revelation 21:22 says no temple is present in the Holy City that descends from Heaven. The Bible gives us no further help. Jewish legend and the Talmud say the priests hid it below the Temple mount, and others state that it was taken to Mt. Nebo. (See below at Heb 9:4).

1 Chronicles 5:26. Pul and Tiglath-Pileser 744–727 BC. Discovery of the Babylonian king list cleared up this perplexing question, when for the year 728 BC the king's name was given as Pulu. Tiglath-Pileser III was his Assyrian name, but he may have used his Babylonian name in Babylon for the benefit of the people. He may have taken the name Tiglath-Pileser from the first famous conqueror of that name. He was not of the royal line, only a general. His father and mother are not mentioned. Esarhaddon mutilated his inscriptions because he had no royal linage, which happened to no other king. However, the statue of Ashurnasirpal II was apparently mutilated by the Medes when they overtook Kalhu or Nimrud in 612 BC (BAR 34(1): 14 [08]). Sennacherib's reliefs of the capture of Lachish at Nineveh also had his face hacked out, probably by the Medes. The next king, Shalmaneser V 726–722 BC also had a Babylonian name, Ululai on the king list.

25:3. From this list of names one name has been lost, and only five are given. His name was Shimei from v. 17 (NUD p. 1184).

25:4. A hidden prayer. The Hebrew names from Hananiah to Mahazioth actually form a prayer that reads, "Be gracious unto me, O God, be gracious unto me, Thou art my God. Thou hast increased and raised up help for him that sat in distress. Do thou make the (prophetic) visions abundant" (IB Vol. II p. 426).

Proverbs 13:24. Corporal punishment of children. Yes, the Bible condones it, if done with an attitude of correcting folly and not to inflict serious injury. Let the courts rethink their position and draw up better guidelines rather than throwing out the baby with the bathwater, which leaves him or her worse off.

Ezra 4:7. Artaxerxes? I Longimanus 464–424 BC. This whole section to v. 24 should probably follow at the end of Chapter 10, due to his late reign. Could refer to the pretender Gaumata also called pseudo Bardiza (a brother whom Cambyses assassinated), or pseudo Smerdis who ruled eight months in 522 BC. Josephus *Antiquities* 11.2.1 p. 229 calls him Cambyses, but this may refer to v. 6.

8:35. When were the lost tribes lost? After the return from exile, the burnt offering of 12 bulls for all Israel indicates that each tribe was represented. The 12 he goats of 6:17 were a sin offering, one for each tribe. Sargon only took 27,290 people from Samaria in 721 BC; this was only a small portion (Finnegan p. 175). Note also that the Lord offered himself to the Nation "the lost sheep of the house of Israel." (See also Mt 10:6; Lk 2:36 (Anna of the tribe of Asher); Acts 4:36 (Levi); 26:7, Rom 11:1 (Benjamin); Jas 1:1). The tradition from the Septuagint ca 250 BC states that six from each tribe (or 72) worked on the translation. After the Roman wars of 70 and 135, little is heard from any tribe except Benjamin and Levi, where the Kohens and priests still derive their heritage from Levi. Gad is mentioned on the Moabite stone, but the tribe of Reuben living in the area of Moab is not. Reuben was the first tribe to disappear about 850 BC.

Nehemiah 5:17. One Hundred and fifty at Nehemiah's table. It was common for the Persians to feed their officers and ministers, but in this case from his own pocket instead of the king's treasury. Xerxes fed 15,000 at his table, costing 400 talents of silver per meal. A thousand animals were slaughtered. The guests usually kept the gold drinking cups. When traveling, the numbers were lower, but the host had to pick up the tab, often costing 20–30 talents (Cook p. 207).

Job 2:8. Boils and the ash pit. Scraping the tops off boils allows them to drain, and putting sterile wood ashes on them is an astringent, from the 10% sodium and 90% potassium hydroxide or carbonates present, which probably did not feel too good.

22:14. Does the Bible teach that the Earth revolves? The Hebrew Hug means circle or revolve. In 38:13 the Earth in v. 14 turns (as a potter's wheel). In Psalm 19:6 the Hebrew Sabab means circuit, or to revolve as in Exodus 34:22 and Isaiah 40:22, again Hug or circle of the Earth. In Matthew 24:40 and Luke 17:34–36 the Second Coming of Christ happens at the same instant. In that "two in the field" is during the day from sunrise to sunset, the "two grinding" occurs in the early morning ca. 6 A.M.; the two in bed occurs at night. A clear understanding of a turning Earth is shown.

Chap. 38. Answer these and win several Nobel Prizes.

38:8–11. What determined the proper amount of water for the Earth? The water/land ratio is crucial. Vary it too much and you get a world desert such as Mars, or a cloudy jungle such as Venus. Cutting the oceans in half would reduce the rainfall by 3/4. Increase it 1/8 and precipitation would increase fourfold. Beware global warming, which has now been shown to be real. From 1906–2005 temperatures have risen 0.74 degree Celsius, carbon dioxide has increased 115 ppm, and sea levels have increased 3.1 mm per year since 1993–2003. Sea level at Fiji has risen 135 cm over the last 90 years (FLIA p. xii; Scientific American Aug. 2007 p. 64).

38:12–13. Why are the Earth's orbit and rotation exactly right for life? A little closer or farther away from the Sun and we would either burn or freeze. Vegetation as we know it would be vastly changed. The same for our orbit, which is based on the mass of Earth and Sun, as stated by Newton's gravitational law: F the force of gravity= $4\Pi^2$ G Ms Mp divided by C^2. Where Π= 3.14159, G is the gravitational constant, Ms is the mass of the Sun, Mp the mass of the planet and C is the planet's orbital circumference. All these can be determined and from this, a planet's mass or the Sun's mass can be calculated. No scales needed (Thorne pp. 563–4). A smaller Earth could not hold sufficient atmosphere due to the weaker gravity, and a larger Earth's gravity would make movement of mankind harder. With water freezing a 0° Centigrade, ice would accumulate at the poles and salt in the sea would be needed to alter its freezing point. Kepler's Laws established why the planets behave as they do (Magueijo p. 119).

38:16. A reference to springs and rivers underwater? Such are known in the Red Sea, Sea of Galilee, the Lost River and others. "Recesses of the deep," is a reference to large underwater canyons before any undersea exploration was done.

38:17. Does science or anyone understand what happens at death? Does the soul have weight? Dr. Duncan MacDougall of

Haverhill, Mass. made one study in this area in 1901. A dying man was carefully weighed both before and after death. It was concluded the soul weighs about 3/4 ounces. Five more terminal patients were weighed over the next two years with a weight loss of 3/8 to one ounce. When the same thing was done on 15 dogs, there was no weight loss. (Reported in Parade Magazine 6-19-83; Mary Roach *Spook* W.W. Norton 2006.) In addition, Dr. Nils-Olof Jacobson in *Life after Death* reports the soul weighs 21g, or 3/4 oz. What are the "Gates of Deep Darkness"?

38:18. Why is the Earth's diameter right for life? As above, it prevents water from being lost and holds the atmosphere.

38:19–20. Where does light originate? Note the Bible states that light does not have a place, whereas darkness does. Visible light of 4000–7700 A° is confined to this narrow range, because substances absorb radiation on either side of this range. UV is harmful and IR heats bodies up too much. Other ranges such as X-rays, gamma rays and microwaves are also harmful. What is light? As a photon particle, it shows photoelectric, photo-conductivity or spectra effects. As a wave, it shows reflection, refraction, interference, diffraction and polarization. Traveling at 186,281.74 miles per second, it cannot have a place as recalculated from Thorne p. 78. No particle can travel faster than light; in the 90s, electrons were accelerated to 0.9999999995 the speed of light (Thorne p. 83). Einstein in 1911 predicted that light could be bent by passing near a large object (the Sun for example), but it was not proved until the eclipse of 1919 by Eddington and Crommelin (Magueijo p. 61).

38:22–23. Large quantities of moisture are available for God to use as snow or hail; as a display of His power ex. Exodus 9:22–26, Joshua 10:11, I Maccabees 13:22 when Trypho's army in 143 BC was delayed due to a heavy snow. The rain for 40 days and nights of Genesis 7:4 or Judges 4:15, 5:4 and 21 are other examples. By the way, raindrops that are too large will split in half. There is a limiting size. Hail with diameters of 15.75 inches fell on Paris on July 13, 1788 (FLIA p. 162).

38:24. Where does light actually come from? In the stars, from fusion of Hydrogen into Helium, but are there other ways? For the Sun: $_1H^1 + _1H^1 \rightarrow _1H^2$ (Deuterium) $+ e^+$ (positron) $+ Ve$ (electron neutrino); $_1H^2 + _1H^1 \rightarrow _2He^3$ (Helium) $+ \gamma$ (light photon); $_2He^3 + _2He^3 \rightarrow _2He^4 + 2$ p (protons). The result is that four protons (the electron of Hydrogen is stripped off) give one helium, which has 0.7% less mass (which appears as energy or light) than the four protons. Four protons cannot collide directly (four body reactions are essentially impossible), thus the series shown. The positron is destroyed by collision with an electron $e^+ + e^-$ (electron) $\rightarrow 2\gamma$; overall $4p \rightarrow _2He^4 + 2Ve + 6\gamma$, the last two being the source of light and heat (Encarta 2000). What is the source of the wind? Why is the east wind more violent in Palestine? The sirocco of the Arabian Desert is a dry, hot, east-to-south wind. In Palestine, it is the *hamsene* or 50-day wind. (See Ex 14:21; Jb 27:21; Is 28:8; Eze 27:26).

38:25–30. How do rain, hail, and lightening originate? We may think we have these answers.

38:31. Can you bind the chains of the Pleiades? Can you draw together the open star cluster called Pleiades, or allow the limits of the constellation Orion to expand? Does cord=band=belt? God revealed that these seven stars were associated before astronomy confirmed it. These seven stars in the constellation Taurus are seen as 40 with a small telescope, but actually consist of 120 stars. M. Medler over a century ago discovered that Aleyone, the brightest star in the Pleiades, is the center of gravity in our solar system. Pleiades or Kimah in Hebrew means hinge, pivot or axle. Do the limits of expansion refer to the Super Nova in the time of Job, which resulted in the Orion nebula?

38:32–33. Can you lead forth the Massaroth (constellations) in their seasons? What determines the seasons? The tilt of the

Earths axis at 23.5° and rotation are responsible. Would life be possible on Earth without this effect on the weather, climate etc. as controlled by the moon?

38:34–35. Can man control the weather or elements? We have had some success in bringing rain, but not much for tornadoes or hurricanes. Are messages sent by lightning (electricity)? Look what Ben Franklin started. Ask AT&T, or turn on your radio or TV.

38:36–38. Is there a constant cloud cover over the Earth? For what purpose? To moderate the earth's temperature, shield UV radiation, etc.? When and why should rain occur? Is there a constant rainfall over the earth's surface? Why? To purify the air of dust, smoke, pollen and carbon dioxide, etc.?

38:39–41. The earth is in balance, each species depending on each other. Who destroys the balance of nature, man or God? Is not God the great ecologist?

39:1–4. What is the gestation period of the Ibex and fallow deer? Science can answer this one, although their shy manner and the difficulty of observing them would have been a mystery to the ancients.

39:5–8. The wild ass (the Asian wild ass is the onager) has a certain type of territory and seems to prefer the desert; why?

39:9–12. Can you domesticate the unicorn? The Hebrew is re'em and it has more that one horn (Dt 33:17). When viewed from the side, it appears to have one horn. This refers to the aurochs or wild ox. Tiglath-pilesar I (1115–1057 BC) pictured it on wall slabs; it existed in Germany during the time of Caesar, who described it. It became extinct in Europe during the middle ages. It was a large (11 feet high at the shoulder) strong and ferocious beast, completely untamable. The bull leaping frescos at Knossis in Minoan Crete are the best-known examples.

39:13–18. Man can study the ways of the Ostrich, but why should it have these traits?

39:19–25. The horse has a certain intelligence and can be taught to run at the sound of a trumpet, for example the cavalry horse or racehorse.

39:26–30. The hawk and eagle or vulture have special eyesight for seeing small objects at a great distance. Would man have known this by observation in that day?

40:15–24. What does man know when God creates nature. The Behemoth or Hippopotamus was native to the coast of Israel and the Jordan River in the past, some of their bones have been found at Beisamoun near Lake Hula; Ubeidiya at the south end of the Sea of Galilee, on the mountain spine at Bethlehem including Elephant and Rhinoceros, as well as the Cave of the Oven at Carmel dated to 80,000–55,000 BC. Most are from Pre-Pottery Neolithic B (7000 BC), along the coast they date from the Middle Bronze Age to the Iron Age, BASOR 280:67(90).

41:1. Leviathan is the Crocodile or an allusion to Lotan the seven-headed monster of the Ugaritic Ras Shamra texts, Riedel p. 32.

41:18–21. The breath and vapor resemble smoke, light flashes from the eyes as coals when seen in the night. It could refer to a fire idol or the god Lotan (Isa. 27:1).

41:31. Due to the rolling action when attacking a victim. The Hippopotamus is his only natural enemy.

Psalm 103:12. East from the West. Before the compass was known, God revealed the fact that east and west never meet. What a disaster to inspiration if it had said, "as far as the north is from the south."

Isaiah 13:20 vs Zephaniah 2:14. Babylon and Nineveh contrasted. "Neither shall the shepherds make their fold there." Arabs believe the site of Babylon is haunted, and they will not go among the ruins after dark. "No Arab will pitch his tent there" Vs. 21–22 under Shapur I, was fulfilled in 363 who turned the city into a game preserve. As late as 1845 when Austin Henry Layard dug at Calah (Nimrud), the Asiatic lion (about half the size of the African lion and shown on the relief's of Ashurbanipal) still roamed the ruins of this site and Nineveh at night, picking off the Bedouins' dogs (RPNF p. 40).

"Flocks shall lie down in the midst of her (Nineveh)." Nineveh is fairly flat over the ruins of the old city, across the river from Mosul, Iraq; flocks can be seen grazing there (Bible and Spade 1: 73 [72]), whereas Babylon is a mass of fallen brick and sand dunes. Saddam Hussein rebuilt part of the city of Babylon as a tourist attraction, and to try to emulate the fame of Nebuchadrezzar, the only one to conquer Jerusalem and the Jews.

Jeremiah 7:18 and 44:17–19, 25. Queen of Heaven. Semeramis was the wife of Nimrod (Tammuz). She was the original impersonation of the Semitic goddess Astarte, identical to the Babylonian Ishtar (the Greek Venus), the Latin Juno, Ashtoreth of the Zidonians and Eostre of the early Anglo-Saxons and the Druids, from which Easter derives. She was a mother goddess of fertility and worshiped chiefly among women. This interest in the spring vernal equinox with Easter, eggs associated with the theology of the Egyptians, Persians, Gauls, Greeks, Romans and Druids. The Babylonians believed an egg fell from heaven into the Euphrates River, where fishes rolled it to shore and a dove hatched out called "the Queen of Heaven," or Ishtar. The egg is her symbol. The Chinese dyed eggs and the German myth of a white hare hiding colored eggs in odd corners of the house completed the Easter fable. The Egyptian word for hare is "*un*," meaning to open. Thus, the hare (born with its eyes open) opens the spring season. The early British considered it unlucky not to wear some new article of clothing at Easter. Put all the loose ends together and you have the garbage of Easter.

Ezekiel 1:5–7 and 10:20. Cherubim. These are mentioned several places in Scripture. Known as Karabu in Babylon, Kuribu in Akhad, and in Assyria the karibu (kirabu} or lamassu figures are shown guarding the portals of gates or throne rooms. The sets of horns on the headdresses are important. Major gods and goddesses have four, such as Shamash on the Code of Hammurabi, Nanna on the Ur-Nammu stele, Ishtar on the palace walls of Mari or Lilith (Lloyd p. 170); the gatekeepers or cherubs at the Oriental Institute from the palace of Sargon III have three, those from the palace of Ashurnasirpal II at Ninrud have only two, those with only two are lesser deities such as archangels, while those with only one are minor deities, door keepers or deified kings such as shown on the water pourer from Mari or the Stele of Naram-Sin (TLBGK pp. 15,33; BR 18 (2), p. 30 [2002]). See also the sarcophagus of King Ahiram of Gebal (Byblos) and the ivory inlay on the throne of a Canaanite twelfth-century king from Megiddo, both without horns [ANE Vol. I fig. 126; BAR 11(4): 46 (1985)]. Such stonework or bas-reliefs were not present in Babylon since ready sources of stone were not available; brickwork was used instead.

8:10. Idols on the walls. No image or idol of Yahweh has ever been found by archaeologists. However, an interesting controversial potsherd found at Kuntillet 'Ajrud in the Sinai reads, "I bless you by Yahweh of Samaria and by his Asherah" with crudely drawn figures, one male wearing a bull mask and one female wearing a cow mask and a third playing a lyre while seated (BAR 27(3): pp. 36–7 [01]).

8:14. Women weeping for Tammuz. He was the ancient god of vegetation who died in the summer heat (June-July) and returned to life with the rainy season. He dates back to ca. 3000 BC in Babylon. This myth was popular and common from Canaan to Babylon.

8:16. Men worshiping the Sun. This was forbidden in Deuteronomy 4:19; 17:3. These men may represent the priesthood worshiping the Babylonian Sun god Shamash. The significance is that the Babylonian gods were defeating Yahweh, God of Israel.

24:1. Ninth year, tenth month and tenth day, see 1:1. The date is Jan. 15, 588 BC, the date Jerusalem is besieged. Ezekiel dates by Jehoiachin's reign in absentia in 597 BC.

29:17–20. Egypt to be captive 40 years (see v. 13). The prophesy is dated in Spring New Year, April 16, 570, or April 26, 571 (v. 17). Nebuchadrezzar invaded Egypt in 568/7 and after 40 years, or 528, Egypt was to be released. Hophra (Apries) was replaced by Amasis II in a coup in 569 BC. Only Pathros or Upper Egypt was to be restored (v. 14); the Delta would be uninhabited and thus a source of weakness (vv. 14–15). The order of events for this period is: July 587, Jerusalem falls; 585–572, Tyre is besieged by Nebuchadrezzar, who played peacemaker during an eclipse (May 28, 585 BC) of the Sun, on the Halys river between the Lydians and Medes (Manda), the conquerors of Assyria. Nebuchadrezzar had no navy; thus the long siege. In 568 Egypt is attacked and in 566 he returns to Egypt to put down a revolt.

Daniel 5:24–28. What mean these words? This section from 2:4–7:28 is in Aramaic, the language of diplomacy in Babylon. Daniel interpreted "Mene, Mene, Tekel Upharsin" to mean Numbered, Weighed and Divided (or Broken). The "U" in Upharsin is "and" in Aramaic. Each word has a double meaning: Mene—Your kingdom is so counted out that it is full—your time has run out. Tekel—You have been weighed and found too light (deficient in moral worth)—you don't measure up. Pharsin—Meaning is not to be divided into two equal parts but to be divided into pieces or dissolved—you are as nothing.

In Aramaic, the vowels would be absent and written from right to left as: NSRPU LQT 'NM 'NM. In cuneiform, the vowels would be included. Since Jewish Rabbis often wrote vertically, they could appear as: P T M M

R Q N N
S L ' '
N

Without vowels, these words could also be read as monetary units: Maneh = $800 equivalent to Nebuchadrezzar, Teqel = Shekel = $16 equivalent to Belshazzar, Peras = half Maneh = $400 equivalent to the Meads and Persians. Peres as a plural is Pharsin and is an Aramaic word for Persian (a Pun?). Mene is probably repeated twice for emphasis. For other words which are changed by a vowel change see Jeremiah 1:11—almond tree; Amos 8:1—summer fruit; and Jeremiah 1:12—watching; Amos 8:2—end. These are also used as puns.

5:20. Who was Darius the Mede? History does not record this name in connection with the fall of Babylon, but rather Cyrus II and his General Ugbaru. Cyrus did not enter the city until 18 days after it was captured on Oct. 13, 539 BC. Ugbaru was also governor of Gutium (Elam). He died eight days after the arrival of Cyrus on Nov. 8, 539 BC.

Another person known as Gubaru or Gobryas was also known to have been appointed by Cyrus as governor, but he is not called a Median, or king of Babylon, and his age is not given in the Chronicle. Some scholars equate Ugbaru = Gubaru = Gobryas, while others identify Gubaru with Darius (Whitcomb p. 5).

D.J. Wiseman contends that an Aramaic translation of 6:28 allows ". . .Darius even the reign of Cyrus the Persian." Thus, Darius would be a nickname for Cyrus. These facts are known:

Darius: from Bible	Cyrus: from History
Was a Mede 5:31	From Elamite land of Anshan
62 years old 5:31	Died in battle 530 BC, age?
A son of Ahasuerus	A son of Cambyses I
(Astyages or Cyaxeres) 9:1	

The archaeologist shovel may shed light here someday. Ahasuerus is the same as the Xerxes of Ezra and Esther. It is a Persian name. No Xerxes has a son named Darius. However, Darius I (522–486 BC) son was Xerxes I (485–465 BC). Could there have been a name switch? Persian names look strange in Greek; compare also Kurush to Greek Kuros or our Cyrus. Cyrus's two sons Kabujiah and Bardiya: we know them as Cambyses and Smerdis (see Cook pp. 65–67).

9:25–26. When will the Messiah come and die? This prophecy is the most important one in the Bible. The 69 weeks of years is 483 years. However, from 9:27 the last week of years or seven years is divided into two parts, the 42 months or 3 ½ years of Revelation 11:2, 12:14 and 13:5, or the 1,260 days of Revelation 11:3. From this, a 360-day year is being used (see also Gn 8:3–4; 7:11 and 24). If the 483 years is multiplied by 360 and divided by 365.25, the corrected figure is 476.06 years or 476 years and 22 extra days. The decree of Artaxerxes I (464–424 BC) to "restore and build" was given in the 20th year, the month Nisan (Neh 2:1, 5, 8), which was Mar/Apr 445 BC. The death of Christ in the month Nisan was 476 - 445 = 32 AD + or - 1 (due to uncertainty of whether the ascension year was being used). In making these calculations, keep in mind there is no year 0 (although some still make this mistake) between BC and AD. The date of 31 to 33 AD is about as close as you can push it. I don't know of any other person who could claim to be the Messiah who died during this time period. What more proof could anyone want? Due to the great time span between the allusions in Isaiah and the coming of Christ, the Jews have had two pictures of the Messiah, one of Aaron and one of Israel as mentioned in the DSS Community Rule Section IX (Vermes pp. 86, 110).

Jonah 1:17 and Matthew 12:40. Great fish. The Greek Ketos or Hebrew Tannim is anything that is not a fish; not necessarily a whale. It could have been a whale shark or rhinodon both of which have been known to swallow a whole human. Alternatively, it could have been a specially prepared or created creature. See the account by Harry Rimmer in *The Harmony of Science and Scripture* (p. 185 Berne 1940). A sailor fell overboard while attempting to harpoon a rhinodon and was swallowed before he could be picked up. It took 48 hours to locate the fish and kill it. He was recovered unconscious, but after a few hours' stay in the hospital, was released as physically fit. Rimmer personally interviewed the man, who also lost all his hair and had yellowish-brown patches on his skin. Ambrose John Wilson records that a sperm whale near the Falklands Islands swallowed a Star of the East ship's crewmember, James Bartley in Feb. 1891, who was rescued three days later, revived from unconsciousness and subsequently lived in good health, although the stomach acids bleached his skin to a deadly whiteness of parchment and never recovered its former appearance. The Cachalot or Sperm whale has swallowed sharks 15–16 feet long, or parts of squid or octopus eight feet in diameter. Anything it can't digest, or if dying, it vomits up. See the account in Princeton Theological Review 25: 630 (1927). The widow of the ship's captain later claimed to reporters that no one fell overboard during the period when her husband commanded the vessel (reported in the *Expository Times* 17 p. 521 [1905/06]; 18 p. 239 [1906/07]). The skin effect accords well with Jonah's reception at Nineveh. He was probably a sight to behold. The porcupine fish (diodon) has been found alive in the stomach of a shark and will eat its way out through the side, unaffected by his Jonah-like experience.

Matthew 2:2 and 9. What was the star the Magi from Persia followed? A nova? Or based on the conjugation of Jupiter, Saturn, and Mars in Pisces in 750 A.U.C. (ab urbe condita "from the founding of the city" of Rome in 753 BC) as predicted by Rabbi Abrabanel from a similar event three years before the birth of Moses, which would also occur before the birth of the Messiah, calculated by Kepler 50 years later as correlated to 4 BC.

(See NUD p. 229.) Keller p. 328 says the triple conjugation occurred from May 29, 7 BC to December 4th. He also says the statement "We have seen his star in the east" is a mistranslation of the Greek "*en te anatole,*" which is singular; usually "the east" is "*anatolai*" in the plural. In an astronomical sense, it means "we have seen his star appear in the first rays of dawn," as a helical rising. This event would have been in the southern sky and appear to be going "before them."

Another event, although appearing to be too late, was calculated when Jupiter passed in retrograde three times around Regulus (the King's star) in Leo on Sept. 14, 3 BC to May 8, 2 BC over a period of eight months. Later on June 17, 2 BC, Venus lined up with Jupiter and at 8:51 P.M., they appeared to kiss. (Reported in Parade Magazine Dec. 23, 2001 p. 9 and Menzel p. 41.) Stars as such don't move.

5:13. Can salt lose its saltiness? Theologians of the 1800s have kicked around this question and its chemistry. The problem is they didn't understand the context. Ancient salt supplies were impure, especially those obtained from the Mt. Sodom diapir. This is one of two salt domes in the Dead Sea region. This one on the West side of the Dead Sea at the South West end is 6.83 miles long by 0.93 miles wide and 820 feet high. The salt is pushed up from the floor along faults and is over 10,000 meters deep. It is still rising at a rate of about nine mm per year or about 72 m for the last 9,000 years (the Avery Island Louisiana salt dome is estimated to go down 40,000 feet). This salt has fine clay interspersed around the crystals, giving it a reddish color. You can enter the Arubotaim (the Chimneys) cave and examine the deposits. The salt would be gathered up and placed in large clay pots with water to dissolve the salt. The clay and grit would settle to the bottom and the saturated salt solution was dipped out for cooking (or evaporation if table salt was desired). More water and or salt would be added and the process repeated until all the salt dissolved and the solution was too dilute to use, with only the clay and grit left. At this point, the waste would be thrown out, as Jesus indicated. The second deposit underlies the Lisan Peninsula several hundred meters down and is 8 x 15 km wide. It has been reached only by drilling (see DSLS pp. 58, 70, 238–9, 241).

5:29–30; 18:8–9. Hand, foot, or eye cause to sin. A perfect case of hyperbole not meant literally. One hand cannot reach out to sin unless both feet carry you within reach from a thought already present in the mind. Unless you only have one eye or are severely astigmatic so that you only have vision in one eye, our stereoscopic vision requires both eyes to see the same object at the same time. Jesus' teaching goes to the root of conflicts that result in sin: always be on guard.

5:43–4. "Hate your enemy." This enigmatic passage occurs in no Jewish writing except the Essene Manual of Discipline. As such, it is possible an anti-Essene answer to the Essenes. (See BAR 10(5): 46 (84) for a summary.)

10:28. Body, soul and (spirit). No single verse links all three. The Egyptians, from the earliest predynastic times had a concept of resurrection and immortality. They conceived of man as composed of eight parts: the physical body (*khat*) that could decay and must be protected. The (*ka*) or double, or personality that was free to move about at will; it could starve if not fed with food and drink (a picture would suffice). The (*ba*) or soul dwelt in the *ka* but was ethereal; like the heart of man (*ab*) it was the seat of life. The (*khu*) was spirit or spiritual intelligence. The (*emsekh*) or power was his vital force personified. The (*khaibit*) or shadow mentioned in connection with the soul (wherever a man went his shadow would follow). The (*ren*) or name and if obliterated was to destroy him also. A nameless being could not be introduced to the gods. To know the names of the gods and pronounce them in the proper tone of voice, caused them to be under his power and they would perform his will. These can be reduced to the three above (BER pp. 189–193).

12:39. Sign of the prophet Jonah. In Jonah 1:5 he was asleep, so it was probably night. The three nights and three days offer no problem here if he was vomited up on dry ground any time before 6 P.M. on the third day. Jesus' statement here cannot be taken literally by our reckoning, knowing he arose early on Sunday and was put into the tomb before nightfall, or 6 P.M., on Friday.

In the parable of 20:1–14 each is hired for a denarius a day, in which any part of a day gets the full day's pay. Therefore, any part of a day counts for a full day by Jewish reckoning. From 3 P.M. at the earliest, allowing for the request of the body from Pilate to a hasty preparation for burial by 5 P.M. Friday, to the onset of nightfall, is one day, Saturday is the second day, and after sunup on Sunday is the third day. Only two nights are present by our reckoning, Friday night and Saturday night. Thus roughly 38 hours equals three days. The Jewish reckoning can even be stretched to include the previous night of Thursday as a part of Friday. Their calendar counted from "the evening to the evening," not from morning to morning. If you are not Jewish living in the 1st century, you are going to get confused. See the Passover Trilogy by J.H. Cohn (Amer. Board of Missions to the Jews p. 24).

American courts do something similar. A criminal is sentenced for three days, so if he enters on a Friday afternoon say before 5 P.M., he is released on Sunday morning as though he has spent three days in jail.

17:15. Lunatic. The Greek is "moonstruck", but usually translated epileptic. The other accounts in Mark say a dumb spirit and Luke, a doctor, says the boy was demon possessed with an unclean spirit. See the section Science and the Bible-Medicine where this could be a case of ergot poisoning. The ancients and healers often couldn't separate the physical effects of foods or toxins and allergic reactions or the effects of hallucinogens in general. Frequently the diagnosis was demon possession.

Matthew 17:21 is missing from the older manuscripts and in Mark 9:29 "and fasting" is omitted.

24:15. History repeated. What is the "desolating sacrilege"? Jesus invokes Daniel 8:9–14 and 9:27, an event is to be repeated in the last days (2 Thes 2:3–4 and Rev 13:5–18). This is the Antichrist. Daniel speaks of Antiochus IV Epiphanes who was on his way into Egypt to put down a rebellion and to take over the country. He was met four miles outside Alexandria by his acquaintance, the Roman envoy C. Popilius Laenus. He was informed that there would be no negotiations until he relinquished all claims to Egypt as ordered by the Roman Senate. Antiochus said he would consider the matter. Laenus, in a masterstroke of diplomacy, drew a circle around him in the sand with his sword and told him to make up his mind before stepping out of the circle. Rather than risk a showdown with the rising power of Rome (who had just destroyed Carthage as well as Macedonia, the first of Alexander's kingdoms to fall), he withdrew, leaving Egypt to Ptolemy VI. He then took out his frustration and anger on the Jews of Jerusalem by sacrificing a sow on the altar, burning copies of the Torah and their owners, and forbidding circumcision of children on pain of death of the child and mother (Tenney p. 32; MBA Map 184). His own country of Seleucia and Egypt were soon to fall to the Romans and end Alexander's empire.

27:51. Veil of the Temple. This was the inner veil visible only to the priests. It was a handbreadth thick and replaced twice a year. After being placed into a *mikveh* to purify it, it required 300 men to carry it. This was the one split from top to bottom, but not by an earthquake (only God could do this), at the death of Christ to open the way directly to God. The outer veil was visible to all. Josephus in War 5, 5, 4, says it was a Babylonian curtain that had embroidered on it all that was mystical in the heavens except the living creatures of the zodiac.

27:65. You have a watch. What did Pilate really mean? That he would provide a Roman guard, or that the Sanhedrin should use the Temple Guards? Due to the chain of command, in either case the guard would report to their commanders and not to the civilian Sanhedrin. If this was a Roman guard this group of four in the squad were already dead men. Any guard detail that let a body be stolen right under their noses could not expect to see the light of another day. See the case of Paul in Acts 16:27. No bribe of the Jews could save them. With the Temple guard, which is probably what we have here, possibly this could be done.

Luke 4:13. When did Satan tempt Christ again? Probably several times in his ministry (Heb 4:15), but most likely in the Garden (Mt 26:39).

21:32. "This generation." Due to confusion of what "this" means. Some hold that Jesus was referring to the generation of the Apostles and that the Second Coming would be within a few years. The Apostles took it this way until about a generation had passed and nothing had happened. At this point, it was realized that current events needed to be written down for posterity. In addition, the Gospels and Letters were put into copies. Now we take it to mean that the generation that is alive when the events begin to unfold shall not pass until all is accomplished.

Since Jesus is talking about the fig tree, Israel is often pictured as a fig tree. If He is saying, when Israel is freshly reborn as in May 15, 1948 as putting forth new branches and leaves, "this generation" born then will see these things. If 65 years is taken as the lifespan of "this generation" then the end should be about 2013 (Hagee p. 92). Compare this to the Mayan Dooms Day of Dec. 21, 2012.

Mark 14:13 and Luke 22:10. The events of the Last Supper. A man carrying a water pitcher? It was unusual for a man to carry water, unless he was a professional water carrier. This was a task for women or slaves. They followed him, apparently without a word being spoken, as part of a prearranged signal.

Luke 22:7. Was this meal the regular Passover meal? John 13:1, 29 and 18:28 indicate that it was not. Some Jews were allowed to partake a day early (in case the new moon witnesses were off by a day). However, since the Temple was in control of the Sadducee High Priest, no lamb could be killed except on the day set by the Sanhedrin (also under the control of the Sadducees), thus there was no lamb present. In Luke 22:1 the Feast of Unleavened Bread (lasted for one week after Passover) was sometimes called the Passover. John 19:31, with 1 Corinthians 5:7, indicates that Christ died at the time the Passover lambs were being slain in the Temple. This would place it as part of the Passover ritual. If Nissan 14 was on Friday, the regular evening sacrifice lamb was slain beginning at 12:30 and the Passover offering was slaughtered after that. Josephus mentions from 9–11 hour or 3–5 P.M.. See the excellent discussion in "A Passover Trilogy" by the American Board of Missions to the Jews.

April 7, 30 or April 3, 33. The start of Jesus' ministry from Luke 3:1 was the 15th year of Tiberius, who ascended the throne on the death of Augustus on Aug. 19, 14. Thus the year 28/29 is indicated, depending on when his imperium commenced. John mentions three Passovers (2:23, 6:4 and 13:1) indicating a three-plus year ministry. Thus, Jesus died in the year 30 or 33 at 3 P.M. at age 33–37 (Herod died in 4 BC; the massacre of the babies of Bethlehem age two and under could push the date to 6 BC for the birth of Christ). The darkness from noon to 3 P.M. might coincide with the partial lunar eclipse of the full moon on April 3, 33, accompanied by a dust storm that caused the moon to be "turned to blood." This was mentioned on a National Geographic TV program on the Tomb of Christ. Most of the known facts appear to be accounted for.

22:12. Furnished. Already prepared for a feast in a city swollen with visitors for Passover. Compare the Motel situation on the day of a big football game. Josephus reports in War 6,9,3, that in 66 AD (which was a time of turmoil with fewer visitors to Jerusalem) there were 256,500 lambs slaughtered, representing about ten persons minimum or as many as 20; at 13 per Passover lamb, there would be 3,334,500 undefiled persons present for this Passover and being housed for miles around.

22:15. "With desire I have desired." A Hebrew idiom to intensify the meaning of the verb, "to eat." The meal should be interpreted in the light of his death (before I suffer).

22:19 and 20. "Which is given for you. . ." To the end of v. 20 is omitted from the Western manuscripts (one of the best which usually amplifies rather than omits). These lines may not belong in the original text of Luke. However, see 1 Corinthians 11:23–26. Also v. 43 and 23:34 are absent from the Western text.

John 1:18. No man has seen God at any time. Needs some clarification; obviously Moses saw Him. And in Exodus 24:1; 9–11 Moses, Aaron, Nadab and Abihu plus the 70 elders of Israel saw the God of Israel, the sapphire under his feet and ate and drank with Him. Exactly what "was seen" is actually not described.

2:2. The marriage at Cana. In spite of the *Da Vinci Code*, this is not the wedding of Jesus. Mary, his mother, was there. A strange statement as one would expect the groom's mother to be present. However, stranger still, it says Jesus and the disciples were invited. The groom is never invited to his own wedding. These are a dead giveaway.

4:6–42. The woman at the well. Sychar of vv. 5–6 is nowhere else mentioned in the New Testament. The Syriac Gospel reads Sychem (Acts 7:16). Shechem does not seem to be occupied to any significant extent during New Testament times (BAF p. 302). In v. 7 she is not necessarily from the city of

Samaria (a woman of "Samaria" indicates a territory). Although some streams are nearby, she comes to the sacred well. She arrives at 6 P.M., the usual time for drawing water by the women. John uses Roman time.

4:9. A Jew. She probably recognized his dress and speech as a Rabbi. She would not have spoken to him if the disciples had been there (vv. 27–30). "Jews do not use vessels in common with Samaritans," fits the situation better. The well is about 100 feet deep, but now only about 85 feet.

4:28. She left her water pot. It would have been quite heavy when full, and it would slow her down. She talked to the men, not the women (v. 7).

4:41. The first revival brought about by a woman.

4:42. Savior of the world. Jesus indicates that Gentiles could be saved.

8:13–59. Escalation of a confrontation. 1. You witness to yourself . . . you are not valid. 2. Who is your father? In v. 20 this was spoken in the Court of Women near the alms boxes (cf. the widows mite, of Mark 12:42; the Greek Lepton or Hebrew Perutah, two of which make the smallest acceptable offering. 3. In v. 41 "we are not bastards (as you are; is the implication)." Mary's registration of the birth of Jesus would be available to anyone wanting to look it up, in the archives of the Temple (located in the vaults under the Robinson Arch stairs). Josephus in War II, 17, 6 said they were burned in the revolt around June 30, 66 to wipe out the records of debts. The father's name was probably left blank unless she indicated YHWH as the father. Either case would indicate to the Jews the father was "unknown" and place a stigma on her (an Apocrypha version said a Roman soldier had raped Mary). This was the basis for the charge of the Pharisees. 4. You are a Samaritan, and demon possessed, in v. 48, is another insult. 5. I am. This is the last straw, in v. 58; blasphemy was a capital charge by stoning. As a religious charge, this and adultery were allowed capital cases under Roman law.

13:2–4. And supper being ended. Can also be translated, "while supper was going on." The materials for washing were present, but no servants were there to serve. Apparently, Jesus had requested complete privacy. A price was already on his head. Why didn't one of the disciples volunteer? See Luke 22:24 and 27. This job usually fell to the last man at the triclinium, a U shaped table (low man on the totem pole). Apparently, this was Peter's position. The places of honor were usually to the left, facing the opening of the U. Judas would have been on the left hand of Jesus with John at the right hand and across from Peter. All were reclining on their left sides, laying down and eating with the right hand. (Information provided by Dr. Jim Fleming, Director of Biblical Resources Jerusalem.) The rivalry for a high post in the anticipated kingdom had not been lost. Christian love had not yet replaced pride.

18:15. John and the High Priest. Another unexplained event. How did John from Bethsaida know Caiaphas well enough to be allowed into his house, followed by Peter? John's fishing business was obviously prosperous for him to have a house in Jerusalem and servants (Mk 1:20). He was apparently better off than we might imagine. His mother's influence in Matthew 20:20 also speaks of some ambitions for her sons.

18:28. The trial of Jesus. Matthew and Mark say the final trial was held early in the morning. John as the only eyewitness indicates they went early to Pilate at the Praetorium, with no mention of the final trial. See the Talmud chapter for illegal details of the trial.

19:17. The crucifixion. John was the only eyewitness and strangely does not mention Simon of Cyrene carrying the crossbar, or of Him falling, even once, let alone the three times of tradition. Jesus was probably in no condition to carry the crossbar. The full cross would not be carried in major cities (see the Mostellaria, a Roman comedy by Plautus), where the crucifixion site was permanently equipped with the upright (crux) and a scaffold for hauling up the body attached to the crossbar (patibulum) from off the ground. Then the feet would be nailed. No, the nails would not be put through the palms. Medically it has been proved that the palms would not carry the weight, and the nails would pull through between the bones of the fingers, not through the nail head, since a wooden washer was slipped over the nail before it was driven in to prevent this. Rather they would be placed between the radius and ulna. The crucified man from Jerusalem, Jehohanan son of HGQWL, found at Giv'at Ha-Mivtar, had a crease on the radial bone showing the nail had been placed in the forearm; the nail in the heal bone was still attached [(IEJ 20: 49 (70); Decision Oct.5, (77)]. At any rate the Greek term for hand (cheias) is not specific and can include the wrist (Jn 20:27, MCOCB pp. 53/4).

20:17. Touch me not. The Greek implies "Stop clinging to me" or holding me back from my task.

20:25. What is belief? What Thomas said and did are two different things. Thomas had not touched him in v. 27, but as soon as Christ spoke to him, he declared that he was in the presence of Deity.

Acts 13:13. Why did Mark turn back? From Perga to Antioch one had to pass through Pisidia. Sir William Ramsey has found numerous inscriptions in the region of Pisidia that refer to armed policemen and soldiers needed to keep the peace. Other inscriptions refer to conflicts with robbers or to a drowning in a river. Compare 2 Corinthians 11:26. Could this be part of the reason (Free p. 316)?

1 Corinthians 14:2–23. Heavenly language or Unknown tongues? This is a place where the KJV italic word should be removed, as causing more damage that it is worth. Tongues are clearly a word for a known language, but those present may not understand it and its use would cause confusion unless an interpreter was present. The gift of speaking a foreign language would be for the edification of those who did know it, as Acts 2:6–12 indicates.

Hebrew 9:4. The Ark of the Covenant. The contents are mentioned here, but the outside dimensions are given in Exodus 37:1. A box 2.5 cubits long or 45 inches, 1.5 cubits wide and high or 27 inches. The thickness is not given; we will assume one inch (if it was thicker the dimensions below would be still shorter). At this time, the cubit was 18 inches; the royal cubit of 20.67 inches was not introduced until the time of the kings. It held the two stones containing the Ten Commandments, an omer of manna, which was 5.1 pints (a day's supply), and Aaron's dry staff that budded (that was a real miracle and now we know the type of wood—almond). A tribal chief's staff was usually quite distinctive and could be easily recognized by the owner (see Gn 38:25); in this case the tribal chiefs names were engraved as well. We are not told how large the staff was, but the usual shepherd staff was six feet. Could it fit into the Ark in one piece? The diagonal of 26 (subtract one inch for the bottom board) x 43 inches (two inches must be subtracted since there is a board on each end) internally is 50.25 inches, using the Pythagorean Theorem. The hypotenuse of the triangle of 26 x 50.25 inches is 56.58 inches using the Pythagorean Theorem, or just under four feet nine inches. Maybe it was this short, but I doubt it. No staff could be longer than this and fit into the Ark. It is strange that we are not told the staff was cut in two. Oh well, it's only details.

So what happened to the Ark? Again, we are not told. Nebuchadrezzar, in 2 Kings 25:15 and I Esdras 1:41, was said to have taken some of the holy vessels to Babylon. Josephus says nothing of its fate. However, II Maccabees 2:4–5 says that Jeremiah took it to Mt. Nebo and hid it. Tom Croster in October of 1981 carried out an illegal excavation in a tunnel under the "grave of Moses" (in the Byzantine church on Mt. Nebo). His photos were fuzzy; except for one, all were shown to Prof. Siegfried H. Horn of Andrews Univ. He concluded the box was a modern fabrication. The excavation by an American team for Tell Jalul was cancelled by the Jordanian government because of this, costing them $35,000 in preexcavation expenses, [BAR 9(3): 66 (83); 9(5): 30 (83)]. The Talmud in Yoma 53b says the Ark was buried under the NE Chamber of Wood in the Women's court of the Temple of Solomon. Both Yoma (other Rabbias took exception with the statement about the Ark) and II Maccabees were written late, and it is not as good a source as I Maccabees. In 1981, Rabbi Yehuda Getz of the Western Wall and Rabbi Shlomo Goren the Chief Rabbi of Israel gave permission for the search of a chamber under Warren's Gate for the Ark of the Covenant. The Arabs discovered the tunneling through the wall of the Temple Mount and the tunnel was sealed with concrete. (Reported in the TV program Secrets of the Bible II.)

CHAPTER 16

NEW TESTAMENT
ARCHAEOLOGY

THE OLDEST NEW Testament fragment, of ca. 125 AD is the papyrus Rylands—John 18:31–33 and on the back 18:37–38—now in the Rylands Library of Manchester England. Codex Vaticanus of ca. 350 AD is our oldest complete New Testament.

The Catacombs of Rome date from 150 BC–410 AD with the sack of Rome by the Goths under Alaric. They extend 550 mi if laid end to end and contain nearly two million bodies. They cover a surface area of 615 acres. These are the oldest preserved places of Christian worship. Inscriptions dated from 72 AD and wall paintings from 150 AD show no trace of a belief in purgatory, socialist gospel, tenets of modernism, cults or isms (Free p. 337; Wight p. 192).

The oldest Christian church dates from 232 AD. It is a chapel found at Dura in Mesopotamia on the Euphrates River; it contains a shallow Baptistery (Wright p. 246). A private chapel at Herculaneum dates from the 79 AD eruption of Vesuvius. It shows a cross as a Christian symbol (KY p. 378). The lower basalt building at Capernaum (excavations have been filled in, but the lowest course of the wall can be seen under the limestone wall on the West) is the one Jesus walked and taught in (Lk 7:1–5, BAR 9(6): 25 [83]).

Matthew 2:23. Nazareth. The city never seemed to have a good reputation. The name implies something insignificant— thus Nathanael's remark in John 1:46 "can any good thing come out of Nazareth." The population at the time of Jesus was only about 400, or at five per family about 80 houses. Joseph probably worked in Sepphoris (population ca 30,000) the nearby district capital of Herod Antipas. Sepphoris was said to be the birthplace of Mary, but it is not mentioned in the New Testament.

5:2. Mt. of Beatitudes. This is not the site presently shown west of Capernaum, except that it may be the site of the sermon on the plain (Lk 6:17). The height is not great enough to be called a mountain. Rather, the Matthew site is probably at the Horns of Hattin (where Saladin defeated the Crusaders on July 4, 1187) on the road from Magdala to Nazareth by way of the Arbel canyon.

16:13. Caesarea Phillipi. Known in 1 Chronicles 5:23 as a Canaanite shrine, Baal Hermon, it was the second pagan place visited by Jesus. The Greeks called it Panias, where a shrine to Pan, inside the cavern at the source of the Jordan, was located. Herod the Great had built a temple to Augustus here (which was also pagan as was everything in town) and Herod Phillip had made it his capital (BAR 24(1): 54 [98]).

17:1. The Mt. of Transfiguration. Jesus was already in the region of Caesarea Phillipi (16:13) and six days later reached this spot. In v. 24 he is in Capernaum. Therefore, it is not likely that Mt. Tabor is involved in the Transfiguration. When Mt. Tabor was excavated, it was apparent that a Hasmonean village had been located on top of the mountain; established probably by Alexander Jannaeus (103–76 BC). Josephus in *War* 4:54–61 also mentions it. It was still occupied by Jews, when captured by Vespasian in 67 (HJP p. 301). It existed until sometime after ca. 100 AD. It would be difficult to envision Jesus and the disciples holding a meeting with townspeople coming and going around them. The tradition for this site did not become established until Cyril of Jerusalem in 348 AD. Rather, look for the area on one of the mountain slopes of Hermon (O'Connor p. 366).

20:29; Mark 10:46 vs. Luke 18:35. "Which way to Jericho?" Matthew and Mark said as Christ left Jericho, whereas Luke said on the way into Jericho.

Excavations have shown that Jericho was a double city. The old Canaanite city was about one mile from the Roman city and Winter palace of Herod the Great. Both Matthew and Mark speak of the old city and Luke of the Roman. One or two different healings are recorded, which is less likely. Thus, leaving the old and entering the new would fit the situation.

Luke 2:1. The census. Emil Schurer ca. 1900 had these objections: (1.) Historical records of Augustus do not record a general imperial census. (2.) Under Roman procedure, neither Joseph nor Mary would have to register at Bethlehem. (3.) A Roman census would not have been conducted in the territory of an associate King. (4.) Josephus *Antiquities* 18.1.1 and 2.1 states that the census took place under Quirinius (Chrenius), after Judea became a Roman province in 7 AD. (5.) The census of Quirinius could not have occurred under Herod, since he died in 4 BC.

Answers: (1.) Augustus's monument at Ankara, Turkey from 14 AD states, "A 2nd time in the consulship of Gaius Censorius and Gaius Asinius, I again performed the Lustrum alone with the consular imperium. In this Lustrum 4,233,000 Roman citizens were entered on the census rolls" (UNT p. 213). The papyri of Egypt show that the censuses were taken every 14 years. Eight cycles would require one for 9/8 BC (Wight p. 149).

(2.) An edict of Gaius Vibius Maximus, governor of Egypt in 104 AD, states that the customary household enrollment was due, and those persons who were for any cause outside their home territories should return to complete their registrations. At least by 104 AD this practice was not exceptional.

(3.) Josephus states that Augustus was already angry with Herod for declaring war on the Arabians without Roman permission. He wrote to Herod that, whereas he had previously treated him as a friend, he would thereafter treat him as a subject. If Augustus wanted a general census, Herod was in no position to refuse cooperation. Herod was old and succession to his kingdom was subject to approval of Augustus. Due to Herod's family problems and the restive and rebellious mood of the Jews, a delay of the census may have occurred under the guise of a Jewish family or tribal census, which would not offend the populace as much.

(4.) Luke does not state that Quirinius was procurator, but rather Hegemoneuontos had "command" over Syria. A fragmentary marble inscription (the Lapis Tiburtinus) found near Tivoli in 1764 tells of a Roman official who was proconsul of Asia and twice the Legatus (governor) of Augustus in charge of Syria. The only likely candidate with these qualifications is Quirinius, having two Syrian governorships. An inscription found at Rome in 1828, and one found by Ramsey before WW I at Antioch in Galatia, imply two governorships (Frank p. 292; Free p. 286). Josephus does not refer to Quirinius's taxing and census as the first, but refers also to a revolt of one Judus, which is the same incident referred to by Gamaliel (Acts 5:37). The census of 7 AD is indicated, whereas Luke specifically mentions the first census of 6 BC.

(5.) The Greek term used in Luke 2:2 is *Protos,* usually translated as "first," but also often meaning "before or prior" as in Luke 11:38 and John 15:18. A more accurate translation would be "this was the census before Quirinius was governor of Syria (BR 18(2): 8 [02]).

Summary: It is known that: (1.) On Jan 1, 12 BC Publius Sulpicius Quirinus was made a consul and was sent to the East to act as overseer and military commander in that year upon the death of Augustus's friend and viceroy Marcus Vipsanius Agrippa. (2.) Tertulian 160–228 AD, states that the first census took place under C. Sentius Saturninus who was governor or Proconsul of Syria from 9–6 BC. (3.) P. Quintilius Varus was Proconsul from 6–4 BC. (4.) Neither of these is mentioned by Luke since Quirinius was the imperial legate or real head of government. (5.) He was reappointed in 6 AD with Coponius Procurator of Judea (Josephus *Antiquities* 18.1.1). (6.) He remained in office until 17 AD when Tiberius appointed Germanicus (UNT p. 63; Tenney p. 134). Both Justin Martyr about 160 AD and Tertullian about 220 AD say that this census record was still in the Rome archives.

Sir William Ramsey said, "Luke's narrative is unsurpassed in respect to trustworthiness . . . You can press the words of Luke in a degree beyond any other historian and they stand the keenest scrutiny and the hardest treatment, provided always that the critic knows the subject and does not go beyond the limits of science and justice" (Tenney p. 16).

2:8. Shepherds in the fields. A statement in the Talmud says that the flocks were in the fields from March to the beginning of November. Christ's birth was not likely to have been in December. December 25 was not called Christmas until 354 AD, which coincided with *Dies Natalis Invicti*, "the birthday of the unconquered," the day of the winter solstice and the last day of the pagan Saturnalia.

2:4–7. Bethlehem. Actually named for the Canaanite war god Lahum. A fairly small town covering ca 100 x 400 yards at the time of Jesus (the massacre of the innocents probably didn't cover more that twenty infants). The cave of the Nativity has been known since the time of Justin Martyr in 130 AD. Hadrian had the spot desecrated in 135 AD by building a temple to Adonis over the cave, just as he did in Jerusalem at Christ's tomb. These are the only places treated this way. The early Church's tradition was still within eyewitness accounts from the time of Mary and John, who would have been able to hand down the actual locations to others.

2:22. Jesus presented at the Temple. Mary brought the baby to be dedicated at the Temple and to be registered in the archives, probably located under Robinson's Arch. After the forty days of her purification, she would have been immersed in one of the Temple *mikveh* located between the two sets of stairs at the Hulda gates before ascending the underground stairs to the Temple Mount. These are the only *mikvaot* known, and Jesus used the stairs in his teaching. An injunction in the Talmud says one should be quick to ascend but slow to leave the temple. The archive (where Jesus' father's name was to be recorded) was probably left blank, and would have been known by anyone looking up the family history. Thus the charge that he was a bastard in John 8:41. These archives were burned in 66 AD at the beginning of the war to wipe out the records of debt for creditors. Remember the Temple acted as a bank and lent out money. (Josephus *War* 2.17.6).

4:9. The Pinnacle of the Temple. See below, where the "pinnacle" was probably at the SW corner rather than the more traditional SE corner, which was much more isolated. Both corners were at the same height above ground. Even though the Kidron valley outside the walls on the east would appear to be a bigger drop, no one could jump from the walls directly into the valley. The outer wall of the city would have been from 20–25 meters east of the Temple Mount wall. The main walkway surrounds the Temple Mount at the bottom of the wall. The western part along Tyropoeon Street is 41 feet wide; the width of the eastern side is not known (not excavated). This walkway, complete with stairs leading up the east side, was a smaller complement to Robinson's Arch stairs on the west side. Part of the arch on the east can still be seen. Thus, the place for the largest number of people to congregate and view a body (for anyone wanting to jump from the wall) would be at the SW corner. This was probably Satan's plan, but it didn't work [Ritmeyer p. 2; BAR 15 (6): 23 (89)].

7:5. The Synagogue at Capernaum. When excavated by Corbo and Loffreda in 1968–77 and 81, remains of an earlier structure built of basalt that dated from 1–4 century were found. Lower strata gave remains from the 2–3 century BC, along with a coin of Ptolemy VIII Eugerates, 146–117 BC. All has been filled in now, but on the west side the basalt foundation can still be seen running off at a slight angle under the limestone foundation. The last basalt renovation was probably that done by the unnamed centurion. At the time of Jesus, this was the highest point in the city (upon which synagogues as a rule were built). However see the one at Gamla (BAR 9(6): 24 [83]).

22:20. Did Jesus drink wine? The so-called communion meal took place after the regular Passover meal, as expressly stated here. Unless you want to invoke that all wine was turned back into juice before Jesus drank any (which scripture never implies), this is a strained attempt to remove Jesus from the usual customs of the day. All juice by the time of Passover in March-April was wine, and no fresh grapes would have been available for fresh juice. Pasteurization was unknown at this time. The wine used in the Passover meal (and at any other time) was always diluted three to one as in the Mishna (Berakoth 7:50a), so that the four cups consumed during the meal only contained one cup of actual wine. In this way, it was not intoxicating when eaten with the meal. The government has stated that any alcoholic drink of less than 3.2% alcohol is not intoxicating and subject to a lower tax. Medical science has also shown that the liver will detoxify the diluted wine as fast as it is taken in. Therefore, that settles that. There is only one scripture (Dt 14:26) that states that strong drink could be freely consumed by those coming to Jerusalem bringing their tithe in cash and repurchasing the equivalent products.

John 1:38 and 20:16. Rabbi or master. Rabbinic scholars state that this term (Greek *Didaskalos* or master) did not appear until the 2nd century, when it appeared in the Mishnah. This was cited as evidence of a late date for John.

E.L. Sukenik, in 1930 found a 1st century ossuary on Mt. Scopus containing the Gr. Didaskalos as a title of a man named Theodotion written in Aramaic characters. Thus, no anachronism is necessary (Free p. 300).

2:20. The Temple. In the process of building for 46 years and still not complete. Yasher Arafat in a meeting with President Clinton made the ridiculous statement that no Jewish Temple ever stood on the Temple Mount. Moreover, Clinton didn't know how to refute him. The surface of the Temple Mount today is devoid of Jewish remains (the Romans took care of that). Anything found by the illegal digging the Arabs do there, is never shown the light of day (except when archaeologists sift through their dumps). How do they explain the outer walls expanded and built by Herod? Historical sources recount the beauty of the Temple as being the "eighth wonder of the world." Josephus would especially have to be thrown out. On one of the stones north of Robinson's Arch, a part of Isaiah 66:14 is carved in Hebrew: "You shall see, and your heart shall rejoice; your bones shall flourish like the grass" dating from ca. 363, when Julian the Apostate gave permission to rebuild the temple in a failed attempt (Mazar p. 94). When the rubble at the SW corner was cleared away from the street leading to the Hulda Gates, a large stone, that had been pushed from the top corner of the wall (probably the "Pinnacle of the Temple") was left where it was found (it can be seen in some of the old photographs of this area, (Mazar p. 136), but has now been moved to the Israel Museum). It originally stood near one of Capt. Charles Warren's shafts that he dug when exploring underground. He actually cracked the stone as he sunk the shaft (the other piece has never been found and his debris pile location is not known today). When it was examined, a beautiful Hebrew inscription, dating to ca. 2 BC, was found which reads: "to the place of trumpeting to distinguish [between the sacred and the profane]." In a niche cut into the stone, a priest would stand and blow a trumpet to announce the beginning and ending of the Sabbath, since the main part of the city was to the west, south and SW (Mazar pp. 138–9). This may be the actual stone Jesus stood on when taken to the Temple by Satan.

These, and the balustrade inscriptions, are the only artifacts known at present associated with the temple. However, the third stone above the frieze, on the east side of the west Hulda gate, is the inverted base of a statue (one of two that was on the Temple Mount of Aelia Capitolina). Said to be of Hadrian, the first line reads "To Titus Aelius Hadrianus." Hadrian's first name was Publius, thus the statue is to Antonius Pius 138–161 AD (J. Wilkinson Palestine Excavation Quarterly 1976, p. 78). The other one was a statue of Hadrian—could its base also be in the wall, but turned inward?

Hadrian in 135 AD deliberately left the Temple Mount in ruins as a testimony that the God of the Jews did not save His people or city. When Titus burned the Temple in 70 AD several artifacts were saved and taken to Rome; these are shown on the Arch of Titus. One is a box, which may have contained the Temple scrolls. Josephus says he had access to these at any time. They were kept in Titus's home for some time. These scrolls may have been the copies prepared by Ezra, as reported in II Esdras 14:42 written in the new square Hebrew letters. Many statements of scripture as recorded in Josephus read better and differently than the Masoretic text. Especially the statements "that such and such was there until this day" are all missing from Josephus.

Two of the balustrade inscriptions warning gentiles not to go any further into the Temple have been found, both in Greek; one is in the Rockefeller Museum in Jerusalem, the other complete inscription is in the Istanbul Museum. These were both found in the cemeteries outside the walls of the Temple Mount near St. Stevens Gate, where the Romans threw the debris over the walls. It is now about 125 ft deep.

5:2. The Pool of Bethesda. Is not actually the two Sheep Pools near St Anne's Church, but is outside the pools in a cave under the center apse of the Byzantine Church. It may come as a surprise to know that this is actually a pagan shrine to the Greek god of healing, Asclepius ([that Jesus was visiting] the Semitic Eshmun). Excavation of this area turned up numerous ex-voto offerings of body parts in clay hands, feet, heads, etc., and a small statue of a woman holding a hand to her breast, which points out the area healed. In addition, part of the serpent of Asclepius with a human head (live serpents who shed their skin were looked on as a symbol of resurrection and were always found in these temples) was part of a statue, as well as numerous pools for bathing, both in caves and outside, were found fed by a spring.

Bethesda, which means "house of mercy" or "temple of mercy," could not be given the actual name of "temple of Asclepius" by the Jews, so the less offensive name was used. Since so many healings were attributed here, the results could not be ignored. The original sheep pools are 45 feet deep with a narrow set of stairs leading down into each from the north for the north pool and from the west side for the southern one. For these to be used, depending on the water depth, if full, the first one into the water on this day would be healed and the rest would drown; if the water was low, the first one would be cured and the others killed by the fall. The stirring of the water in v. 4 (the verse is not present in many of the older manuscripts) is thought to be due to a rush of clay tinted water brought down to the subterranean spring by the winter melt in the spring, probably near the feast of Purim near Passover (see Jn 6:4). There is also evidence that these pools went out of active use when the Pool of Israel at the NE corner of the Temple Mount was constructed (ABR 2: 24 [89]).

John 9:1–11. The Pool of Siloam. For years, we thought the pool emptying out of Hezekiah's tunnel (but known to date only from the fourth cent AD) was the correct place. However, 75 m to the SE, repair on a sewer line brought to light the real pool with three sets of five steps 225 feet long. Also discovered were four coins of Alexander Jannaeus 103–76 BC along with twelve coins of years 2, 3 and 4 of the first revolt against Rome. This shows that the pool went out of use at that time and slowly filled with silt (BAR 31(5): 16 [05]). More can be expected, as this is an ongoing dig.

10:40. Bethany beyond Jordan. Not identified here, but the same as in 1:28. Beyond means on the east side of the Jordan. Also known as Beth Abara (House of the Crossing or ford). This site has now been identified as Tel el-Kharrar (BAR 31(1): 34 [05]). The closest site in Israel is Qasir-al Yahud. This is the southernmost crossing point of the Jordan, but the bridge is long gone in the conflict with Jordan. Jordan does not want it rebuilt, since tourists visiting from Israel would not remain in Jordan to spend dinars, dollars or shekels for any length of time.

18:28. Praetorium. While it is true that this was the governor's official residence as well as a prison, there is some controversy as to its location. Herod's palace near Joppa Gate or the Antonia fortress are options. Jesus was sent first to Herod Antipas (Lk 23:8), who was staying in the family palace (it is not clear whether this was Herod's palace at Joppa Gate or the old Hasmonean palace south of the Street of the Chain and near the bridge at Wilson's Arch. This building was used by Herod Agrippa and Bernice in 65 AD (Josephus, *War* 2.16.3). This palace and the house of Ananias the High Priest were burned at the start of the war (Josephus *War* 2.17.6).

There is no mention of Herod being summoned to Pilate at the palace, nor are we sure that both could stay in the same location. Since this was a Jewish building, would this defile a Jew to enter before the Passover, or was the gentile presence defiling? Actually it was because the premises had not been cleansed of leaven. Nor do we know how many prisoners could be held there. The Antonia, on the other hand, makes a better location, holding a cohort of troops. It would have a large prison. It was a gentile building in all respects. From Pilates' perspective, being near the Temple was imperative. Riots always started here; to control the situation required him being where the action was, and getting from the palace to the Antonia in a timely fashion would be next to impossible in the crowed streets of Jerusalem in the time of the festivals (MBA p. 149). Pilate already had three strikes against him. Any procreator who could not keep the peace was due to be banished. He had allowed the cohorts' eagles and images of Caesar to be brought into Jerusalem at night (to avoid detection), resulting in a riot; he appropriated (Corbin) Temple funds to construct an aqueduct and had gold shields with images and names of deities in his palace—the emperor ordered them removed. Either the debacle of Jesus or the crushing of a Samaritan revolt caused them to complain to Vitellius the governor of Syria. He was sent to Rome to answer charges, but the new emperor Caligula had him banished to Gaul where he committed suicide in 36 AD.

One of the towers guarding Herod's palace, known as David's tower, can be seen inside the Citadel; it was previously known as Phasael's (Herod's brother), but Hillel Geva (IEJ 31: 57 (81) has identified it rather as Hippicus (a friend of Herod). This is the only actual remnant of the palace area now known.

18:29. Pontius Pilate (26–36 AD) Prefect of Judea. The first inscription known, mentioning Pontius Pilate as well as Tiberius, was found in 1961 at the theater at Caesarea (a statue base recut and reused as a step). His correct title of Prefect is given. Claudius changed it to Procurator in 48 AD, and this was the title used in the Gospels, which were written after this date (Mazar p. 81).

20:1–12. Tomb of Jesus. The description here is a perfect example of a Herodian type tomb. The stone across the mouth could as easily be a plug type (weighing 600 pounds and impossible for one person to push out) rather than a rolling stone. These are harder to sit on, and usually roll back into covered slots (see the one at Queen Helene's tomb) with little or no space above them (Mt 28:2). Rolling stones would give no handhold for the person inside to try to move and would be impossible under any conditions. The edges would be on the outside and not reachable from the inside. So forget the swoon theory as a way for Him to get out in His condition. They had to stoop to see into the tomb. Again, perfect for the plug type opening which is less than two feet high. The main burial bench could be seen immediately behind the door with a burial bench on each side. There would be a maneuvering pit immediately behind the door so those moving the body inside could stand up. The two angels' feet would be hanging inside the pit. In v. 7 the folded face cloth lying by itself signifies that the host will be back and is not yet finished. From the other grave wrappings, the body had simply vanished and had not been unwrapped. Not mentioned here, but usually present, are kokhim slots cut back into the rock for additional later burials, as many as three to nine for small tombs, or up to seventy for larger ones. At the back of each bench are frequently carved semicircular recesses (arcosolia). In the west Syrian Chapel alcove behind the traditional Tomb of Jesus (which is the right location at the Church of the Holy Sepulcher), there is a Herodian tomb you can go into (another is present in the Coptic monastery to the north). The tomb of Jason at 12 Alfasi Street in Jerusalem (the only tomb with a street address, open Mon. and Thur.) also has a plug.

The Garden Tomb is actually an Iron Age tomb extensively reworked in the Byzantine period. The door is five by two feet four inches wide making stooping unnecessary, and the main burial bench, which is off to the right in a second chamber, could not be seen from the open door (see above, another reason why this is not the tomb of Christ). The openings of these tombs are frequently tall enough to walk into standing up, or as small as the Herodian type. There are about 12 IA tombs in this area, the largest and most elaborate two are on the grounds of the Ecole Biblique, which you can visit with advance notice [these have been identified as the tombs of Kings Amon and Manasseh BAR 13(4): 54 (87)]. Another is bricked up in the open bus station across the street from the Garden Tomb. Two were excavated in Suleiman Street near Nablus Road and then recovered. The rest are mostly inaccessible. (See O'Connor p. 45; McBirnie for a full discussion.)

The large rolling stone and opening at "Herod's family tomb" is unusual. The type at Queen Helena's tomb on Nabulas Road is more common; there are others in Israel; the third one in Jerusalem is at Bethphage behind the Franciscan church (McBirnie p. 22).

The recently rediscovered "family tomb of Jesus" shown on the History Channel is not connected with Jesus in spite of the ossuary inscriptions. He was buried in a borrowed tomb, as he didn't have two shekels to rub together.

Acts 8:9–10. Simon. A forerunner of Marjoe or Garner Ted Armstrong. Justin Martyr (150 AD) states that Simon Magus came from Gitto, a village of Samaria, and moved to Rome in the days of Claudius (41–54 AD) where he was defied by a statue inscribed "Simoni Sancto Deo."

Irenaeus (180 AD) says the same, and that he started a Gnostic sect served by profligate (prodigal or wasteful) priests who practiced magical rites and worshiped Simon as Jupiter and his ex-slave Helen as Minerva.

Hippolytus (170–236 AD) a disciple of Irenaeus adds, "Simon claimed that the originating principle of all things is fire, which is imparted to man through sexual generation. Such generation is a manifestation of the emanation of world power, by which Mind fructifies (makes fruitful) Intelligence. Simon indulged in mystical interpretation both of the Old Testament and the Homeric poems. He allegorized the story of Helen of Troy, maintaining that she was the lost sheep who was claimed by the powers of the world. When he visited Tyre, he purchased a female slave named Helen, who, he said, was a reincarnation of Helen of Troy, whom he had to reclaim. He concluded his career by avowing that if he were buried alive, he would rise on the 3rd day. His disciples accordingly interred him, but he failed to rise. His cult vanished shortly afterwards, for Origen (225 AD) states it could be found nowhere in the world" (Tenney p. 192).

12:21. Herod Agrippa I and the Third Wall. He was killed by God at Caesarea for not giving praise to God. His third wall in Jerusalem has generated some controversy. Many sources and maps show the third wall running under Damascus Gate and the walls built by Suleiman.

In 1925 Sukenik and Mayer and later by Ehud Netzer in 1972–74 have now uncovered 4,125 feet of the 13.8-14.1 foot thick wall. Kathleen Kenyon in 1961–67 tried to call it the siege wall (circumvallio) built by the Romans in 69 AD. But Netzer found eight towers 198 feet apart running for 2,132 feet facing to the north (towers always faced the enemy side), with pottery shards of the Herodian period in the fill on the south side. The Romans with Marsus governor of Syria under Claudius got the work stopped. The patchwork job using all available stones shows this was a hurried-up job by defenders prior to the first Jewish war. Part of the wall can be seen south of the Paz gas station on Nablus road at the old American Consulate, then over to the Albright Institute along St. George Street [IEJ 24: 97 (74)].

13:7. Sergius Paulus. A Roman Proconsul who became a Christian, v. 12. Sir William Ramsay in 1912 found a paving stone at Antioch, which read "To Lucus Sergius Paullus the younger," one of the four commissioners in charge of the Roman streets, "tribute of the soldiers of the VI Legion, etc." At Paphos the capitol of Cyprus, an inscription on a monument of Apollonius dedicated to his parents about 55 AD, states that he "Revised the Senate by means of assessors in the time of the Proconsul Paulus. At Soli, Cyprus a Greek inscription dated to the 13th year of Claudius (52–3 AD) reads, "Under Paulus the proconsul" (UNT p. 261). Another inscription mentioned a woman, Sergia Paulla. These were the son and daughter of the Proconsul of Cyprus. Ramsey believes the inscription hints that she may have been a Christian along with her children. Her husband dropped out of public life (probably because he became a Christian).

Latin always used Paullus whereas Greek used Paulus, thus Luke is accurate. Cyprus was originally an imperial province in the Roman State, but in 22 BC, Augustus transferred it to the Roman Senate to be governed by proconsuls. A brief rundown of the Roman system follows:

Consul—One of two joint chief magistrates in the Roman Republic.

Praetor—Magistrate next to Consul in rank. A Judge. After serving as Consul or Praetor, he became eligible for Procurator.

Proconsul—Governor of a district appointed by Senate.

Prefect—Governor of a district appointed by Emperor. Changed in 48 by Claudius to Procurator.

Procurator or Propraetor—Governor of a district or fiscal agent or administrator appointed by the Emperor.

Aedile—A peace officer and supervisor of public works, roads, latrines etc.

Quaestor—Petty official, usually financial.

Military:

Tribune or Chilliarch (Greek) —Leader of 1,000 men with six per Legion. In Acts 21:31 he is called a chief captain.

Equivalent to a Colonel. Each commanded a Legion in turn
with the rank of General or Legate.

Centurion—A captain or leader of 100 men.

Legion at full strength = 6,000. Numbers could drop to
4,000 with corresponding decreases in the rest of the units.

Cohors= Cohort of 600, there were ten per Legion. In Acts
10:1, called a band.

Maniple= 200; there were three per Cohort.

Centuries= 100; there were two per Maniple. (See Acts 10:1,
22: Mt 8:5; 27:54, Time-Life Books: *Imperial Rome* p. 40.)

Acts 14:6. Relationship of Iconium, Lystra and Derbe.
Luke indicates that Lystra and Derbe were cities of the province
of Laconia [which was true only between 37–72 AD, Bible and
Spade 3: 2 (74)]. Roman writers, Cicero (106–43 BC) and others,
and the Greek Strabo (63 BC–21 AD) indicate that all three
were in this province. Xenophon (445–355 BC) and Pliny the
Roman (23–79 AD) list Iconium as a Phrygian city. Thus, critics
discounted Luke as the author, with a late date for the writing.

In 1910, a monument was found by Sir W. Ramsey in
Turkey, which indicates that Iconium (present day Konia) was
a Phrygian city. Other discoveries showed that the Iconians
considered themselves as citizens of Phrygia, and Phrygian was
still spoken as late as 250 AD. Thus, Luke was vindicated.

The site of Derbe was proved by two inscriptions found at
Kerti Huyuk NW of Lystra in 1956 and 62. Since Derbe is now
known to be 60 mi from Lystra, Acts 14:20 should read "on the
next day he set out with Barnabas for or toward Derbe" (Free
p. 317; Tenney p. 229). Lystra was discovered in 1885 by J.R.S.
Sterrett near Khatyn Serai, 18 mi SW of Iconium.

16:11. Troas. Luke joined Paul at this point "from Troas
we . . ." Troas Antigonia (built by Antigonas) became Troas
Alexandria in 300 BC in honor of Alexander the Great by
Lysimachus (his General). It was a direct continuation of cities

from the Troy of Homer's Troy—Illium of 1250 BC (city VIIa, the 4th from the top of nine old cities excavated in 1870).

16:20 and 35. Chief Magistrates. Luke uses the title that they called themselves by; their official title was only Magistrate. Ramsey found an inscription in a nearby colony, which records that the Magistrates usurped a higher title than they were given [Bible and Spade 3: 6 (74)].

17:6. Rulers of the city. Literally Politarchs, this term was known in Greek only from Plutarch's *Lives of Themistocles* (p. 22 of the Harvard Classics Edition) until an inscription dated 1st century AD from the Vadar Gate at Thessalonica was found listing six politarchs. This gate was removed in 1876; the inscription is now in the British Museum. Since then 16 other occurrences have been found [Bible and Spade 2: 71 (73)].

17:18. Babbler. This term is also used for "sparrows" that picked food from the gutters, thus "gutter picker" [Bible and Spade 3: 3 (74)].

18:4. Synagogue at Corinth. A stone door lintel has been found on the Lechaeum Isthmus road bearing part of the title "Synagogue of the Hebrews." Paul also used several other Corinth references in 1 Corinthians 3:16. "Body as temple of the Holy Spirit" refers to the temple on the Acropolis; in 1 Corinthians 6:15–16 "A member of Christ is not to be joined to a harlot" refers to the 1,000 temple priestess prostitutes there; 1 Corinthians 9:24 "Running a race" refers to the Isthmian games (Olympic) held in the vicinity of Corinth.

18:12. Gallio and date of Paul's stay in Corinth. Gallio became proconsul on July 1, 51 AD and lasted one year. He was the eldest brother of the Stoic philosopher Seneca. An inscription from Delphi (across the Corinthian Gulf from Corinth) placed by the Emperor Claudius in his 26th imperatorship (Jan.-Aug. 52 AD) mentions Lucius Junius Gallio "my friend and proconsul of Achaia." Thus from Acts 18:1, 11 Paul came to Corinth ca. 50 AD, after the Jerusalem Council of Acts 15:1–35.

The elevated platform or Bema (Latin *rosta*) in the Agora has been excavated, which was the site where Paul faced his Jewish accusers before Gallio (vv. 12–17).

Another inscription in the Agora calls the meat shops "markets" from the Latin *macellum,* whereas Paul used the Greek *makkellon* (1 Cor 10:25, Tenney p. 276).

19:23. Temple of Diana or Artemis. One of the seven Wonders of the World. A shrine to house the meteorite (v. 35) was built ca. 800 BC. Enlarged by Croesus of Lydia (from an inscription on a drum of a column) in 559 BC and it was later destroyed by fire in 356 BC (the day Alexander the Great was born). The Alexandrian architect Dinocrates started a new temple in 356 BC, and Alexander the Great offered to pay the cost to complete it in 334 BC. It was 340 x 160 ft with 200 columns, 55 ft high. It was finally destroyed by the Goths in 262 BC. Scopas worked on the sculptures both here and at the Mausoleum of Halicarnassus, another of the seven Wonders of the World.

19:29. The Great Theater of Ephesus. It was 495 ft in diameter and seated about 24,000. The present ruins were rebuilt after Paul's day on the same floor plan. It stands at the head of the 1/3 mi long marble paved 36 ft wide thoroughfare, the Arcadian Way, rebuilt and named for the Roman Emperor Arcadius who reigned 395–408 AD, and ends at the harbor. The street was lighted at night with street lamps. During the Christian persecutions under Decius 249–251 AD or Diocletian 283–304 AD, according to legend, seven young men took refuge in the Cave of the Seven Sleepers, fell asleep, and did not awaken until the reign of the Christian Emperor Theodosius II 408–450 AD (or 104 years later). Rip van Winkle was a piker.

Conscious of having slept only one night, they were amazed to find a new generation in the city, with everyone Christian. The youths all died naturally on the day of their awakening, the tradition says, and the Emperor had them buried in their cave and erected a church on the spot (UNT p. 256).

23:2. High Priest Ananias. During the period 40–70 AD there were 28 high priests, coming from four families: Boethus (including the Cantherus family), Hanan (Annas), Phiabi and Kimchit (Kanthros). A little folksong in the Talmud Pesachim 57:71 relates:

> Woe is me because of the House of Boethus; woe is me because of their staves. Woe is me because of the House of Hanan; woe is me because of their incantations (sharp tongues). Woe is me because of the House of Kathros; woe is me because of their pens (famous for their libelous slander). Woe is me because of the House of Ishmael, the son of Phiabi; woe is me because of their fists. For they are the High Priests, and their sons are treasurers, and their sons-in-law are trustees, and their servants beat the people with staves.

Through corruption, nepotism and oppression these families had abused their positions [BAR 9(6): 66 (83); Mazar p. 84].

From the Hasmonean period of 165 BC, almost all High Priests were Sadducees especially in the time of Christ, when they were backed by the Romans. They also had complete control of the Temple and the rituals.

In the Burnt House, in the Upper City of Jerusalem inhabited by the wealthy, was found a stone weight with a two-line inscription: Belonging to bar Kathros (Dbr Kthrs), most likely his very house. In a room on the east under a pile of rubble, blocking a door was found the arm and hand of a 20-year-old woman, when the house went up in flames on Sept. 20, 70 AD.

23:26. Claudius Lysias and Roman law. From Acts 21:31 he was a Tribune or Ciliarch a leader of 1,000 men. His name in 21:37 is probably Greek, which he took when he purchased his citizenship (22:28). He had taken the Roman surname Claudius.

Little is known of Roman law for this period, but a papyrus from Oxyrynchus of 300 AD forbid scourging free men, even for purposes of questioning. In matters of arrests, imprisonment and examination by flogging, the accounts are similar. Protection of the accused under Roman control was guaranteed (Acts 23:35). The procurator could pass a death penalty so long as his fitness for office was above imperial suspicion. He had no superior except the emperor, who personally appointed him. Roman authorities were conciliatory to the Jews' warning notices in the Temple courts, alternating in Latin and Greek, the two main languages of the gentiles; so much so, that even a Roman citizen was libel to the death penalty if he went beyond them. Two of these warning notices have been found, both in Greek, one in 1871, the other in 1935. The last one is in the Rockefeller Museum

Antonius Felix (v. 26) was the brother of Pallas, a favorite of the emperor Claudius. Tacitus said of him, "He exercised the power of a king with the mind of a slave." Josephus recounts his evil career. He put off Paul's case, hoping to be bribed either by Paul or his friends (Acts 24:26), and to please his Jewish wife, Drusilla, sister of Bernice. The two years of v. 27 refers to his governorship or to the imprisonment at Caesarea (Wight p. 331).

Porcius Festus succeeded Felix under Nero, probably in 60 AD. When Paul appealed his case to Rome, Festus was obliged to send a report along with the prisoner (Acts 25:26-7); thus he welcomed the advice of Herod Agrippa II, a great-grandson of Herod the Great, on the Jewish charges. Agrippa's incestuous relationship with his sister Bernice began to create a scandal according to Josephus. During the Jewish-Roman conflict, he fought on the side of Vespasian and died in 100 AD in Rome as a Praetor (magistrate next to Consul in rank). Luke appeared to be present and accompanied Paul to Rome (Acts 27:1).

The Augustan band or Cohort was a group of intelligence-liaison branch of officer-couriers. They were part of the Diplomatic Corps and it was an honorary title (UNT p. 298).

28:7. Chief man. Two Maltese inscriptions, one in Greek and one in Latin, use this very term for an official. Whether a local man or Roman is not known (Boyd p. 190).

Romans 16:23. Erastus the chamberlain (treasurer). This was written from Corinth. In excavations near the Greek auditorium, an inscription on a paving block was found: "Erastus procurator, aedile (building superintendent later treasurer), laid [the pavement] at his own expense." This pavement existed in the 1st century (Wight p. 263).

Revelation 2:1–3:22. The Seven Churches of Asia. John uses facts well known to the residents of these cities, to remind them where they have gone off track.

Consider if a modern person, writing about Washington DC, mentioned: "Let her cherry buds flourish as a maiden in the springtime of her youth. Let her reflection pool mirror her deeds of life. May her honored dead sleep in peace and the watch fires burn eternally. Let not her proud dome or obelisk as of Egypt fall into decay. Whitewash the fire-scarred black stains of sin with a holy covering. Moreover, let her five sides be protection against your enemies, and that your river may flow forever." Would a reader 2,000 years from now know what was implied?

By Roman road, itinerary runs clockwise:

- # Ephesus to Smyrna is 41.5 miles
- # Smyrna to Pergamun is 64.5 miles
- # Pergamun to Thyatira is 44 miles
- # Thyatira to Sardis is 33 miles
- # Sardis to Philadelphia is 26 miles
- # Philadelphia to Laodicea is 47 miles
- Laodicea to Ephesus is 98.5 miles.
- # City still exists.

2:4. Ephesus had lost its "first" love. Ephesus, Smyrna and Pergamun claimed to be the "1st [City] in Asia." Its maximum population was 500,000. The Temple of Diana (Artemis) was considered the 1st among the Seven Wonders of the World. The temple burned to the ground in 356 BC the night Alexander the Great was born. In Ephesians 2:19–22 the "temple of the Lord" would contrast the "temple conscious" readers. J.T. Wood discovered the temple on Dec. 31, 1869 at a depth of 20 ft. Some 4,000 objects were found in the foundation deposit of the altar in 1905 by D.G. Howard.

By John's time, Emperor worship had already arrived as a rival to Diana.

2:8. Smyrna. The old population was 200,000. This city still flourishes as Izmir (a Turkish corruption). It is said to be the birthplace of Homer.

2:10. Some to be tested and ten days of tribulation. Polycarp, Bishop of Smyrna was burned in 155 AD in the Stadium; the Jews (v. 9) desecrated their Sabbath in order to bring wood to make the fire. "Ten days" may refer to the ten Emperors Domition-Diocletian. "Crown of life" refers to the hill Pagus, whose slopes and top were covered with stately public buildings from which the phrase "Crown of Smyrna" became a familiar nickname for the city. This "coronus" or crown of buildings was sometimes shown on silver coins. The cup found at Caesarea shows Tyche wearing the battlements of Caesarea as a coronus (HHBR pp. 13, 15).

2:13. Pergamum. The old population was 200,000. The name perpetuates the word parchment, which was invented here when Ptolemy II Philadelphus of Egypt in 282 BC cut off the supply of papyrus to prevent the 200,000-volume library from outstripping the one at Alexandria. Anthony later gave this library to Cleopatra. The famous health center dedicated to the god Asclepius, who was worshiped as a serpent, was at its height in the 2nd century, when Galen practiced here. The present city Bergama is a Turkish corruption. Arabic has no "P"; they use "B" instead. "Satan's throne" refers to the great altar of Zeus (now in E. Berlin) and one of the Eight Wonders of the World as listed by Ampelius, a Roman in the 2nd century, or to Emperor worship which was started here and to which three temples were dedicated [BAR 32 (3): 26 (06)].

2:18. Thyatira. Very little is known about the old city; no excavation had been done here. The town of Akhisaar, population 25,000, occupies the site. "Burnished bronze" may refer to the bronze workers, one of the largest trade guilds or labor unions, which also functioned as funeral societies. Others were the woolworkers, linen makers, tailors, leather workers, tanners, potters (v. 27), bakers, slave dealers, and dyers (Lydia, Acts 16:14, belonged to this guild). The famous "Turkey Red" was made from the madder root. A Christian tradesman would have been hard pressed to stand fast to Christ, when guild meetings concluded with banquets of revelry and sin. Thus the compromise with Jezebel (v. 20).

3:1. Sardis. This old capital of Lydia was considered impregnable by King Croesus, since it was built on a hill with three straight sides, except for the South side, which was quite steep. It fell to Cyrus in 546 BC after an unusual winter attack. Gold found in the sand of the Pactolus River, which traversed the city, provided much of the wealth of Croesus. A small village, Sert (a Turkish corruption), occupies the site. "Alive and you are dead" and "strengthen what remains and is on the point of death"—Probably refers to the earthquake of 17 AD, which destroyed the city along with Ephesus, Smyrna, Philadelphia and Laodicea. Tiberius remitted the taxes for five years and gave a gift of 10,000,000 sestercis, but the city never regained its former glory. It was ready to die. Tacitus (Annals II, 47) states that this was the hardest hit of all the neighboring ten cities. In v. 3, "thief . . .you will not know at what hour"—This reference may go back to when Cyrus took the city by having a soldier scale the unguarded wall.

3:7. Philadelphia. Was named for Attalus II Philadelphius 159–138 BC (brother lover—because of his loyalty to his brother). In v.8 "an open door"—Refers to the new role of this City as a missionary church for Christianity, just as it had been for 250 years, a missionary center for Hellenism and Greek culture. In v. 10 "I will keep you"—The present city Alah-Shehir (City of God), population 9,000, is still a Christian town and the residence of a Bishop. Most of the others have entirely lost their Christian roots to the Moslems. With v. 12 "a pillar in the temple"—Ruined temples and broken pillars were a characteristic sight, especially in this unstable city, which was located on a fault. "He shall go no more out [of the city or temple]"—A reference to the quake of 17 AD and the recurring shocks over the next 70 years, which caused the people to dwell outside the city for some time. "I will write upon him the name of my God, and the name of the city. . .New Jerusalem"—After the quake the city was renamed Neokaisareia (New Caesar) in honor of Tiberius, both cases honoring the imperial cult. Imperial consent was necessary according to Roman regulations and was, in effect, "the Emperor writing his name upon the city."

3:14. Laodicea. Named for Laodice, wife of Antiochus II (261–254 BC). It was also a Greek missionary city. Ramsey found a tax document for 62 BC indicating there were 7,500 adult Jewish freemen in the district. Flaccus the propraetor seized a collection of more than 20 pounds of gold for the Jerusalem temple. In v. 15 "neither hot or cold"—The city water supply came from the South by a six mile aqueduct, either from hot springs which cooled on the way, or from a cooler source which warmed up. In v. 17 "rich, prospered, need nothing"—The city was a rich commercial and banking center; Cicero cashed drafts there in 51 BC. After the 17 AD quake, and particularly the one in 60 AD under Nero, the citizenry declined help from Rome or the provincial government in rebuilding the city. In v. 18 "buy gold"—Alluded to the banking industry in the city. "White garments"—The black glossy wool was world famous. It was woven directly into garments, rather than bolts as in modern factories, which included a rain-resistant seamless outer-garment, the *Paenulea* (2 Tm 4:13). The short cloak *Chyamydes* and the dalmatic *Paragaudae* both had purple borders. The wool came from a special breed of black sheep, or was dyed (the Lycus river water is suited for dyeing). "Salve for the eyes"—The medical school in the city produced the famous Phrygian Powder mentioned by Aristotle. In v. 20 Christ is on the outside of his own church! In addition, in v. 22 "He who has an ear to hear"—A famous ear ointment was also produced here. See Wycliffe, Wight and UNT.

Rev 13:18. The Beast. . .666. Two graffiti wall scribblings found at Pompeii, which was destroyed Aug. 24, 79, read: "The number of her honorable name is 45" and "I love her whose number is 545." Dr. Deissmann says of these: (1.) They are concerned with names or persons, which for some reason are to be concealed. (2.) Converting it into a number concealed the name. (3.) Single letters were given their usual values as numerals and then added them together. (4.) The Revelation riddle would not necessarily be Semitic, which would be foreign to Greeks. (5.) To solve the apocalyptic numbers it is feasible to start with the Greek alphabet. The number of the letters of the antichrist's name in Greek should add up to 666 (Wight p. 197). The value of the Greek numbers can be found at www.geocities. com/~lasttrumpet/greek.html. The Ephraemi Rescriptus Codex C has 616, which was known to Irenaeus, but is the only one out of some 400 manuscripts to contain this number.

14:19. Bad grammar in Revelations? "The great winepress"—Winepress is in the masculine and the word great is in the feminine gender. A modifying adjective should agree with its noun in gender. This represents a "solecism," as in English "between you and I" should be "between you and me."

The Egyptian papyri in Greek from the New Testament era contain this exact expression. Other texts show the New Testament writers used merely grammatical forms common among the middle classes of the 1st century AD.

The expressions characteristic of the Hebrew language were also shown by the papyri to be expressions, which had been picked up and used by the non-Jewish population of the apostolic period (Free p. 333).

Bible Personages from Inscriptions

Caiaphas from an ossuary in Jerusalem [BAR 18(5): 38 (92)].
Pilate from a pedestal in Caesarea.
Others are mentioned in the text.

CHAPTER 17

PROPHESY AND CURRENT EVENTS

THE FAILURE TO understand prophecy is explained in Daniel 12:4, 8–10. But much has already been fulfilled and some is becoming clearer as events unfold. Israel has been reestablished as a nation and awaits only the rebuilding of the Temple for the rest to start to fall into place. For a more complete listing of every prophesy in the Bible, see Walvoord.

Leviticus 26:43–44. Israel and the Jew are not forgotten. Compare Deuteronomy 7:1 and Jeremiah 31:35–37. The Hittites by about 800 BC were extinct (1 Kgs 11:1). The Girgashites, one of the Canaanite nations, lived west of the Jordan (Jos 24:11). The Amorites (the high ones or highlanders) lived around Hebron (Gn 14:13), and later east of the Jordan (Dt 3:9); extinct by 800 BC. Canaanites (belong to the land of red-purple), essentially the same as the Phoenicians along the coast. But their territory covered all Palestine. A remnant remained until the Roman period at Carthage. Perizzites lived in Judah and Ephraim (Jos 17:15–18). They were extinct by 800 BC (2 Chr 8:7–8). Hivite, their main area, was in the north near Tyre and Mt. Hermon (Jos 11:3 and 2 Sm 24:7). Not as warlike as others, Jebusites lived in and around Jerusalem (Jos 15:63). The city may have been captured (Jgs 1:8), but was not held by Israel until the time of David (1 Chr 11:4–8). **Numbers 24:20. Amalekites to cease to exist.** This was fulfilled in 1 Chronicles 4:43. **Deuteronomy 28:15–68. Things to come.** Verse 25 fulfilled in 2 Chronicles 29:8, v. 32 fulfilled in 2 Chronicles 29:9, v. 33 fulfilled in Judges 6:1–6, v. 36 fulfilled in 2 Kings17:4, 6; 24:12, 14; 26:7, 11; Daniel 6:11–12, v. 38 fulfilled in Haggai 1:6, v. 41 fulfilled in Lamentations 1:5, v. 42 fulfilled in Joel 1:4, v. 53 fulfilled in 2 Kings 6:24–29, v. 64 fulfilled in Daniel 3:6; v. 68 fulfilled in Hosea 8:13. **33:18. Zebulun to prosper.** The port of Haifa is in the old territory of Zebulun and was not started until 1934. **33:19 "Suck. . . hidden treasure of the sand."** The old pipeline from Kirkuk was not opened until 1935. Iraq closed it with the establishment of the new State of Israel. **33:24 "Asher to dip his foot (toe) in oil."** The old pipeline crosses the territory between Asher and Zebulun at Haifa, just about where the toe of the foot-shaped territory would be. **Judges 9:45. Shechem sowed with salt.** A symbol of perpetual desolation. However, Shechem was rebuilt (1 Kgs 12:25), as was Jericho (1 Kgs 16:34), although it had been cursed in Joshua 6:26–27, which was fulfilled. This is to be contrasted with true prophecy: Samaria in Micah 1:6 "A place for vineyards." Nineveh in Nahum 1:9–12. Ashkelon in Zephaniah 2:4 is now a new port for Israel. Tyre in Ezekiel 26:3, 14, has a fine spring which would support a large city, but is only used for washing fishnets. The cities of Edom in Ezekiel 35:9, except for the new tourist hotels at Petra, none of the old cities are rebuilt. Chorazin was cursed in Matthew 11:20, Bethsaida in 11:21 and Capernaum in 11:23; all were foretold in Matthew 24:35. **1 Kings 5:17. Great Stones.** One of the great foundation stones nearly 39 feet long is the chief cornerstone of the Mosque of Omar (The Dome of the Rock) built by Abd el-Melik in 686 AD. It contains Phoenician markings, as do several in the bottom course of the SE temple mount wall, probably salvaged from Herod's projects. Note Hiram and most of the stone masons were from Tyre (see Amp. Bible).

2 Kings 9:25–26. Prophesy fulfilled by remembrance (compare 1 Kgs 21:19).

Isaiah 7:14. A virgin shall be with child. "Almah" simply means a young woman of childbearing age. However, Genesis 24:42, Proverbs 30:18 and Psalm 68:25 assume a virgin. The Greek LXX translates this by the Greek *Parthenos,* equivalent to virgin. Almah is from the root AWLAHM, to be hid or secret. Thus an Almah is hidden or kept from experience with men. Other than Mary, the only other so called "virgin birth" was Christabel, Lady Ampthill in 1920, who bore Geoffrey Russell as a confirmed virgin (Time Dec. 9, 1935; newspaper articles of April 1976; internet)?

60:5. Wealth of the Sea. In 1935 G.T.B. Davis wrote in *Rebuilding Palestine* the computed wealth of the chemical salts of the Dead Sea including salt, potash, bromine (chlorine and sodium hydroxide) from salt is estimated as four times the wealth of the U.S. The Dead Sea is God's bank and savings account. Isaiah did not know this, but God caused this record to reveal it. In January 1979, evaporation from the top 40 meters caused the Dead Sea to turn over (in that the mean density of this top layer finally equaled that of the bottom layer); separation into two parts had already occurred in 1976 at the Lisan. Other geochemical processes are also occurring. New materials are precipitating, oxygen is penetrating to the depths, hydrogen sulfide has disappeared from the deeper waters, and except for the top ten meters the temperature is uniform. Trace metals such as iron, manganese, and lead are uniform to the bottom. The Dead Sea has dropped some 60 feet since 1950. It is now dropping at three feet per year. It is time for reconsideration of the Med-Dead Canal as a means of generating hydroelectric power and raising the level of the Dead Sea. This could be a great economic boon for Israel (DSLS p. 5).

66:8 and Ezekiel 37:19–22. Israel to be born in one day. May 14, 1948 saw the new state of Israel established in one day, as a preview to a rebirth under the Messiah. Until 1900 only a very few Jews lived in Israel. Travelers in Palestine could see it as a "valley of dry bones." By 1960 1/6 of the Jewish world population was again in Israel (LaHaye p. 67); Ezekiel 37:22b–25 is yet to be fulfilled in the near future.

The Arabs have vowed to "drive Israel into the sea." In the War of Independence, Israel was outnumbered by 100,000 experienced troops vs. 30,000 trained Israelis. On Feb. 14, 1949 Abdul Nasser's unit was encircled at Faluja east of Ashkelon. The armistice of Jan. 12 ended the First War and freed him. The Sinai Campaign of Oct. 26, 1956 was a six-day war that was over in actually three days. Egypt suffered heavy losses and 6,000 prisoners at the Mitla pass. The Six Day War of June 5–11, 1961 had Israel facing the Egyptian army of 100,000 men and about 600 tanks. The Sinai tank battle proved that Israeli's mobility, training and ability of its inferior tanks were superior to the more modern Egyptian tanks. In the Yom Kippur War of Oct. 6, 1973 the Syrians had five divisions of 45,000 men, 1,200 tanks and 300 planes on the Golan Heights against the initial two Israeli tank brigades of 4,500 men and 180 tanks. Syria lost 3,500 men, 370 prisoners and 1,200 tanks. Egypt lost 15,000 men, 8,000 prisoners and 1,000 tanks. Both lost the greater part of their air force and navy. Israel lost only 2,500 men, 350 prisoners, 100 planes and 600 tanks (many damaged tanks were put back into service during the night). These two tank battles were among the greatest in history. Israel has still not been driven into the sea. Every advantage Israel had gained in their wars has been lost through diplomacy, even having to put up with the PLO on its shores (HJP pp. 1062–1088). It's amazing and a miracle they can hang on at all. Col. Richard Meinertzhagen's proposals (to give the Palestinians the Sinai) if adopted at the end of WW I (captured territory was at the disposal of the British in this case) would have avoided all this. See his *Middle East Diary* 1917–1956, with many cited references. The U.N. resolutions 242 and 338 recognize Israel's right to the captured land of the West Bank: A state acting in lawful exercise of its rights of self-defense may seize and occupy foreign territory as long as such seizure and occupation are necessary to its self-defense. As a condition of its withdrawal from such territory, that state may require the institution of security measures reasonably designed to ensure that the territory shall not again be used to mount a threat or use of force against it of such a nature as to justify exercise of self-defense. When the prior holder of territory had seized that territory unlawfully, the state which subsequently takes that territory in lawful exercise of self-defense has, against that prior holder, better title.

Just as England had no desire to honor the Balfour declaration and voted in 1947 against Israel becoming a state (many high level British officers actively aided the Jordan Arab Legion), the U.N. has had no desire or fortitude to help Israel, seeming to prefer the PLO, and now Hezbollah in Lebanon.

Jeremiah 26:18 and Micah 3:12. Zion to be plowed. After Titus destroyed Jerusalem in 70 AD the walls were not rebuilt until 1542, by Sultan Suleiman the Magnificent. For defense purposes the architect and engineers omitted Mt. Zion (the old city of David) from the enclosure. Dr. William Thomson in "*The Land and the Book*" wrote in the 18th century, "Mt Zion is now for the most part a rough field. From the tomb of David (at the Upper Room) I passed on through the fields of ripe grain. It is the only part of Jerusalem that is now or ever has been plowed." Even in 1967 old furrows could be seen in photographs. This area still has few houses (see Amp. Bible).

31:38–40. Jerusalem to be rebuilt. Destroyed by Nebuchadrezzar in 587 BC; by Titus in 70 AD; Hadrian razed it and rebuilt Aelia Capitolina in 135 AD; by Chosroes II the Persian in 614 AD. It was captured by Caliph Omar in 638 and in 1072 by the Seljak Turks. It changed hands six times from 1099–1517 during the Crusades. Since 1099 to nearly 1800, travelers reported it as an almost deserted city, its buildings in ruin and filled with rubble. Its inhabitants ranged from 1,000–6,000.

The prophecy states that the growth will be mainly to the NW; from 1935 to 1970 this has been the main direction of growth. Now it is to the SW. Years ago some commentators said that so unlikely was the fulfillment of this prophecy that it should be interpreted "spiritually."

Ezekiel 26:2–21 and 27:1–36. Tyre. The land city was destroyed by Nebuchadrezzar after a 13 year siege 585–572 BC with some rebuilding after 70 years. The land city was swept clean by Alexander the Great and the island city destroyed in Aug. 332 BC (Free p. 263). The city was probably larger than Jerusalem at the time of Christ's visit in Matthew 15:21. Eusebius (*History*, 10:4) says that "when the church of God was founded in Tyre . . . much of its wealth was consecrated to God . . . and was presented for support of the ministry." Jerome in the 4th century said the wealth of the church of Tyre "was not treasured up or hidden, but was given to those who dwelt before the Lord (Amp. Bible p. 786; LaHaye p. 64).

26:19. After the Crusades and Arabs destroyed the city; the ruins were still visible in the 13th century. Earthquakes caused the western end of the island to sink, and travelers told of seeing "houses, towers and streets far down in the deep." Today the population of 6,000 (no census has been done since 1932, but estimates have shown a loss in population due to the wars) is mostly made up of fishermen, but the city as such has never been revived. At the land site only the springs remain plus a few houses. Population pressures have encroached on this area since then.

The more than 25 prophecies concerning Tyre were all fulfilled. The Law of Compound Probability gives odds of one out of 33.55 MM against its accidental fulfillment. The authenticity of God's Word leaves no chance for sane denial.

44:2. The East Gate to be shut. The Golden Gate was the main eastside thoroughfare until 70 AD. In 1642 Sultan Suleiman the Magnificent built the present walls; after the Crusaders were expelled in 1187, the road was not used and the Gate was walled up, along with four others on the east and south side of the Haram Esh Sherif. St. Stephen's Gate is now the east entrance (Moody Monthly, Oct. 1973).

Matthew 24:15. Desolating sacrilege in the Temple. Until the time of the Gentiles are fulfilled (Lk 21:24). Antichrist to be crowned in the Temple (2 Thes 2:3–4). All these indicate that the Temple is to be rebuilt in the (near?) future.

Emperor Julian "the apostate" in 363 tried to prove much of Christ's words false by rebuilding the Temple as a center for a new Jewish colony. With everything favoring the success of the plan, the work began. Wealthy Jews provided spades and pickaxes of silver. Rubbish was removed in mantles of silk and purple. Yet the combined power of the empire and the enthusiasm of the Jews were in vain. An earthquake on 5-20-363, "a whirlwind and a fiery eruption, (of some sort of inflammable gas) which overturned and scattered the new foundation of the temple" are reported with some variations by contemporary and respectable evidence.

Ammianus Marcellinus reported "horrible balls of fire, breaking out near the foundations, with frequent and reiterated attacks, rendered the place . . . inaccessible to the scorched and blasted workmen." The work was abandoned.

The infidel historian Edward Gibbon (1734–1794) in *"The Decline and Fall of the Roman Empire"* (Vol I pp. 374–377) said

"Such authority should satisfy a believing, and must astonish an incredulous mind" [Moody Monthly Oct. 1973 p. 32; BAR 7(2): 23 (81)].

Luke 21:6. Stones of Temple to be thrown down. Titus gave orders that the Temple was not to be harmed. But it was set on fire anyway. The heat melted the gold overlay, which ran down into the cracks between the stones. After the ruins had cooled, the soldiers pried the stones apart to get it, and also because they had heard that treasure was hidden in underground vaults. The Romans sold the recovered gold at half price (Josephus *Wars* 5.14.4 and 6.6.1). For others see LaHaye pp. 115–124.

21:20–21. Jerusalem encircled. . . flee. How does one flee from a besieged city? In 66 AD, Nero sent the XII Legion and others totaling about 30,000 under Cestius to besiege Jerusalem. He set up his headquarters on Mt. Scopus and completely encompassed the city. The Jews were ready to surrender because of the hopeless situation, but because winter was approaching, for which Cestius was unprepared, "he recalled his soldiers from the place and by despairing of any expectation of taking it he retired from the city without any reason in the world" (Josephus War 2-19-7). In the retreat via the Beth Horon pass 8,795 Romans were killed by the Jews. The golden eagle was lost, which was unforgivable. The Legion was reconstituted and fought well under Titus in 70 AD, but because of the loss of the eagle, was banished from Syria to Melesine in Armenia on the Euphrates (in other words to the boondocks).

The Christians then fled to Pella in the Decapolis for safety. Apparently none were present when Titus destroyed the city in 70 AD. During the siege 1.1 MM Jews died. In the previous seven years of the war 1,337,490 died and thousands were sold into slavery at a reduced price, but none would buy them (Dt 28:68) due to the glut. They died of starvation in confinement (Josephus and Hertz p. 872).

Current Events

Genesis 1:28. Population explosion, the beginning. The end is Luke 23:29. In Isaiah 4:1 the proportion of men to women is becoming smaller, even though more boy babies are born than girls; in 1960 nine men died for every seven females. In 1970 there were 13.9 old women for every ten old men. Everything is now in an exponential growth curve since the last 200 years; at a 1.9% increase per year the world's population doubles every 40 years. Electricity consumption and publication of scientific articles doubles in less than 40 years. By 2600 the world population will stand shoulder to shoulder and the Earth will glow red-hot from the electricity consumption. Obviously this trend cannot continue, and the 2nd coming will occur before 2600. Huge economic and human suffering problems are on the horizon. The sick joke in scientific circles is that we have not been contacted by extra terrestrials, since we should self-destruct when we reach this stage (SHUN p. 158).

Exodus 15:3. War. The Lord is a man of war. Everything is in God's hands (Eph 1:11). Civil war and strife in the U.S. are ordained by God (Is 19:2–4). God uses heathen nations to punish the wayward elect (Jer 5:15, 17). Hitler was used by God to restore Israel on May 14, 1948 after 1878 years to fulfill Daniel 9:27 (a functioning government is needed to have a treaty). The Arab and Jewish problem from Galations 4:22–30 goes back to Genesis 16:15 and 21:2, 9–10. Consider the Jewish situation in the War of Independence of 5-1948; the Jews were outnumbered 50:1; in the Yom Kippur war June (5–10) of 1973 they were outnumbered 6:1—another modern miracle.

Deuteronomy 30:4. Could be used and applied for Apollo 13.

Ecclesiastes 1:10–11. Does history repeats itself? Is anything new?

Esther 1:10–19. Women's lib first appears.

Isaiah 24:1, 3, 5, 19, 20 and Jeremiah 2:7. Pollution—the cure is in Exodus 15:23–26.

Daniel 2:33 and 43. Looks to the European Common Market. As steps to unity: (1.) Defense against a common enemy, which was Communism. Jean Monnet, father of the Common Market said, "as long as Europe remains divided, it is no match for the Soviet Union. Europe must unite." (Look Nov. 26, 1968). (2.) Economic facts of life. Servan-Schreiber author of "The American Challenge" says, "a successful response to American technology, organization and research demands a united European effort" (N.Y. Times Mag. 5-19-68). (3.) Political. Dr. Walter Hallstein (former president of EEC) "at about 1980 we may fully expect the great fusion of all economic, military and political communities together into the U.S. of Europe." This process is still going on as the European Common Market.

Who will be the ultimate leader? The Anti-Christ? (1.) He comes up out of the sea and stands on the sand of the seashore (Rev 12:17b–13:1; compare Rev 17:15). (2.) This symbolic beast has ten horns and seven heads (Rev 13:1 and Dn 7:24). (3.) He is like a leopard (speed), had feet of a bear (powerful), and a mouth of a lion (regal oratory, Rev 13:2). (4.) The dragon gave him his power, throne and great authority (Rev 13:1, 2—compare Rev 12:9, 2 Thes 2:9 and Lk 4). (5.) One head as if it had been slain and the fatal wound healed (Rev 13:3 and 14). We sometimes make idols of people—compare J.F.K., Gandhi, Sister Teresa and a multitude of others. (6.) He will have a magnetic personality, be attractive and a powerful speaker, with answers to all the world's problems (Rev 13:4—compare 1 Thes 5:3). (7.) Christians will be translated (Rapture: 1 Thes 4:13–18). Note the church is not mentioned after Revelation Chapter 6–19 (Tribulation period). (8.) He will deify himself (2 Thes 2:4) in the rebuilt Temple (on the site of the Dome of the Rock?) in Jerusalem (Mt

24:15 and 2 Thes 2:3–4). (9.) He has absolute authority as a dictator for 3½ years (Rev 13:5). (10.) He will blaspheme God and heaven [to discredit the Christian belief and to explain away the Rapture (Rev 13:6)]. (11.) He makes war with the new converts of the 144,000 Jewish evangelists (Rev 13:7). (12.) His cohort or Minister of Finance will be a Jew, known as the False Prophet (Rev 13:11–18; 19:20; 20:10). (13.) Russia defeats the Arabs (Dn 11:40–45), invades Israel, and the Anti-Christ defeats Russia (Eze Ch. 38–39). (14.) Armageddon, between China's 200,000,000 troops (Rev 9:16) and the Anti-Christ (Rev 14:20; Zec 12:2, 3 and 14:1–2 also Is 63:1–4) by Atomic War? One third of mankind will fall (Rev 9:18). (15.) Christ's Second return (Mt 24:29–30) with the Millennium. (16.) Judgment Day (Rev 20:11–15). See the slightly different account in Walvoord, pp. 400-1.

12:4. Revolt and descent. Solution is 2 Chronicles 7:14. Knowledge and wisdom increased:

1. Some 90% of all scientists ever born are alive today. But Psychiatrists have the 2nd highest suicide rate among professional men. With their help there is a 3% remission rate and without their help the rate is still 3%!
2. Computers can calculate in a minute what would require a man 20 years to answer, working 24 hours per day.
3. Enzymes, proteins and insulin are synthesized and analyzed by machines that would require days—years to achieve by the old methods.
4. Archaeology has only been around since 1900 to confirm the Bible. See the separate sections, also LaHaye p. 264.

Acts 1:8. The Great Commission here and in Revelation 14:6 says the Word must go out to the ends of the earth before the Second Coming. Wycliffe estimates that in 2005 there were 6,739 different languages in the world. Only 405 had the entire Bible, 1,034 had the New Testament, only 2,563 had a translation in progress, and 2,737 had no portion of the Bible. From the start of translation to final printed copies is estimated to take ten years. Using this as a guide indicates the Second Coming is quite a while off (www.wycliffe.org.).

Revelation 6:8. Peace vs. war, prosperity vs. famine, conquest of disease vs. pestilence (old diseases recurring or new strains such as polio in Africa and Aids, super bugs, Ebola, and its cousin Marburg hemorrhagic fever in Africa, Anthrax, Herpes, Asian bird flu H5N1, swine flu H1N1 and a host of others) (Hagee p. 87). Animals multiply. What happens if the wild game parks of California, N.J., and Texas, etc., let the animals get out? After guns are outlawed!

We are probably closer to the end of mankind than we think. Exponential population growth is putting a cap on food production (the cost of which will skyrocket) as agricultural land is taken out of production for housing, roads and other uses. There is estimated only 100 years supply of phosphates left for fertilizers, so somewhere near 2,100 could be the end. The climate effects of the greenhouse gases will also take their toll. Problems will mount faster than they can be cured (the switch to electric or hydrogen powered cars or hybrid ones will be too little, too late to cut into carbon dioxide production), such as rising sea levels (most coastal cities will have to be moved to higher ground or abandoned), and weather effects, the costs of which will bankrupt all governments. The Northwest Passage, in 2007, was free of pack ice for the first time in recorded history. Jesus alluded to these in Matthew 24:7. A good summary is Chapter 12 of FLIA.

For the 44 prophesies of the Messiah fulfilled in Jesus Christ see the Open Bible pp. 1236–42. For a fuller discussion see LaHaye pp. 97–109.

False Prophets

False prophets were dealt with by God in Ezekiel chapter 13. Do we have false prophets today? Consider Mohammed's statement in the Koran on the apocryphal stories about Jesus' youth in making a sparrow out of clay in the Table 3:110 and the Imrans 3:49. The confusion of Mary and Miriam, Moses' sister in Imrans 3:36 as sister of Aaron, was used by several Western scholars as a charge that Mohammed had made a mistake. But this could be an Arabic idiomatic expression similar to Jesus being the son of David. Other more serious errors exist. Such that Jesus was not crucified in Women 4:154. Or that he was not the Son of God, and that God is not a triune being. Claiming that Abraham was to sacrifice Ishmael rather than Isaac in the Ranks 37:100–107. Then confusing Saul with Gideon at ein-Harad (Jgs 7:1–7) in the Cow 2:249. It also refutes claims that Christians have never made, such that Mary was a part of the Trinity. The common Arab view maintains that Allah would not let any of his prophets die by crucifixion. The Koran scoffs at the very idea in Women 4:157. Muslims do not accept the prophet's ignorance for these discrepancies (he was illiterate); rather, Muhammad and the Koran are correct and that Christians and Jews have corrupted every copy of their Scriptures. See James A. Beverly in Christian History 31(2): 10 (02); www.religionwatch. ca. The Koran was first written about 613, or about 580 years after the death of Christ. Thus it is late and Jesus had already spoken on His final authority in John 14:6: "I am the way the truth and the life. No one comes to the Father except through Me." If God is the author of prophesies, then the Koran has not kept up to date. The Koran makes for dull reading in that the battles of Badr (where all the Jewish males were killed and the women and children sold into slavery, is perhaps the blackest mark against early Islam) and Mecca take up much space along with many repetitions. In The cave 18:83–98 appears, as an epithet or a parable, the mystical character Dhul al Qarnain (the two horned one), which for 1300 years has been treated as Alexander the Great. He is often shown on Greek coins with the horns of Amon (TLBG p. 159). This would make him a Muslim 946 years before the Islamic period. Modern Muslim scholars are backing away from this identification due to the belief in the infallibility of the Koran and prefer to rely on the parable approach.

Only hinted at in the Koran, The Imrans 3:195, but expounded in the supplemental writings, commentaries, sermons and lessons (the Hadith) when things were at a low point, the flight from Mecca to Medina prompted Muhammad to develop a more militant theology. He formed "the Mystic Fighters," a cutthroat squad who were guaranteed eternal life and paradise for martyrs killed in battle, with 70 virgins for each (I don't know where this places today's female Jihadists) to keep them company, complete with all the pleasures of the flesh at their disposal. Their bloody excursions intoxicated his Bedouin followers to a frenzy; now covered in a religious pretext.

The beauty of the Golden Rule and "to love your enemies" is lacking. The section, Repentance 9:23, says clearly "believers should not take as friends or protectors, even their own fathers or brothers if they love Infidelity above Islam." The closest one can get is in the Hadith # 13 of Al-Nawawii's 40 Hadiths or Bukhari 1.2.12, where the prophet said, "None of you will have faith til he wishes for his (Moslem) brother what he likes for himself." The claimed version: "Do to all men as you would wish to have done unto you, and reject for others what you would reject for yourselves," has no authentic reference in the Koran or Hadith as to its location. They have been known to make statements that cannot be verified. The building of the Kabah was said to be by Abraham and Ishmael (Abraham was never at Mecca) and contains a meteorite built into a corner of a wall. The god of the stone was said to be Allah. According to a Koranic legend, it fell from heaven and the angel Gabriel brought it to Abraham during the reconstruction of the Temple (only no Hebrew Temple existed at this time, unless the term refers to the Kabah). Any could enter in safety, except no infidel could enter (a type of contradiction). www.messengers-of-truth. org/Articles/ fundamental_islam.html

The events taking place in the Middle East with the likes of Osama Ben Laden and other Islamic fanatics basically represent an east v. west mentality often played down by the press as politically incorrect, to keep from stepping on toes. The claim that Islam condemns terror killing must be modified. In the chapter Women 4:92–3 the statement is made that it is unlawful for an Islamic believer to kill another believer except by accident. There were Islamic believers in the World Trade Center on 9-11-01. Since this was not an accident, those guilty "will burn in Hell forever" according to the Koran. Any other infidel people simply do not count and are of no consequence. Any Mosque, once established cannot be abandoned and must be reestablished at the first opportunity. Moorish Spain is on notice. Any land that the foot of an Islamic believer touches becomes Islamic land. Thus the U.S., Asia, Africa and Europe beware. During the Arab conquest the believers in the Book (Jews the Torah, and Christians the Gospels) were exempt from converting to Islam but were held in contempt (The Table 5:13–82). All other idolaters were given "an offer they couldn't refuse"—convert or die on the spot. Compare the recent remarks that got the Pope in trouble.

The Mormons also have fabricated several myths. In the Book of Mormon the compass (called Liahona) is described in use in 600–590 BC by Nephi son of Lehi, who escaped from Judah (Nephi 16:10, 18:12, 19:21, II Nephi 5:12, Moshia 1:16 and Alma 37:38). The horse was found in America in 589 BC in II Nephi 29:3 in spite of the fact that they first escaped from Coronado's troops in 1540–42. Use of the word Bible in 559 BC in II Nephi 29:3. Linen in America in 178 BC in Mosiah 10:5. Jesus born of Mary in Jerusalem in Alma 7:10. Coins found in America in 82 BC in Alma 11:4–20, although none have been found. Cement in America in 46 BC in Helaman 3:7. The earth being in darkness for three full days at Christ's death in Helaman 14:20–27; III Nephi 8:23. Horses and elephants in America are described in Ether 9:19. Ancient towers and cities, although other than the cliff dwellings of the American Indians, no such ruins are known except for the Toltec, Aztec and Maya of Central America and the Incas of South America, none of whose beliefs are similar to the Israelis.

The Olmec calendar, known as the Long Count, which some think began with the beginning of time, of the Fifth Sun, on Aug. 13, 3114 BC and includes the end of time on Dec. 21, 2012 (do they know something we don't?) and continued until the records stopped in 900 AD. (See also Science and the Bible.) Hancock p. 499 gives Dec. 23, 2012 (Herbert J. Spinden in *Mysteries of the Mexican Pyramids* p. 286 gives Dec. 24, 2011). Some events recorded allow a synchronization of these events in Mesoamerica with European history (Gallenkamp p. 77; Time Life *Lost Civilizations: The Magnificent Maya* p. 14, 30, although it gives Aug. 11, 3114 as the start of the Fifth Sun.) But no arrival of the Israelites can be found. The polytheistic beliefs of these people are also at odds with Israeli beliefs. The Mormons also equate the Aztec Topiltzin Quetzalcoatl with the resurrected Jesus in America. This leaves their last mystery unsolved: the 24 gold plates, the Urim and Thummin and the breastplate found on the hill Cumorah in New York. These gold plates are supposed to be the source for the Book of Mormon in 1830, later claimed to have been taken back to Heaven (BAR 11(5): 54 (85); Wilson pp. 278–285). Needless to say, there was a court case in 1826 and 1830 in which Joseph Smith was accused of bank fraud, pilfering of funds, as well as money digging by hiring out as a "glass-looking" treasure hunter, using the above

Urim and Thummin [W.P. Walters in Westminster Theological Journal 36: 123 (73/4)].

The Mormons under John D. Lee also caused over 100 pioneers "on their way to California" to be massacred on Sept. 11, 1857 at Mountain Meadows, Utah after a five-day battle (they had laid down their arms and were offered safe conduct out of the area). Only some children below the age of eight were spared. The charge was they had trespassed on Holy Ground "Zion" and were in need of "blood atonement" as required in the Book of Mormon, Mosiah 3:11. The first trial was a hung jury with eight Mormons voting acquittal and the other four non-Mormons voting guilty. The second trial, delayed by the Civil War, found him guilty when several of those present turned against him. It was felt that Brigham Young had a hand in the decision, but no one would implicate him. Lee was shot by firing squad at the site where a memorial now stands (History Channel 2-8-05).

To round out the picture: Inca pyramids have been found in Peru at Casma and Caral dated by C-14 to 2600 BC. These are now the oldest known in the Americas or Egypt and have rewritten the history for this age (from a National Geographic TV program).

The National Inquirer likes to run stories on the leading psychics of our day. Dr. D. James Kennedy followed up on a story they ran on *50 Prophecies of Ten Leading Psychics for the Next Year*. Ten years later he checked the results. Not a single one came about. Lahaye similarly tested the spirits from an article in the Sun on 4 Sept. 2001 pp. 24–27, on *101 Predictions and Prophecies for You and Your Loved Ones from World's Leading Seers and Psychics*. Did any hint at the 9/11 disaster? No, not one (Lahaye p. 29).

Other psychics who bombed are Harold Camping in 1994, who said Jesus would return in Sept. of 94, then recalculating it to Oct. 2. Still no luck. Edgar Whisenant sold 4.5 million books titled *88 Reasons Why the Rapture Will Be in 1988*. When that didn't work he said he forgot to account for the year 0 (he was wrong again; there is no year 0 between BC and AD) and changed it to 89. Score zero (LaHaye p. 256). In addition you may remember Sun Myung Moon, Mary Baker Eddy, founder of Christian Science and the psychic advisor to the royal family, the Very Reverend Horace Bartholomew's prediction that Palestinian separatists would send life-like robots on suicide bombing missions (LaHaye p. 30). There are also the practitioners of Transcendental Meditation, Scientology (Tom Cruise's version, which led to a woman's death, as she was deemed not needing psychiatric treatment), Herbert W. Armstrong's Worldwide Church of God, Edgar Cayce, Hare Krishna or Zen. Take your pick. More recently we have Jeane Dixon who predicted that Jacqueline Kennedy would not remarry in 1968, that the Vietnam War would end in 1966, that Walter Reuther would run for President in 1964, plus other bloopers. The problem of her name (she was born Lydia Pinchert in 1904), where she was born, wed or attended school were also claimed to be unknown (The National Observer issue of Oct. 27, 1973). Even her brother couldn't confirm some of her claims.

Michael Travesser (a.k.a. Wayne Bent), a self proclaimed Messiah, prophesied the end of the world on 10-31-07 at midnight.

Among those in the current or past healing movement are: Maria Beulah Woodworth-Etter, who started the "slaying in the Spirit" movement and predicted in 1890 that San Francisco would be destroyed by an earthquake and tidal wave; Aimee Semple McPhearson, who had multiple affairs, two divorces, and died of a drug overdose; Kathryn Kuhlman and her love affair with money and jewels, and who also had an affair with a married evangelist, who in turn divorced his wife to marry her, until she also divorced him; and A.A. Allen, who was a chronic alcoholic and died of cirrhosis of the liver, and who likewise divorced his wife—his unique claim was that he could turn $1 bills into $20's (of which the IRS would not approve), not to mention that he could raise the dead, though unburied bodies of his followers failed to comply. Then there was William Branham, who predicted the end of the world in 1977. His followers believed he was God and that he would rise from the dead.

Jack Coe was ousted from the Assemblies of God, and while he taught that medicine was the mark of the beast, he readily took the mark himself when he got sick. His wife, after his death, published an expose of his many fraudulent healing claims and financial excesses.

And of course there was Oral Roberts, whose $8 million death threat from God raised the money, but did not save his hospital, nor did it document a single healing. On TV he claimed Paul Crouch had been healed of chest pains, only to be hospitalized with a heart attack that same night.

Kenneth Hagin, founder of the Word Faith Movement, claimed that the healing teachings in his books were revelations from God—this though they were actually plagiarisms from books by E.W. Kenyon, who in turn admitted that his teachings were directly from Christian Science cults.

Benny Hinn has taught that there are actually nine in the Trinity. He was responsible for the death of one elderly woman, when he slew someone in the Spirit that landed on top of the woman and broke her hip. He couldn't heal the woman.

Paul Cain claimed that God took away his sexual desire for 40 years, but an affair caused him to leave the ministry for 25 years. He sparked the "laughing revival" movement associated with the Vineyard Movement and the Pensacola, Florida Revival (Yates pp. 452–3).

Edward Cayce, the "Sleeping Prophet," claimed to be a reincarnation of the Egyptian high priest Ra-Ta and that the lost records of Atlantis were buried under the front paws of the Sphinx. His Edgar Cayce Foundation has even conducted research at the Sphinx backed by the Stanford Research Institute, Dr. Mark Lehner, and Recovery Systems International, all above reproach. Cayce has some 1,159 readings (delivered during a trance) concerning Ra-Ta. Dr. Zahi Hawass of the Egyptian Antiquities Organization working in some underground tunnels near the Sphinx actually found one that led under the Sphinx and was featured in a TV program (HBMS pp. 85–99). The Freemasons, AMORC Rosicurcians of California, and the Theosophical Society of London and Madras have all proposed the Atlantis Hall of Records at Giza, and have spawned a multimillion-dollar New Age industry about the Pyramids and the Sphinx, complete with crystal power.

The biggest scam today is the Universal Life Church. Essentially it is a tax dodge where for $1 you can become an ordained minister, and with two others as members you can qualify for tax advantages, be exempt from being inducted into the armed forces, and park in Pastors' spaces, etc. They won one case against the IRS in 1974. On the internet at ULC.net there is now no cost for becoming a minister.

Cults still do their damage—just recall the Jim Jones Guyana fiasco in which 913 died. Or there is David Koresh and the Branch Davidians of Waco, Texas, where another 87 and four law officers died. A more recent tragedy is The Heaven's Gate and their UFO's Hale-Bop comet, culminating with another 40 dead. Now the FBI is after the polygamist FLDS cult of Warren S. Jeffs who has claimed never to be taken, but was.

CHAPTER 18

BIBLE QUANDARIES

GENESIS 10:20–25. NEGRO race is cursed? An old racist argument with no basis. Ham's son or descendants the Canaanites were cursed. Ham's licentious character would be in full bloom in the Canaanites (and others who had close contact with Canaan, such as the Amorites, Philistines or Phoenecians). Carthage was a depraved colony to the Romans. (See also Gn 15:16; 19:5; Lev 18 and 20; Dt 12:31.) This curse was basically religious in that Shem's blessing was also religious. Other than the blessing of fruitfulness in Genesis 9:1, there was no blessing on Ham or his other sons (Cush, Mizrain and Put), indicating that they were implicated. Note the Arab problem today, as well as general African paganism, witch doctors and morbid fear of demons.

    Exodus 13:18. Red Sea. The translation of the Hebrew Yam Suph as Red Sea is incorrect, since Reed or Marsh Sea is meant. No reeds grow along the north arm of the Gulf of Suez or Mediterranean Sea or in any salt water. The march was from Rameses to Succoth (means tabernacles, Ex 12:37), then to Etham (wall or rampart) at the edge of the desert east of the

Suez Canal, then to Pi-hariroth (house of marshes), then to Migdol (fort or watchtower) a Canaanite name, then back to Baal-Zephon (Ex 14:2 Lord of winter or north) also a Canaanite name. The proximity of Succoth to the Reed Sea is indicated. The Papyrus Marsh according to Egyptian records was near Rameses (now Tanis). The body of water crossed was probably around Lake Timsah, probably brackish but able to support papyrus growth (UOT p. 137; KOROT pp. 266–272).

Some maps show crossing of the Gulf of Suez. Not withstanding the above, if the water of the Gulf of Suez was removed, the cliffs to the bottom would be about 200 feet high, with no way to get down or back up. Do not look for any crossing in this area. The shallowest portion is at the north end for about 30 miles, where it is only 60 feet deep; the cliffs would still present an insurmountable problem.

Jeremiah 8:22. Balm of Gilead. The shrub (Commiphora Opobalsamum or B. Gileadense) has never been found in Gilead proper. It comes from Arabia and the east coast of Africa. It was imported to Jericho and En-Gedi, the groves covered 20 mi²; it was a principal source of revenue for Herod (Perroe p. 68).

Matthew 16:18. Peter the Rock? An interesting sermon from St. Catherine's Monastery at Mt. Sinai, dates to around the 6–9 century AD:

> O Petros, thou wast convicted of fault by Paulus thy colleague. How do men say that upon Petros … I have built [the Church which] is not shaken … O Petros, after that thou didst receive the keys of heaven, and the Lord was seen by thee after he arose from amongst the dead, thou didst let go of the keys, and thy wage is agreed with thy Master when thou saidst to him, Behold we have let go of everything and have come after thee. What then shall be of us? And he said to him, Ye shall be sitting on twelve thrones and judging the tribes of Israel, and after [all these signs, O Petros], thou wentest away again

to the catching of fish....Thou didst deny me! (See Cobern pp. 279–80.)

At least by some at this date, Peter was not considered the Rock.

This is a typical "play on words" in Greek. Christ says: "Thou are Petros (a stone) and upon this Petra [the statement that Peter just made (a massive rock)], I will build my Church . . ."

Matthew 21:1. Palm Sunday. Only John gives the chronology (12:1). Six days before the Passover is Sunday, when a meal was prepared. He came from Ephraim (John 11:54, 19 miles NNE of Jerusalem by way of Bethany) where he stayed until Saturday the Sabbath. He traveled almost all day Sunday (he could not travel on the Sabbath until it was over), arriving before evening (v.2). In v. 12, the next day, Monday, he presented himself for examination for four days. Note a type of lamb (Ex 12:3). The lamb is selected and examined for blemishes for four days before Passover. Thus, this is Palm Monday—so much for Palm Sunday. See the excellent booklet by The American Board of Missions to the Jews: A Passover Trilogy.

Mark 16:9. Mary Magdalene. She is not called a harlot in the Bible. She is never mentioned except in connection with her home town (Magdala), thus she is not the woman of Luke 7:37, since Luke names her in 8:2, 23:49 and 55. Matthew and John also distinguish her from the many other Marys (Unger p. 823).

Luke 2:7. Mary a perpetual virgin? Christ is called her first born, not her only son. Otherwise first would not be stressed. See: Luke 8:19 "brothers"; Matthew 13:55 and Mark 6:3 where four brothers and at least two sisters are mentioned; 1 Corinthians 9:5 "brothers of the Lord" are married brothers; Galations 1:19 "James the Lord's brother"; Jude 1:1 "a brother of James." There is no reference known where "first born" can be equated with "only begotten." The Catholic position that these are half brothers from Joseph's first marriage is only tradition from apocryphal works and cannot compete with actual Scripture.

2 Corinthians 5:1–10. Soul Sleep? Compare Philippians 1:21–23, it is the body that sleeps and it will be changed. "Moment" is *atomos* in Greek (1 Cor 15:52). "Last trumpet" refers to the Old Testament march from Egypt in which seven trumpets would blow, Numbers 10:1–7: (1) prepare to break camp, (2) fold up tents . . . (7) move out.

1 Thessalonians 4:13–18. Rapture vs. Second Coming of Christ. Same Event?

1. In Old Testament, evangelizing was the task of the Jew. In Church Age evangelizing is the task of the Church. During the tribulation the Jew is responsible for evangelizing again (Rev 7:1–4).

2. The second coming is visible to the whole world during the height of a global war (Rev 1:7). The Mount of Olives will split during an earthquake (Zec 14:4). A spring will open up and flow east and west (Zec 14:8).

   In the rapture only the Christians see Christ, not necessarily at a time of war. No conditions in Scripture must be fulfilled for the Rapture to occur.

3. At the 2nd coming, Christ will divide on earth the believers from the unbelievers.

   At the rapture, all living believers will be caught up to join him in the clouds.

4. During Christ's reign, there will be mortal humans on earth over which He will rule.

   At the rapture, the body is changed, it is not mortal. During the seven year tribulation other people will become believers (Rev 3:10). The Philadelphia type Church will be "kept out of trial," not "safeguarded through."

5. Note in Revelation chapters 1–5 (chapters 4–5 are scenes in Heaven) the Church is mentioned 30 times; in chapters 6–19 (describing the tribulation) the Church is not mentioned once—because it is not on earth. It is in Heaven.

Each chapter in 1 Thessalonians has a verse or promise about the Rapture or 2nd coming.

1:10 To wait . . . for the rapture. We do not wait for Him at the 2nd coming—we are with him.

2:19 In presence of Lord—Rapture. From Rapture to 2nd coming we were already present.

3:13 Coming with all his saints—2nd coming.

4:16–17 Caught up together—Rapture.

5:23 Soul, spirit and body to be preserved (compare v. 2) —Rapture. Not necessary to preserve these at 2nd coming.

Note before Christ's death, Paradise was *down*; after His death He led captivity (death) captive (Eph 4:8); and Heaven was *up*. In Luke 16:19–31 Abraham's bosom (v. 22), Paradise and Hell were side by side with a great gulf between. Lazarus's soul was in torments and heat, yet his body was in the grave. The soul carries the senses and feelings.

James 5:16. Confess sin. Not to a priest, but to one another so that we may pray (duty of a priest, 1 Tm 2:1–3, 5) for one another. (Compare Mt 21:23–43). Those saved are priests (1 Pt 2:5, 9; Rev 1:6).

The rite comes from Matthew 16:18: the power to bind or loose, to impose penance and pardon sins. Also Extreme Unction comes from James 5:14. One who is sick is not necessarily near death. Purgatory is not taught in the Bible; this concept was not known to Christians of 100 AD, as shown by Catacomb inscriptions in Rome. Prayers for the dead, sin offerings, and to make atonement for sins come from II Maccabees 12:43–45.

The old statement "Cleanliness is next to Godliness" is also not in the Bible.

Likewise, another unbiblical aphorism is "God helps those who help themselves."

The Seven Sacraments of the Catholic Church: these are first mentioned by Dionysius Areopagiticus in the 5th century. Luther does not mention matrimony as a sacrament:

Baptism.

Communion.

Holy Orders. This and the above two were the only sacraments in the 1st century.

Confirmation.

Penance and Confession.

Matrimony was a civil ceremony.

Extreme Unction.

Kwanza, of course, was not invented until 1966 (might as well end on a humorous note).

The Old Testament Today

And so God talked to Moses and said, "Moses, there's good and bad news.

Your staff will change into a serpent.

The Nile will turn to blood, and the fish in the Nile will die and stink.

The Nile will bring forth hoards of frogs, which will die and stink.

From these, mounds of dead frogs and the ground will come forth clouds of gnats, flies and insects to infect the Egyptians' cattle so that they die.

Boils will break out on the Egyptians.

Great hail mingled with fire will kill every exposed animal, man, tree and plant; the entire flax and barley crop will be ruined, except in Goshen.

Locusts will consume what is left, only to be finally drowned in the Reed Sea.

Then for three days a thick darkness or smog that can be felt will cover Egypt, except for Goshen.

Then the entire first born, both of people and cattle, will die.

Finally I will part the Reed Sea so Israel may cross, but the Egyptian Cavalry will be drowned.

Later 3,000 men will die at Mt. Sinai, where the 2.5 million Israelites will camp for about one year, and each family must have its own privy.

Over the next 40 years the people will wander over Sinai and all but four over age 20 will die—over two million people.

Finally you will destroy the people of Ammon and Bashan, and Joshua will lead the people over Jordan to subdue the Canaanites.

That's the good news."

Moses said, "Lord, that's wonderful; but what's the bad news"?

God replied, "You must write the Environmental Impact Statement."

REFERENCES

ABR. *Archaeology and Biblical Research.* Published by Associates for Biblical Research. Conservative, limited distribution. Name changed to Bible and Spade.

ADHL. *Archaeological Discoveries in the Holy Land.* New York 1967. Easy reading but slightly dated. Short articles by the excavator.

Albright, William Foxwell. *The Archaeology of Palestine.* Maryland 1956. Debir is misidentified and some of the archaeological data is out of date. Otherwise an excellent scholar.

ANE. *The Ancient Near East,* Vol. I & II. Edited by James B. Pritchard, New Jersey 1975. Earlier versions known as ANET. All the important Historical and Biblical texts are covered. A must read if you want to know about the Moabite Stone, The Rosetta Stone or the Code of Hammurabi and the Amarna Letters, etc.

AO. *Archaeology Odyssey.* Covers other areas, not primarily the Holy Land. Published by Biblical Archaeology Society along with BAR and BR.

ARAB. *Ancient Records of Assyria and Babylon,* Vol. I & II. Edited by D.D. Luckenbill, Illinois 1926. Anything not covered in ANE or ANET will be found here. Also a must read for the specialist.

Arch. *Archaeology.* Not as technical as others.

Ashton, John F. ed. *In Six Days.* Arkansas 2000. Fifty scientists who believe in the six days of creation and why. References are a good source for the creationist view.

BA. *Biblical Archeologist.* Current research published here.

BAR. *Biblical Archaeology Review.* Washington D.C. Popular Journal, some authors are quite liberal, but the best source for the public. Available in some public libraries.

Barber, E.J.W., *Prehistoric Textiles.* New Jersey 1991. Covers everything about the role of women in society.

Barnes, Thomas G. *Origin and Destiny of the Earth's Magnetic Field.* I.C.R. Tech. Monograph No.4 1973. Conservative with interesting consequences for the age of man.

BASOR. Bulletin of the American Schools of Oriental Research. Current research published here.

Baumann, Hans. *The Land of Ur.* New York 1969. Many interesting facts.

Baxter, J.S. *Studies in Problem Texts.* Michigan 1975. Conservative., only 12 selected texts covered.

BER. Budge, Wallis, *Egyptian Religion.* New York 1959. From the 1900 edition but still a good source.

BR. *Bible Review.* Covers text problems. Same publisher as BAR, same comments apply.

Bible and Spade. *Same as ABR.* Published by Associates for Biblical Research. Conservative, limited distribution.

Bowman, Sheridan, *Radiocarbon Dating.* California 1990. Only 64 pages but factual.

Boyd, Robert T., *Tells, Tombs and Treasure.* New York 1969. Conservative but somewhat breezy style written for the layman.

Bryan, Betsy M., *The Reign of Thutmose IV.* Maryland 1991. Complete scholarly treatment.

Budge, Wallis, *The Egyptian Book of the Dead (The Papyrus of Ani). New York 1967.* From the edition of 1895. As of 2007 the only copy in print.

Buswell, J. Oliver, *Systematic Theology of the Christian Religion.* Michigan 1962. Conservative.

Burrows, Millard. *The Dead Sea Scrolls.* New York 1955. The first account of finding the Scrolls.

Campbell Jr., Edward Jay, *The Chronology of the Amarna Letters.* Maryland 1964. Best account for the letters.

Carter, Howard. The Tomb of Tutankhamen. New York 1972. Some of the things he did, such as to the body of King Tut, are not reported, but were learned later.

CBMW. *Ebla.* Chaim Bermant and M. Weitzman. New York 1979. One of the first works published before the names of Jerusalem, Sodom and others were removed. Still fascinating reading.

Chouraqui, A., *The People and Faith of the Bible.* Massachusetts 1975. Somewhat liberal but interesting comments in other areas.

Cobern, C.M. *The New Archaeological Discoveries.* New York 1929. Oxyrhynchus papyri, which include early hymns, sermons, inflation, taxes. Archaeological material is dated and Lachish is misidentified.

Coppedge, James F., *Evolution Possible or Impossible?.* Michigan 1973. The most thought out book on the subject, a goldmine of information and statistical conclusions.

Cross, John R., *The Stranger on the Road to Emmaus.* Canada 2002. Resources in the appendix are a good source of information on Genesis.

Curtis, Helena. *Biology.* New York 1975. College textbook.

DSLS. *The Dead Sea: The Lake and its Sitting:* Tina M. Niemi, Z. Ben-Avraham and J.R. Gat. Oxford Univ. Press 1997. Very good technical discussion on all points of the Dead Sea. Source of sulfur is not identified.

Dunbar, Carl O. *Historical Geology.* New York 1953. College textbook.

EAEHL. *Encyclopedia of Archaeological Excavations in the Holy Land.* Edited by Michael Avi-Yonah. New Jersey 1976. This, and the better new edition is "the Bible" for sites in Israel. If you can't get to other sources, use this.

ECIAT. *Egypt, Canaan and Israel in Ancient Times.* Donald B. Redford. New Jersey 1992. Ties up the Near East quite well, covers 10,000–586 BC. Takes issue with some of the history of Israel.

Edwards, I.E.S., *The Pyramids of Egypt.* New York 1972. Very complete account.

EHB. *Eerdmans Handbook to the Bible.* Michigan 1992. Conservative, excellent special sections.

Engels, Donald W., *Alexander the Great and the Logistics of the Macedonian Army.* California 1978. Excellent logistical summary of the campaigns of Alexander.

ET. *Tutankhamun: His Tomb and its Treasure.* Edwards, I.E.S. New York 1976. There are no page numbers in this photo edition.

Eydoux, Henri-Paul, *In Search of Lost Worlds.* New York 1971. Good overall information.

Fagan, Brian, *The Rape of the Nile.* Colorado 2004. The fascinating characters of the comings and goings, mostly of the artifacts. Most of the early excavations, until Petrie, were deplorable.

FLIA. Fagan, Brian, *The Little Ice Age.* New York 2000. Climate effects from 1300–1850.

FRB. Fagan, Brian, *Return to Babylon.* Massachusetts 1979. More on Assyria and Mesopotamia than Babylon. Interesting details of Archeologists and the early digs. The references are a good summary of starting points.

Finegan, Jack, *Encountering New Testament Manuscripts.* Michigan 1974. Excellent reference and information.

FLAP. Finegan, Jack, *Light from the Ancient Past.* New Jersey 1959. Very good information.

Franck, Adolphe, *The Kabbalah.* New York 1940. First translated from the French of 1843. This is a new retranslation. There are very few readable works on the Kabbalah; this is one. Or try the Dummies book.

Frank, H.T., Bible Archaeology and Faith. New York 1971.

Free, Joseph P., *Archaeology and Bible History.* Revised, Michigan 1992. Revised and expanded by H.F. Vos.

Gadd, C.J., *The Stones of Assyria.* London 1936. An account of the early sculptures removed from Assyria, etc. The parsimonious and poorly equipped expeditions resulted in about 30 sculptures being damaged by Arabs while unguarded, and over 100 slabs lost from a boat wreck in the Tigris. The Museum acquisition numbers are all right, but the other numbers used are not explained. There is no index, and the artifact description text is not keyed to the plates.

Gallenkamp, Charles, *Maya.* New York 1985. Includes glyphic decipherment.

Garfinkel, Yosef, *The Goddess of Sha'ar Hagolan.* Israel Exploration Society 2004.

Grant, F.C., Hellenistic Religions: The Age of Syncretism. New York 1953.

GRE. Grant, Michael, *The Roman Emperors.* New York 1997. Covers 31 BC to 476 AD.

Gurney,O.R., *The Hittites.* London 1990. Laws, languages and literature.

Hadingham, Evan, *Lines to the Mountain Gods (Nasca and the Mysteries of Peru).* New York 1987. Archaeology at Nasca and the religion of the Inca.

Hagee, John. *Beginning of the End.* Tennessee 1996. End times associated with the assassination of Yitzhak Rabin. By a conservative pastor.

Hancock, Graham, *Fingerprints of the Gods.* New York 1995. The Admiral Piri Reis Map made in Constantiople in 1513, showing an ice free Antarctica. Plus other information that the Olmec culture, Great Pyramid and Sphinx could be much older than first thought.

Hawass, Zahi, *Secrets from the Sand*. New York 2003. New finds from the Giza plateau.

HBMS. *The Message of the Sphinx,* Graham Hancock, and Robert Bauval. New York 1996. Astronomical evidence that the Sphinx dates to about 10,500 BC.

Hertz, J.H., *The Pentateuch and Haftoras. Second Edition.* London 1992. Includes an interesting commentary with the comment, "Accept the truth from whatever source it comes." This version by the late chief Rabbi of the British Empire is the source used as the pew Torah in many Synagogues, especially on the East coast and elsewhere.

HHBR. *King Herod's Dream: Caesarea on the Sea.* Edited by Kenneth G. Holum, Robert L. Hohlfelder, Robert J. Bull and Avner Raban. New York 1988. Excavation methods discussed briefly.

HJP. *History of the Jewish People.* Edited by H.H. Ben Sasson. Massachusetts 1976. Historical background for the development of Israel to the Yom Kippur War. Most of the historical texts are correlated with the Bible texts; problem areas are emphasized.

IB. *Interpreter's Bible.* New York 1956. Liberal but good Hebrew language points and scholarship.

IEJ. *Israel Exploration Journal.* Current research published here.

Jacobsen, Thorkild, *The Treasures of Darkness.* Massachusetts 1976. Excellent history of Mesopotamian Religion.

JNES. *Journal of Near East Studies.* Evangelistic in approach.

Johnson, Paul, *The Civilization of Ancient Egypt.* New York 1978. Good source material.

Josephus. Complete Works, Translated by William Whitson. Main source for the Jewish wars.

Kenyon, J. Douglas Editor, *Forbidden History.* Vermont 2005. Additional information on prehistoric technologies and the suppressed origins of civilizations. Book has no index.

Keller, Werner, *The Bible as History.* New York 1981. A scientific journalist. A ten million copy best seller. Errors of fact occur on pp. 89,91,95,235,256,261,305,331,334,345, 347,349;378. Debir is misidentified and the smelters at Tell el-Kheleifeh did not have flues.

KY. Kee, H.C. and Young, F.W., *Understanding the New Testament.* New York 1959. Conservative.

Kitchen, Kenneth A., *Ancient Orient and Old Testament.* Illinois 1968. Excellent conservative scholar. Only thing wrong, the book is about five times too small in material.

KOROT. Kitchen, Kenneth A., *On the Reliability of the Old Testament.* Michigan, 2003. Fills out the material noted in the one above. Puts the minimalists in their place.

KPT. Kitchen, Kenneth A., *Pharaoh Triumphant.* England 1982. The life and times of Rameses II.

Kunin, R., *Ion Exchange Resins.* II Ed. New York 1958.

LaHaye, Tim, *The Merciful God of Prophecy.* Canada 2002. Conservative.

Lewis, C.S., The Inspirational Writings of C.S. Lewis, The Business of Heaven. New York 1987.

Livingston, David, *Khirbet Nisya: The search for Biblical Ai 1979-2002.* Pennsylvania 2003. The final excavation report by the Associates for Biblical Research. My chapters on the tombs and Greek lamp inscriptions were not included due to a time element. I can furnish these on request.

Lloyd, Seton, *The Archaeology of Mesopotamia*. London 1978. Good chronology of ancient sites.

Maier, Paul L., *Eusebius the Church History*. Michigan 1999. New translation and commentary.

Magueijo, Joao, *Faster than the Speed of Light*. New York 2004. A radical new theory not disproved at this time. His writing needs to be cleaned up.

Maqueen, J.G., *The Hittites*. Colorado 1975. Good general source.

MBA. *Macmillin Bible Atlas*. Edited by Y. Aharoni and M. Avi-Yonah. New York 1978. Good source material and maps for Bible events. Mt. Tabor is mislocated on maps 227, 228, and 230. The Gadarene swine incident is mislocated on the West side of the Sea of Galilee in map 231. Other minor errors are present.

Matthews, V.H. and Benjamin, Don C., *Social World of Ancient Israel 1250–587 BCE*. Massachusetts 1993. Interesting concept of protocols for the family and how to understand the ancient near east.

Mazar, Amihai, *Archaeology of the Land of the Bible*. New York 1990. Covers 10,000–586 BC.

Mazar, Benjamin, *The Mountain of the Lord*. New York 1975. Chief excavator around the South and Southwest corner of the Temple Mount. A Jewish scholar I do not argue with.

McBirnie, William S. *The Search for the Tomb of Jesus*. California 1981. Examines both sites in detail, historically.

MCOCB. Metzger, B.M. and Coogan, M.D., *The Oxford Companion to the Bible*. New York 1993.

Menzel, D.H., *Astronomy. New York 1970*. Usual information on Solar System, and calculations for eclipses.

Metzger, Bruce M., *The Text of the New Testament.* New York 1968. Excellent Greek scholar.

Michener, James A., *The Source.* New York 1965. Required reading in Jewish circles. Contains everything in archaeological and historical novel form that you wanted to know about the Jews but were afraid to ask. Covers 9834 BC to 1964. The research is astounding—he must have used 20 research assistants.

Moore, Raymond Cecil, *Introduction to Historical Geology.* New York 1949. College textbook.

Montet, Pierre, *Lives of the Pharaohs.* London 1968. Contains some little known information. Some of his theories are not supported by others. Has a low opinion of the Exodus as a historical document.

Murnane, William J., *The Road to Kadesh.* Illinois 1990. The definitive study of the battle reliefs of Seti I at Karnak.

NIB. *New Interpreter's Bible.* New York 1998. Comments not as good as in IB.

Noblecourt, C. Desroches, *Tutankhamen.* New York Graphic Society 1969. Very good account.

Oates, Joan, *Babylon.* London 1979. Excellent scholar.

O'Connor, J.M., *The Holy Land.* New York 1998. An excellent tour guide by a Catholic priest at the Ecole Biblique. Generally supports the Catholic position with exceptions.

Oppenheim, A. Leo, *Ancient Mesopotamia.* Illinois 1964. Excellent, more facts presented than in other books.

Phillips, Wendell, *Qataban and Sheba.* New York 1955. An oilman's excavation account, but he had Prof. Albright and Dr. Albert Jamme along to read the inscriptions.

Pfeifer, C.F., *The Qumran Community.* New York 1969. Good general reference.

Rapport, Samuel and Wright, Helen, *Archaeology.* New York 1963. Brief accounts of discoveries from Thomas Jefferson to the Dead Sea Scrolls.

Redford, Donald B., *History and Chronology of the Eighteenth Dynasty of Egypt.* Univ. of Toronto Press 1967. A definitive study by an Egyptian scholar.

Reeves, Nicholas, *The Complete Tutankhamun.* London 1990. More up to date information.

RD. Readers Digest, *The World's Last Mysteries.* New York 1987. Atlantis, Nasca, Tiahuanaco, and other sites. Mostly facts and no UFO stuff.

Riedel, E. et al, *The Book of the Bible.* New York 1979. Liberal but good source of definitions and terms for people and plants, etc.

Ries, H. and Watson, T.L., *Engineering Geology.* New York 1948. College textbook.

Ritmeyer, Leen & Kathleen, *Secrets of Jerusalem's Temple Mount.* Washington DC 1998. Available from Biblical Archaeology Society, reprinted from BAR.

Rohl, David M., *Pharaohs and Kings.* New York 1995. A chronology revision for the conquest.

RPNF. William Ryan and Walter Pitman. *Noah's Flood.* New York 1998. Evidence for the drying of the Mediterranean Sea and the Black Sea breakthrough, and the legends in back of Noah's flood.

RW. Nicholas Reeves and Richard H. Wilkinson, *The Complete Valley of the Kings.* London 1996. Complete information on excavations, excavators, tombs and all things found. The "source" for the 88 tombs and pits found so far.

Saggs, H.W.F., *The Babylonians*. London 1988. Most complete source. Includes the older Mesopotamian versions of the flood dating to 2200 BC or 800 years before Moses, the tree of life, and the Tower of Babel.

Scofield, C.I., Reference Bible. *New York 1967*. A KJV with conservative notes and modernized words. Good commentary notes.

Simons, J., *Jerusalem in the Old Testament*. Netherlands 1952. A good summary of all excavations up to K. Kenyon (1961–67) and Y. Shiloh (1978–85). A good source for problems in the Hebrew and interpretation of the various results and theories.

SHUN. Stephen Hawking. *The Universe in a Nutshell*. New York 2001. Not much math needed, but keep your brain open. The wit is superb.

SMM. *Student Map Manual*. Part of the Wide Screen Project. Pictorial Archive. Jerusalem 1979. The very best source material for the Holy Land. The one resource I cannot do without. The 2500 35-mm color slides are cross-referenced to the Manual. Generally available to Seminaries, Bible Schools and Churches, but was for sale in the book stores in Jerusalem. Listed on New Orleans Baptist Theological Seminary Home page, possibly others (unless Katrina wiped it out). Possibly by interlibrary loan.

Stern, Ephraim, *Archaeology of the Land of the Bible Vol II (from 732–332 BC)*. New York 2001. Takes up where Mazar leaves off.

Strobel, Lee, *The Case for a Creator*. Michigan 2004. A former atheist. Interviews many agnostic scientists who are now believers. A must read. "Faith Under Fire" is a current TV program.

The Koran. N.J. Dawood. Penguin Books New York 1985. Revised translation of 1973.

TEEB. Shana Priwer and Cynthia Phillips. *The Everything Einstein Book*. Massachusetts 2003. All of Einstein's works, ups and downs, and life.

Tenney, M.C., *New Testament Times*. Michigan 1965. Conservative.

TFFK. Tommy Tenney. *Finding Favor with the King*. Minnesota 2003. Conservative insights on Esther.

Thiele, E.R., *The Mysterious Numbers of the Hebrew Kings*. Michigan 1965 revised. A masterful working out of chronology in a confused area. The "source" for this information.

TLBG. Time Life Books, *Lost Civilizations: Greece*. Virginia 1994.

TLBGK. Time Life Books, *The God Kings*. Virginia 1987.

TLBM. Time Life Books, *Lost Civilizations: Mesopotamia*. Virginia 1995.

TLBCC. Time Life Books, *Cradle of Civilization*. New Jersey 1970.

TLLC. Time Life Books, *Lost Civilizations: The Celts*. Virginia 1994.

Tompkins, Peter, *Secrets of the Great Pyramid*. New York 1971. All the main information needed.

Thorne, Kip S., *Black Holes and Time Warps: Einstein's Outrageous Legacy*. New York 1994. A romp from Einstein in 1915 to 1994 on the historical developments of Astrophysics using the depth of Einstein's theory to explain black holes before any had been discovered, based only on the basis of thought. The best example of its kind.

Trever, John C., *The Untold Story of Qumran.* New Jersey 1965. Good general reference.

TWLSGF. *The Word of the Lord Shall Go Forth.* A Festchrift to David Noel Freedman Ed. by C.L. Meyers and M. O'Conner. Indiana 1983.

Walvoord, John F., *Every Prophecy of the Bible.* Colorado 1999. Of 1000 prophecies, some 500 have already occurred. Offers an explanation of the major ones and some alternate views.

WBF. Wilson, Ian, *Before the Flood.* New York 2001. Details the information that the Black Sea breakthrough in 5600 BC may represent the original flood. The flood accounts from other cultures are also listed here.

Weeks, Kent R., *The Lost Tomb (KV 5).* New York 1998. The rediscovery of the tomb of Ramesses II sons. Good background information.

Wellard, James, *Babylon.* New York 1972. Good general information.

WERE, *When Egypt Ruled the East,* George Steindorff and Kieth C. Seele . Illinois 1971. Excellent Egyptian history.

Whitcomb, J.C. Jr., *Darius the Mead.* Michigan 1959. Conservative.

Wight, Fred H., *Highlights of Archaeology in Bible Lands.* Illinois 1955. Dated, but good information.

Wilber, Donald N., *Persepolis.* New York 1969. Good account of the remains.

Wilkinson, John, *Jerusalem as Jesus Knew it.* London 1978. Dated in a few areas, but a lot of good information.

Williams, Larry, *The Mountain of Moses*. New York 1990. An adventurer illegally explores an off limits area in Saudi Arabia.

Wilson, E., *The Dead Sea Scrolls 1947–1969*. New York 1969. Other early cult leaders, including a background on Joseph Smith and the Mormons.

Wiseman, D.J., *Illustrations from Biblical Archaeology*, Michigan 1958. Conservative.

WMGF, *The Genesis Flood*, J.C. Whitcomb and H.M. Morris. Michigan 1961. Conservative.

Woolley, Sir Leonard, *Excavations at Ur*. New York *1954*. Report on the only excavation at Ur.

Wright, G.E., *Biblical Archaeology*, Pennsylvania 1957. Somewhat liberal but good historical information. Some data ex. Sodom and Debir are out of date.

WW, *Women's Work: The First 20,000 Years*. Elizabeth Barber. New York 1994. The role of women and their contribution in society. A must read for feminists.

Wycliffe. *Historical Geography of Bible Lands*. Edited by C.F. Pfeifer and H.F. Vos. Illinois 1967. Conservative; slightly dated, but good.

Unger, Merrill F., *The New Unger's Bible Dictionary*. Illinois 1988. Conservative, excellent.

UNT. Unger, Merrill F., *Archaeology and the New Testament*. Michigan 1962. Same as below.

UOT. Unger, Merrill F., *Archaeology and the Old Testament*. Michigan 1954. Dated but good information, conservative.

VSE. Van Nostrand's Scientific Encyclopedia. New Jersey 1968.

Vermes, Geza, *The Complete Dead Sea Scrolls in English.* New York 1997. Everything except the Biblical Scrolls (these were published earlier) is covered.

Verner, Miroslav, *The Pyramids.* New York 2001. Everything about the 96 known pyramids. Doesn't think much of Hancock's ideas.

Yates, John, Faith Bible Institute New Testament Vol. IV, 1 Corinthians. Unpublished.

ENDNOTES

Introduction

1. To elaborate more fully could add from 50–300 pages
   for each point. For example, Marvin Pope's Anchor Bible
   Commentary on the Song of Songs requires 410 pp. of
   explanation just to cover the 117 vs. or 4½ pages in the
   KJV. Grouping the material by topic brings all pertinent
   verses together, but makes location harder, since the point
   could be covered in more that one area. The Scripture index
   can be used to see if any particular verse is referred to and
   where it is located. The result is to give new information to
   explain and especially to document where this information
   can be found, for anyone who has an interest in these areas.
   It is meant to whet the appetite rather than rehash the entire
   train of evidence. The reference material will do that. Each
   section covered will give the verses in question from Genesis
   to Revelation. It will help to find the verse in question in
   a KJV to see how it reads and compare it to the improved
   version. The pioneering work of the late Dr. J.P. Free of

Wheaton College, listed in the references section, was the first along this line (out of print, but revised in 1976), but no later compiled works of this type are known; although the information on select verses is available in scattered references and journals. Many of the references would be available by interlibrary loan. Some from the internet are also listed, and is the most useful source.

2. For instance, for some differing views on the Exodus and Conquest and historical setting, see ECIAT pp. 257–69; 299–309.

3. Views of other scientists affiliated with Christianity can be found in the Journal of the American Scientific Affiliation. I recommend *In Six Days* edited by Dr. John F. Ashton Master Books, Green Forest, Arkansas, 2001. He has 50 Ph.D. scientists from various fields explain numerous problems, and why they are believers in creation verses evolution.

4. The reference section also contains notes on the implications of the reference itself, as well as that author's position.

Chapter 1

5. See 2 Kgs 18:26, set in 702 BC; compare v. 13.

6. See II Esdras 14:42.

7. Prior to the Dead Sea Scrolls, the oldest manuscript is the Babylonian, a Jewish center of learning ca 400 AD. (Book of the Prophets 895 AD, Trevor p. 184.) Fragments of 1 Sm 23:9–16 from Cave 4 at Qumran date to ca 280 BC.

8. Some pages were burned during the riots of Dec. 2, 1947. The next oldest, the Leningrad Codex, is complete, and dates to 1010 [BR 13(4): 32 (97)].

9. See Development of the Old Testament, Chapter 5, or Dead Sea Scrolls Bible Chapter.

10. Tradition says 72 scholars were sent, six from each tribe (see Josephus *Antiquities* 12.2).

11. Ex, James in Acts 15:16 quotes from Am 9:11–12.

12. Some examples: 1 Cor 5:7 reads, "Purge the old leaven that you may be a new paste, as you are asymes," Heb 9:23 has "the exemplars of the celestials," and in 13:16 reads "Beneficence and communication do not forget, for with such hosts God is promerited."

13. 54 initially

14. One verse is still uncorrected in Mt 23:24—strain "at" a gnat should be "out." The Jews were careful to strain out these critters, but ate the largest nonkosher animal of all. The NKJV has corrected it.

15. English Lev 6:8 is 6:1 in the Hebrew, English Jer 9:1 is 8:23 in Hebrew and Mal chapter 4 in English is combined with chapter 3 in Heb.

16. Due to Reuben's sin, his tribe never became large; it disappeared before 849 BC, and it is not mentioned on the Moabite stone of king Mesha of about the same date.

17. Some of our Charismatic friends have latched on the "unknown" of 1 Cor 14 as a reference to a heavenly utterance of "unknown" type, instead of leaving it out and recognizing the tongues as a known language such as Greek, Arabic or Coptic, which is what tongues actually refers to.

18. Not all translation challenges are due to anachronisms. As an example, Mt 23:13 reads, "Woe to you scribes, Pharisees . . ." In an Arabic translation in 1973, a mistake in Pharisees became "Frenchmen." And it proved hard to convince the Arab printer to make the proper correction, since Arabs and the French did not get along (from a lecture by Prof. Bruce Metzger in E. Windsor, New Jersey on 2–17–74).

Chapter 2

19. Especially see 2 Sm 23:2 and Heb 3:7–11; "The Holy Spirit saith" refers to Psalm 95:7–11, written by David or someone

else, but contains no reference to a human author.) Over 50 times in New Testament is the Old Testament spoken of as of divine origin and authority (see Mt 22:29, Mk 14:49, Lk 24:25–27; 44–46 and Rom 3:2).

20. Examples: in Jn 8:58, it is the present tense rather than the past tense. In Jn 10:34–36 inviolability of a single word, Gal 3:16 the singular number of the noun rather than the plural, Gal 4:9 the passive voice rather than active for the verb "you have known" and Heb 12:27 as the Amplified Bible has it "Now this expression, Yet once more,"

21. Distinction between revelation and inspiration: revelation is "the what" (1 Cor 2:9–10), inspiration is "the how" (vs. 13).

22. See also 1 Pt 1:10–12; Zec 9:9; setting is 30 AD, but 9:10 looks to the 2nd Coming.

23. See especially the Interpreter's Bible notes on Lamentations Vol. VI as an example; on p. 5, he misses the point on Jer 31:29–30 where v. 31 speaks of the New Covenant after Christ's coming. The conclusion was that Jeremiah could not have written Lamentations ca 530 BC if he died ca 580 BC.

24. See the same problems in the Interpreter's Bible discussion on Mi 5:2 where Christ is not even mentioned as coming from Bethlehem, but rather is interpreted as a reference to David only.

25. Gn 4:10, 11–2 Ch 24:21 are inclusive, where the Hebrew Old Testament actually ends with 2 Chr.

Chapter 3

26. Thus in Prv 3:5 "embracing" should be linked to "stones." The Midrash Qoheleth Rabbah explains it as a metaphor for marital intercourse, a time to engage and the seven days

when it is prohibited, rather that the act of making a field unsuitable for chariots as in 2 Kgs 3:19.

27. As the state of Israel being created in one day: May 14, 1948 (per Is 66:8). This is one of the few we have lived to see.

28. By Jewish usage this period could have been as short as 14 months since any part of a year was counted as a year)

Chapter 4

29. Gn 31:47; Jer 10:11; Dn 2:4–7:28; and Ezr 4:8–6:18; 7:12–26

Chapter 5

30. Copies will be found mostly at theological schools or major libraries.
31. These three "Babas" are civil law.
32. This and Shebu'oth (oaths) are criminal law.
33. Actually, the last is backward.

Chapter 9

34. 1Q28a (the Messianic Rule) says that this occurs at age 20 when he may take a wife, Vermes p. 158

SCRIPTURE INDEX

General Index

CPSIA information can be obtained at www.ICGtesting.com
Printed in the USA
241933LV00001B/9/P